Racing to the Top

Racing to the Top

How Energy Fuels Systemic Leadership
in World Politics

WILLIAM R. THOMPSON AND LEILA ZAKHIROVA

OXFORD
UNIVERSITY PRESS

OXFORD
UNIVERSITY PRESS

Oxford University Press is a department of the University of Oxford. It furthers the University's objective of excellence in research, scholarship, and education by publishing worldwide. Oxford is a registered trade mark of Oxford University Press in the UK and certain other countries.

Published in the United States of America by Oxford University Press
198 Madison Avenue, New York, NY 10016, United States of America.

© Oxford University Press 2019

CIP data is on file at the Library of Congress
ISBN 978–0–19–069969–7 (pbk.)
ISBN 978–0–19–069968–0 (hbk.)

1 3 5 7 9 8 6 4 2

Paperback printed by Sheridan Books, Inc., United States of America
Hardback printed by Bridgeport National Bindery, Inc., United States of America

WRT: For co-authors no longer with us

LZ: For my beloved dad – my role model

CONTENTS

PART III   THE FUTURE

ACKNOWLEDGMENTS

We would like to thank the Newgen folks (Sarah Vogelsong and Damian Penfold) for their excellent copyediting services.

An earlier version of chapter 2 was published as "Revising Leadership Long Cycle Theory," in W. R. Thompson, ed., *Oxford Encyclopedia of Empirical International Relations Theory* (New York: Oxford University Press, 2018).

An earlier version of chapter 12 was published as "Racing to a Renewable Transition?" in T. Devezas, J. Leitao, and A. Sarygulou, eds., *Industry 4.0-Entrepreneurship and Structural Change in the New Digital Landscape* (Berlin: Springer, 2017).

Racing to the Top

PART I

INTRODUCTION

1

Systemic Leadership and Energy: The Argument

A complicated and disheartening paradox characterizes the futures of systemic leadership and energy. Systemic leadership has increasingly become reliant on an energy transition to make and fuel new technological innovations relatively inexpensively. The incumbent systemic leadership appears to be eroding. Many observers nominate China as the likely successor. Given the finite supply of coal and petroleum and the high costs of consuming them (for both the consumer and the environment), renewable energy has been pitched as the best alternative to these fuel sources and the likely focus of a new phase of energy leadership. However, most governmental and corporate forecasts do not foresee renewable energy becoming the predominant energy source in the next fifty years, if not considerably longer. If the forecasts prove to be accurate (and there are reasons to expect that they will not), there is less reason to anticipate a change in systemic leadership in this century, because such a shift in the past has been predicated on a transition to new energy sources.[1]

If no economy can be expected to take the lead in (a) developing radical new technology that is (b) fueled by a new and relatively inexpensive source of energy, there is much less reason to expect the emergence of a powerful new lead economy, as has occurred several times over the past millennium. In the absence of a new lead economy, the transition away from fossil fuels will be all the slower. Currently, the world's leading CO_2 emitters just happen to be the incumbent system leader and its possible successor. If they find it difficult to decarbonize, CO_2 emissions will continue to be too high. Presumably, that will only make global warming impacts more severe. Should it prove increasingly difficult to rely on coal and petroleum through 2050, we may anticipate major energy shortfalls, global economic crisis, and the failure of new systemic leadership to emerge. Even if these shortfalls do not materialize, accelerated environmental deterioration in response to rising or persistent hydrocarbon consumption seems likely. Thus we still end up with a shortage of renewables, one form of global crisis or another, and no new systemic leadership. Such a situation might facilitate a greater leadership role for international institutions, but such an outcome is hardly guaranteed. Nor is there much reason to be optimistic about international institutions, particularly in the absence of strong systemic leadership.

On the other hand, system leaders have not always been around. They began to emerge only in the last millennium as a result of states' possessing the world's lead economy for a finite period of time (Modelski and Thompson, 1996) in an era in which the world was starting to become a smaller place. Today, on the basis of their concentrated technological innovation and global power projection capabilities, system leaders play preponderant roles in managing the world political economy. They set examples for others to emulate. But they also have the most to gain from a smoothly functioning world economy. As a consequence, they encourage (verbally and materially) others to behave in ways that further collective interests. They also use coercion on occasion.

Scholars disagree about which states have earned the label of "system leader."[2] The further back in time one travels, the more difficult it becomes to compare the predominance of various candidates. As a consequence, few would dispute the United States' contemporary claim to the distinction—although whether the claim holds true to this day is a different matter. Similarly, many would accept Britain's claim to systemic leadership in the nineteenth century. Before that, choices become increasingly more controversial. However, the Netherlands in the seventeenth century has considerable support among those who have examined the question.

We suggest that there is a reason why only three states can lay a relatively strong claim to the systemic leadership label. These three states have some distinctions that no other states can claim. The unique nature of their claims can be demonstrated quickly by looking at the broadest slate of possible candidates. Leadership long cycle analyses are based on a narrative of modern economic growth in which the main technological problem of the last millennium has been to break free of agrarian constraints based on the limitations of human/animal muscle and a reliance on solar radiation for plant growing. Song China made the first attempt in the tenth to twelfth centuries to industrialize but ultimately failed. Information on many of its innovations was subsequently passed on to Europe and played an important role in stimulating later European industrialization. Three of the principal intermediaries in this exchange between Asia and the West were Genoa, Venice, and Portugal, which successively dominated East–West trade by organizing new trade routes and monopolizing the distribution of Asian commodities in Europe. Their commercial successes were also predicated on harnessing and improving maritime technology beyond the competencies of their European and Asian rivals.

The situation in Europe began to change in the seventeenth century with the Netherlands' rise to technological leadership in a variety of industries, based in part on an energy foundation of peat and the deployment of thousands of windmills.[3] The Dutch were soon eclipsed by their neighbors, however, in particular the British, who developed coal-based industries and moved toward industrialization. Britain, in turn, was eclipsed by the rise of the United States, which led the way in innovating petroleum-based industries in the twentieth century. China could continue this trend of eclipsing predecessors, but we should be cautious about projecting the pattern into the future given other significant changes that have or have not occurred at the same time.[4]

Table 1.1 clarifies the leadership pattern that characterized the past millennium. Each state had some claim to a commercial lead in at least some territory, with the scope of the trade gradually expanding to encompass the entire globe. Each state had some claim to technological prowess that differentiated it from its rivals. Minimally, their technological leads were concentrated in the naval sphere—building new types of ships, developing navigational skills, and pioneering new trade routes. Increasingly, though, other technological innovations contributed to their ability to develop desired manufactures for trading purposes, especially those that depended on intensive heat processes for their creation. These intensive heat processes, in turn, were based on harnessing the interaction between new technology and new sources of energy—successively, peat/wind, coal, and petroleum. As a consequence, the Netherlands' seventeenth-century lead, the second British lead, and the United States' lead stand out in table 1.1.

Table 1.1 **Attributes of Successive System Leaders**

	Commercial Lead	*Technological Lead*	*Energy Lead*
Song China	No	Yes	No
Genoa	Yes	No	No
Venice	Yes (Europe)	Yes (Europe)	No
Portugal	Yes (East–West trade)	Yes (maritime)	No
Netherlands	Yes (Europe and East–West trade)	Yes (Europe)	Partially (peat/wind)
Britain I	Yes (Europe and Atlantic trade)	No	No
Britain II	Yes	Yes	Yes (coal)
United States	Yes	Yes	Yes (petroleum)

Only these three states were able to combine leads in all three areas—commerce, technology, and energy.

Leads do not last forever. They are constructed gradually and often erode fairly gradually as well. The rate of erosion, however, may vary, and the slower the rate of erosion, the more difficult it is to discern relative decline. This tendency helps explain the disagreements about the position of the United States. Not only was its concentration of leads more strongly established than those of its predecessors at the time of its rise, but its relative decline, partially as a consequence of that strength, has also been slow. Nonetheless, other states and their economies have been catching up to the U.S. position. Figure 1.1, for instance, shows the fluctuations in the U.S. share of world knowledge and technologically intensive industries as a marker of technological leadership. According to this figure, the United States has maintained its lead, but other states have narrowed the gap. European economies, in general, are closest, followed by Japan, which has fallen behind in the competition. We can anticipate that the European Union's position will decline as well, presuming that the United Kingdom follows through on its announced Brexit plans.[5] China is moving up but still has some way to go. Thus, based on these indicators, the United States' technological lead is slowly declining, although the gap between it and other nations remains strong.[6]

A second dimension of systemic leadership is the ability of the lead state to project force throughout the system in order to protect its predominance in

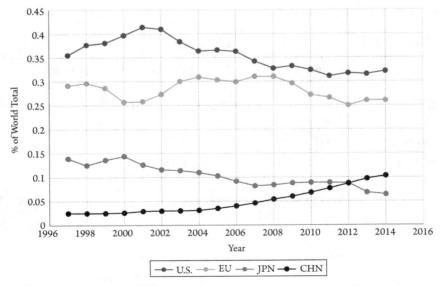

Figure 1.1 World Shares of Value-Added Knowledge and Technologically Intensive Industries. Source: Data from U.S. National Science Board (2014, 2016).

the world economy. Global reach capabilities have varied over time, but prior to the twentieth century, they were exclusively naval in nature. Technological change in the twentieth century permitted forays into the air and outer space. Consequently, any index of global reach must adjust for technological change. The power projection scores shown in figure 1.2 combine distributional information on blue water naval capability (ships of the line, battleships, heavy aircraft carriers, nuclear submarines and their ballistic missiles) and information on strategic bombers, land-based ballistic missiles, and military satellites.

While not demonstrated in figure 1.2, the United States' lead in global reach capabilities was and still is much more impressive than its British predecessor's position. At the same time, though, the U.S. lead has hardly been static. The nation's strategic preeminence emerged abruptly during and immediately after World War II, was maintained into the 1960s, and has been declining slowly since then relative to other states' attempts to narrow the military projection of force gap. The Soviet Union made some headway in closing this gap but stopped well short of catching up. Its successor, the Russian Federation, is trying once again, and so is China—although it will take time for either to become genuinely competitive in this sphere.

The two figures demonstrate something similar: a still predominant United States that is gradually losing its relative technological and power projection leads. Given the impressive heights of concentrated power to which the United States rose, it may not be surprising that its trajectory of decline has been slow. At

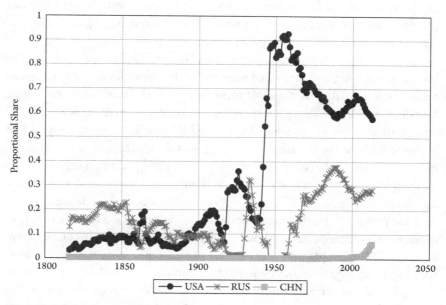

Figure 1.2 Global Power Projection.

the same time, relative decline has been slower in the area of military capability than in technology. One of the distinctive properties of the current era is that the economies that have made the most headway in narrowing the technological gap have shown much less interest in narrowing the military capability gap. At the same time, the economies that have shown the most interest in narrowing the military capability gap have struggled to narrow the technology gap.[7] Yet neither gap-narrowing process has stopped, and presumably further inroads into the United States' leads can be anticipated in the years to come.

The continuation of the United States' relative decline as system leader, however slowly it might be occurring, sets up an expectation of eventual succession. The natural question is who is the most likely candidate, and many observers have put China forward as the state with the best chance of becoming the next system leader. Much of this argument, however, is predicated on China's economy becoming the largest in the world. Such an emphasis is misplaced and misunderstands the nature of the processes at work. Possessing a large economy can be advantageous, just as having the world's largest economy can be an asset, especially when it comes to creating markets for the consumption of commodities. More important, though, is the technological lead—and that is not something that is conferred by possessing the world's largest economy.

Moreover, it is fairly clear that it is not just the technological lead that is critical in determining system leadership. Over the past few centuries, the radical new technologies produced by states possessing the technological lead increasingly required relatively inexpensive fuels that were capable of converting organic and inorganic materials into powerful sources of energy. Both the low price and the power of these energy sources proved critical to successful production and finding markets for those products' consumption.

Therefore, it is not enough to ask who will have the largest economy or even the most technologically advanced economy in the twenty-first century. It is also necessary to ask whether the most technologically advanced economy will be founded on a new, relatively inexpensive energy base. One thing is abundantly clear: coal and petroleum, which have fueled the rise to power of the past two systemic leads, will not suffice. Their supply is disappearing (with petroleum dwindling faster than coal), and, consequently, their price is rising. For both reasons, the next system leader—should there be one—cannot depend on either resource to provide cheap and reliable energy. Inasmuch as dependence on coal and petroleum has led to unsustainable environmental costs, the incentive to move to a different, non-carbon-based, source of energy seems all the more paramount. Natural gas may seem to be a useful compromise, but it is carbon-based and only slightly less environmentally harmful than coal or petroleum. By the middle of the current century, gas may also face its own supply and pricing problems.[8] Our questions then are twofold: (1) Which of the likely candidates for technological preeminence in the future are moving toward developing a non-carbon-based economy? and (2) Is any candidate moving fast enough to make a difference

To make such claims, we need a strong theoretical foundation, one that is well anchored in the political and economic fluctuations of the past millennium. We have a candidate for this foundation: leadership long cycle theory, which has been around for some forty years. This theory has its uses, but it needs refinement. Therefore, our first order of business involves the improvement of this theoretical perspective. Once we have an improved theoretical foundation, we can turn to a close examination of the rise and fall of concentrations of economic and technological leadership over the past one thousand years. The lessons learned from that exercise can then be applied to our current and future dilemmas concerning energy, climate, and world politics.

In chapter 2, we reexamine our framework for assessing systemic leadership. This revised framework is then applied to the political–economic evolution of the past thousand years to consider the factors underlying the rise and fall of a sequence of system leaders and to examine the evidence for the linkage of energy transitions and technological leadership. The evidence for such a linkage is fairly strong; it is difficult to imagine the ascent of the last three system leaders (the Netherlands, Britain, and the United States) had they had significantly different energy foundations. In other words, without peat, coal, or petroleum/electricity, respectively, these episodes of systemic leadership would have been far less likely to have occurred. With this baseline assumption in place, we turn in the last third of the book to a consideration of its current ramifications. Today, the linkage of energy and systemic/technological leadership is further complicated by climate change brought about by increasing reliance on carbon-based fuels. Thus, systemic leadership is no longer a matter of who is ahead in utilizing fossil fuels, as it was in the nineteenth and twentieth centuries. Somehow, economies must be weaned off of emitting carbon dioxide into the atmosphere lest their economic growth destroy the planet's environment. That proposition suggests the need to make a transition to non-carbon-based fuels as expeditiously as possible.

Within the twin transitional context, that is, ongoing and simultaneous transitions in the systemic leadership and energy regimes, we review in chapter 10 the evidence for a strong relationship between global warming and fossil fuels and what might be done to forestall the consequences of such a relationship. A second question concerns whether the emergence of unconventional extraction methods for the production of shale oil and gas are likely to make a significant difference in the relative standings of the United States now and China perhaps later. We argue in chapter 11 that fracking is unlikely to create a foundation for renewed or new systemic leadership. More likely, this innovation will only protract the transition away from fossil fuels. In chapter 12, we turn specifically to the question of renewables development, examining who is leading that race and whether it matters all that much that the transition appears to be so far in the future. In our view, a partial transition to renewables focusing on transportation and electricity generation is more probable than a full-scale transition. At what pace this will take place and whether it will be sufficient to address global warming concerns remains to be seen. Whether a partial shift to cleaner energy can create the foundation for new systemic leadership is also not clear, because the innovations involved may be readily emulated by rivals. Systemic leadership has been predicated on gaining an economic edge over the competition. If that edge is no longer achievable, world politics will either need to move toward new political leadership patterns or make do with the eroding older ones.

Thus, if our understanding of the technological leadership–energy transition and forecasts are correct, there is little reason to anticipate much movement toward a systemic leadership transition in this century. If the reserves of coal and petroleum remaining to be extracted and exploited economically have been overestimated, we are likely to be confronted with major energy shortfalls by roughly midcentury, compounding major energy problems with even more major environmental problems in about the same time frame. The only solution to these problems is to accelerate the energy transition. Who leads in that effort might be rewarded with systemic leadership—assuming that this traditional institution of global political governance continues to exist. Yet even if that prize is unattainable, the ensuing decarbonization will still benefit the planet immensely.

Nonetheless, we do not expect readers to accept these assertions without first strengthening the case for coming to these conclusions. Leadership long cycle arguments tend to be supported fairly strongly by the data. Such an evaluation hardly means, however, that the interpretation cannot be improved upon. In chapter 3, we suggest that greater attention to energy sources will produce positive payoffs. All of the lead economies in the Northern Song to U.S. sequence have been treated as if they have been similar in terms of weight in world politics—yet clearly that cannot be the case. Genoa or Portugal did not exert the same influence over global politics in earlier centuries that Britain in the nineteenth century or the United States in the twentieth did. What differentiates Britain's second phase of leadership and that of the United States from Britain's first phase and those of the Netherlands and Portugal? One answer has to do with energy bases. The energy foundations of the British and American cases were vastly different than those of their predecessors. An appreciation of that difference leads to a better understanding of why it matters and what it tells us about the future of systemic leadership and energy.

In the process of examining the technology–energy relationship, we will also need to move beyond an exclusive focus on the existence of technological edges. In chapters 5 through 9, we investigate other factors that were important to the emergence of technologically based leads—or, in other words, how technological leads came about. The answer is energy and energy transitions. New sources of energy give selected states increasingly decisive edges over their competitors. This broader focus will give us more solid footing in addressing the question of the extent to which technology and energy have become intertwined. This same foundation will assist us in discussing the near future in chapters 10 through 12, which examine global warming, shale energy, and renewables. In chapter 13, we conclude by recapitulating our argument and evidence.

2

The Leadership Long Cycle Framework

In this chapter we summarize the most pertinent parts of long cycle theory and underline the problems associated with ignoring energy and treating all system leaders as if they were fundamentally similar. The role of energy deserves more prominence in long cycle theory than it has received. The solution to this problem, fortunately, is not difficult to devise. Demonstrating how technology and energy transitions have interacted closely in the past should take care of the energy oversight.

Leadership long cycle arguments are highly compatible with Gilpin's (1975) initial articulation of hegemonic stability theory, identified in box 2.1.[1] The theory is not complex. According to this view, radical technological change is the main vehicle for generating economic growth, which in turn leads to uneven wealth concentration and hierarchy. Such change further contributes to wealth concentration because it has historically been monopolized by one country at a time. The greater the consequent edge of this lead economy, the more probable it is that it will be drawn into various management problems associated with the functioning of the world economy. Consequently, the lead economy will construct a political order for the world economy that is finite in its duration. As the lead economy loses its lead or edge over the rest of the world, its political ordering capacity will also wane.

The first assumption expressed in box 2.1 is critical. Every economic system comes with a political order of some sort. Governance of the world economy is primitive but can be traced to concentrations of wealth and power. The most wealthy and powerful states in the world economy provide it some order, if only to protect their own extensive activities. For example, most states view piracy as a nuisance that needs to be eliminated. This problem is linked to many others, including rights of passage and interference with transit through international waters; how far national sovereignty should extend from the coastline; and the ensuring of continued access to vital commodities, such as timber or petroleum,

> ## Box 2.1 Gilpin's Initial Hegemonic Stability Theory
>
> **Assumptions:**
> 1. Economics and politics are reciprocal processes in international relations. Economic processes transform power relationships, which lead to new hierarchies and political frameworks of economic activity that serve the interests of the most powerful. Thus, economic systems do not arise spontaneously. Every economic system rests on a political order.
> 2. Economic systems require a leader to manage and stabilize the system because the benefits of economic interaction are not sufficient to induce actors to pay the costs of sustaining the economic system or to forgo opportunities to advance individual interests at the expense of the collectivity.
> 3. System leaders are defined by variable mixes of size, technological superiority, and function (banking, trading system construction, investment, and rule making/enforcing).
>
> **Theory**
> 1. Uneven economic growth leads to centers of concentrated wealth, industry, and economic activity.
> 2. Concentrated economic growth is achieved via discontinuous (in both space and time) and radical technological innovation but tends to be singularly focused in one central economy (lead economy) at a time.
> 3. The greater the lead in developing new technology, the more dominant the relative economic position of the lead economy.
> 4. The more dominant the relative position of the lead economy, the more likely it is that this economy will also take the lead in economic activity and management of the world economy.
> 5. As the relative position of the lead economy declines, the framework of political–economic relations evolves, initially producing less hierarchy and/or fragmentation into regional blocs, until a new order emerges based on a reconcentrated lead economy.

needed for the continued functioning of the world economy. Resolving these problems invariably requires some political leadership to coordinate or impose preferences. After all, the problems will not simply go away or resolve themselves. At the same time, one cannot assume that sufficient leadership will be available to address these problems or will be successful in doing so. Such insufficiency is one of the reasons that governance in the world economy has been so limited.[2]

Yet expressing a hegemonic stability theory is not enough. One must test it, and to do that one must develop a historical script that interprets it. Leadership long cycle theory is a version of hegemonic stability theory with both a distinctive historical script and a very strong commitment to operationalization and assessment. Its initial historical focus was the past five hundred years of major-power activity.[3] A five-hundred-year perspective may not have been all that conventional by international relations standards, but it did resonate with the Eurocentricity of world politics analysis at the time of the theory's development. According to this view, a structured, regional European international relations could be said to have begun emerging with the onset of the Habsburg–Valois feud and the early extension of European force to non-European theaters. Therefore, it made some sense to begin at the "beginning" of contemporary international relations.

Less conventionally, perhaps, it could also be argued that the distinctions between global and regional layers of interaction became more distinct after 1500. At the time that Portugal entered the Indian Ocean and created a predatory trade regime there, it was not intensely engaged in European international relations. Yet what Portugal did in the Indian Ocean had ramifications for European international relations, as manifested by Venetian opposition to Portuguese movements. The same could be said about the later Spanish discovery of Peruvian silver (roughly mid-sixteenth century). One difference between these two examples, however, is that the Portuguese movement into the Indian Ocean was an interregional reflection of the decay of the Venetian political order in the eastern Mediterranean, while the Spanish discovery involved a global political–economic aspect. In the former instance, Portuguese decision-makers and adventurers were responding to the decline of a Venetian–Mamluk monopoly on the Western supply of Eastern spices. That same Venetian decline encouraged French intervention into Italy and Spanish resistance to the French intervention, actions that highlight the regionality of European international relations in the 1490s and thereafter.

As the world economy became less regionally focused, or, alternatively, the regions became more fused, the global layer began to take on more appeal as a focus of analytical attention. What political order would characterize this emerging global layer? There was no reason to assume that such a political order would be identical to that of any of the regions nested within the nascent global system. More likely, global politics would be governed by the actors who were involved in global activities. These actors were not necessarily those who were most wealthy and powerful at the regional level. A distinction between regional and global elites had to be made. Leadership long cycle analysis did this by positing that the minimal threshold for an actor to be considered global was that the actor have the capability to engage in global activities (commanding at least

10 percent of the pool of global reach resources, which were largely naval after 1494) and that the actor have actually operated outside regional theaters. This last criterion meant that navies qualified as global by having operated away from their home regions.

So, we can claim that the 1490s were a turning point in the development of a global layer of political–economic activity. But does a turning point necessarily provide the best place to begin analysis? Just where that "beginning" point should be located has never been obvious to international relations analysts. Other scholars have favored major events such as the bombing of Hiroshima or the Industrial Revolution as the demarcation point for the beginning of modern or contemporary world politics. The rise of nuclear weapons and the onset of industrialization both had serious impacts on how international relations worked. Reasonable arguments can be constructed to justify looking at post-1815 or post-1945 developments as somehow markedly different from pre-1815 and/or pre-1945 processes.[4] That the arguments can be plausible, however, does not make them "right." Questions inevitably arise about how beginning structures and processes evolved. What preceded the ostensible beginning and is it important enough to bring into the analysis? If so, should the beginning point be pushed back in time?

Such questions encouraged a reframing of leadership long cycle theory's historical script. Beginning conventionally around the 1490s was always awkward. If one thinks Portugal represented the first manifestation of wealth and power concentration at the global level, it is rather difficult to ignore the close to a century of developments that led to the Portuguese ascendancy. That is, the Portuguese did not simply or abruptly discover a way around the African continent but fumbled around the issue for nearly a century before they were successful. That history suggests that the fifteenth century could be an interesting focus of a study of global emergence.

Then there is the question of the Venetian–Mamluk monopoly that the Portuguese managed to break. Where did that regime come from? It turns out that the Venetian position in the fourteenth and fifteenth centuries was the outcome of a Genoese–Venetian struggle to monopolize Asian commodities coming into Europe on the overland and maritime Silk Roads from China and Southeast Asia. The rise and fall of the Mongol Empire was important to this story, because the empire's emergence reduced transaction costs for overland Silk Road activities, while its demise favored maritime Silk Road activities and could also be said to have facilitated the reemergence of the Ottomans, an event with its own implications for eastern Mediterranean–based political orders. All that implies that processes unfolding in the thirteenth and fourteenth centuries were also significant for the emergence of a global layer of activity.

Once one ventures back to the thirteenth century in Asia, it is difficult to overlook Chinese developments in that the Chinese were seemingly destroyed by the Mongol assault on the Song empire. Earlier in the tenth and eleventh centuries, China seems to have had an opportunity to break free of the constraints of agrarian political economy, although it did not do so. Moreover, many of its technological accomplishments appear to be linked to subsequent European technological developments. Should not that also be part of the story leading to the 1490s and beyond—especially if Chinese activities a thousand years ago resembled later activities of global powers?

It was this kind of reasoning that led to the reframing of the leadership long cycle argument that is explicit in Modelski and Thompson (1996).

The Modelski and Thompson Argument

Modelski and Thompson (1996) developed an interpretation of world politics that focused on lead economies, growth waves, and the emergence of strong concentrations of violence related to lead economy succession. This interpretation's historical script begins more than a thousand years ago with developments in Song China that ushered in a new phase of politico-economic history by attempting the first serious break from the economic limitations of the agrarian system. In developing gunpowder, expanding coal and iron production, accelerating economic commercialization with the creation of paper money, and developing extensive commitments to maritime trade and sea power, Song China came close to accomplishing the type of industrial revolution led by Britain in the eighteenth and nineteenth centuries. But the empire, beset by expanding nomad neighbors, instead succumbed eventually to the Mongols.

The demise of Song China created an opportunity for others to pick up where the Song economy left off. The maritime and land routes connecting China and the Mediterranean gave advantages to northern Italian city-states, which became the transmitters of Chinese wealth and technology to western European markets. First Genoa and then Venice created Mediterranean commercial empires that used bases and highly systematized fleets to move goods from the Black Sea or the Indian Ocean (transported across the Middle East or up the Red Sea) to European consumers.

Portugal managed to break this monopoly by finding a maritime route down the coast of western Africa, around the Cape of Good Hope, and up the eastern coast into the Indian Ocean. While Portugal was not able to hold on to its own coerced monopoly in the western Indian Ocean for long, Portuguese activities altered the reliance on traditional Silk Road routes by completing the maritime circuits. The Portuguese were succeeded by the Dutch, who went one step further and developed routes across the Indian Ocean (as opposed to staying near the southern Eurasian coastline) to the Spice Islands. The English, forced out of the Spice Islands by the Dutch, eventually managed to take over increasing amounts of South Asian territory and ultimately succeeded in penetrating the Chinese market in ways that the Portuguese and Dutch had never been able to do.

The 1996 interpretation of long cycle theory focused primarily on adding another five hundred years to the existing historical script. What happened prior to 1494 was not exactly like what happened after 1494, but the pre-1494 developments resembled the post-1494 processes, as emergent phenomena often do. Some of the conceptualization that was applicable and already in use for the post-1494 material could now be extended further back in time, but only to a point beginning with Song China, and not before then.

Anchoring the historical script are two sets of theoretical conceptualizations that predate the 1996 modifications. The common denominator of this string of actors from the Song through the British (and the United States) is their claim to being the lead economy of their time. Lead economies are not necessarily the largest economies or even the wealthiest. Rather, they are the most innovative economies, and they utilize their innovations to specialize in long-distance trade, industrial production. and global reach capabilities, which for much of the time period under consideration meant blue water naval capabilities. The sequence from ships of the line to battleships, nuclear submarines, and aircraft carriers has been the iconic manifestation of global reach for hundreds of years. Air and space capabilities are more recent extensions of this sequence.

The lead economy concept is not all that common to international relations discourse. It was explicit in Wallerstein's (1974, 1980, 1982, 1989, 2011) hegemonic states and Gilpin's (1975, 1980, 1987) initial hegemonic stability theory, which relied on "leading states." However, Gilpin was always reluctant to extend the concept beyond nineteenth-century Britain and the twentieth-century United States. Other scholars have since made similar conceptualizations, in which the leaders tend not surprisingly to overlap, as shown in table 2.1.[5]

Of the five sets of authors, Wallerstein envisages the shortest tenures but the strongest influence for his hegemonic states. Both characteristics derive from his insistence that hegemons develop first their agricultural lead, then their commercial/industrial lead, and finally their financial lead. Hegemony exists only when all three leads are possessed simultaneously—hence the brevity of their tenure.

Kindleberger (1996) begins his argument on primacy by noting that focusing on the lead state of any era can turn economic history into a mechanical dog race. Yet he asserts that the concept of a race in which economies compete with one another to be first is not a bad metaphor for what takes place, as long as one does not worry too much about precision in dating or causation. Such an

Table 2.1 **Five Views of Economic Primacy**

Approximate Century	Wallerstein (1974)	Gilpin (1975)	Modelski and Thompson (1996)	Kindleberger (1996)	Maddison (2001)
10th–11th			Northern Song		China
11th–12th			Southern Song		
13th			Genoa		
14th			Venice	Italian city-States	Venice
15th–16th	Habsburgs		Portugal	Portugal and Spain	Portugal
17th	Netherlands		Netherlands	Netherlands	Netherlands
18th			Britain I	France	Britain
19th	Britain	Britain	Britain II	Britain	Britain
20th	United States	United States	United States	United States	United States

Note: While there may appear to be some chronological progression in this table, it is misleading. Wallerstein, Gilpin, and Modelski and Thompson were all writing about their versions of structural change by 1974.

assertion, of course, does not make it easy to summarize his argument. However, he does stress Perroux's (1979) dominance concept as part of his emphasis on rivalry and emulation. That is, rivals try to emulate their counterparts to the extent that they seem to be getting ahead in some way. Dominance in this context means that the dominated have to pay attention to whatever the first country has done, but the dominator can ignore what followers do. From this commentary, Kindleberger arrives at the statement that economic primacy falls short of dominance (and certainly hegemony, which is more familiar in international relations discourse). A state with economic primacy does not dictate what others must do. Rather, it establishes new benchmarks of success that persuade followers to follow the same path. Primacy therefore means leading primarily by example.

Primacies themselves go through national life cycles in which the normal course is to move from an emphasis on first trade to industry and later finance. Trade tends to be aggressive abroad and protected at home. Industry is said to be imitative at first and then more innovative. But the successful innovators become large, resistant to change, and defensive. Finance begins to promote trade and industry but gradually evolves toward a focus on amassing wealth for its own sake.

> Merchants and industrialists graduate from risk-taker to rentier status, and conserve flagging energy. Consumption out of given incomes rise, savings decline. Various interests push their concerns at the political level, and if enough do, they block effective government action. Income distribution tends to become more skewed, the rich richer, the poor poorer. With greater access to the reins of political power, the wealthy are likely to resist some ethically appropriate sharing of national burdens, such as the costs of defense, reparation, infrastructure, and other public goods. (Kindleberger, 1996: 213)

Hardening of the economic arteries of growth thus sets in, bringing the national cycle full circle.[6] An opening is created for challengers to replace the declining leader, although it may or may not be exploited.

Maddison's (2001: 18) argument is much more parsimonious than Kindleberger's. Clearly, Maddison is interested in focusing on the long term. Three interactive processes/variables are put forward to explain "advances in population and income over the past millennium":

a. Conquest or settlement of relatively empty areas with fertile land, new biological resources, or the potential to accommodate transfers of population, crops, and livestock
b. International trade and capital movements
c. Technological and institutional innovation

In elaborating what these processes are about, Maddison's discussion tends to highlight how historically each factor has advantaged one or more states in distinctive ways. Conquest and settlement benefited China between the eighth and thirteenth centuries. Trade underwrote the rise of Venice, Portugal, the Netherlands, and Britain. Technological innovation is described as slow prior to 1820, but Maddison also notes that Venice had its Arsenal, Portugal's preparations for entering the Indian Ocean required extensive experimentation, the Dutch had the fluyt, and British trade was facilitated by navigational and medical innovations.[7]

We have interrupted our discussion of the 1996 modifications with this vector on Kindleberger and Maddison for three reasons. One is to clarify that the lead economy concept is not so unique. Others employ it under different names. The second is that Kindleberger's views on economic primacy are worthwhile in underlining what lead economies do not do as a rule. They do not necessarily dominate the worlds they inhabit. To be sure, wealthy and powerful actors are likely to dominate in some parts of the world, but primarily they lead by doing things first. Yet there is more to systemic leadership than simply providing an economic model to emulate. System leaders also lead by addressing global public goods, although they do not always address them intensively, thoroughly, or neutrally.[8] As a consequence, the world order is primitive. Nevertheless, the impact of such involvement in public goods issues can be quite significant even if these instances tend to be restricted to conceptualization of what it takes to maintain the continued functioning of the world economy, focusing on tasks such as policing sea-lanes to keep world trade moving smoothly, encouraging free trade, and ensuring open access to critical resources (such as petroleum). Finally, Maddison's argument about the three sources of getting ahead will reappear later in chapter 3. His account is an excellent partial summary of how states become predominant for a finite period of time, although it is missing the critical energy component—an issue to which we will return with some frequency in subsequent chapters.

In any event, not only are lead economies the most innovative for their time, but they are also the principal sources of new technologies. They do not necessarily invent all of these technologies. Rather, lead economies put them into application first and reap the lion's share of the profit benefits. Other economies are able to copy these new techniques, subject to some developmental lags, and may even improve upon them, but only some are able to operate close enough to the technological frontier to make use of them. Others have to wait to buy the new products when they can. Thus technological diffusion, like economic development in the first place, is uneven and increasingly so as time passes (Reuveny and Thompson, 2004; Thompson and Reuveny, 2010).

Technological production is also uneven in the sense that its introduction is (a) spatially concentrated in the lead economy and (b) subject to waves of S-shaped emergence.[9] A second revision associated with the 1996 reframing of the leadership long cycle argument is the idea that each lead economy in the sequence experiences two growth waves. The first one tends to involve more novelty and gives the lead economy a decisive head start in the activities or industries that it is pioneering. This imbalance contributes to increased international conflict; historically, such tensions gradually metamorphized into global wars—long (roughly thirty-year) periods of intensive conflict—that determined who would make rules governing long-distance trade.[10] These conflicts were also linked to European regional conflicts between small sea powers and large land powers in which one or more land powers were periodically defeated by a coalition of sea powers and some land powers. Defeating the land powers that seemed to threaten to become regional hegemons was crucial to the smaller sea powers being able to continue to specialize in long-distance commerce and production (a dynamic most pronounced in the Dutch and British eras).

Over the centuries, each lead economy has experienced at least two growth waves, with Britain enjoying a full quartet. The United States may be going through a third one, but that does not guarantee a fourth. As noted, halfway through the lead economy iteration, global wars (1494–1508, 1580–1609, 1688–1713, 1792–1815, and 1914–1945) separated the two waves. Leading the winning coalition in such wars became increasingly helpful in bringing about a second postwar wave. Yet the second-wave era in general tended to be marked by other states eventually catching up to the lead economy's head start, while the first wave was distinguished by the lead economy jumping ahead of the field of rivals.

Also associated with this mid-millennial development has been the gradual emergence of the global system leadership status for the lead economy. After the global wars resolve questions of which state/economy has moved successfully to the head of the global hierarchy, the new system leader has a window of opportunity to shape some of the rules and institutions concerning long-distance trade and industrialization.[11] As the system leader solidifies its status, it also tends to develop a commanding lead in global reach capabilities (Modelski and Thompson, 1988). After all, it is in its own best interest to possess the types of capabilities necessary for policing and protecting maritime trade routes and access to resources deemed vital to the continued functioning of the world economy.

As noted earlier, the leadership long cycle approach is geared toward measuring and testing its assertions. A lot of that testing has been carried out in other examinations. We confine our look at empirical evidence in this chapter to three questions:

1. Is there evidence to support singling out the leads of the lead economies—that is, do the lead economies genuinely lead in terms of trade and industrial production?
2. Is there evidence to support the two spurts of growth associated with each lead economy?
3. Is there evidence to support the relationship between economic leads and leads in global reach capabilities?

To spoil the suspense, the answer to all three questions is yes.

There are various obstacles to empirically verifying our claims over a time frame of a thousand years. The biggest one is that the data that do exist must be interpreted. However, relevant data are more available than one might imagine. China's technological lead at the beginning of the second millennium CE is not really contested by anyone. There are arguments about how long the lead persisted, but no one puts forward a candidate that was competitive with the wealth and power of China in the tenth to twelfth centuries—which is just as well, because empirical data are not abundant for those centuries. There is also little debate about the edge gained by Italian city-states in Europe during the late medieval period. That there were more Italian city-states involved in the competition for control of Mediterranean trade than Genoa and Venice cannot be denied. At the same time, it is rather difficult to argue that Florence or Pisa was as successful as Genoa and Venice, and few would deny Venice's status as the leading Italian city-state, especially in the late fourteenth to early fifteenth centuries. There are intermittent data on Genoese and Venetian trade volumes, but they do not lend themselves to close comparison.

Putting aside the arguments for China, Genoa, and Venice found in Modelski and Thompson (1996), we can be more specific in isolating the leads from fifteenth-century Portugal on. Figure 2.1 plots the ups and downs of the economic leads established by Portugal beginning about 1494 through the United States up to the present.[12] Portugal's lead was relatively abrupt, peaked early, and was in decline by around 1530. The Dutch lead began to be established after the 1590s, plateaued and peaked in the second third of the seventeenth century, and then proceeded to decline. Britain did well between 1690 and 1730 and then did even better later in the eighteenth century, with a peak within the first half of the nineteenth century. The United States surpassed the British position prior to World War I and peaked in 1960, with an interruption to its relative decline

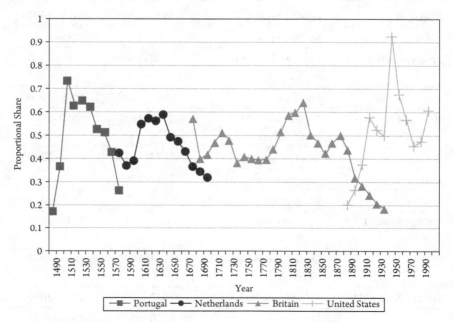

Figure 2.1 Lead Economy Succession.

around the beginning of the twentieth century. None of this reading of figure 2.1 sounds too far off the mark based on what is said in pertinent economic histories. We can certainly quibble about whether the data get every decade exactly right. Roughly, though, the picture that emerges seems fairly accurate. There is evidence for a Portuguese lead, a Dutch lead, two British leads, and, so far, a U.S. lead.

The second question concerns whether each lead economy experienced two growth spurts per period of leadership. Table 2.2 lists the sequence of leads and matches them to periods of predicted and observed growth spurts. The indicators examined are listed by leader. The predicted growth spurts are based on a calendar developed prior to pursuing this question and a four-phase pattern for each leadership in which a period of coalition building is followed by a period of global war, then a period of maximum impact of the global leader in structuring the system's rules (the execution or world power phase, and finally a period of delegitimization and agenda building. Since the argument is that the two growth spurts are interrupted by a period of intense conflict (global war),

Table 2.2 **Leading Sector Timing and Indicators, Fifteenth to Twenty-First Centuries**

Lead Economy	Leading Sector Indicators	Start-up Phase	High-Growth Phase
Portugal	Guinea gold	1430–1460	1460–1494
	Indian pepper	1494–1516	1516–1540
Netherlands	Baltic and Atlantic trade	1540–1560	1560–1580
	Eastern trade	1580–1609	1609–1640
Britain I	Amerasian trade (especially sugar)	1640–1660	1660–1688
	Amerasian trade	1688–1713	1713–1740
Britain II	Cotton, iron	1740–1763	1763–1792
	Railroads, steam	1792–1815	1815–1850
United States I	Steel, chemicals, electronics	1850–1873	1873–1914
	Motor vehicles, aviation, electronics	1914–1945	1945–1973
United States II?	Information industries	1973–2000	2000–2030
	?	2030–2050	2050–2080

the coalition-building and execution/world power phases are designated as the most likely periods of high growth.[13]

In this context, table 2.3 specifies the indicators examined, the predicted phase of high growth, and the phase of peak growth of the designated activity. The four phases for the Northern and Southern Song dynasties in China are not really testable because there are no appropriate series to examine. We think cases

Table 2.3 **Predicted Versus Observed Growth Peaks in Global Lead Economy Industries**

Global Lead Economy Indicators	Predicted High-Growth Period	Observed Growth Peak
Northern Song		
Printing and paper/woodblock book printing	960–990	
National market/Champa rice/iron casting (coke)/paper currency	1030–1060	
Southern Song		
Public finance/reformed tribute system	1090–1120	
Maritime trade	1160–1190	
Genoa		
Champagne Fairs	1220–1250	Second quarter, 13th c.
Trade volume	1275–1300	1290s
Venice		
Romanian galley fleet traffic	1325–1350	1330s
Levantine galley fleet traffic	1390–1430	1390s
Portugal		
Guinea gold (volume of imports)	1460–1492	1480s
Indian pepper (volume of imports)	1516–1540	1510s
Netherlands		
Baltic trade	1560–1580	1560s
Asian trade (value of Dutch East Indies Company Asian imports)	1609–1640	1630s
Britain I		
Tobacco, sugar, Indian textiles (volume of imports)	1660–1680	1670s

(continued)

Table 2.3 **Continued**

Global Lead Economy Indicators	Predicted High-Growth Period	Observed Growth Peak
Tobacco, sugar, tea, Indian textiles (volume of imports)	1714–1740	1710s
Britain II		
Cotton consumption, pig iron production	1763–1792	1780s
Railroad track laid (absolute amount and per square kilometer)	1815–1850	1830s
United States		
Steel, sulphuric acid, electricity production	1873–1914	1870s/1900s
Motor vehicle production, aerospace sales, semiconductor production, civilian jet airliner seat production	1945–1973	1950s

Note: Sources for these indicators are found in Modelski and Thompson (1996).

can be made for the activities peaking as predicted, but since we know more about the introductions of innovations than about their impacts, we cannot really say much about the timing of maximum impact.

In the other fourteen cases, it is possible to be more empirically specific. In every case, the predicted high-growth phase corresponds to the observed high-growth phase. Thus the idea that each lead economy has experienced two growth spurts before and after a period of global war or intense conflict (prior to 1494) seems supported to the present day.

It might look better if we did not have to change the indicators by time period. But that is the way technological innovation proceeds. Different sectors of the economy rise and fall in terms of their novelty, significance, and even existence. Asian pepper was a "hot" and highly profitable commodity in the sixteenth century but by the eighteenth century had become a more common sort of product. Steel was iconic in the late-nineteenth-century U.S. economy, but by the late twentieth century, it was hard to find much steel production in the same economy. Our tests have to correspond to changes in economic production in the same way that examinations of naval technology cannot give the same weight to the ship of the line or the battleship across time. What was first-class for frontline naval technology in the early nineteenth or twentieth century was relegated to the scrapyards later in the same century.

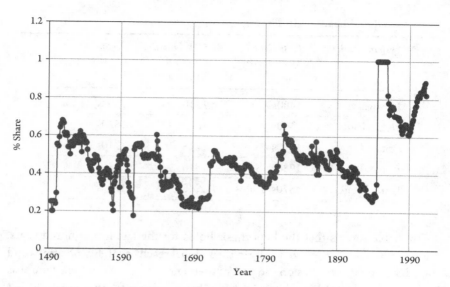

Figure 2.2 System Leader Global Reach Concentration, 1494–2013.

The third hypothesis examined here is the relationship between fluctuations in the concentrations of economic and global reach capabilities. Figure 2.2 plots the fluctuations in the share of the global system leader for the post-1494 period, for which we have reasonably good annual information. The picture portrayed seems only slightly different from the one plotted in figure 2.1. Portugal's rise is as abrupt as its decline. There is some short-lived reconcentration toward the end of the sixteenth century, when Spain absorbed the Portuguese country and fleet, that is not found in figure 2.1. After that interval, though, figure 2.2 resembles figure 2.1 relatively closely. The Dutch rose quickly and then fell in a steplike fashion. Britain experienced two periods of rise and decline in which the declines seem more protracted than those of its predecessor. The U.S. rise was abrupt, declined, and then got a second wind after the collapse of the Soviet Union. So there are similarities and differences.[14] The question is whether they are closely related.

Table 2.4 offers a quick test of the hypothesis that lead economies and global reach concentration are closely related. We should expect global system leaders to emerge just before the global war phase, with their peak global reach capability position between the two growth phases examined for the second hypothesis and probably around the time of the intervening global war. The normal shape of global reach capability concentration resembles the letter "N" without the third leg. Table 2.4 establishes when each global system leader attained or exceeded a 50 percent position in global reach capability concentration. The expectation was that the year identified in the third column should fall between the years shown in the second and fourth columns.

Table 2.4 **Global Leadership Timing**

System Leader	First Growth Spurt Peak	50% Naval Threshold Attained	Second Growth Spurt Peak
Portugal	1480s	1510	1500s/1530s
Netherlands	1560s	1610	1620s
Britain I	1670s	1715	1710s
Britain II	1780s	1810	1830s
United States	1870s/1900s	1945	1960s

The table reveals that the hypothesis holds for the last five hundred years. Global system leaders peaked early in their global reach capability positions and then, barring catastrophes on the part of their enemies, rode out their tenure as leaders with a decaying position. Historically, one reason for this pattern is that most global reach capability has been developed during periods of emergency (global war). Until more recent times, it has been difficult to find the money needed to develop increasingly expensive capabilities in peacetime. Cold wars have helped override this propensity. Thus, economic and naval concentration are seen to be related overall, but the two spurts in economic fluctuation are not necessarily mirrored in the naval data.

The leadership long cycle framework provides a useful foundation for examining systemic leadership questions. But it has at least one flaw that can be fixed with attention to differences among system leaders and the role of energy. This problem constitutes the primary focus of chapter 3. The first half of that chapter will elaborate the nature of the problem, and the second half will outline how we proceed to address it.

3

Revising the Framework: Energy and Eurasian History

This chapter has two different foci and parts. In the first part, we theorize as if each system leader has been similar in terms of what sorts of resource foundations they have brought to the arena and what they have been able to do with those foundations. It is clear that earlier leaders were much weaker than later leaders. What accounts for the difference, and what should we make of it in terms of deciphering international relations? Our answer is that system leaders have had variable claims to leads in commerce, technology, and energy. When they have combined all three, they have been very powerful. If they have only had a lead in commerce, they have still been able to play significant roles, but there have been very clear constraints on their systemic leadership capacities. Historically, it is only quite recently that system leaders have been able to combine all three. The process has been very much evolutionary.

In the second part, we consider how we might best track that evolutionary process and still contribute to a better understanding of the changes that have occurred. There are various research designs that we might employ. However, we have chosen to embed our approach in one of the central issues of Big History (see, e.g., Christian, 2011): the swinging of the socioeconomic, military, and political lead from western Eurasia to eastern Eurasia and back to western Eurasia and North America in what is sometimes referred to as the "Great Divergence." This oscillation was put in motion by the discovery of agricultural techniques— first in southwest Eurasia and then in China a few thousand years later. That gave the West a lead to innovate all sorts of things, such as cities, armies, irrigation, and beer. Gradually the East caught up and developed its own cities, armies, and irrigation projects. Exactly at what point the region caught up is debatable, but one position that is easy to defend is the era in which both the Roman and Han empires coexisted. After this point of rough equality, Rome declined and the Han Empire fragmented, but China came back in the Sui–Tang–Song dynasty period, while western Europe remained fragmented. Today, the pendulum may be swinging back to eastern Eurasia once more.

We seek to address these two issues simultaneously, explaining the leadership shift from the West to the East and back to the West while at the same time explaining the differential tendency for a long sequence of system leaders to develop commercial, technological, and energy leads. That goal may sound overly ambitious, but our response is that we think they are largely the same question. In this view, it is the sequence of systemic leadership that has played the vanguard role in the West–East–West organizational lead shifts.

To best reach this goal, we will start with Rome in chapter 4, instead of Song dynasty China, the first system leader in the leadership long cycle theoretical tradition. Rome is celebrated in Western annals as a powerful model of achievement in the ancient world, but it also represents the swan song of the ancient Western lead. Moreover, it represents in many respects the epitome of the agrarian land empire. As such, its economic foundation alerts us to look for different foundations among states in the post-Roman era, for Rome did not develop leads in commerce, technology, or energy. Such leads came later, with different powers. How that happened is the story told in chapters 5 through 9.

Not surprisingly, we think Modelski and Thompson's (1996) framework did some things right. It pushed back the origins of contemporary international relations to encompass a thousand-year development trajectory. It linked activities in the West to activities in the East as part of an even longer-term process lasting some five thousand years. Western developments (defined as those in the Middle Eastern/Mediterranean region) unfolded most intensely early on, before the pace of development shifted to the East and then back to the West, this time to Europe. Contemporary international relations is a product of these shifts and may be in the throes of still another shift back to the East.

Implicitly and explicitly, this framework links international relations to ongoing arguments about economic development. The two fields need each other. Economic development often tends to be too inward-oriented. International relations often does the opposite, neglecting critical internal changes. The framework does more than simply provide a development narrative. It generates a precise sequence of shifting technological concentrations that takes the story from China through the eastern Mediterranean to the Atlantic (moving from Portugal to the United States). The theory also elaborates the relationships between global economic leadership and political leadership by declining to focus on those states with large populations and armies that have played primarily regional roles, arguing that it is lead economies that matter most at the global level of interaction. For that matter, this approach emphasizes the differences between regional and global politics and political economy. Moreover, it attempts to buttress its arguments with empirical verification of its various claims. Strong and repeated concentrations in technology and global reach are not merely matters of opinion; they are hard to miss in the relevant data when one knows what to look for.

More than twenty years after the introduction of this framework, however, it has come time to admit that there is a problem that needs to be remedied. Modelski and Thompson's framework gives the impression that all system leaders have been similar in constitution, when clearly they have not and could not have been. No state in the eleventh or sixteenth century could approximate what powerful states could do in the twentieth century or can do in the twenty-first. The 1996 framework also ignored the role of energy. Remedying this oversight should help differentiate how system leaders have evolved over time as their energy foundations have changed markedly alongside their political, military, and economic clout.

Leaders and Their Energy Foundations

Treating the lead economy as if all lead economies have been generically similar when in fact they have come in all sizes and shapes is a problem. A more defensible generalization is that lead economies have packaged variable leads in commerce, technology, and energy. A commercial lead implies predominance in long-distance trade, often of a maritime nature. A technological lead means that the lead economy has been recognized for its distinctive ability to create software and hardware that make economic production and exchange more feasible. Technology thus encompasses machines that have made workers more powerful and effective (e.g., windmills or assembly lines) as well as the development of new ships and trade routes that have made exchange possible in ways that did not exist before. Transportation innovations (trains, cars, and planes) have been central to this history.

Energy leads, finally, involve some type of breakthrough in developing new energy sources that have not been absolutely necessary for the emergence of radical new technology but in the absence of which it would be difficult, if not impossible, to optimize the new technology's impact.[1] Relatively inexpensive energy is necessary to attain the scale of production required for broad market distribution. Otherwise, the new technology may remain restricted to elite consumption—which can still matter, but not as much as if consumption were to move beyond elite circles. The automobile is the best example from the twentieth century. Once assembly line innovations were introduced, motor vehicles could be turned out quickly and inexpensively. Experiments were conducted with steam engines and electricity, but petroleum combined with internal combustion engines won out as the most readily available and reliable fuel source.

Another new generalization is that it makes some difference how lead economies combine commercial, technological, and energy leadership. Those lead economies that have managed to combine all three have had the most impact on the world economy of their times. Additionally, one can also say that the nature of these technological leads has meant that each of these "trifecta" lead economies has outperformed and had a greater impact than its predecessor(s), especially in the case of the most recent examples (see table 3.1).[2]

Of course, it is easy to make such pronouncements. It is another matter to justify them in a theoretical fashion. To do that, we turn to Goldstone's (2002) efflorescence theory. Goldstone's concerns are not the same as ours; he is more interested in how analysts think about the general transition from premodern to modern economies. If it is assumed that (1) intensive economic growth is associated exclusively with modern economies, and (2) premodern economies only experienced extensive growth when they acquired larger populations or

Table 3.1 **Attributes of Successive System Leaders**

	Long-Distance Commercial Lead	*Technological Lead*	*Energy Transitional Lead*
Song China	No, but developed later, and limited to Eastern zone	Yes, and maintained later at times	No
Genoa	Yes, but limited to Western zone	No (European maritime lead)	No
Venice	Yes, but limited to Western zone	No (European maritime lead that became more industrial)	No
Portugal	Yes, but limited to Western zone	No (European maritime lead)	No
Netherlands	Yes (Europe and East–West trade)	Yes (Europe)	Only partially (peat/wind subject to important constraints)
Britain I	Yes (Europe and Atlantic trade)	No	No
Britain II	Yes	Yes	Yes (coal)
United States I	Yes	Yes	Yes (first coal and then electricity/petroleum)

territories, the transition from premodern to modern economies seems somewhat mysterious and forces analysts to fall back on how the places that first made the transition are different from the places that were slow to follow.

Goldstone thinks that this type of thinking is erroneous. In his view, significant periods of economic growth, called "efflorescences," are not restricted to modern economies but could be experienced by premodern economies as well. The difference between modern and premodern economies is that growth in premodern economies could occur for a number of decades but could not be sustained. Sooner or later, expanding premodern economies would run out of steam and enter a crisis period in which growth stagnated or was reversed. Modern economies have short-term crises too, but they are still able to sustain economic growth in the long term. Thus, the question is what was missing from the premodern economy that precluded sustained economic growth. For Goldstone, the answer is a sufficient amount and concentration of energy generators that ultimately produced energy bottlenecks. Premodern economies could muster only so much energy, and what they could muster tended to be dispersed. Remove one or both barriers, and more work could have been accomplished. Box 3.1 lays out the theory more fully.

Goldstone's theory does more than "merely" specify the key to the transition from premodern to modern economies. It also addresses when periods of efflorescence and crisis are more likely. In particular, efflorescences are linked to external contacts and ideas developed through trade. Goldstone does not elaborate on this notion, but he is clear that isolation is bad for growth—excluding, as it does, not only Smithian growth, which is based on gains from divisions of labor across borders, but also Schumpeterian growth, which is predicated on technological innovations (assuming that innovators can benefit from ideas generated in foreign economies by avoiding ideas that do not seem to work and copying and improving on those that do). Trade generates power and wealth in its own right to be sure. But it also enhances opportunities for borrowing ideas from others and developing technological leads that promote growth.

Energy needs to be both expanded and concentrated to support the development of manufacturing complexes and urban areas. While not explicitly stated in Goldstone's theory, it also helps if the energy is relatively inexpensive. Otherwise, there will be severe constraints on how productive novel combinations of energy sources and technological innovations can be. To build an economy capable of becoming the predominant global supplier of technologically sophisticated goods, a state's energy supplies must be very large, highly concentrated, and inexpensive. Again, although not emphasized in Goldstone's theory, economic gains of this scale are usually associated with a state's either leading the transition to a new fuel source or better exploiting the prevailing primary energy source than predecessors.

Box 3.1 **Goldstone's Efflorescence Theory**

Most premodern economies intermittently pulsated up (efflorescence) and down (crisis) in terms of growth without achieving modern, sustained economic growth.

Crises are more likely to emerge in the context of wars, climate reversals, population growth that proceeds faster than economic innovation, and/or harvest failures. They are characterized by declining living standards and population growth.

Efflorescences are characterized by increases in per capita income, accelerated urbanization, expanding trade, and significant population growth.

Efflorescences are more likely to occur in trading centers focused on meeting commercial demands and in places subject to sustained cultural and ideational interactions with other economies. They are also more likely during periods of reconstruction following some kind of shock that unleashes new energies, groups, or territories to exploit. Efflorescences are less likely toward the end of long periods of stability that stress conformity or in relatively isolated societies.

The ultimate bottleneck in premodern economies involved the amount and concentration of energy available. Premodern economies had limited amounts of energy, and their energy sources were difficult to concentrate in order to support equally concentrated production, consumption, storage, and urbanization.

Whenever these premodern energy bottlenecks were overcome, economic growth generally followed (and the greater the extent to which the energy bottlenecks were overcome, the greater was the economic growth that followed).*

However, overcoming bottlenecks was not sufficient to attain sustained growth. While there was no general pathway from early to fully modern economic growth, the transition to sustained economic growth could be achieved by developing technology that turned sources of heat into considerably expanded productivity, as well as by embracing an "engine" culture open to continuing experimentation with the application of transformed heat to manufacturing and transportation.

---

*The statement in parentheses is not found in Goldstone's explicit argument, but it does seem to follow it implicitly.

Long-distance commerce, technology, and energy are all linked. If one state can monopolize or develop a substantial lead in one, two, or all three of these arenas for a period of time, its political–economic power will increase relative to competitors, particularly as more of these activities are controlled simultaneously. This is all the more true if the lead economy acts as a pioneer in developing new sources of heat generation for manufacturing, transportation, and warming/cooling purposes. The lead economy that also leads the way to new levels of "modernity" will be more powerful than states that fail to do so.

Klein (2007) has generated a list of ten factors that he thinks were involved in the industrialization of the United States. The list is striking because, with a few adjustments and additions, it can be applied as a template to efflorescent growth over the past two millennia (or even further back). The list, which appears in box 3.2, begins with the replacement of muscle with machinery and the infiltration of productivity-enhancing technological innovation. Dramatic improvements in transportation and communications and the reorganization of firms then facilitate scalar increases in production and the expansion of the

---

Box 3.2 **Klein's "Hothouse for U.S. Economic Growth" Model**

1. Power-driven machinery replaced human and animal muscle as a source of energy for doing all kinds of work.
2. Technological innovations infiltrated every area of business and economic activity, greatly increasing productivity and expanding the range of goods that could be produced.
3. Production increased in scale by moving from scattered homes and shops to factories or other centrally located facilities.
4. A transportation revolution regularized and sped up the flow of goods and people.
5. A communications revolution regularized and sped up the flow of information, enabling firms to do business across the nation while maintaining a centrally located headquarters.
6. A full-blown market economy emerged and extended its reach beyond the local level to the regional and national levels.
7. An organization revolution restructured American business enterprise, enabling it to reach unprecedented size and scale of operation.
8. Specialization came to characterize nearly every aspect of economic activity.
9. Population increased at unprecedented rates.
10. The number of cities and towns increased sharply, as did the proportion of Americans living in them.

market economy and specialization within it. Finally, rapid growth in population and urbanization responds to the positive environment of economic
growth.

All of these factors were not equally present in the four national cases that
came closest to energy breakthroughs—Song China, the Netherlands, Britain,
and the United States. The reorganization of firms, for instance, was more strongly
evident in the U.S. case than in Song China. Communications revolutions, of
course, work differently in different eras depending on the starting point. Full-
blown market economies can only be created so many times.

Despite the strength of Klein's model, several additional factors are needed.
One is energy transitions that interact with such factors as muscle-replacing machinery and technological innovation. A second is trade, which was only intermittently critical in the U.S. case but far more so in earlier cases. A third factor
is something we call "frontier exploitation," or a hitherto untapped source of
resources (Maddison's fertile empty areas) that can be utilized to benefit the
economic growth of the larger unit.[3] Thus, Klein's original model would resemble figure 3.1, while our model of economic growth can be sketched as displayed in figure 3.2. In Klein's model, all ten factors "compete" for effect. Ours,
in contrast, relies on a two-phase model in which the first phase can generate

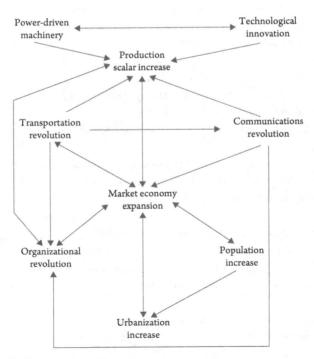

Figure 3.1 Klein's Ten Primary Factors.

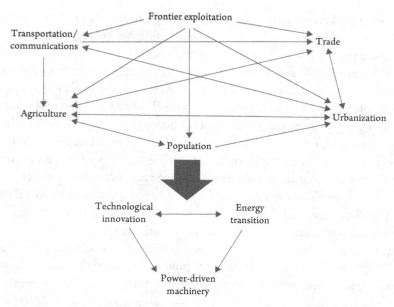

Figure 3.2 Our Revision of Klein's Model.

economic growth of the Smithian variety without an energy transition or even much technological innovation. Without some significant interaction between technological innovation and energy transition in the second phase, there are limits to the type of economic growth that can be achieved, meaning that the economy stops short of registering a full breakthrough from the type of political economy that preceded the transformation. Song China remained an agrarian economy despite prescient moves to industrialize. The Netherlands made considerable headway in utilizing peat and wind but still fell short of becoming the first modern economy. Britain made use of coal, steam, and iron to do what the Netherlands had failed to accomplish. The United States closely followed and eventually surpassed the British lead, first with coal, steam, and iron and later with petroleum, internal combustion engines, electricity, and information technology.

Perhaps the most glaring missing variable in these models is political structure. An easy explanation for this absence is that Klein's U.S. case was characterized by limited government intervention most of the time, making political structure not an obvious variable of interest for his single case study. When one compares different states across one thousand years, political structure might seem a more obvious factor. Economists have always stressed that strong political centralization is bad for economic innovation. We are willing to accept this generalization with caveats; however, all of the cases that we will be examining possessed governments that either were facilitative of economic growth or at least were not barriers to growth in the eras of greatest economic innovation. In some cases, governments later became less facilitative. Yet it is not always clear which came first: economic decline or the less facilitative role of government. As a consequence—and admittedly quite ironically, because the authors are trained as political scientists—we have chosen not to explore this issue much in this chapter or the next five, although it is much harder to avoid in the last few chapters on global warming and the transition to the next energy foundation. The reason is that we simply did not find it to be a critical variable in our four main case studies.[4] Perhaps if we had engaged in more explicit comparisons of cases of failure and success, politics would have been more significant. However, we centered our discussion on what the more successful cases have in common. Thus, we have assumed that governments were at the very least not significant obstacles in a given state's ascent to technological centrality.[5]

At the same time, our entire explanatory apparatus is very much attuned to the interactions between international politics and international economics. System leaders are political–economic actors that engage in some minimal level of governance over a widely dispersed economic system. Various factors are important to the rise of system leaders. One is some level of insularity that prevents the leader from being overwhelmed by powerful neighbors with stronger armies. China relied on rivers to keep the Mongols at bay for a while. The Dutch had their dikes and canals. Britain had the English Channel, while the United States enjoyed the Atlantic and Pacific bulwarks. A second factor, previously emphasized in chapter 2, is the influence of global war as a facilitator of new system leader regimes. Once global wars emerged after 1494, winning these intensive conflicts and leading the subsequent reconstruction efforts became necessary ingredients in the "inauguration" of system leaders. But our emphasis in this examination is technological centrality, not system leadership per se. Thus, geopolitics is also compartmentalized away from the model displayed in figure 3.2.

Our revision of the Modelski–Thompson (1996) framework will focus primarily on demonstrating the distinctions among the cases of China from about 500 CE to 1800 CE, the seventeenth-century Netherlands, nineteenth-century Britain, and the nineteenth- to twentieth-century United States. We do not propose to ignore the other actors singled out as system leaders in the original framework. As suggested in table 3.1, our plan is to discuss three main types of leads: long-distance commerce, technology, and energy. The central argument is that systemic leadership that has been founded on leads in all three categories has led to the most impactful global leaders. Less impactful leaderships have been based on one or two of these categories, and they have come with caveats about where these leads were maintained. Genoa, Venice, and Portugal, for example, were not unimportant, but they were mainly commercial leaders in the

Western zone. With hindsight, we can also say that they were transitional agents in moving from the early Chinese lead to an eventual European lead. Britain I shared a great deal with these transitional agents, as did the Netherlands in some respects. The movement from medieval China to the twenty-first century was not as linear as a China to United States sequence might otherwise suggest.

The interaction between technology and energy helps to explain one analytical disagreement in international relations discourse. Only the leadership long cycle argument makes a case for nine successive lead economies, albeit of uneven significance, over a millennium. Most approaches to the structure of world politics either assume the absence of hierarchy altogether or focus on some combination of the Netherlands, Britain, and the United States as worthy of special distinction. Of these three, the United States is usually viewed as possessing the strongest claim to the system leader/hegemon status, with Britain trailing in a weak second position. World system analysts (and long cyclists) add the Netherlands to this group, but most other schools of thought do not. The reason for these disagreements about the historical script has to do with the generalization that lead economies that combine all three types of lead (commerce, technology, and energy) have the strongest foundation for impacting world politics and economics. We remember these economies because they made a bigger impression than the other lead economies, with the most recent cases making the biggest impression.

Song China made considerable headway in breaking free of agrarian constraints on economic development but ultimately failed to make a breakthrough. Genoa, Venice, and Portugal were transient leaders that specialized in long-distance trade, controlled trade routes, and focused primarily on maritime technology. The Dutch followed their path in dominating European trade and, to a lesser extent, Asian–European trade. But the Dutch also pursued the Chinese path of developing technology that depended on converting heat into mechanized power, thereby enhancing what the Netherlands had to trade. However, their energy combination of windmills and peat could only do so much in terms of heat conversion. The British, like most of their predecessors, initially specialized in Asian and American trade, but their heating needs led to an increasing reliance on coal, which, in turn, led to the development of steam engines.[6] The combination of coal and steam engines produced the breakthrough that had eluded both the Chinese and the Dutch. The United States initially piggybacked on the coal–steam engine breakthrough to make its own energy transition contribution in terms of electricity and petroleum. Unfortunately, today we have to figure out a way to make up for the negative side effects of developing carbon-based economies in the next iteration.

Returning to new generalizations associated with revising the older framework, another proposition is that only very enthusiastic advocates of renewables foresee the advent of a new energy transition away from carbon-based fuels prior to the end of the twenty-first century. The implications of such a protracted transition away from carbon fuels for the world environment are not clear. At the very least, more unpleasantness as opposed to less should be a more likely outcome of the acceleration of global warming. These circumstances also suggest a lesser probability of either system leader transition in the twenty-first century or, alternatively, a transition to a new, strong systemic leadership that would require inexpensive energy as a prerequisite (Zakhirova and Thompson, 2015). They may even mean that we will discontinue relying on a rather primitive leadership structure determined by technological preeminence, a decisive edge in energy per capita, wealth, and military–political power.

There are of course other reasons for thinking that a singular lead economy might be an endangered species.[7] But if the hierarchical structure of the system is changing fundamentally, the absence of a singular lead economy might translate to the introduction of less new technology or the introduction of new technology in a less concentrated way—both temporally and geographically.[8] Multiple lead economies in partially autonomous zones might once again set up equally multiple technological life cycles that do not move together in a synchronized way.

Nonetheless, one of the principal motivations for revising the Modelski and Thompson (1996) framework, besides correcting what are now seen as analytical errors, is to underline the close connection between systemic leadership and energy transitions. If we can make this connection as explicit and persuasive as possible, a novel foundation for speculating about the twenty-first century and a possible systemic leadership transition will have been established. We think that the likelihood of a leadership transition will be pegged to the likelihood of an energy transition. Since this transition currently appears to be forecast for some eighty years into the future, we predict that regardless of whether the institution of systemic leadership survives intact, a systemic leadership transition is not likely in the near future and possibly not even in this century.[9]

Still, there are other possibilities. The nature of the next energy transition may not give any particular state the kind of edge or lead that was possible in earlier years. Less hierarchy might thus be expected. For that matter, it is not inconceivable that the ravages of global warming will outpace the onset of an energy transition. We may be too late to salvage the environment in which we live. Precisely what will happen in the twenty-first century is not easy to forecast.

Our first task in this effort is to establish the historical linkages among systemic leadership, technology, and energy. Only then will we have a more solid footing for speculating about the rest of the twenty-first century. Even then, we can only proceed using information that may very well change at some point down the road. However, we think this approach will provide a better foundation for speculating about systemic leader transitions than a comparison of Chinese and American populations or economies. There is more involved in generating system leaders than has been realized to date.

In the next chapter, we discuss the Roman Empire case as an agrarian baseline from which subsequent cases deviated. In chapters 5 through 9, we look at medieval China, the transitional Western lead economies (Genoa, Venice, and Portugal), the seventeenth-century Netherlands, nineteenth-century Britain, and the twentieth-century United States. For the main cases, we particularly examine whether, and to what extent, their developments as technological centers approximate the general scheme outlined in figure 3.2. In general, the schematic template proves useful. Each case is not exactly like the one that preceded or followed it, but the main factors that propelled their development into technological centrality can all be found in the model.

Convergence and Divergence in Eastern and Western Eurasia

Agriculture was discovered independently in several places, but the first two places were located in southwest and East Asia. As a consequence, Eurasia led the rest of the world in transitioning away from the hunting-gathering era. But Eurasia's lead was uneven. Southwest Asia was the first "active zone" of the agrarian era, with many developments emerging from Sumer or southern Mesopotamia in the period between roughly 4000 and 2000 BCE. Some of these Mesopotamian-type innovations began to emerge in East Asia after 2000 BCE. We and others argue that the two regions converged in the Roman–Han empire era (circa 200 BCE–200 CE). Thus, the two ends of Eurasia initially diverged with a Western lead, then converged, and finally diverged again with an Eastern lead for at least a millennium. The divergence in the favor of the East was later reset by what is sometimes called the Great Divergence of the late eighteenth century CE, in which Western industrialization created a massive power gap between West and East.

Yet before the two divergences of the last two millennia, there was a brief but remarkable period of convergence that is well-summarized in the Gizewski (1994) Qin–Han–Roman model delineated in table 3.2. The model begins by noting that both Rome and Qin emerged on the western frontiers of their respective regions roughly at the same time, with one difference: Rome was not linked to Greece or other Mediterranean powers, while Qin was a component of the Western Zhou hierarchy. Otherwise, both states emphasized military prowess and survived in tough neighborhoods in part thanks to protection provided by physical barriers. Gradually, the two states acquired military–political dominance

Table 3.2 **Gizewski Qin–Han–Roman Phase Model**

Phase	Timing	Activities
1	To c. 500 BCE	Creation of polities at western margins of much wider ecumene with emphasis on military capability. Qin already embedded in Western Zhou feudal network; Rome further removed from Levantine power centers
2	5th/4th centuries BCE	Qin and Rome grew into autonomous middling powers and conflicted with comparable competitors. Both retained independence because they were shielded physically (sea and Alps in Italy and mountain ranges in Qin and Sichuan) from major-power conflicts in more developed regions farther east and were able to increase military capability without encountering the superior capacity of more powerful states.
3	4th/early 3rd centuries BCE	Acquisition of hegemonic power over large sectors of respective ecumene, with Rome adopting an Italian focus and the Qin a Sichuan focus. Growth occurred without triggering major conflicts with leading powers, but clashes were brought closer by encroachments on leading-power territory.
4	3rd–1st centuries BCE	Hegemony achieved over entire core ecumene in series of high-stakes wars. Qin bureaucracy facilitated direct rule, unlike the limited bureaucracy of the Romans. Large-scale conquest triggered violent adjustment processes. In the East, the war machine state of Qin shifted to the less overtly centralized early Han regime; in the West, a more protracted transition took place as Rome shifted from oligarchy to military monarchy. Both transitions produced monarchies with militarily strong aristocratic participation.

Table 3.2 **Continued**

Phase	Timing	Activities
5	2nd century BCE to 2nd century CE	Slowing expansion and increasing internal homogenization characterized imperial processes, while powerful but cooperative local elites were strengthened at the expense of imperial action ranges.
6	3rd century CE	Warlordism and temporary fragmentation crisis, more readily contained by Roman professional military than by warlords of Three Kingdoms China
7	Early 4th century CE (northern China)/early 5th century CE (Rome)	Attempted restoration (much more prolonged and temporarily successful in Rome) followed by barbarian conquest.
8	Late 5th/6th centuries CE	Division of Rome into eastern and western wings; division of China into Chinese south and northern barbarian successor states. In both cases, conquerors merged with local elites. Christianity and Buddhism made considerable progress in their respective spheres. Sixth-century reunification efforts more successful in China than in the Mediterranean.
9	7th century CE on	Sharp divergence. In the East, Tang regime consolidated, while the eastern Roman state was nearly destroyed by Persians and Arabs, followed by prolonged and intensive Islamic and Frankish fragmentation. Europe characterized by state polycentrism, while China underwent the Song–Yuan–Ming–Qing sequence.

Note: Model based on Gizewski (1994) as recounted in Scheidel (2009).

over first Italy and Sichuan, respectively, and then over the Mediterranean and China. Qin was replaced by Han shortly after hegemony was established, but both states remained or became highly centralized at the turn of the millennium.

After this period of expansion, both empires became relatively stationary and by the third century CE were confronted with the threat of fragmentation by warlords. Rome managed to overcome this tendency for a century or two, while the Han Empire disintegrated. Nonetheless, both states were overrun by barbarians in the fourth and fifth centuries CE and left divided. Western Rome never reemerged, though an eastern wing based in Constantinople managed to persist to the fifteenth century. In China, which was divided on a north–south axis, indigenous dynasties regained control gradually. By the seventh century CE, imperial China had been restored.[10]

The differential outcomes of the two empires help considerably to explain the shift in organizational momentum eastward. When both empires were strong, they possessed similar-sized populations, very large imperial domains, military dominance, and technological supremacy, with the important exception that the Eastern hub was more open to innovations than the Western hub, which emphasized engineering over science and technological innovation (unless such innovations were due to the Greeks). After dissolution, the Eastern colossus regained its momentum. The Western colossus fragmented into a number of small and relatively weak states with limited tax-collecting capabilities and a feudal dispersal of military capability. Disease lingered in the West, while it was largely absent in the East. Urbanization was not renewed in the West for quite some time after fragmentation, while in the East, a number of large cities subsequently emerged, with some approaching the size of Rome. Finally, the Chinese were able to hold their barbarian invaders at bay for several centuries until being completely overrun in the thirteenth century, while in the West, the barbarians had taken over everywhere except Constantinople by the sixth and seventh centuries and soon were at war with Islamic forces expanding upward from the south. In many respects, the shift in organizational momentum was overdetermined by events working out much differently in the East and the West.

One byproduct of this asymmetrical outcome was the continued operation of east and west Eurasia as two separate development zones. Although agriculture developed in these two regions separately, the zones subsequently interacted. The Western zone emerged first, and its early influence on the East can be seen in Eastern archaeology (e.g., iron and chariots that came from the West). After the Eastern zone caught up and surpassed the Western zone by the second half of the first millennium CE, a number of Western industrialization innovations were based on Eastern inventions. Western industrialization in turn boosted the West ahead of the East and led to the gradual subordination of the East to the West via a combination of military and economic conquest. Europeans moved first into the Indian Ocean and the Eastern islands producing spices before expanding to South Asia, followed by southeast Asia and then the Chinese core itself in the nineteenth century. Thus, the two regions were never entirely separate autonomous zones. But they were autonomous enough to develop differently in the period leading up to the mid-nineteenth century, after which they no longer possessed much autonomy.[11]

Underlying this discussion of connectivity is the notion that there are different types of interaction. Chase-Dunn and Hall (1997) suggest four main types: information, bulk goods, prestige goods, and political/military. While they do not specify any thresholds for such interaction, we can posit a system in which actors regularly engage in, respectively, the exchange of ideas and technological principles (information), food and raw materials (bulk goods), luxury commodities (prestige goods), and military conflict or alliances (political/military). Systems may focus on only one of the four types of interaction, or some combination of the four may be nested in an overlapping pattern that need not possess exactly the same boundaries.

In this respect, Afro-Eurasia became a single system very early on in terms of information exchange. Prestige goods were also being exchanged fairly early, if somewhat intermittently, as demonstrated by the silk trade linking Rome and China in the second century BCE. Yet an Afro-Eurasian political/military integration took quite some time to develop, in part because Western actors were unable to project force into East Asia before the sixteenth century CE, and in part because China chose not to project its own military force beyond East Africa in the early fifteenth century CE. Mutually exclusive military boundaries were reinforced by occasional clashes on land (survivors of a decimated Roman legion may have been used as slave mercenaries in Central Asia, and Chinese and Muslim forces fought in the eighth century CE), but the only genuine exception to the political/military separation of West and East was associated with the Mongol expansion. Yet even this spectacular undertaking stopped short of penetrating all or even most of the Western system in a military sense.

Chase-Dunn and Hall (1997: 205) have developed a figure (see figure 3.3), jocularly described as the "Kissing Coyotes," that summarizes their interpretation of East–West interactions. In general, they say:

> All world-systems pulsate in the sense that the spatial scale of integration, especially by trade, becomes larger and then smaller again. During the enlarging phase, trade networks grow in territorial size and become more dense in terms of the frequency of interactions. During the declining phase, trade slackens and local areas become less connected and reorganize around self-sufficiency. Local identities and the cultural distinctions between local groups and outsiders are emphasized.

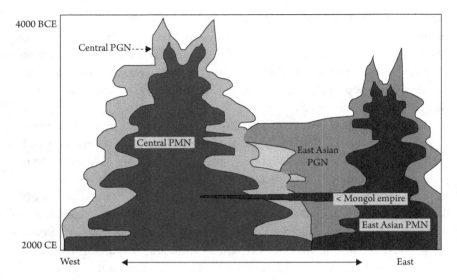

Figure 3.3 East and West Interactions in Eurasia Source: Christopher Chase-Dunn and Thomas Hall.

In the case of two adjacent or nearly adjacent systems, internal pulsations overlap with external pulsations. In the typical pattern, initial contact comes in the form of indirect information flows across boundaries. Next, the systems' prestige goods networks establish linkages. Later their political/military networks may merge. Finally, even the bulk goods networks are integrated. This is the way the Western (Chase-Dunn and Hall say "central") and Eastern systems have come together. Information flows developed quite early, followed by trade in prestige goods. The lighter areas in figure 3.3 represent trade networks, and the darker areas political/military networks. The Eastern and Western systems pulsate in their own right, as do their cross-system interactions. Other than the Mongol penetration in the thirteenth century, the two political/military networks did not fuse until the nineteenth century CE.

Hence, one can argue that one single system encompassing both eastern and western Eurasia existed from a very early date, but it was initially confined to the exchange of information (and some technology). Prestige goods were added to the mix more systematically after about 200 BCE. In the Chase-Dunn and Hall perspective, fuller integration came only with the Opium Wars. One implication of this model is that we do not have to worry too much about explicitly comparing what was going on in the West when our focus is on the East, and vice versa.

Before we get to that point, however, a very low-level baseline needs to be established. We create that baseline by examining the last Western empire of the ancient world, Rome, in the next chapter. It is not fully part of our story, but it provides a good contrast with what took place after the fall of Rome and the slow passage toward the emergence of system leaders in world politics. Rome was certainly a system leader in the ancient world. However, it was not part of the modern lineage of system leaders.

PART II

THE PAST

4

Rome as the Pinnacle of
the Western Ancient World

A series of increasingly impressive empires characterizes the history of the Western ancient world. Beginning with Sargon's Akkadian Empire in Mesopotamia and moving on to the Assyrians, the Persians, and the Macedonians, the successive Western empires became larger and more powerful. Rome followed in this tradition, becoming even larger and more powerful. Yet, in the end, the decline of Rome almost brought the sequence of Western empires to a halt.[1] It also signaled a transition in economic innovation toward the East that was to persist for at least a millennium.

Ancient Rome is thus an important turning point in Eurasian history. But it is also an interesting test case in its own right. Previously, the standard view (Finley, 1973) was that ancient economies operated on a subsistence production basis and lacked technological innovation, and that therefore, economic growth in the modern sense—as opposed to intermittent efforts to seize additional farming territory from neighbors—was highly unlikely.[2] Yet we have the sense that Rome was wealthy, and, as Scheidel (2012: 12–13) expressed it, how could economic expansion "have failed to occur" given the expansion of the Roman republic and and then the empire throughout the Mediterranean and Western Europe? In support of his argument for Roman expansion, Scheidel provides a long list of growth-promoting factors associated with the empire, including capital inflows, slave inputs, violent redistribution of assets, reduced transaction costs, widespread resource mobilization, knowledge transfers, underexploited mines supporting monetarization and other activities, climate optimum, and an absence of pandemics. Given all these factors, it is hard to imagine some economic growth not taking place.

Was this growth simply another example of the efflorescence that has been possible at various times in history without regard to innovations in either technology or energy? Our answer is yes. The Roman Empire most likely did enjoy a spurt of economic growth. However, its absence of technological and energy

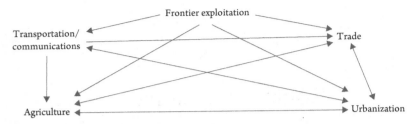

Figure 4.1 Roman Economic Growth.

innovations sets Rome apart from the next two millennia of efforts to escape the constraints of organic economies. In that respect, it provides a useful baseline with which to compare the evolving nature of global power—military, political, and economic. Rome belongs in this story not so much because it was part of the lineage of the more powerful states to come—for of course it was and later powerful states remembered its legacy. Rather, Rome belongs in this story for what it did not do: it made little effort to escape the constraints of an agrarian political economy. Thus, it is something of a negative template for what was to come in the next one and a half millennia.

Figure 4.1 resummarizes our economic growth model without the technology–energy–power-driven machinery triangle.[3] From the perspective of this model, the Roman story revolves around frontier exploitation and its linkages to agrarian production, urbanization, and trade. Roman economic growth was about coercive expansion that could not, or at least was not likely to, go on forever. Similarly, the Roman growth spurt was finite and could not be sustained any more than the Roman Empire was likely to endure for a very long time. That it did last as long as it did is an impressive achievement, one firmly embedded in an agrarian political economy from which it could not escape. Nor did it try to escape from an agrarian regime. That makes it very different from some of the states that followed. It is this characteristic that explains why figure 4.1 has no technological innovation–energy transition–power-driven machinery bloc. They are simply not pertinent to an understanding of the Roman phenomenon.

Frontier Exploitation and Agrarian Development

In some respects, the Roman achievement was the product of a distinct type of frontier exploitation. Conventionally, frontier exploitation is about accessing and making use of new and untapped resources. Rome fulfilled these aims by building an empire focused on the Mediterranean and extending north into Europe. The resources it tapped were new to the Romans, if not to the people who were subordinated by them. Conquest brought new resources into Italy, and these new resources transformed the political economy of that region, if not the entire empire. Paradoxically, though, Rome would ultimately be hoisted by its own petard, because these political–economic changes contributed significantly to its eventual decline. Imperial success ultimately had major implications for the long-term survival of the Roman Empire.

A good place to begin is Mann's (1986) core–periphery contradiction model (figure 4.2) and his emphasis on the "legionary economy." The Romans, once subordinate to Etruscan overlords, were situated on a frontier themselves—one separating Italy from Celtic intrusions from the north. Initially, Rome had little success in fending off Celtic attacks, but gradually it changed its tactics and developed a military capability that few adversaries could defeat. The core of that capability was the Roman army. Focused on an infantry recruited from a population of farmers who served part-time and then tended to their land, the Roman system abandoned the Greek phalanx for a more flexible organizational format that centered on a combination of javelins, large shields, short swords, and various types of artillery.

For Mann, the army legions represent the state and the economy. Thanks to elite apprehension about power concentration, the state was kept to a minimal size and its leadership was rotated frequently. Its primary purpose was to supply and support the army. Consequently, the Roman economy was equally fixated on the same purposes—supplying and supporting the army's need for provisions and salaries. Yet the army itself was dependent on societal cohesion,

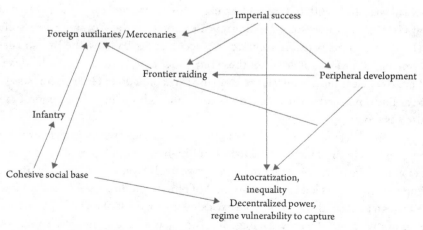

Figure 4.2 Mann's Core–Periphery Model. Source: Modified from Mann (1986): ch. 9.

which ensured a regular supply of men who were willing to serve and could rely on one another to carry out their military mission.

These initial conditions contributed to the success of the Roman legions in creating a very large empire over several centuries, but they were always unlikely to be sustained indefinitely.[4] Rising military costs, population decline, the need for cavalry, and frontier raiding led to an increased reliance on foreign troops and mercenaries. Actually, the use of part-time farmer volunteers had begun to weaken as early as the Punic Wars, which began in the mid-third century BCE. Full-time professionals were increasingly demanded to wage imperial warfare continuously. However, heavy infantry have always encountered supply problems when operating in empty deserts and steppes far from home bases, and forests also have historically made it difficult to operate in large units. Therefore, conquest armies have inevitably confronted spatial limitations beyond which they cannot move successfully. As the Roman Empire assumed its maximal shape, it was hemmed in by forests in the north, deserts in the south, an ocean to the west, and deserts and steppe to the east, with the latter exacerbated by the enemy's combination of heavy cavalry and horseback soldiers with rapid-firing bows, which was hard to beat. Offensive expansionary approaches had to give way to increasingly expensive defensive tactics that demanded more mobility than could be expected of infantry, especially when the northern and eastern frontiers were under attack simultaneously.

Table 4.1 is designed to provide some support for these assertions. Focusing on actual fighting between Romans and non-Romans and ignoring civil wars, revolts, and political turmoil involved in overthrowing emperors, the columns on the left-hand side encompass selected BCE events, while the right-hand columns look only at CE events. Before the Common Era, Rome gradually expanded its control in its immediate backyard, went on to conquer Italy, and then spread west and south to take on Carthage, north to seize Gaul, and east to pick off Greece and the eastern Mediterranean littoral. In the Common Era, some relatively minor expansion occurred in places like the Balkans, the British Isles, Armenia, and Mesopotamia. Yet these territories could not always be held, and there were clear limits to what the Roman army could do in German forests and Near Eastern deserts. The defensive flavor of the fighting in the Common Era is also easy to discern.

Another facet of the Roman undermining-its-own success problem emphasized in the Mann model that is not highlighted in figure 4.2 is depicted better in Hopkins's (1978) model of the growth of slavery, outlined in figure 4.3. Imperial conquests led to a large amount of plunder finding its way back to Italy. Although some of this loot may have trickled down, most of it was kept by elites. Part of the spoils of war was a huge influx of slaves, who eventually comprised as much as a fourth or third of the Italian population. Given this ample supply

Table 4.1 **The Rise and Fall of Rome: Selected Highlights, 396 BCE–410 CE**

Date	BCE Events	Date	CE Events
396 BCE	Etruscan city of Veii captured	7 CE	Roman border expanded to Balkans
343–341	Roman–Samnite fighting	9	Rome withdraws to Rhone after Teutoburg Forest defeat
340–338	Roman–Latin League fighting	43	Invasion of Britain
328–305	Roman–Samnite fighting	58	Conquest of Armenia
298–290	Roman–Samnite fighting	77	Conquest of Wales
295	Gauls/Celts defeated in northern Italy	80	Invasion of Caledonia (Scotland)
283	Defeat of Etruscans, Boii, and Senones	106	Dacia and Arabia (Nabatea) become provinces
280–272	Pyrrhic War leads to conquest of most of southern Italy	116	Mesopotamia conquered
264	Roman–Carthaginian fighting	122	Hadrian's Wall built in Britain
241–238	First Punic War—Carthage surrenders claims to Sardinia and Corsica	161–166	War with Parthians
229–228	Illyrian fighting	167–178	First invasion of German barbarians
225–222	Invading Gauls defeated	194	Palmyra annexed to Syria
219	Illyrian fighting	198	Northern half of Mesopotamia annexed
218–201	Second Punic War	202	Southern frontier of African expanded
214–205	First Macedonian War	214	Edessa declared a colony
200–196	Second Macedonian War	230–233	Roman–Sassanid fighting
192–180	Roman–Seleucid War	244	Roman–Sassanid fighting
172–167	Third Macedonian War	255	Goths invade Macedonia, Dalmatia, and Asia Minor
150–148	Fourth Macedonian War	256–260	Sassanids defeat Rome and conquer Armenia and parts of Mesopotamia

(*continued*)

Table 4.1 **Continued**

Date	BCE Events	Date	CE Events
149–146	Third Punic War	269	Gothic invasion of Balkans forestalled
146	Macedonian and African provinces established	279	Fighting with Vandals in Illyricum
133	Pergamum willed to Rome, giving Rome control of Mediterranean	344	Roman–Sassanid fighting
128	Province of Acquitania (southern France) established	357	Roman–Alemanni fighting
111–106	Numidia defeated	363	Roman–Sassanid fighting
91–88	Social War (Italian rebellion)	376	Goths cross Danube fleeing Huns
87–85	First Mithridatic War	376–382	Roman–Gothic fighting
81	Second Mithridatic War	406	Vandals, Alans, and Suibi cross Rhine
73–63	Third Mithridatic War	410	Rome sacked by Visigoths; Britain abandoned by Rome
69	Invasion of Armenia		
64	Syria becomes Roman province		
57	All of Gaul conquered		
53	Roman–Parthian fighting		
47–30	Invasion and annexation of Egypt		
36	Invasion of Persia attempted		
20	Roman–Parthian border fixed at Euphrates		
13	Roman border expanded to Danube region		
12	Rome crosses Rhine into Germania		

Source: Information partly drawn from Piero Scaruffi, "A Time-line of the Roman Empire," www.scaruffi.com/politics/romans.html.

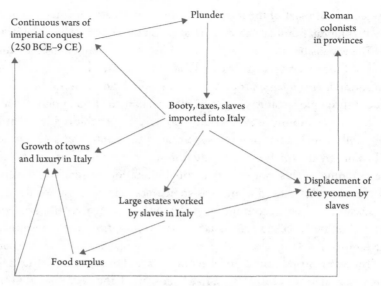

Figure 4.3 Hopkins' Growth of Roman Slavery Model. Source: Based on Hopkins (1978: 12) and simplified somewhat.

of cheap labor and the agrarian economy, elites' most common investment was the purchase of land in Italy, on which they constructed villas. That land could be used to grow food for consumption in Rome and other growing cities. But it also meant the displacement of the farmers who had once been the army's core recruiting base.[5] As agriculture became more commercialized, farmers without slaves could not compete and in many cases could not hang on to their land. Their choices were to become full-time, professional soldiers; move to the city, especially Rome; or become colonists somewhere in the empire that needed a cluster of loyal residents to feed the army.

Liebeschuetz (2002) argues that this Roman villa system spread to wherever Roman rule was extended and in the process helped diffuse an agricultural revolution that permitted the efficient generation of a food surplus.[6] But there was a downside as well. Agricultural productivity later declined, albeit differentially in time and place, beginning first in Italy in the early imperial era and then moving to North Africa and the eastern part of the empire in the later imperial era. Some of the decline may have been due to overexploitation, but it is hard to assess in the context of the competing contributions of waves of disease (beginning in the mid-second century CE), invasions, and climate deterioration.[7]

Imperial plunder thus had many effects. It helped fund more wars while contributing to the decline of a semiprofessional military cadre. It encouraged the elimination of subsistence farming in favor of commercialized agriculture.

The retention of most of the loot by the elite accentuated inequality considerably, with plunder funding elaborate buildings in the cities in which the rich elite lived. The expansion of Rome and other cities was also encouraged by the migration of former farmers and slaves. One of the consequences of this type of urbanization is that a large proportion of the population will not be able to be productively employed and will require state welfare to ensure political stability.

Still, some economic growth could also have been achieved by what Bang (2009) calls a "tributary empire" operating in the context of an agrarian political economy in which most production was consumed close to its source. If the outcome of this system was a conglomeration of small, relatively isolated communities engaging in subsistence economics, how would it have been possible to create economic growth? One path involves imperial victors commanding resources made available for consumption by the wealthy elite of the empire. As Bang notes, "By imposing tribute, empires forced resources out of the semi-closed cells of local economies and brought them into a wider sphere of circulation" (2009: 104). In a later work, Bang (2012) goes even further by suggesting that given the low productivity of a preindustrial economy, the predatory violence of conquest may have been the only way to unlock Mediterranean growth potentials.[8] Coercively moving wealth from one place to another is at least one way to stimulate and also increase the integration of a regional economic system. Increased circulation of the most desired commodities could be expected to have expanded the size of the Roman economy and to have encouraged a division of labor among different parts of the empire, thereby contributing to the efficiency of production. Moderate division of labor is likely to have fallen short of economically integrating the empire substantially. But unified rule, along with the introduction of piracy suppression policies, would have decreased the transaction costs associated with moving commodities from place to place.

Tribute flows, unfortunately, do not have an infinite life, because the imperial control that an empire is able to project rarely remains constant. A quick spurt of conquest loot is apt to taper off to some lesser level of flow dependent on demand, the ability of individuals to pay for the goods, and the ability of the empire to stay intact. Of course, some war plunder keeps on giving. Iberian gold mines underwrote state expenditures in the first two centuries CE only to exhaust themselves in the third century (Wilson, 2012: 148). As noted in Hopkins' agrarian slave model (figure 4.3), tribute can also be used to stimulate productivity in other spheres. By financing the purchase of large areas of land in the vicinity of Rome and other large cities, conquest loot helped lead to finite agrarian efficiency gains in Italy.

Another kindred argument is that the imposition of Roman rule hastened the emergence of a monetarized economy.[9] Subsistence economies tend to make exchanges in kind—trading several chickens for a young goat, for example—as needs develop. Imperial economies, on the other hand, do not wish to have taxes paid in kind, because such payments are too cumbersome to collect and process for the imperial treasury. Like other empires, Rome soon demanded that taxes be paid in coin. For subsistence farmers to do so, they needed to develop surplus crops that could be marketed. The fiscal imperatives of imperial rule thus meant that the state had to rely less on subsistence and more on commercialized agriculture.

These multiple changes—the unification of the Mediterranean, increased commodity circulation, monetarization, and the construction of enlarged and more efficient villas—in turn contributed to the urbanization of the Roman Empire in a two-way process. The creation of surplus food made large cities possible, and large cities encouraged commodity circulation, monetarization, and agrarian efficiency. The question is whether these combined factors led to a one-time spurt or a period of continuous economic growth. The evidence appears to point strongly in the direction of a finite spurt that lasted two or three centuries at most before decaying (Sallares, 2002; Scheidel, 2009; also see figures 4.4 and 4.5).[10] Modern growth, stimulated by successive waves of technological change, tends to be more continuous, if unevenly so. The Romans would have had to construct new empires at regular intervals to have that kind of growth pattern.

Other factors intruded on these gains. The Roman climatic optimum began to wane in the third and fourth centuries CE. The Roman republic and early empire had been bolstered by temperatures and rainfall ideal for growing crops.

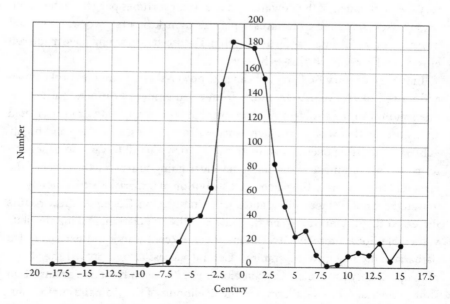

Figure 4.4 Known Mediterranean Shipwrecks. Source: Data taken from Morley (2007: 572).

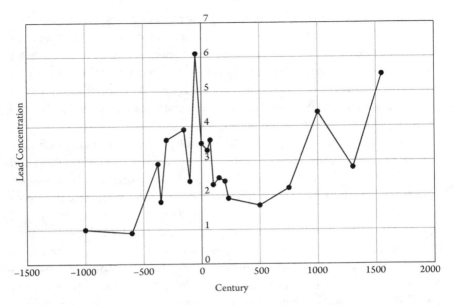

Figure 4.5 Lead Concentration in Greenland Ice Cores. Source: Data reported in Kehoe (2007: 548).

The later empire was less fortunate. Temperatures began to cool after 180 CE, while rainfall peaked in 100 BCE and declined through 300 CE (Malanima, 2011b: 10–11). Disease began to play a more prominent role in the second century CE, with much of the downturn in economic fortunes pegged to the population losses associated with waves of plague. To make matters worse, Italian soil in the vicinity of Rome was fertile but thin. Deforestation would have made soil erosion and productivity losses highly probable.

In the last century BCE, republican elite power-sharing schemes broke down and moved toward monarchy in the form of an emperor. Autocratization was one solution to the problem of endemic civil war among elites, but it created an institution that was increasingly isolated from the rest of society and highly vulnerable to being overthrown by the Praetorian Guard. It was also expensive to maintain, with most of the state's revenues going to pay for the costs of the army and the emperor. The narrow redistribution of imperial wealth severely aggravated economic inequalities and social stratification. Together, these factors increased the distance between the state and the population, making the state vulnerable both internally (to legionary coups/civil wars) and externally (to barbarians moving into the empire). Central success also improved the ability of the periphery to emulate the center and use its own advantages against it. In short, imperial success undermined the likelihood of the Roman Empire's survival in its optimal form. The more the central empire developed and became complex, the more the periphery's ability to take over the center increased—which is exactly what happened in the west.

That this process did not unfold in the same way in the eastern part of the Roman Empire suggests some limitations on the application of the model. However, the eastern segment of the Roman Empire survived in part because it was better at bribing its adversaries and encouraging them to look for easier pickings in the west. Ultimately, it also succumbed to its own periphery, but only after a very long run.

We can thus conclude that the economic success of Rome was predicated on its coercive exploitation of a frontier that was a combination of old but affluent societies and new and underdeveloped northern territories. As Jongman (2002: 47) puts it, "An underdeveloped economy was driven hard towards con-centrated support of one of the few world-empires of pre-industrial history." To acquire and exploit these frontiers maximally, Rome became a war machine (Cornell, 2003). Fighting was initially concentrated in Italy and then expanded throughout the Mediterranean littoral. The booty extracted from these wars made elites, who retained the lion's share of it, even richer. In the process the farmers who supplied the bulk of the army became poorer and could not hold on to their farms, which were bought by landowning elites and farmed by the slaves that poured into Italy thanks to the wars. Yet war, which had by and large moved to non-Italian battlegrounds in the second century BCE, returned to Italy in the first century BCE to settle disagreements among the ruling elite. The war machine was subsequently transformed into a more professional, full-time orga-nization that owed its loyalty to the emperor.

Moreover, the war machine began to encounter limits to Roman expansion. Increasingly, the empire needed to defend its borders from barbarian incursions in the north and strong resistance in the Near East. Armies became larger but not necessarily more well trained or armed. Nor could they draw on the successful infantry tactics that had built the empire, since more mobility was needed to move from one hotspot to another quickly. More cavalry were needed, and more taxes to pay for them.[11] At the same time, less economic surplus was available to meet the rising protection costs, and fewer Romans were available for army recruitment, as demonstrated in table 4.2.[12] As a consequence, there was less commitment to defend Rome against attacking enemies. Armor was abandoned because soldiers preferred not to wear it anymore. Unit discipline and tactical routines were lost. Ferrill (1991: 62) argues that the barbarization of the Roman army threw away the tactical superiority it once enjoyed as the strongest heavy infantry force in the ancient world:

> Barbarization of the army, which began on a large scale with Constantine, also undermined the old Roman discipline. Barbarian troops, under

Table 4.2 **Origins of Legionary Recruits**

Time	Italy	Upper/Lower Danube
1–4 CE	51.1%	5.5%
41–68 CE	63.6%	12.6%
68–117 CE	24.6%	17.0%
117–300 CE	3.2%	38.7%

Source: Based on MacMullen (1988: 54).

their own commanders and their lax discipline, were often treated with greater favor and received more pay than Roman forces. When Roman troops petitioned the Emperor for relaxation of discipline, and for a reduction of the heavy armor they had always worn, he was in no position to deny the request. By the fifth century, there was no one left alive in the Empire, according to Vegetius, who knew the old Roman system. It had to be learned from books. (Ferrill, 1991: 51)

The once-successful war machine had become a far less successful one, and its resource base, not unlike the institution of the army itself, was increasingly hollowed out by disease, climate change, and declining agrarian productivity. It is not too surprising that control over western Rome was eventually lost to the tribes (Franks, Goths, Huns) coming in over the border. The offensive threat was greater than it had been for some time, and Rome's defensive capability was sorely diminished. The "barbarian attack constituted an insurmountable threat not because the barbarians were so many and so strong, but because the defense was so weak" (MacMullen, 1988: 191).

There was still a war machine. It had evolved with changes in the Roman environment, but the odds were increasingly against it functioning successfully. It no longer enjoyed a substantial martial edge over its opposition. The nature of the threat environment had also changed considerably with increasing pressures at the borders. Despite growing in size, the war machine was now very much on the defensive. Furthermore, the effectiveness of the agrarian and state infrastructures supporting the army were also not up to the defensive task.

Population and Urbanization

Urbanization accelerated in the Roman period. Jongman (2002: 28) notes that in 1500, Europe had only four cities with populations exceeding 100,000. The Roman Empire had at least seventeen, according to Modelski's (2003) estimates, reported in table 4.3. The table suggests, furthermore, that once Carthage and Greece were eclipsed, Rome was the only state in the Western ancient world to have cities with more than 100,000 inhabitants. Alexandria in Egypt remained large after it was conquered by Rome but never exceeded its

Table 4.3 Cities with 100,000 or More Population

Cities	500 BCE	400 BCE	300 BCE	200 BCE	100 BCE	1 CE	100 CE	200 CE	300 CE	400 CE
Memphis	100	100	100							
Carthage	100	200	500	200						
Agragas	100									
Syracuse	100	120	200							
Athens		100								
Rome	100	150	250	210	400	800	1,000	1,200	1,000	800
Capua			100							
Jerusalem				100	100	100				
Alexandria			300	600	1,000	400	500	600	500	200
Antioch				100	125	270	330	400	330	270
Ephesus				100	100	200	200	200	125	
Pergamum				200	100	160	140	170		
Apamea					100	130	100	120		
Cibyra					100	100				
Ceasarea Maritime.							100	100	140	130
Ceasarea IOL.							100	110	100	
Smyrna							125	100		
Ceasarea Mazaca								100		
Trier									100	
Milan									100	
Emerita									100	100
Nicomedia									100	
Constantinople										400

Note: Populations expressed in thousands.

Source: Based on information reported in Modelski (2003: 49).

preconquest peak of 1 million. Rome, on the other hand, reached 800,000 at the end of the first millennium BCE and met or exceeded this number through 400 CE. These urban sizes were not exceeded in Eurasia for nearly a millennia, until the rise of Kaifeng in Song dynasty China in the East and nineteenth-century London in the West.

This increased urbanization through the second century CE reflects the population increase, improved agricultural output, and heightened commercial exchange seen throughout the empire (Kron, 2012: 160). The outbreak of disease in 165 CE may have been most responsible for the urbanization decreases that occurred between 200 and 300 CE. At the same time, the cities were quite capable of killing people with or without epidemics. According to Smil (2010: 135), "For an ordinary Roman citizen the city was not a stunning cosmopolis of marble temples. . . . [I]t was a squalid, fetid, unsanitary, noisy, and dangerous amalgam of people, animals, wastes, germs, diseases, and suffering." Large ancient cities like Rome were petri dishes for filth and contamination, incapable of taking care of their sewage and dead in a sanitary fashion. Even so, Wilson (2008: 312) argues that Rome's large cities would have been smaller without the empire's capability to supply its cities with water. The maintenance of a water supply for drinking and cooking purposes, however, does not mean that most cities were connected to widespread sewage discharge systems.

Transportation and Communications

The Romans excelled at engineering and especially road construction. While the initial incentive for road construction was military usage, others could profitably use the same roads. Greene (1986: 169) notes that "Roman transportation was not excelled in scale or effectiveness until the advent of canal and railway networks and steam powered ships." Yet it could also be argued that the costs of moving commodities by water in ancient times were so much less than those of moving commodities by land that maritime shipping functioned something like railroads in more modern times. Brown (1971: 12–13), for example, suggests that it was cheaper to ship grain from one end of the Mediterranean to the other than it was to send it seventy-five miles inland. Those differential costs put economic constraints on the expansion of interior traffic. This does not detract, however, from the equal fact that the Roman Empire did make it possible to move throughout the interior of the empire. Some increase in internal transportation and interaction must have occurred, even if we have no reason to assume that it was ever steady or heavy.[13]

Trade

After widespread drought gave rise to the "dark ages" that stretched from the end of the second millennium BCE (circa 1200 BCE) into the first two centuries of the first millennium BCE, the Mediterranean became an increasingly active trading zone. Etruscans, Phoenicians, Carthaginians, and Greeks competed fairly strenuously as traders in the Italian/Sicilian area. The Romans replaced the Etruscans initially, while the Phoenicians were absorbed by the Persians. Later the Carthaginians and Greeks were defeated and their territories occupied by the Romans, giving Rome centrality in the Mediterranean trading zone, which encompassed Europe, the Near East, and North Africa and was connected indirectly as far east as China.

Grantham (2015: 88) makes the important point that Rome did not create the Mediterranean-centric economy of the West. In his view, it would be more correct to say that it was able to capitalize on nearly a millennium of trade development:

> The Roman economy of the first century BC did not spring fully formed from a subsistence economy like Minerva from the head of Jupiter. The emergence of a spatially integrated economy stretching from the shores of the North Sea to the Euphrates occurred over eight to nine centuries during which trading connections between the eastern and western Mediterranean and between the Mediterranean and northwest Europe were intermittently knitted together. (Grantham 2015: 88)

Yet Rome's centrality in this large system paid off for only one or two centuries, as figure 4.4 hints. Shipwreck data admittedly are not ideal in this context because shipwrecks tend to be found in relatively shallow waters where they are easiest to find. But that liability is offset by the fact that most ancient shipwrecks likely occurred in relatively shallow waters because coastal hugging was the most common approach taken for sea voyages. Moreover, figure 4.4 has face validity in that it resembles other charts of Roman activity (see, e.g., figure 4.5). It also approximates Hopkins' (1995/1996) estimate of trends in Roman economic growth: rising in the last two centuries of the first millennium BCE, plateauing in the first century CE, and then declining gradually in the second and third centuries CE. Similarly, figure 4.4 shows sea trade activity picking up after 750 BCE and gradually rising to a peak between 100 BCE and 100 CE before declining successively through the next six centuries.

To the extent that Mediterranean traffic accurately captures the trajectory of Roman trade, the profits of this activity seem to have been rather short-lived and to correlate with Roman conquests that ended around 100 BCE. Mediterranean traffic serviced the largest cities of the empire. Less known is how much traffic penetrated inland into Europe. As mentioned earlier, overland trade was clearly more expensive. Johnson (2017: 140) contrasts overland trade costs of 50 percent of commodity value with 2 percent trade costs at sea. Not surprisingly, then, it was easier for Roman provincial trade to remain localized—a tendency that was only accentuated by the gradual qualitative superiority of provincial goods compared to Roman goods. As Brown concludes:

> So, the Roman empire always consisted of two, overlapping worlds. Up to AD 700, great towns by the sea remained close to each other; twenty days of clear sailing would take the traveler from one end of the Mediterranean, the core of the Roman world, to the other. Inland, however, Roman life had always tended to coagulate in little oases, like drops of water on a drying surface. The Romans are renowned for the roads that ran through their empire; but the roads passed through towns where the inhabitants gained all that they ate, and most of what they used from within a radius of only thirty miles. (1971: 13)

Roman production could hardly remain central if it lost its edge in manufactured goods, and even in this respect the initial Roman production edge was narrowly focused on commodities such as wine. There may also have been some tradeoff involved in normalizing conquest areas. Before Gaul became a Roman province in the second century CE, for example, it could trade raw materials and slaves for wine with Rome. Once it became a province, the focus shifted to paying taxes and men for imperial protection (Bang, 2002). Gaul subsequently developed its own wine production as well.

McLaughlin (2014) stresses the fiscal importance of long-distance trade after the conquest of Egypt (30 BCE) in terms of the wealth gained not only from Egypt, but also from the taxation of eastern trade coming in through the Red Sea. As Egyptian wealth was moved to Rome, it encouraged a consumer boom, while trade customs almost doubled Roman state income in the last century of the first millennium BCE and then doubled it again in the next century. Since the main charge on the Roman treasury came in the form of army costs, McLaughlin (2014: 20) contends that the empire's ability to maintain its army at its peak was only possible because of taxes levied on incoming silk and spices. Yet this claim must be offset somewhat by the inflows of Carthaginian loot and especially the takeover of the Spanish silver mines in roughly the same time period. Figure 4.5 captures the ancient peak of lead pollution in Rome, which is attributed largely to silver production at the end of the republican era and the beginning of the imperial era. Silver and gold were critical to the Eastern trade because the Romans had little else to offer Eastern markets. This trade eventually shifted away to Constantinople, either due to more aggressive trading practices in eastern Rome or due to the alternation of land and sea routes connecting the Mediterranean and China. Constantinople was the main western terminus of the overland Silk Road.

Technological Innovation

One of the more curious features of the Roman era was the marked disinterest in technological innovation. This statement is not meant to imply that no novel techniques were developed or applied.[14] Agricultural technology related to seed cultivation and crop rotation was strong. Army artillery and siegecraft tended to be superior to anything enemies could muster. But these and other innovations were based on technology developed by the Carthaginians (farms worked by slaves) or the Greeks (most everything else). The century before the Roman ascent, the fourth century BCE, is considered a high point for technological innovation, but its locus was in Alexandria. After that high point, nothing much changed in the West that mattered for economic production purposes for centuries. As Hodges notes:

> The year 300 BC represents in antiquity almost the end of one aspect of technical development in the Near East and indeed in the whole of the Western world. It is true to say that virtually no new raw material was to be exploited for the next thousand years and that no really novel method of production was to be introduced. What new advances were made were to be almost entirely in the field of engineering, and most of the principles involved had themselves already been discovered and applied, although usually on a smaller scale. Thus, during the entire period in which Rome dominated the civilized Western World one of the few really novel means of production that appears to have been developed in any industry was that of blowing glass. (1970/1996: 208)

The glass-blowing innovation, moreover, occurred in the provinces (the Levant) and not in the Italian imperial center.

Han China was much more technologically innovative than Rome. Smil (2010: 95) recounts a long list of early Chinese accomplishments including iron casting; steel production from cast iron; papermaking; the introduction of the horse collar harness and iron plows; percussion drilling; the creation of watertight ship compartments, batten-strengthened lug sails, stirrups, and porcelain; and the use of coal in smelting.[15] Why eastern Eurasia should have been so much more technologically innovative than western Eurasia at this time is not clear.[16] But it is certainly one strong clue as to why the organizational lead shifted across the continent in the early centuries of the first millennium CE. It also helps account for the absence of sustained economic growth in the Roman case. As Schneider observes:

> Technological change in the ancient Mediterranean never changed production in agriculture and craft as fundamentally as did the Industrial Revolution and never increased productivity to a degree that would have resulted in change to the economy or social structure. On the contrary, technological progress in antiquity always took place within the framework of the agricultural society and never achieved the same dynamic as the innovating processes of modern industrial societies. (2007: 170–171)

Energy

Energy is critical to understanding what political-military organizations can accomplish within their milieu. Even if a state is much more powerful than all its rivals and therefore can be said to have a lead on the competition, its prevailing energy format makes a difference. As Smil (2010) notes, societal capacity is a function of the kind and quality of inputs that can be utilized to create desired outputs:

> All systems . . . are nothing but highly organized (simple or complex) convertors of energy. . . . Levels of energy use (more precisely, the availability of useful energy) circumscribe the economic, military (and to a lesser extent) social capacities of any society and are the key determinants of the prevailing quality of life. Higher, more varied, and more efficient throughputs result in more desirable, that is, richer and more differentiated outcomes. (2010: 79)

On the question of what kind of energy the Roman Empire relied upon, there is little controversy. Its agrarian political economy was fueled by muscle and solar radiation. Human and animal muscles were substituted for motors. Sunlight provided the main fuel for plant growth and, indirectly, the feed for animal growth. Jongman has noted that in Rome, "technology changed little; it made abundant use of labour that was cheap as a result of population pressure and legal oppression. Rome was and remained what has been termed an organic economy, without the technology to use fossil fuels for heat and power" (2002: 32). Similarly, Wilson has observed, "The Roman world, like all other pre-industrial societies, was an organic economy and suffered the same constraints; the available energy budget in each year was a fraction of the solar radiation emitted in that year that could be captured, principally via photosynthesis" (2012: 151).

The Romans might conceivably have made the breakthrough to utilizing fossil fuels in order to escape the energy constraints associated with relying primarily on photosynthesis, although such an outcome would have been improbable. More factors worked against the Romans than worked for them in such an enterprise. While coal did not have to be the principal transition fuel, it was the most likely one. Since we know how the coal adoption story proceeded, it is possible to list the most likely ingredients needed for such a transition to occur. These include cold weather, large coalfields, at least one large city demanding fuel for heating, coal mines that penetrated below sea level and thus flooded, some ongoing experimentation with steam engines, and someone to make the connection between the steam engine's potential for pumping water and the coal mining problem. Given the size of the Roman Empire, it should not be surprising that only the first two of the six ingredients—cold weather and large coalfields—were at hand, although they were located in the far north, far from the center of the empire. Coal was used to heat homes in Britain during the Roman occupation, but its consumption did not continue at the same pace once the Romans abandoned Britain. The Romans had large cities, but they were all located in warmer climates and in places that lacked ready access to high-quality coalfields. The lion's share of these cities' heating needs were taken care of by firewood (Wilson, 2012).

The Romans also had problems with flooded silver mines but did not lack cheap labor in the form of slaves to combat the problem.[17] There had been some very early experimentation with steam engine principles in Alexandria several hundred years before the Romans invaded (Bresson, 2006), but little in the way of experimentation can be discerned during the Roman era.[18] Without some ongoing experimentation, the last ingredient, entrepreneurs to connect steam engines to water-pumping problems, was also largely moot in the Roman Empire.

Conclusions

We concur with Jongman's (2007: 597) verdict that "however impressive the Roman economic achievement may seem it was not an aborted beginning of the modern world." Rather, Rome's path was highly traditional. In an agrarian age, economic growth meant acquiring control over more territory to facilitate the growing of food and to support more population. Rome did that with a vengeance until it could do it no more. Serious resistance to further expansion, along with the onset of less favorable conditions (disease and climate change) and the undermining of the superior army institution that was fundamental to conquest, slowed Rome's imperial momentum and the development of its capability.

Table 4.4 **Presence and Absence of Key Economic Growth, Ancient Rome**

Frontier Exploitation	Agriculture	Urbanization	Trade	Transportation/ Communication	Technological Innovation	Energy Transition	Power-Driven Machinery
Present	Present	Present	Present	Present	Relatively absent	Absent	Relatively absent

When the external threat environment worsened, Rome had few resources and instruments with which to defend itself.

Rome did, however, experience a coerced spurt of economic growth in the late republic and early empire periods. By exploiting its frontier in the Mediterranean basin and Western Europe, Rome altered its agricultural productivity and efficiency, built roads, supported large cities, and stimulated commercial interactions within and outside the Mediterranean area. Thus, it relied on at least five of the traditional key processes in table 4.4: frontier exploitation, agriculture, urbanization, trade, and transportation/communication. None of this economic expansion necessarily led to technological innovation, energy transition, and the development of power-driven machinery. Thus, Rome remained embedded in the constraints imposed by its reliance on solar radiation as its principal fuel source.

Ironically, Rome was actually better able to withstand its barbarian threats or at least to hold them off longer than the Han Empire. But the difference was that the Chinese were able to overcome their fragmentation, embrace imperial unification, and resume expansion. Western Rome never was able to repel the new groups that entered western Europe and North Africa. Instead, these groups stayed and constructed multiple competing weak states that operated on equally weak economic foundations for centuries. China, on the other hand, encouraged technological innovation and the more traditional processes of economic growth until it was overrun by steppe invaders in the thirteenth century CE. This Chinese story is the focus of the next chapter.

5

China: The Incomplete Transition

Modelski and Thompson's (1996) framework takes as its Chinese focus the medieval Song dynasty. Yet the technological lead demonstrated by China during the Song dynasty was not necessarily restricted to the Song era. Some of this lead was achieved in the preceding T'ang dynasty, while some, as in the case of maritime commerce, was achieved only after the Song dynasty. China did not lose its technological lead once the Song dynasty gave way to Mongol rule but continued to be the clear lead economy in East Asia. As a consequence, a number of analysts have argued that it is difficult to compare China to Venice, Genoa, Portugal, or the Netherlands in terms of technological complexity. None of these critics' arguments are identical, but for present purposes, we will restrict our attention to what is probably the most strenuously voiced critique, John Hobson's manifesto (sketched in box 5.1), although it is a close call with Frank's (1998) equally Sinocentric analysis or Pomeranz's (2000) more measured attack on European-centric interpretations of the European economic ascent.[1]

Hobson's position is that virtually nothing about the later European ascent to predominance was due to European attributes or developments. All improvements in status were based on borrowing and adapting earlier Chinese accomplishments. Moreover, the claim that Song China had a chance to industrialize but was stopped short by the Mongol conquest misreads the evidence for continued Chinese technological preeminence through the Yuan, Ming, and Qing dynasties.

There is much to agree with in Hobson's critique, but he overstates his case. China's technological precocity in iron manufacturing, transportation, maritime shipping and navigation, weaponry, market commercialization, and agriculture cannot be denied. Nor can it be denied that European industrialization borrowed extensively from Chinese practice. The problem, however, is that there was no energy revolution in China prior to the mid-nineteenth century, when Hobson reluctantly concedes that Britain outpaced China. China's mere use of coal, petroleum, or natural gas, however early, did not constitute an energy revolution. What was needed was a conversion to some type of carbon fuel as the

Box 5.1 **The Hobson Critique**

China experienced the first "industrial miracle" over a period of 1,500 years, culminating in the Song revolution. The subsequent diffusion of Song technological and ideational breakthroughs significantly informed the rise of the West.

Cast iron dates from 513 BCE, and steel production from the second century BCE. Between 806 and 1078 CE, iron output may have increased sixfold. British iron production did not match Song production in terms of volume until late in the eighteenth century. Song iron was produced to make tools, not just weapons. Pioneering production techniques included the use of cast iron, smelting using blast furnaces, and the substitution of coke for charcoal (eleventh century CE).

Petroleum and natural gas were used for cooking and lighting probably as early as the fourth century BCE; their use constituted an energy revolution.

The Chinese silk industry began as early as the fourteenth century BCE. The Chinese textile industry developed water-powered spinning machines for silk and hemp in 1090 CE.

The development of a canal system to distribute goods from north to south constituted a transportation revolution.

An agricultural revolution was in place in China by the sixth century CE and was not matched by Britain until the seventeenth to eighteenth centuries. Chinese agriculture continued to improve throughout and after the Song era.

Propelled by a tax system based on cash, paper money (predicated in turn on the development of printing and papermaking) was introduced in the ninth century CE, thereby facilitating the commercialization of a market economy that strongly encouraged all members of the population to produce for the market. Commercialization also encouraged urbanization.

A navigational revolution was achieved via the invention of the compass (around 1000 CE), the production of highly accurate maps by the fifteenth century, and the construction of strikingly large and numerous ships that incorporated rudders, fore and aft sails, and watertight compartments long before comparable European developments.

The European military technological revolution of the sixteenth and seventeenth centuries was based on gunpowder, the gun, and the cannon, which were all introduced in China between 850 and 1279 CE. Other Chinese military applications included flamethrowers, bombs, grenades, rockets, land- and sea-mines, and fire-lance guns. Naval vessels were heavily weaponized, and some had iron plating by Southern Song times.

After 1100 China's standing was second to none in the world. The Chinese economy did not regress or sink without a trace after 1279. Its vibrancy enabled China to stand at or very near the center of the global economy as late as the nineteenth century. Iron and coal production were revived after 1420. After 1434, government regulations limiting trade were circumvented by disguised trade in the form of "tribute." By the sixteenth century, Chinese agriculture had recovered from the Black Death, was highly commercialized, and was important to Chinese trade. The Chinese population expanded between 1700 and 1850 phenomenally, suggesting an equally major increase in the food supply. Before 1800, China was the world's leading power, although it did not dominate the polycentric trading system linking Asia and the Middle East. China's per capita income remained roughly equal to Britain's up to 1750, its gross national product was as high as Britain's in 1850, and its share of manufactures was higher than Britain's up to 1860.

Source: Based on Hobson (2004).

primary source of energy in response to demands by prime economic movers.[2] Moreover, China's expansion of iron production volume per se did not equate to an industrial revolution. If Britain had only expanded iron and textile production in the late eighteenth century, it probably would not have pioneered in industrialization either. What was needed for a breakthrough to sustained industrialization was the marriage of an energy transition and new technology that demanded greater energy inputs and yielded greater productivity as a consequence. Such a development, first realized in the steam engine after a century of modification, was absolutely necessary if one requires economic transformation as a corollary to an industrial revolution. Otherwise, iron and textile production might well have expanded in volume for a time before reaching some natural limits and stagnating in terms of growth. Instead, they were supplanted by even better versions of iron and textile production, as well as by other new industries.

Clearly, Chinese technology was ahead of comparable developments in Europe. It is hard to imagine the European breakthroughs having occurred without the Chinese foundations on which many, if not all, of them were based. But the fact remains that China still failed to achieve a full break from the constraints of the agrarian economy, whereas Britain, for whatever reasons, successfully made this transition. We thus need to decipher what transpired in China before the Mongols came.

The analysis of China offers the first opportunity to apply our segmented model (figure 5.1) to the development of technological leadership. In the first cluster, all six categories play some role, with external trade being the least persistent factor. Internal trade between different regions was vital in China early on, but external trade only gradually became significant. Its greatest significance, in a negative sense, may have been associated with its discouragement during the Ming dynasty era (fifteenth century) and the state's subsequent diminished contact with the outside world, circumstances that hardly favored continued innovation.

What looms large in the China story is the shift in economic gravity from the traditional north to the south. Medieval China's exploitation of its southern economic potential and its integration of north and south via the construction of the Grand Canal (prior to its loss of control over the north) encouraged some division of labor and increased specialization among the leading macro-regions. Kaifeng, as the central site of urbanization, seems to have played a role similar to that of London in Britain—as a singular large and expanding city that placed demands for its sustenance on the rest of the country. Even the two cities' demands

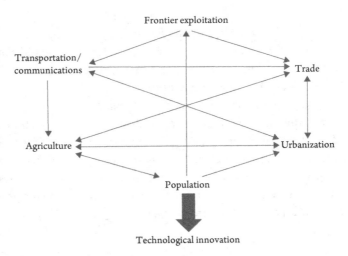

Figure 5.1 Factors Underlying Chinese Technological and Economic Leadership.

for coal for heating purposes were similar. But the difference between London and Kaifeng was that the latter's political–economic centrality was destroyed by invaders in the twelfth century, who forced the Song dynasty to retreat to the south. Ultimately, more invaders defeated the Southern Song as well, setting up nearly two centuries of poor conditions for continued innovation.[3] Economic growth did not resume until the fifteenth century, only to be discouraged by Ming dynasty decision-makers who favored internal stability over an expanding external role. Subsequent centuries witnessed an expanding Chinese population, indicating extensive economic growth. During this time China maintained its technological leadership, but largely by default, since the state's economic growth after the fifteenth century was not noticeably characterized by technological innovation. At some point in the nineteenth century, if not before, Japan's technology surpassed China's, but by this point both Japan and China had been shown to be deficient in technological innovation compared to Western powers.[4]

What looms just as large as the importance of southern frontier exploitation in the China story is the absence of a transition to a more powerful energy source. China increasingly used coal until the fall of Kaifeng but then seemingly backed away from it. It also used a variety of powered machinery, but none of these innovations led to sustained scalar increases in production. We think this was not coincidental. One of the keys to China's constrained role in world politics prior to recent times was the state's failure to develop technology that depended on coal. Without that interaction between technology and fossil fuels, no industrial revolution was probable. Consequently, China remained an agrarian empire that was large and more technologically proficient than its equally agrarian neighbors for a long time. Eventually, its early technological advances created a foundation for technological advances at the other end of Eurasia. Western Europe was ultimately the beneficiary.

Frontier Exploitation and Population Dynamics

Early Chinese economic and societal developments were concentrated in the north, leaving the south relatively underdeveloped. About 80 to 85 percent of the Chinese population resided in the north for the first seven hundred years of the first millennium CE. During this millennium, the climate continued to favor northern development. Beginning in the twelfth century, however, decreased rainfall began to make the northern plains less attractive for growing food, especially millet. Rice was not new to the south, but the tenth century saw the introduction of a new type of Champa rice that allowed the number of crops that could be harvested in a single year to double or even triple. A hundred years later rice had replaced millet and wheat as China's primary grain source. Furthermore, the south offered better coastal harbors than the north. These harbors opened up new trade possibilities with Korea, Japan, Southeast Asia, and the Middle East, particularly in the Tang dynasty era. Military conflict with the invading Jin and later the Mongols provided a third stimulant for movement into the south.

There were three main waves of migration into southern China.[5] The first two took place during the Tang dynasty (618–907) and were encouraged by a combination of newly drained land, food, and the convenience of the Grand Canal. Increasing conflict in the north facilitated the third wave. Hartwell (1982: 385) has sketched a rough timetable of this shift, estimating that during the Sui dynasty, 15 percent of the population resided in the south, with the percentage rising to 26 percent in the mid-Tang dynasty, 50 percent by 1080, 54 percent by 1200, 59 percent by 1391, and 60 percent by 1542 (with a drop to 42 percent by 1948).

At the beginning of the seventh century, as much as 85 percent of the Chinese population was concentrated in the north. By the end of the eleventh century, internal migration had altered the north–south split to something more like a 50–50 proposition. At the end of the Southern Song era, 90 percent of the Chinese population could be found in the south thanks to the loss of control over the north. This extreme asymmetry was remedied by the Mongol conquest. It was not until the sixteenth century that the population ratio began to return to a more balanced distribution (although roughly 60 percent of the population still resided in the south at that point).

Various benefits notwithstanding, the movement to the south represented the exploitation of an underdeveloped frontier. As Barbier notes:

> The Sung Dynasty propelled China into a phase of economic growth that would sustain it as the richest and most advanced country in the world for the next several centuries despite the major upheavals such as the Mongol invasion of the thirteenth century and the Black Death of the fourteenth century. In fact, the intensive growth of the Sung period could be considered the prime example of successful frontier-based development during the 1000–1500 era. (2011: 169)[6]

Elvin (1973) argues that this southern frontier, which for several centuries served as a major source of economic dynamism, had been fully exploited by about 1500. By that time, most of the land that could be cultivated in the south had been made productive by the large influx of migrants from the north. Southern agriculture could thus no longer function as a high-growth sector in the Chinese economy. P. J. Smith (2004: 279–280) also argues that the "primary engine of medieval transformation was undoubtedly the shift in the demographic center of gravity from North China to the frontier regions drained by the Yangzi River." His slightly different twist on this theme, however, is that movement into the south encouraged the search for innovative approaches to cultivating rice. In turn, the increased supply of food broke the cycle of agrarian self-sufficiency, creating opportunities for interregional specialization. Wong (1997) completes the story by suggesting that later Qing rulers merely adapted to the constraints imposed by an expanding population and limited resources.[7]

Hartwell (1982) has developed a more general model that seems to fit Chinese dynamics fairly well.[8] An important assumption of his model is that states encompass multiple macro-regions that experience differential growth dynamics at different times. Thus, instead of talking about changes in China, one needs to specify the macro-region(s) in which the changes occurred. He posits four phases that each Skinnerian Chinese macro-region experienced: frontier settlement, rapid development, systemic decline, and equilibrium.[9] Critical factors in a macro-region's movement in and out of each phase are fluctuations in population density and the emergence or deterioration of complex market hierarchies. According to the model, each macro-region initially possesses little in the way of marketing networks. Almost all of the population are either subsistence farmers or farm laborers. Few towns exist. Movement toward the rapid development phase gets underway as towns grow and population densities increase through natural processes and/or immigration. Higher population densities increase demand for food from rural hinterlands. Farmers and their products become more commercialized. City growth also implies that the size of the nonfarming population is expanding. Specialization is likely to emerge at both the individual and the regional levels. Just how wide the networks extend will be variable, but the wider they reach, the greater will be the demand for products and the incentives to respond to the increased demand. As the market networks become more complex and more hierarchical, different-sized towns will come to serve as hubs for surrounding areas, connected in turn to other hubs of varying size. Greater demand for agricultural and industrial products will then lead to innovations in production technique and organization as the scale of output becomes greater.

Population densities in towns will subsequently wax and wane. When macro-regions are hit by floods, rebellions, war, or disease, city size may decline. The exploitation of flora and fauna may reach limits imposed by agrarian technology and experience, diminishing marginal utilities. If the decline in density persists, the macro-region will enter the systemic decline phase, during which the processes encountered in the expanding phase virtually reverse themselves. Towns will become smaller, either gradually or abruptly, depending on the nature of the problems besetting them. The least developed peripheral areas will become more depopulated as cultivation in the hinterland becomes less sustainable. Market hierarchies and networks will collapse. Output scale will diminish, and therefore the incentives for innovation will disappear. At some point, the decline will slow until the macro-region has attained equilibrium characterized by limited growth and innovation.

Hartwell's model aligns well with the core principle of Smithian growth dynamics. If groups, regions, or states are isolated from one another, there will be a tendency toward constrained specialization. If the geographical scope of the markets is expanded, incentives for specialization will emerge as the hitherto unconnected markets fuse. Economic growth should ensue (Kelly, 1997) until or unless blockages or market interruptions emerge—in which case, stagnation may set in.[10] There are differences of opinion, however, on what might trigger such an acceleration. Hartwell (1962, 1966, 1967a, 1982) pegs the Northern Song acceleration to the centralized urbanization of Kaifeng, which became the largest city in the world for a time. Kelly (1997) pins the Song commercialization upswing to the national waterway network, which was actually constructed during the Sui dynasty (and in fact made the enlargement of Kaifeng feasible). It is not clear that we really have to choose between the two types of causal path, however, since both seem to have worked together in the tenth and eleventh centuries.

The most helpful aspect of the Hartwell model is that it bases China's early technological lead on changes that took place in eastern macro-regions. After the fourteenth century, some of the same changes were extended to western macro-regions, but not exactly in the same way, and without effects of the same magnitude. Another way of putting this is that what transpired between the eighth and twelfth centuries in some Chinese macro-regions could not be duplicated exactly in later centuries. The critical difference is that the exploitation and integration of the western frontiers did not possess the same potential to produce transformative effects that the initial integration of the southern frontier did.

More generally, post-Han population decline was arrested by the advent of the Sui–Tang dynasties midway through the first millennium CE (see figure 5.2).

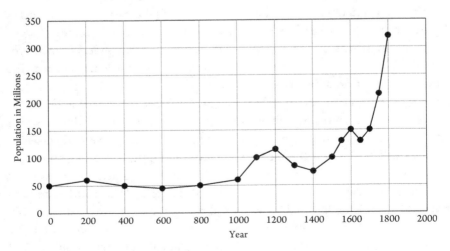

Figure 5.2 China's Population Growth. Source: Based on McEvedy and Jones (1978: 167).

Although population numbers were increasing in the post-Han era, an acceleration of population growth did not take place until after the expansion of the food supply brought about by the introduction of Champa rice. The size of the Chinese population nearly doubled in the eleventh century and continued to expand in the following century before peaking early in the thirteenth. Subsequently, two centuries of conflict, disease, and rebellion led to two waves of population decline, the first ensuing after 1200 during the conquest era and the second in the mid-fourteenth century with the advent of plague.

Transportation and Communications

South and north China were connected by the Grand Canal, completed in the seventh century by the Sui dynasty. In particular, food from the south could be moved north as needed. While the primary motivation for the canal may have been military and political control, connecting the administrative center in the north to the emerging resource base in the south, it also had the effect of encouraging the economic integration of several regions. Hartwell (1982) argues that interregional commercial transactions were negligible prior to the Tang dynasty that followed the Sui. This observation does not imply that all of China was abruptly integrated in the eighth century. It means only that the cores of several macro-regions were brought into closer contact by an improved conduit that made the movement of goods more feasible at a lower cost. While this development began in the eighth century, canal locks and improvements in ship technology concerned with construction, operation, and navigation are dated to the eleventh century. In the Southern Song era, the Yangtze River replaced the Grand Canal as the main artery, functioning, according to Ibn Battuta, along the lines of the Egyptian Nile (Adshead, 2000: 116).

Agrarian Development

Between 400 and 750 CE, the climate of Eurasia became colder and wetter. In Europe, which was already experiencing increased plague, the impact was largely negative, with too much water damaging the prospects for good grain crops. In China, there was far less plague, and more rain was good for crops in the north. The transition to Tang China was therefore possible, while Europe fell into a form of dark age (Adshead, 2000: 58–59).[11]

Elvin (1973: 129) describes Chinese agriculture in the thirteenth century as "probably the most sophisticated . . . in the world." Four developments are credited for this outcome, and they help to explain what happened between the

Tang and Song dynasties. First, the quality of the soil was enhanced by improved tools and fertilizers. Second, new seeds increased output. Third, further advances were made in moving water to crops and crops to market by rivers and canals. Fourth, the three principal regions (the north, centered on Kaifeng; the less centralized south; and the Chengdu-centered southwest) increased their interdependence through specialization in production. Agricultural developments therefore created the foundation for most Chinese economic development in the medieval period. In particular, these developments greatly benefited population growth and urbanization, which would have been unlikely to have proceeded in the absence of improvements to the food supply. Hartwell echoes these sentiments:

> During the period between 750 and 1550, there were major changes in the relative positions of the macro-regions of China owing to [catastrophes, political decisions, transport and communication improvements, and agricultural innovations]. The shift in the comparative advantages of the regions and their combined growth in population and wealth not only brought about changes in the intraregional development process, but also had an aggregate impact on empire-wide political and social structures. (1982: 425–426)

After the sixteenth century, the Chinese agrarian economy was sufficiently rich and diverse to support an expanding population and a political–economic strategy that privileged agrarian improvements over all else, including technological/energy innovation, colonies, and foreign trade.[12] Between the late fourteenth century and the mid-nineteenth century, the amount of cultivated land increased by a factor of 3.24, while the population increased by a factor of 3.7 (Barbier, 2011: 271). This strategy thus appears to have been relatively successful, at least until new land that could be cultivated dwindled in a more contemporary (late-nineteenth-century) version of frontier closure.

Urbanization

According to Elvin (1973), interregional trade within China and international trade made intensive urbanization and the "urban revolution" of the twelfth and thirteenth centuries feasible. In this early period, urbanization focused on central cities. Much later, it became more dispersed and even rural in nature, with new towns in the periphery created and expanded at the expense of growth in the older cities.[13] Around 400–300 BCE, Linzi had a population of 350,000 (table 5.1). In 700–800 CE, Changan had 1 million (a number matched and perhaps exceeded by Kaifeng in the Northern Song period).

Table 5.1 **East Asian World City Networks**

400–300 BCE	700–800 CE	1300–1400 CE	1500–1600 CE	1700–1800 CE
Linzi	Changan	Nanking	Peking	Peking
Xiatu	Luoyang	Hangchow	Osaka	Canton
Louyang	Guangzhou	Peking	Kyoto	Yedo (Edo)
Daliang	Suzhou	Kamakura	Hangchow	Hangchow
Yiyang	Chengdu	Canton	Canton	Osaka
Qufu/Lu	Xin Jang	Kyoto	Sian	Kyoto
Yenhiatsu	Youzhou	Soochow	Soochow	Soochow
Shangqui	Kaifeng	Sian	Seoul	Sian
Xinzheng	Nara	Seoul	Chengdu	Seoul
Handan	Kyoto	Kaifeng	Sumpu	Kingtehchen
Suzhou	Lsasa (Lhasa?)	Wuchang	Changchun	Tientsin
Anyi	Wuchang	Yangchow	Fuchow	Fuchow
Yong		Fuchow	Kaifeng	Foshan
Yianyang		Chuanchow	Yamagushi	Chengdu
				Nagoya
				Lanchow
				Shanghai
				Ninghsia
				Changsha
				Ningpo
				Kaifeng

Source: Drawn from Taylor, Hoyler, and Smith (2012: 14–20); Chinese cities in bold.

Nanking in 1300–1400, however, had only 487,000 residents, while Peking expanded from 706,000 in 1500–1600 to 1.1 million in 1700–1800—in other words, not much different from Changan in the eighth century. Thus, one strong clue to the differences between pre-fourteenth-century China and post-fourteenth-century China is a fundamental shift in how urbanization worked. After the fourteenth century, Chinese urbanization was less likely to have the same positive effects on intensive economic growth that it had prior to the Mongol invasion.

Rosenthal and Wong (2011) have a distinctive and alternative interpretation of the role of Smithian growth in China's trajectory, taking China as a whole and focusing on the type of urbanization that occurred there as opposed to its scope. They argue that conditions initially favored China as a beneficiary of commercial dynamics but later favored Europe. Intermittently, but increasingly, China, seen as a large eastern Eurasian region, was pacified. The Han Empire represented a major consolidation of the region comparable to the position assumed by the Roman Empire in western Eurasia. Unlike the Western experience, however, subsequent dynasties in China were able to re-create pan-regional empires (the Sui, Tang, Northern Song, Yuan, Ming, and Qing). Granted, by the time of the Southern Song, China had once again become a multipolar region with multiple states, but this situation was only temporary. The Mongol conquest restored and extended the imperial boundaries. Throughout these periods of unified rule, the internal empire was usually at peace, with conflict concentrated on the frontier. While internal warfare disrupted both interregional economic transactions and foreign trade, internal peace was good for the smooth functioning of Smithian commercial dynamics before and after Mongol rule.

The downside of imperial peace was that there was far less incentive for China to build the walled cities found in western Europe. As a consequence, Chinese manufacturing remained largely rural-based after the Ming era and therefore was situated in a context of low wages that did not encourage the development of labor-saving innovations. The failure of the Roman Empire to be restored in western Europe meant that industry there was more likely to be clustered within city walls and in higher wage contexts. In this way, Rosenthal and Wong's (2011) answer to why the Industrial Revolution occurred in Europe and not in China is that political circumstances in China often favored Smithian growth, while those in Europe in the last five hundred years or so favored industrial technological innovation, or Schumpeterian growth.

The main problem with this interpretation is that Europe did not initiate industrialization—Britain did. British industrialization, moreover, was not situated within a tradition of walled cities, because Britain had been invaded only infrequently in the last millennium.[14] It would be easier to argue, as we will later (see chapter 6), that Smithian economic growth made Britain's industrialization more likely rather than that political circumstances made Smithian growth less likely. Still, Rosenthal and Wong (2011) are probably right to note that urbanized Smithian dynamics were more likely to arise in the more pacified setting of eastern Eurasia than in western Eurasia, and did in fact do so. It may be that Britain's internal peace in the eighteenth century more closely resembled circumstances in China than it did those in western Europe. If so, it does not seem to have precluded the emergence of substantial Schumpterian impulses in the British economy.

Maritime Commerce and International Trade

The threads of commerce which linked the Sung capital with other parts
of the empire and with the leading states of much of the non-Chinese
world formed a giant web with strands of varying degrees of thickness.
The multiplication in function and the rapid increase in size of the me-
tropolis had their greatest impact on economic development in the
immediate market area [Kaifeng]. But the growth of this urban center
affected, with varying degrees of intensity, the agricultural and industrial progress of the whole Chinese empire. And foreign commerce
linked the city . . . with Japan, Korea, Tibet, Manchuria, Mongolia,
Central Asia, India, the Near East, Africa, and possibly even Europe.
(Hartwell, 1967b: 143)

Hartwell's web of foreign commerce did not emerge overnight. It expanded
slowly. Limited coastal activity in the Han dynasty era became more ambitious
under the Tang dynasty, which also saw improvements in ships, maps, and navigational skills. Even more expansion occurred during the Song dynasties era, in
part because the blockade of land routes by hostile neighbors made maritime
trade the only possible outlet for foreign commerce between the tenth and thirteenth centuries. Once the Mongols controlled all of China, the land routes were
reopened, but maritime commerce was still encouraged through the end of the
thirteenth century, despite or because of the destruction of several large fleets
involved in attempts to invade Japan and Vietnam (Champa and Annam). Over
the next sixty to seventy years, naval and maritime activities were depressed by
deteriorating circumstances within China (floods, disease, conflict, etc.). In the
second half of the fourteenth century, trade and the Chinese navy were revived
with the ascent of the Ming dynasty.

Lo argues that China peaked as a sea power in the first third of the fifteenth
century and "achieved political hegemony over the states of the maritime Asia,
from Japan in the east to Ceylon in the west" (2012: 339). While *hegemony* may
be too strong a word to describe the extent of China's relative influence from
Japan to the Indian Ocean, Lo has in mind the seven fleet voyages of the Ming
dynasty that ultimately reached East Africa. His point is that, in good Mahanian
style, Chinese fleets had gradually (or intermittently) become the dominant
naval influence in an expanding area from the East China Sea to much of the
Indian Ocean. This development took time; it was hardly an abrupt phenomenon. Chinese shipping had begun to emerge in the Tang era but did not break
through Arab commercial predominance until the Southern Song period.[15]

Once gained, the Chinese maritime lead (which was both commercial and military) prevailed through the Yuan and early Ming dynasties.

At the same time, Chinese naval fortunes fluctuated in a way that perhaps presaged what happened in the Ming dynasty. In Lo's (2012) survey, once the Southern Song rulers made peace with the Jin invaders in the north, naval funding and ship construction were reduced until they once again became priorities to counter the Mongol invasion. The Yuan navy is also described as declining after 1294 and Qubilai Khan's death. The Ming dynasty some seventy-five years later rebuilt the navy but then reduced its significance when its services seemed less critical. Thus, the Chinese commitment to a blue water navy was never consistent even when (or because) it had little competition at sea.

Demonstrating a reinvigorated Ming Chinese power certainly was one of the missions of the now-famous Zeng He expeditions, which are summarized in table 5.2. Tributary relations had fallen off in the late Yuan dynasty. China believed that a show of force could revive the hierarchy that once characterized East Asia. Strengthening linkages with the Chinese diaspora in Southeast Asia, constructing bases, and removing recalcitrant rulers elsewhere were other goals (see Levathes, 1996; Dreyer, 2007). The size and power of the fleets sent out from China could not be matched by any other power in the world, let alone Southeast Asia and the Indian Ocean. Thus, it does seem fair to regard the first third of the fifteenth century as China's sea power peak.

Table 5.2 **Chinese Voyages in the Ming Dynasty, 1405–1433**

Years	Number of Ships	Number of Personnel	Places Visited
1405–1407	62	27,000	Champa, Java, Sumatra, Calicut
1407–1409	n.a.	n.a.	Siam, Sumatra, Java, Calicut, Cochin
1409–1411	48	30,000	Sumatra, Malacca, Quilon
1413–1415	63	29,000	Champa, Java, Sumatra, Hormuz, Red Sea, Maldives, Bengal
1417–1419	n.a.	n.a.	Java, Ryuku Islands, Brunei, Jormuz, Aden, Mogadishu, Malindi
1421–1422	41	n.a.	Sumatra, Aden, East Africa
1431–1433	100	27,500	Vietnam, Sumatra, Java, Malacca, Ceylon, Calicut, Hormuz, Aden, Jedda, Malindi

Source: Based on Maddison (2001: 67).

Sea power in China, however, had not had a long history by the time of the Ming voyages. Prior to the Southern Song, China had not even had a regular state navy. Occasional Chinese attacks on Vietnam and Korea had utilized sea power, but these fleets depended on ships pressed into service to move troops to the place of combat. River- and lake-based naval fighting had a longer history. The Northern and Southern Song dynasties specialized in this type of warfare, but their opponents, especially the Mongols, learned how to fight the same way and ultimately used Song tactics to conquer China.[16]

A major reason for China's initial limited sea power was its relative absence of maritime commerce. Maritime commerce connecting East Asia and the Middle East had increased after about 900 CE, yet most of this trade was controlled by Persians and Arabs. The loss of northern China helped the Southern Song focus more on maritime trade, since the state's access to imports by land had diminished considerably. Increased Chinese participation in oceanic trade was complemented by the establishment of a standing navy. Chinese ships improved in size and durability. Cotton sails, rudders, and iron nails and anchors appeared. Charts, compasses, and navigational skills were developed. Special-purpose boats also emerged, including "whales," larger commercial vessels converted to military purposes, and "sea hawks," designed especially for naval combat. These ships carried various kinds of armaments (including something like Greek fire, bombs, rockets, guns, and, eventually, cannon).[17] Once a regular Song navy was in operation, it faced little competition at sea. Probably in part for that reason, and in part because of severe threats on land, the Song oceangoing navy was not well maintained, despite a doubling in maritime trade between the eleventh and twelfth centuries. Song–Mongol fighting, moreover, was most likely to take place on rivers, not oceans.

Later, the Mongol conquerors were quite ready to make use of oceangoing vessels in attacks against Vietnam, Japan, and Korea. The Yuan dynasty managed to destroy a number of Chinese ships in these unsuccessful attacks but lost interest in maintaining a blue water navy after the death of Kublai Khan (1294). The task of rebuilding trade networks and the Chinese navy fell to the Ming dynasty after its 1368 overthrow of the Yuan. As Wagner records, "After the 'commercial revolution' of the early Song and a period of economic stagnation in the Southern Song and Yuan periods, the Ming was a period of economic expansion. Trade, both inter-regional and international, developed greatly in the course of this period" (2008: 326). The rebuilding proceeded until 1433, when the third Ming emperor decided to end China's Indian Ocean voyaging. Maritime trade had come by this time to be seen as potentially destabilizing. Focusing on the continuing Mongol threat on land also seemed more pressing. The Chinese navy was thus again allowed to decline, and maritime trade was discouraged by imperial edicts after China explicitly decided to exploit internal frontiers at the expense of external ones (Barbier, 2011: 270).

The subsequent decline was rather abrupt but seems to have been temporary, if over a century can be described that way. Wilson (2009) recounts how the Chinese navy was treated poorly through part of the sixteenth century and was then revived once again by Ming decision-makers when naval capabilities were once more needed. As in other cases of states with both continental and maritime ambitions, priorities wobbled back and forth, with continental security issues usually gaining the upper hand.

Technological Innovation and Power-Driven Machinery

New technology created in China made it the world's most advanced economy by the end of the first millennium CE and into the beginning of the second millennium. This conclusion is based on the technological developments highlighted in Table 5.3.

Interestingly, it seems that the Chinese may have even had a steam engine from about the fifth century that worked in reverse of the eventual Western models. Moving water drove wheels, which then moved pistons to sift and shake flour. At later points, the idea was applied to the use of waterpower to smelt metal and operate furnace bellows.[18] Elvin (1973) goes even further to suggest that if medieval China had continued to make advances in textile-spinning machinery, a full-fledged industrial revolution could have come about hundreds of years earlier than in the West.[19] According to him, the tenth through fourteenth centuries were years of discernible emphases on scientific experimentation; mechanized industry; and advances in math, astronomy, medicine, metallurgy, pharmacology, dentistry, and warfare, all of which were undergirded by printing that allowed information to be codified and transferred. There does not seem to be much dissent that China possessed a technological edge up to the early medieval era. Yet something happened in the fourteenth century to cause scientific and technological innovation to stagnate and dissipate.

Two hundred years of intermittent economic decline and depression had something to do with this shift.[20] Economic growth returned in 1500 and persisted into the early nineteenth century, but it was more extensive in character and not marked by much innovation.[21] Elvin's idea of a high-level equilibrium trap that discouraged innovation after the fourteenth century is predicated on the coming together of several developments, including an end

Table 5.3 **China's Technological Developments**

Time Period	Development
2nd century BCE	Abacus
3rd century CE	Porcelain (peaking in Song dynasty era)
4th century	Petroleum and natural gas as fuel
6th century	Co-fusion steel (combining wrought and cast iron) made possible by high blast furnace temperatures developed to deal with the demands of ceramics and weapons
9th century	Gunpowder (may have emerged from experimentation in alchemical medicine)
8th–9th century	Woodblock printing and clockwork
11th century	Paper money
11th and 13th centuries	Movable type
11th century	Spinning wheel
12th century	Water-powered machine for spinning hemp thread

Notes: More parsimoniously, Adshead (2000: 156–162) characterizes the one-way exchange as taking place in five areas: (1) nautical (rudders, compasses, multiple masts lug sails), (2) metallurgical (blast furnace), (3) mechanical (waterpower in textile production), (4) chemical (explosives), and (5) horological (clocks). The first four appear to be well-substantiated. The clock transfer is more disputed, since Europeans later introduced (or reintroduced) clocks to China. Most of these lists of innovations stem from Needham's work published in the 1960s and early 1970s. See, e.g., Debeir, Deleage, and Hemergy (1991: 52–53).

to the benefits realized from exploitation of the southern frontier, decreased international trade and contact with the outside world, and a general shift to cultural introspection that discouraged experimentation. This interpretation underlines the boosts to productivity realized from having a frontier to exploit in the first place and the material and ideational gains derived from external contacts. It thus describes a situation that is not so much an equilibrium trap as it is an arrival at a place in which the primary sources of getting ahead (a frontier and trade to exploit) are either played out or explicitly prohibited to be tapped. With the advantage of hindsight, we can add the failure to undergo an energy transition to this list. Here again, the potential was certainly there, but circumstances worked against the replacement of wood by coal as the principal energy source in medieval China.

Is the absence of an energy transition sufficient to explain China's failure to continue its technological development? Mokyr (1990: ch. 9) offers a critical review of a slate of hypotheses explaining why post-Song China did not return to its earlier, more innovative ways. Fifteen arguments are discussed and, in the main, rejected:

1. Technological slowdown after 1400 was natural; what was unnatural was Europe's rapid ascent (Hucker, 1975).

2. Technological change in labor-intensive rice economies was different from what occurred in labor-saving Europe. Labor-intensive economies focused on labor-intensive approaches to agriculture (Bray, 1986). Mechanization was discouraged by the small production scale and the difficulty of creating machinery that would not also reduce yields (Bray, 1984).

3. Textile-spinning machines were not developed because they would have been unsuitable for household production (Chao, 1977).

4. The decline of ocean shipping was due to a political victory by the antinaval faction at the Ming imperial court.

5. A lack of fertilizer was a cause of productivity stagnation in agriculture, unlike what happened in Europe.

6. Internal migration into southern forestlands operated as a safety valve but also enticed entrepreneurs away from technological innovation (Bray, 1984).

7. Population growth shifted demand from nonagricultural goods to agricultural goods and reduced the supplies of wood and metal indispensable to technological change (Elvin, 1973).

8. The shift from wheat to rice may have led to increased protein deficiency, malnutrition, and lethargy/lack of energy.

9. Parasitic disease stemming from an increased number of farmers working in southern warm waters tainted by the use of human wastes as fertilizer may have devastated the labor force (Jones, 1981).

10. Chinese philosophy was inward-looking and not compatible with scientific and technological progress (Feng, 1922, cited in Needham, 1969).

11. Chinese logic was based on historical analogy and not the hypothetico-deductive method found in the West (Hartwell, 1971).

12. Chinese science became increasingly characterized by obsolete traditionalism (Gilles, 1978).

13. Chinese agriculture encountered diminishing returns in the absence of scientific breakthroughs that were associated with earlier trial-and-error experimentation (Tang, 1979).

14. Merchants in Europe financed research in order to develop new production, trade, and profit, but merchants did not rise to power in China (Needham, 1959).

15. As an empire, China was governed by tight bureaucratic control in which the bureaucrats favored stability over technological progress (Needham, 1969).

Mokyr rejects most of these arguments and puts forward a sixteenth explanation: Chinese governments were more supportive of technological innovation before 1400 than after 1400. It is very difficult to argue with this statement, but why this was the case is less clear. Autocrats tend to prefer stability, and the Ming and Qing dynasties appear to have shared that preference. Such a position also seems to overlap considerably with the fifteenth argument attributed to Needham (1969). Alternatively, European innovations needed less state support, making the issue not as germane in western Eurasia. Still, the Tang and Song rulers were also autocrats and yet were more supportive of innovation than the autocrats that came later. Autocratic preferences per se would therefore not seem to be the ultimate key to the China puzzle. The question remains why these preferences changed and changed so consistently from one set of dynasties to another.[22]

Lipsey, Carlaw, and Bekar (2005) have a more satisfying answer.[23] They suggest that Chinese scientific culture lacked a number of aspects found in the West, including mathematical proofs, deductive geometry, and trigonometry. Chinese understanding of hydrostatics (buoyancy, leverage principles) was underdeveloped, and there was a lack of curiosity about Arab/Hellenic science. More importantly, China lacked relatively independent universities with collective memories of discoveries. Scholars were dependent on state support that may or may not have been forthcoming but was rarely sustained. When discoveries were made, they were often lost or not followed up on. Finally, a lack of familiarity with Newtonian mechanics and the interactions between heat and steam made it unlikely that Chinese innovators would have developed steam engines. Even if they had, the absence of systematic work in chemistry and electronics would have made it equally unlikely that the late-nineteenth-century technology wave would have originated in China. So, it was not simply a matter of on-and-off imperial support for science. Rather, the Western form of scientific infrastructure and basic information base was largely missing in the East. Without it, technological innovations that required variable amounts of scientific input were far less probable in early modern China.

Some of the fifteen or sixteen explanations critically reviewed by Mokyr probably have some applicability. The tenth through twelfth, for instance, overlap with the very plausible position taken by Lipsey, Carlaw, and Bekar (2005). Yet none of them are ultimately as satisfying as the basic answer supplied by Goldstone's efflorescence theory. In this view, Chinese technological innovation became more scarce after the Song dynasty because China failed to experience a transition in energy fuels. If Song China had had a technological reason to commit to coal as its primary fuel, continuing technological innovation would have been more probable—if for no other reason than that new technology that makes use of new sources of energy tends to be so inefficient early in its development that users are compelled to try to improve it. But while Northern Song China had ample access to coal, it did not develop technology that depended on it. No doubt, invoking the absence of an energy transition does not explain everything about China's missing innovation, but it would seem to have more explanatory leverage than the slate reviewed by Mokyr. We say a bit more about this factor in the next section.

Fuel Innovation

Coal was being carved as early as 4000 BCE and used as a fuel for iron production at least by the Han Empire era (first or second century CE).[24] Increasingly employed for both industrial and home heating purposes through the tenth century, the eleventh century witnessed a dramatic increase in coal consumption, especially in the Kaifeng area, where there were major coal deposits nearby, and the population demanded the fuel for heating purposes. Hartwell (1962) is even more specific, establishing a peak in coal production between 1050 and 1125. Immediately prior to this peak (between 998 and 1078), iron output had quadrupled, which in turn led to major reductions in its price (Hartwell, 1966). Coking with bituminous coal was introduced in the twelfth century as well. Hartwell's main point is that these developments resembled later British Industrial Revolution developments in quantity and quality.[25]

After Kaifeng was lost, first to the invading Jin and later the Mongols, the demand for iron and coal declined precipitously. Hartwell thinks that the iron ore and coal deposits in the north were abandoned once demand from Kaifeng disappeared. But some iron production did reemerge in other areas after the Yuan dynasty.[26] Pomeranz (2000: 63) speculates that since the new iron production centers were located some distance from coal deposits, the production may have been fueled by wood and charcoal. Coal, on the other hand, does not seem to have made much recovery after the Mongol invasion.[27] Pomeranz notes:

> It is unclear how much knowledge about the extraction and use of coal was wiped out amid the catastrophes of the twelfth through fourteenth centuries—a distinct possibility since . . . [knowledge] was often passed orally from master to apprentice rather than written down—and how much ceased to be used or developed further as the area housing most of China's coal became a backwater, far from major markets and far from invigorating interaction with other sorts of craftsmen. Although coal-mining remained significant in China, it was never again a cutting-edge sector: instead, various fuel-saving innovations (including stir-frying in

a wok instead of boiling food in heavier vessels) became increasingly important. (2000: 63)

Nonetheless, the critical element is not so much the considerable decline in coal production as the absence of interaction between coal and technology. In Britain, this interaction occurred because a problem needed to be solved: water needed to be drained from deep coal mines. To get more coal, steam engines were developed to remove the water. There is some disagreement about whether drainage was a problem in Chinese coal mining. Pomeranz (2000: 65) contends that the main Chinese problem had to do with ventilation to preclude spontaneous combustion. Golas (1999: 186), however, states that water removal was "perhaps the biggest and most widespread problem in Chinese coal mining." He attributes this argument to the tendency for Chinese coal to be found in limestone, which also often contains large reservoirs of water. If so, then the problem may have been resolved in medieval China by simply moving to another portion of the coal deposit when water interfered with mining operations (Podobnik, 2006: 19). Still, it is not clear that these generalizations apply to all Chinese coal deposits and all periods of time. Eighteenth-century coalmines were described as small and shallow. Perhaps they were similar in Song times. Whatever the reasons for the absence of an energy–technology interaction, it is clear that a transition to coal as the primary energy fuel did not take place in medieval China. It might have happened, but it did not—and since it did not, an early industrial revolution did not occur and probably could not have occurred.

Conclusion

The two factors that loom so large in the Chinese story, summarized in table 5.4, are frontier exploitation in the Tang–Song era and the absence of a successful energy transition to coal. The movement of population south as a result of external military pressures is certainly part of the picture, but there was never any reason to assume that Chinese processes had to combine the exploitation of southern resources (underexploited land, rice, and access to the sea) with the increased integration of north and south via canal traffic. Population growth and urbanization could have been sustained. A third factor is the early technological innovativeness of the Chinese economy, the subsequent stagnation of this precocious lead, and its eventual diffusion to western Europe. Some of the ingredients for an early industrial revolution were present. Coal was being exploited. Iron demand and production were expanding in scale. The only thing that presumably was missing was the steam engine—even though the basic principles underlying such engines were known at least in the abstract. As a consequence, the most

Table 5.4 **Presence and Absence of Key Economic Growth and Technological Centrality Factors—Medieval China**

Frontier Exploitation	Agriculture	Transportation/ Communications	Trade	Urbanization	Population Growth	Technological Innovation	Energy Transition	Power-Driven Machinery
Present	Present	Present	Present	Present	Present	Present	Absent	Absent

important missing element was an interactive transition to coal utilizing technology that required coal as fuel.

We close this chapter with an interpretation that subsumes some of what has been discussed and also helps to bridge the transition from China to Europe in the next chapter. Feuerwerker (1995) has developed a macro-framework for Eurasian population demographics that is centered on five logistics, briefly summarized in table 5.5.[28] The timing of the changes in the logistics are quite close until the nineteenth century, when they diverge. The sequence begins with a relatively small rise and fall of population in both the Han and Roman empires just prior to the beginning of the first millennium CE. Compared to later growth, the bumps in figure 5.3 are barely discernible. But Chinese population increased from 42 million in 200 BCE to 63 million in 200 CE before declining to 50 million in 800 CE, while European population increased from

Table 5.5 **Parallel Eurasian Population Logistics**

Stage	China	Europe
1	Han Dynasty—peaked at c. 60 million; logistic interrupted by imperial fragmentation	Roman Empire—peaked at c. 36 million; logistic interrupted by imperial fragmentation
2	Han peak not exceeded until Northern Song, but growth resumed after 800 CE; Southern Song peaked at 120 million; Mongol invasion interrupts logistic	Medieval population growing after 800 to c. 1300; Black Death interrupts logistic
3	Recuperation and slow growth in Ming Dynasty—150 million in 16th century; 17th century crisis (civil war and Manchu invasion) ends logistic	Recuperation in late 15th and early 16th centuries; 17th-century crisis centered in central and southern Europe and largely evaded by northwest Europe
4	Growth resumed in Qing dynasty, peaking at 430 million in 1840; logistic interrupted by series of rebellions in mid-19th century	Mid-18th-century growth begins and continues despite two world wars
5	Growth resumed in 20th century with emphasis on reduced mortality rates—population more than doubles	n.a.

Source: Based on discussion in Feuerwerker (1995).

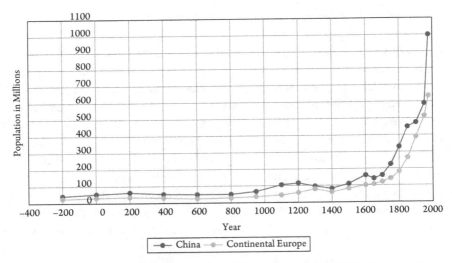

Figure 5.3 Chinese and European Population Growth, 200 BCE–1975 CE. Source: Based on population data reported in Feuerwerker (1995: 50).

26 million to 36 million and then declined to 26 million in roughly the same time span.

Feuerwerker (1995) links each of these successive population logistics with economic growth by arguing that population growth may exceed economic growth but cannot take place without some economic growth that stimulates it in the first place. For instance, the first Chinese logistic is attributed to a shift from millet to wheat as the primary food source, just as the second Chinese logistic is understood to have been fueled to some extent by a shift from wheat to rice. These shifts, occurring in agrarian economies, are considered to be fundamental technological innovations.

Eastern and western Eurasia fragmented politically in similar and roughly simultaneous fashions. Five to six centuries of stagnation and conflict followed before population growth resumed in the second logistic that began around 800 CE at both ends of Eurasia. In China, reunification took place under the Tang and Northern Song dynasties. Europe, of course, did not become reunified. In China, population growth peaked during the Southern Song dynasty, which was subsequently toppled by the Mongols. European population growth peaked just prior to the advent of the Black Death, which was spread by the Mongol expansion into Eurasia.

Mongol rule in China oversaw nearly a 50 percent drop in population size. In the Ming restoration, the population slowly recovered and peaked at about 30 million in the sixteenth century, exceeding the earlier Southern Song peak, before the onset of crises in the seventeenth century and the Manchu takeover.

Europe experienced its own gradual recovery from the waves of plague only to encounter its own seventeenth-century crises, which ravaged western Eurasia with the exception of northwestern Europe. Population growth resumed at both ends of Eurasia in the eighteenth century, with one major difference. In China, a series of rebellions halted or reversed the fourth logistic in the mid-nineteenth century before a fifth logistic commenced in the twentieth century that continues to the present. In Europe, population growth was not interrupted and continued through the twentieth century.

These interruptions to population growth are seen by Feuerwerker not as exogenous interventions but as indicators of deteriorating standards of living in response to population growth exceeding economic growth in a Malthusian rhythm.[29] Internal warfare was not inevitable. Other responses were observed, particularly migration from rural areas to cities and out-migration to less developed areas in both China and Europe.[30] In Europe, marriages were also postponed to later ages, and celibacy was more evident. In contrast, Chinese population controls did not occur until later in the fifth logistic. Instead, Chinese farmers doubled the amount of land under cultivation.

The remarkable parallels in logistic timing become less remarkable if one puts aside the myths of separate continents. The events that unfolded on the opposite ends of Eurasia were not identical, but they were similar in large part because China and Europe were both subject to agrarian political economies and governed by population–resource tradeoffs and overlapping climate regimes.[31] It is the deviation in behavior during the fourth logistic that is more interesting. Feuerwerker's (1995) explanation for this divergence is not unlike Elvin's (1973) argument, but it is broader in scope, if less fleshed out. Basically, he argues that China's technological responses to population growth and other demands initially were more successful than Europe's. Early Chinese technological developments in agriculture, water control, and metallurgy were good enough to work more or less unchanged into the nineteenth century. To be sure, the Song (and Tang) foundation was improved upon, but it was not fundamentally altered for nearly a millennium. Eventually, these developments did prove to be inadequate, but until then, the political–economic foundation more or less sufficed.

European responses are judged by Feuerwerker (1995) to have been less impressive and certainly less advanced than those made by China. In fact, he claims that European agrarian technology up to the early modern period did not surpass what was known during the Roman era. If the Chinese had fewer incentives to change their technological foundation throughout most of the second millennium CE, the Europeans had much more incentive to do so, since their foundation was a millennium older than its Chinese counterpart. Improvements in agrarian technology began to emerge in the Low Countries in the seventeenth century and were copied by the British. With a larger population and greater control of farming land as a result of the enclosure movement, the British were able to apply Dutch techniques to boost the efficiency of their agricultural output and provide surplus labor for industrialization purposes.

Feuerwerker (1995) goes on to add that in Europe the competition among multiple states in an environment characterized by scarcity was more likely to generate institutions that were facilitative of economic growth (such as property laws and public debt) than was the case in China. The early modern environment in China was less characterized by scarcity, and competition within a unified empire was likely to be discouraged strongly. Moreover, the Europeans had their "phantom acreage" in the New World and Asian markets to exploit at a time when the Chinese were simply not all that interested in the outside world. The Europeans also had an interest in science and experimentation at a time when the Chinese did not. Thus, Feuerwerker concludes:

> Before modern times, then, we can "award" technological and institutional leadership to China and demographic flexibility to Western Europe. In the early modern world scientific and technological discovery advanced in Europe but not in China. Institutional innovation swept over Europe, but China offered the sacred "'virtue" of its emperor to all who came from afar and sought to be civilized. (1995: 63)

We will see that the story of the China–Europe technological lead is a bit more complicated than that, but it is not a bad quick interpretation.[32] Simply put, Chinese technology gained an early lead and made the Chinese more complacent. Europeans had less reason for complacency and were able to catch up and surpass this early lead. The only thing that is omitted from such an account is the critical shift in energy sources that occurred in Europe. If the Europeans had only reformed their agriculture and tinkered scientifically, it is most unlikely that the British and French could have penetrated China so easily in the mid-nineteenth century. At the same time, these agricultural reforms and experimentation certainly did facilitate Europe's movement to a carbon energy foundation.

A technological bridge was needed from the eastern zone of Eurasia to the western zone. This conduit was provided sequentially by Genoa, Venice, and Portugal—all three of which specialized in creating trading regimes that were critical in transferring Chinese technology to the West and, ultimately, in moving Europeans from the Mediterranean to the Atlantic Ocean and then back to the Indian Ocean and more direct Asian–European maritime interactions. Chapter 6 continues this saga.

The Netherlands: Not Quite the First Modern Economy and Its Immediate Predecessors

In this chapter, we look at four cases: Genoa, Venice, Portugal, and the Netherlands. Genoa, Venice, and Portugal acted as transitional agents over a five- to six-hundred-year period, creating sea power and trading regimes to move Asian commodities and innovations to and from increasingly organized European markets. While Genoa and Venice were primarily Mediterranean-centric, Portugal led the breakthrough from the constraints of the inland sea and inaugurated Europe's Atlantic focus. At no time did any of these actors possess the power of China or subsequent global actors, but for their time, they were critical technological leaders, presaging the bigger things that were to come in the eighteenth and nineteenth centuries.

Asian–Mediterranean Linkages

Genoa and Venice

Genoa, Venice, and Portugal played pivotal roles in linking Chinese/Asian trade and ideas to the European marketplace.[1] To simplify the basic pathways along which this trade flowed, there were three routes from Asia to Europe prior to the 1490s. The overland route by caravan wound its way through mountains, deserts, and numerous predatory obstacles from China to the Black Sea. Control of or influence over Constantinople was politically critical to European attempts to monopolize the Black Sea outlet into the Mediterranean, with Genoa and Venice acting as the main European competitors in this contest. Venice had the initial edge because it had convinced participants in the Fourth Crusade to take Christian Constantinople in 1204 along their way to the Middle East. This influence, however, was short-lived. A 1261 civil war overturned the ruling elite in Constantinople, and the new rulers had been backed by Genoa, which then proceeded to become the primary European trader in the Black Sea area.[2]

Two maritime routes offered alternatives to the land route(s). Both of these routes transited around India and then either landed in Persia or the Gulf area or traveled farther to the Red Sea. The first of these routes then used land caravans to move commodities to the Levant—one of the reasons Italian city-states were heavily involved in transporting crusaders to the Levant. The other route was controlled by Egyptian Mamluks.

The Mongol conquest of much of Eurasia affected all three routes, albeit in different ways. The overland route became more attractive because the Pax Mongolica reduced predatory transaction costs (Abu-Lughod, 1989). The once-multiple sovereignties through which traders had had to pass were eliminated by the imposition of a new empire that looked on the overland trade favorably. In contrast, the Mongol attack on Baghdad and Muslim resistance to both crusaders and Mongols in the Fertile Crescent area discouraged use of the Middle Eastern maritime route. The decline of Chinese maritime trade during the Mongol rule also did not help the maritime Silk Roads (Lewis, 1988; Huang, 1990). The more distant Mamluks and the Red Sea route prospered, but once the Mamluks had fewer enemies to fight, their need for new recruits, the Circassian slaves who had been supplied primarily by Genoa, fell off. Genoa subsequently lost its favored position in Egypt and was replaced by Venice.

Genoa emerged from these fluctuations in East–West trade route fortunes as the leading Mediterranean trading power in the thirteenth century. Scammel (1981) dates Genoa's lead from 1200, although other authors stress its continuing rivalries with Venice (Lane, 1973) and Pisa (Negri, 1974). Ashtor (1983) views Genoa as being supreme in the second half of the thirteenth century and peaking toward 1300, although Venice failed to surpass Genoa prior to 1370. Throughout this period, Genoa's trade volume soared, doubling between 1214 and 1274 and quadrupling in the last quarter of the thirteenth century (Luzzato, 1961; Lopez and Miskimin, 1962; Kedar, 1976; Scammell, 1981).[3]

Genoa's primary role in retrospect was to organize new routes from East to West. The city-state played a major role in organizing the Champagne Fairs, a circuit of fairs connecting six cities in France, each of which was active for one to two months. They were made possible by a local count willing to provide protection for their functioning for a fee.[4] Gradually, the Fairs became the central market for European trade interactions, both within the region and in exchanges involving Asian goods. But this role was limited in duration. After the success of the Fairs attracted French royal interest and interference, non-French traders encountered discrimination. The Levantine supply of Asian goods also fell off as Crusader control in that part of the Middle East was lost.[5]

Genoa was active during this time in pursuing alternative routes. It helped loosen Muslim control of the Gibraltar choke point in 1290, allowing European maritime trade between the Mediterranean and Baltic areas. This maneuver also opened up Atlantic ports as competitors for the Champagne Fairs' position as the central node in European trade. Scammel (1981) argues that after the Champagne Fairs began to decline, Genoa needed an Atlantic base to facilitate the exchange of northern European textiles for Asian goods coming into the Black Sea terminus. Bruges became the main Atlantic base of Genoese trade, but Genoa had by this time constructed a large Mediterranean–Atlantic trading network stretching from Genoa to the Black Sea and on to Beirut, North Africa, Spain, Bruges, and Southampton. At least one Genoese attempt to circumnavigate Africa was made. Genoese traders also attempted to break into the North African gold circuit and worked with Mongols in Persia to try to block the Red Sea route.

The last quarter of the thirteenth century also initiated a period of general maritime technological innovation in the Mediterranean (McNeill, 1974; Bernard, 1976; Lopez, 1987). Compasses, improved charts, rudders, and new types of sails and masts were all introduced. Ships became larger, faster, and more likely to reach their destinations. Cargo capacity increased sevenfold. Crew size actually decreased. Shipping costs therefore declined. Thus, European trading networks and volume expanded in conjunction with vastly improved ship and sailing technology.

In the last quarter of the fourteenth century, Venice pulled ahead of Genoa as the most important European trader, a lead that was only strengthened in the early fifteenth century (Scammell, 1981; Ashtor, 1983; Van der Wee, 1990). Genoa and Venice had fought a number of wars at sea in the thirteenth and fourteenth centuries in which Genoa had prevailed until its fleet was weakened by the coming of the Black Death in the 1340s. It is not that Venice went unaffected by the plague, but it somehow withstood the widespread population and trade ravages better than its primary competitor did. Regionally, the late 1340s through the early 1380s was a period of economic depression and conflict. Venice, however, outlasted Genoa in 1381 and went on to experience a renewed bout of trade expansion in the first half of the fifteenth century.[6]

The Venetian approach to constructing a Mediterranean-centric network was not unlike the Genoese approach, but it was more regulated and centered increasingly on the Mamluk/Red Sea connection.[7] Venice utilized the new maritime technology to construct a state-owned and state-built fleet of merchant galleys with multiple masts for sailing purposes. The ships were leased annually and required to sail in convoys and to move all trade through Venice. In this fashion, competition among Venetian traders could be constrained while their efforts away from Venice could be concentrated and protected by the state, giving them a further edge over the non-Venetian competition. The galley lines, which were inaugurated in the early fourteenth century, continued to operate into the six-teenth century. The number of ships at sea in any given year fluctuated (Ashtor, 1983: 55, 79, 116–117, 318, 474) but stabilized in the fifteenth century with the rise of a focus on Alexandria and Beirut.[8] Their cargo capacity continued to ex-pand as well. The 20-ton ships of the period prior to 1300 expanded to 150 tons by 1320 and 300 tons after 1450 (Lane, 1987).

Nonetheless, the basic point is that the expansion of Italian economic activity in the first half of the second millennium did not simply mark the endogenous beginning of a rebirth of the West. Rather, as Gernet argues,

> the Italian cities which took on new life at the end of the Middle Ages were at the terminus of the great commercial routes of Asia. . . . [They] profited from the new waves of trade and borrowings set in motion by the creation of a vast Mongol empire extending from Korea to the Danube. What we have acquired the habit of regarding—according to a history of the world that is in fact no more than a history of the West—as the beginning of modern times was only the repercussion of the upsurge of the urban, mercantile civilizations whose realm ex-tended, before the Mongol invasion, from the Mediterranean to the Sea of China. The West gathered up part of this legacy and received from it the leaven which was to make possible its own development. (1982: 347)

The Genoese and Venetians, in other words, served as the conduits for the trans-mission of Chinese advances made prior to the Mongol invasion but via the good offices of the Mongol Empire.

Portugal

One of the indirect consequences of Genoa opening the Mediterranean to the Atlantic in 1290 was that Portugal hired a Genoese admiral to organize its own fleet. Lisbon also became a natural stopover on the run up and down the Atlantic coast of Europe. While the Italians kept Asian trade going in the Mediterranean and Europe and probably were the principal agents for diffusing Chinese tech-nological innovations throughout the region, the Portuguese were pivotal in making the Asian–Atlantic economy a growing concern. The circumnavigation of Africa in the late 1490s forged a direct link between the Indian Ocean and the Atlantic and broke the Venetian–Mamluk monopoly on Asian spices in the Mediterranean. For that matter, it turned the Mediterranean, and especially the Middle East, into something of a backwater in international commerce for a few generations.

The Portuguese role in these developments was only partially premeditated. Portugal's involvement began as part of the continuation of Iberian conflict with Muslims. Once Christians had pushed the Muslims out of Portugal, Morocco became the next target. Tangiers was invaded in 1415. However, the inability of the Portuguese to make much headway in penetrating into Morocco encouraged maritime movement down the North African coastline. As the Portuguese moved farther south, their goals expanded to include penetration of the North African gold and silver exchange circuit and later the trade in Guinean pepper and slaves—all of which were found about halfway down the West African coast in Guinea. Still, the Portuguese kept pushing down the coastline looking for a maritime route to the east. In doing so, they innovated one of the building blocks of the Atlantic economy. Currents and wind patterns made direct voyages between Europe and the Americas difficult. However, the Portuguese discovered that longer, more circular voyages could be made in the southern and northern Atlantic zones.

The more premeditated dimension of the Portuguese effort involved the systematic collection of information on navigation and shipbuilding to aid African exploration. The caravel was a Portuguese-designed ship based on Arab fishing vessels once used in the Algarve region that drew little water and was useful in shallow coastal voyaging from the 1420s on. But once it was realized that these small ships were not likely to survive a trip around the Cape of Good Hope, larger multimasted ships (called *naus* and galleons) were developed that could be used for both commercial and military purposes (Devezas and Modelski, 2008).

Lipsey, Carlaw, and Bekar (2005: 170) describe this process of technological development as a form of positive momentum: "The further they got, the more they needed better navigational aids and better ships; the better the navigational aids and ships that were available, the further they could go." In the process, the Portuguese accessed North Atlantic fishing; discovered the African route to the Indian Ocean, India, and an alternative way to obtain Asian spices; acquired Brazil; and were the first to circumnavigate the world.

Since the Portuguese had little to offer as traders in the Indian Ocean, they fell back on their military capabilities. Armed ships could impose a protection racket in the western Indian Ocean in which merchants were required to purchase licenses to sail and do business in Portuguese-dominated waters. A network of fortified bases were established on the coasts of Africa, the Middle East, India, and Southeast Asia, where they could be relieved by Portuguese fleets when they came under local attack.[9] This coastal network represented the physical outflanking of the Venetians and Mamluks.

The Portuguese movement into the Indian Ocean disrupted the functioning of the older maritime Silk Roads, but not permanently. The Portuguese were sufficiently powerful to defeat Ottoman, Mamluk, and various Indian powers that attempted to resist the initial European penetration into the Indian Ocean.[10] The Portuguese ships carried more cannon and could outsail the oared galleys sent by the Mediterranean powers and the local sailing vessels. But the Portuguese were not numerous enough to maintain their European trade monopoly for long. Spices did return to Middle Eastern markets by more traditional routes in the late sixteenth century. Nonetheless, the Portuguese were able to profit from their control of the European spice market for almost a century—from 1497 to 1591 (Duncan, 1986).[11]

Another facet of the Portuguese movement into the Indian Ocean was that the Asian goods Portuguese vessels brought back were better marketed in northern Europe than in Lisbon.[12] Antwerp became the entrepôt for Portuguese commodities in the early sixteenth century, further facilitating the gradual adoption of the Netherlands/Low Countries as the European trading focus, a shift first initiated by the Genoese when they adopted Bruges as their northern focal point.[13] The Portuguese also introduced sugar into Brazil, which attracted Dutch interest and eventually led to the introduction of sugar cultivation to English colonies in the Caribbean—one of the contributors to Britain's rise to ascendancy in the eighteenth century.

Thus, Genoa, Venice, and Portugal fill in the blanks between twelfth-century Song China and the seventeenth-century Netherlands. Genoa and Venice kept the Asian commodity flow to Europe alive and helped to reorganize European markets. Portugal destroyed the Mediterranean position in this East–West exchange system and connected the Atlantic and Indian Oceans. There is no need to downplay the importance of Spanish silver from Mexico and Peru in providing liquidity for this exchange (and in exacerbating Western warfare) after the 1550s. The Spanish even took control of Portugal and its fleet, but not its empire, in the succession struggle for the Portuguese throne in the 1580s. But at no time could anyone attribute the European maritime technology lead to the Spanish. The same cannot be said of the Genoa–Venice–Portugal sequence. In different centuries, each of the three demonstrated considerable innovation and maritime technological leadership. Yet none of them became economic powerhouses on the scale of China, Britain, or the United States. They did bear some resemblance to the Netherlands in terms of their heavy emphasis on trade and sea power, but the Dutch went beyond their southern European predecessors in developing an agrarian and industrial base to bolster their trading regime. In that respect, the seventeenth-century Dutch more closely resemble Britain and the United States. It is to the Dutch case that we move our attention next.

The Netherlands Case

In one of the most recent explanations of seventeenth-century Dutch (and later British) economic leadership, Broadberry et al. (2015) combine a number of the factors that we emphasize and add some that we exclude. They argue that the edge gained by northwestern Europe (essentially the Netherlands and Britain) after the sixteenth century can be attributed to a combination of two major shocks and several structural factors. The first shock was the Black Death, which appeared in the mid-fourteenth century, with recurrent bouts into the seventeenth century. High mortality rates led to higher per capita gross domestic product for the survivors. The distinctiveness of northwestern Europe is that it managed to keep its greater affluence per capita when the effects of the plague began to wear off and population growth began to resume, as shown in table 6.1.

Three or more structural factors enabled the Netherlands and Britain to take advantage of the second shock—the shift away from the Mediterranean

Table 6.1 **Selected European GDP Per Capita**

Year	England/Britain	Netherlands	Italy	Spain
1280	679			
1300	755		1,482	957
1348	777	876	1,376	1,030
1400	1,090	1,245	1,601	885
1450	1,055	1,432	1,668	889
1500	1,114	1,483	1,403	889
1570	1,143	1,783	1,337	990
1600	1,123	2,372	1,244	944
1650	1,110	2,171	1,271	820
1700	1,563	2,403	1,350	880
1750	1,710	2,440	1,403	910
1800	2,080	1,752	1,244	962
1820	2,133	1,953	1,376	1,087
1850	2,997	2,397	1,650	1,144

Note: Data expressed in Geary-Khamis 1990 international dollars.

Source: Based on Broadberry et al. (2015: 375–376).

as the outlet for Asian goods to the Atlantic, which became the main maritime starting point for access to both the East and the Americas. The first structural factor was that the northwestern economies had agrarian components that were capital- and animal-intensive; employed powered mills that ensured familiarity with cogs, gears, and hydraulics; and incorporated sufficient food processing to warrant millers, bakers, and brewers. It also helped that farming equipment contributed to the demand for iron manufactures.

A second structural factor involved later marriage and time of first birth for women, patterns that again seem to have been concentrated in northwestern Europe. Exactly why that was the case is debated, but it may well have had something to do with high wage rates. Broadberry et al. (2015) argue that the later marriage rates led to higher wage rates, but it seems like the causal arrow could point both ways (i.e., higher wage rates could also have led to later marriage rates). Higher prices and standards of living encouraged people to work harder to be able to afford consumer goods, a linkage that even leaves a place for Weber's (1930) Protestant ethic as a legitimizer of working harder. Most importantly, though, later marriage helped constrain population growth rates so that population gains were less likely to outpace economic gains.

The third structural factor involved the political differences that characterized Europe and China. China was often unified, whereas Europe remained fragmented after the decline of the Roman Empire. This characteristic made for greater transaction costs in Europe but allowed for different economic and political development trajectories. Some states could grow faster. Others could specialize in trade and colonial exploration and settlements. Some could create highly authoritarian regimes, while still others could construct more representative political systems in which executive policies were constrained by legislative institutions and commercial interests.[14] This diversity facilitated the Netherlands' and Britain's adoption of other states' positive elements to further their own economic growth.

Still, there remains the question of why Britain industrialized first. Broadberry et al.'s (2015) answer is that the Dutch domestic and colonial markets were too small in scale to encourage economic innovation, despite both states possessing high wage rates that should have encouraged the development of labor-saving innovations. Furthermore, Britain had plenty of inexpensive coal which allowed Britian to focus on manufacturing. The Dutch, by contrast, specialized in services (financial, commerce, and shipping). Therefore, for all three reasons, Britain was more likely than the Netherlands to build steam-powered machinery.

This argument is certainly plausible.[15] Yet it downplays the element of surprise involved in the ascendancy of the Netherlands captured in the following statement:

> It is a wonder that the Dutch Golden Age happened at all. The period during which structural conditions were enhanced by accidental

circumstances could only be a short one. The wealth of the Dutch Republic depended on a positive combination of many factors in a favourable context, and that could only have been a temporary phenomenon. (Slicher van Bath, 1982: 34–35)

It is one thing to explain why Britain industrialized more successfully than the Netherlands. It is another to explain how the small and initially not very powerful Netherlands came to be in a position in the seventeenth century to claim centrality in commerce, industry, and technology. As suggested by Slicher van Bath (1982), this rise did hinge on a number of factors coming together at just the right time in a way that would have been incredibly difficult to see in advance.

It is helpful to view this case in terms of the interaction among factors displayed in figure 6.1. Whereas China was able to exploit its underdeveloped southern frontier, the Dutch had to virtually create the northern Netherlands by draining enough water to make the area inhabitable. Once inhabited, its agricultural output proved insufficient to feed its population unless farmers commercialized and sold most of their specialized output to the expanding cities and abroad. Urbanization, fed by labor not needed in agriculture and migrants from less peaceful areas, in turn led to the development of various industries that depended on heat energy fueled by peat and wind power. Closely connected to these interactions was the trade network that allowed the Netherlands to tap into food and industrial resources first from the North Sea and the Baltic states and later from the Mediterranean, Asia, and the Atlantic economy. Yet the ability to

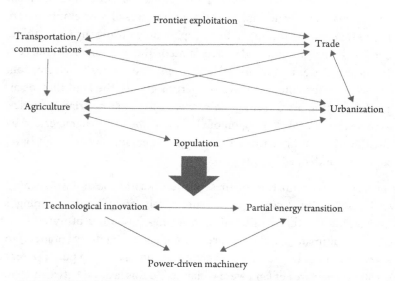

Figure 6.1 Factors Underlying Dutch Technological and Economic Leadership.

develop these trade–industry–commercialized agriculture interactions in highly urbanized settings depended on the distraction of more powerful neighbors. Once these neighbors realized that the Netherlands was profiting at their expense and had resolved some of their domestic problems, they moved to restrict trade with the Dutch. These trade restrictions decreased demands for industrial and agricultural products. At the same time increased external threat and a series of wars beginning in the second half of the seventeenth century and ending only in 1713 bankrupted the Dutch and also slowed down their trade-led economic growth machine. Peat and wind had helped greatly to power machinery and produce heat energy to expand the Dutch trade network, but neither peat nor wind was sufficiently powerful to generate the kind of interaction needed between technology and a new type of fuel to produce an industrial revolution.

Frontier Exploitation

One of the advantages genuinely peripheral areas have is that they tend to be left alone, thereby encouraging more developmental autonomy. The price one pays for such autonomy is an uphill struggle against the developmental odds. The Netherlands fit both generalizations. For nearly two thousand years, there was little to attract European imperial attention to the region. Soggy marshland simply did not invite agrarian development. Only in medieval times did some limited and scattered settlement begin by both farmers largely free of feudal obligations and a strong aristocracy.

> Except for a few patches of habitation along the dunes and the main rivers, this swampy and inhospitable region was almost empty before the tenth century; it came to be occupied only during the high middle ages, when it was colonized and reclaimed. The reclamation of the central peat area was accomplished by farmers who received their freedom and almost absolute, exclusive property rights to the land they occupied as a stimulus to settle and a reward for their clearing activities. And so the central peat region of Holland came to be characterized by medium-size family farms worked by free peasant-owners. (van Bavel and van Zanden, 2004: 504)

The principal preoccupation of these settlers was to make both farming and survival possible by lowering the water levels on potential farming lands and preventing the threat of flooding from nearby bodies of water. Drainage concerns led ultimately to the construction of encircling dikes (polders) to regulate water levels and increasing reliance on windmills to help pump water away. Over 150,000 hectares of land were reclaimed in this fashion between 1540 and

1665 (de Vries and van de Woude, 1997: 32).[16] The Dutch had to first literally construct their frontier before it could be exploited.

Taming a boggy frontier proved a struggle against nature. Removing water caused the land to sink, making it easier to flood. A premium was thus placed on developing technologies that could efficiently manage water levels. Two climatic factors aided this struggle. Storm activity, which had compounded the highly threatening environment, declined after the sixteenth century. The colder climate of the Little Ice Age also lowered sea levels, which reduced the treadmill exercise to some extent after the 1500s. A second problem, however, was that the peaty part of the marshlands proved highly useful for fuel purposes. Its extraction contributed further to sinking ground levels and the creation of lakes that threatened to flood nearby settlements and cultivation.

At the same time, this man-made frontier encompassed little in the way of natural resources (other than peat). As a consequence, the Netherlands became highly dependent on importing raw materials and exporting what it could make. Haley (1974: 59) notes that cotton, bar iron, and coal—all of which were important to later British industrialization—were entirely absent from the Dutch economy. In that respect their absence worked as a form of structural discouragement of a British-style industrial revolution. The Netherlands' heavy emphasis on commercial trade in turn made the Dutch economy highly vulnerable to external interruptions and commercial rivalries.

Population

There are two movements of population that occurred in the Netherlands worth noting. First, the challenge of agrarian development in the marshy lands contributed to increased urbanization in the 1400s. A number of small cities located on the coast drew population away from the rural interior, making the northern Netherlands unusually urbanized for its era. The second shift involved the movement of skilled workers and merchants from the southern Netherlands, Sephardic Jews from Portugal, and Huguenots from France in reaction to religious persecution and financial instability. A fairly large number of people migrated to the northern Netherlands in the seventeenth and eighteenth centuries, but only half of them stayed in the country. The other half moved elsewhere, often in the employ of one of the Indies companies. Still, the influx of so many people in comparison to the total population of the Dutch state (which was roughly twice the size of the in-migration group) needs to be counted as definitely significant, especially in a country that suffered from a deficit of adult men after the seventeenth century. Many of the migrants clearly contributed to the skill pool in the Dutch coastal towns, but it is not clear that they can be credited

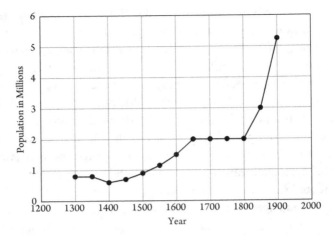

Figure 6.2 Dutch Population Growth. Source: Based on McEvedy and Jones (1978: 65).

with any strong exogenous push toward technological preeminence in specific industries. The migrants more generally reinforced trends already in progress.

As shown in figure 6.2, the population of the United Provinces of the Netherlands doubled between 1500 and 1650 before leveling off for the next 150 years. There would appear to be an unsurprisingly close relationship between prosperous times and Dutch reproduction. Black Death losses were quickly followed by a growing population until about 1650, when population growth literally flatlined until expansion resumed in the nineteenth century.

International Trade

Northwestern European coastal cities were well placed to take advantage of two changes that occurred at the end of the fifteenth century and the beginning of the sixteenth century. As population numbers recovered from the fourteenth-century plagues, demand for food increased. Baltic grain was an important source for this demand, and maritime transport from Poland and Prussia offered an efficient way to move bulky grain into western European markets if middlemen emerged to take on the distribution task. Dutch merchants, especially those located in Amsterdam, competed with their Hanseatic League counterparts and won a monopoly on Baltic trade with Europe.

Not long afterwards, Asian spices began to enter the European market via the new Portuguese routes around Africa and through the Indian Ocean. Because Lisbon was unsuitable as a marketplace, Antwerp emerged as the Portuguese entrepôt of choice for redistributing Asian goods. Antwerp was not Amsterdam, of course, but the prominence of its market flourished through most of the sixteenth century until it was seriously disrupted by a Spanish mercenary mutiny in 1576. In the wake of this uprising, merchants fled Antwerp for other cities, and many ultimately resettled in Amsterdam in the last decades of the sixteenth century.

The Dutch did not merely trade in the Baltic but came to dominate the transfer of commodities from the region to the Atlantic coastline of Europe. In the early sixteenth century, Dutch ships constituted more than two-thirds of the vessels that paid Danish tolls to enter the Baltic and may have controlled as much as half of the total Baltic trade. Moreover, the volume of Dutch trade in the Baltic expanded sixfold between 1500 and 1565. Half of the Dutch merchant fleet was committed to Baltic traffic as late as 1580, but this proportion had declined to a quarter by 1636 (van Zanden, 1993: 8), reflecting a movement away from bulk grains to an increased focus on Asian–American goods.

In looking at the case of the Netherlands, one can choose to emphasize either Dutch efforts to achieve trade centrality or what happened to other states to make the Dutch almost the last European trading hub left standing in the late sixteenth century. As usual, the best course seems to be a combination of both emphases. Israel (1989) stresses the Dutch default position in explaining the origins of its trading primacy. He argues that in late-fifteenth- and early-sixteenth-century European expansion was polycentric.

> The markets and resources of the wider world . . . were subject not to any one but rather to a whole cluster of western empires of commerce and navigation. Portugal, Castile, France, England, the Hanseatic League, the great south Germany emporia, the Italian trading republics of Venice, Genoa, and Florence, and last but not least the Netherlands, especially the southern provinces of Flanders and Brabant (including Antwerp), were all active arms of the West's expanding apparatus of world-trade dominance. (Israel, 1989: 4)

Israel readily acknowledges that not all of these actors were of the same type or operating in the same markets. But his origins explanation stresses that by the seventeenth century most had stumbled, been absorbed, or dropped out of the competition. The Hanseatic League was in full decline by 1590. Many of the rest followed:

> By 1650, Italy, Spain, Portugal, Germany and the South Netherlands had all ceased to form part of the controlling heartland of the European world-economy. These countries had all been reduced to subservience to a tiny number of more developed economies. Even France was . . . lapsing into a semi-subordinate role, with some important

sectors of her trade subject to the Dutch. Only the preciously marginal commercial empire of the North Netherlands maritime provinces, and that of England, continued to expand and grow in vitality during the early and mid-seventeenth century, inexorably gaining ground as the rest receded. (Israel, 1989: 6)

But even England entered a period of domestic instability and economic stagnation that sidelined it in the early seventeenth century. As a consequence, "most of the lost leverage over markets, routes, and commodities was picked up by the Dutch. The Dutch maritime zone moved to the top of the global hierarchy of exchanges, emerging as the hub of what was now definitely a 'mono-nuclear' system" (Israel, 1989: 6).

Yet Israel also acknowledges that in terms of bulk trade, the Dutch had already gained the status of lead "carrying" nation of Europe by the mid-fifteenth century. What they gained in part by default was the rich trades with Asia and the Americas, markets into which they moved directly thanks to their industrial base and aggressive state. Thus Dutch maritime technology had put the state in a good position to take advantage of the decline or distraction of most of its European competitors—a window of opportunity that did not remain open (see table 6.2).

The Netherlands' rise to economic supremacy was not simply a matter of technological advancement leading to shipping centrality. Becoming a leading trade entrepôt also made technological development more likely. As Davids notes,

Table 6.2 **Dutch and Selected Other States' Maritime Carrying Capacities (Metric Tons)**

State	1470	1570	1670	1780	1824
Netherlands	60	232	568	450	140
Germany	60	110	104	155	
Britain	n.a.	51	260	1,000	2,350
France	n.a.	80	80	700	
Italy, Portugal, Spain	n.a.	n.a.	250	546	
Denmark, Norway, Sweden				555	
North America				450	

Source: Based on Maddison (2001: 77). This source provides only the Dutch entry for the 1824 column. The British number is taken from Mitchell (1980: 646) but is not in metric tons (a metric ton is slightly lighter than a nonmetric ton).

Frontrunners in technology between the late Middle Ages and the nineteenth century commonly started their life-cycle in leadership in achieving a key-position in a far flung trading network. Being the core of such a trading network brought . . . a number of advantages compared with places which were not in the centre of a network . . . and would confer on it a cumulative edge in the development of technology. (2008: 534)

Davids (2008) elaborates this observation by listing six specific advantages core members of trading networks enjoyed: capital accumulation, the availability of raw materials, a supply of supplementary energy resources, the ability to gather information on best and novel practices elsewhere, the encouragement of specialization to become more competitive in wider markets, and the attraction of skilled immigrants to trade centers.

Obviously, not all trade hubs go on to establish technological leadership, but those that do can reinforce their centrality by applying technological and fuel innovations to the creation of commodities useful for trade. A hub's reliance on goods that are less expensive to make will facilitate its maintenance of trade centrality. The other side of the same coin is that the failure to maintain trade centrality is unlikely to encourage industrial scalar expansion and continuing technological innovation. The Netherlands' trade window of opportunity began to close in the second half of the seventeenth century (Price, 1998: 52–54).

During the first half of the seventeenth century, the [Dutch] Republic had been the conspicuous beneficiary of the unrest and internal difficulties that preoccupied the surrounding states. The Thirty Years' War not only brought disorder to the German market, it also diminished the strength of potential competitors in Central and Baltic Europe. As long as domestic religious and social conflicts kept France tied up in knots, the large French market lay relatively open to Dutch merchants. The English also had their hands full at home, as domestic tensions prevented the state from pursuing a consistent commercial policy. Once both England and France had secured domestic political stability, it could not be long before they turned their attention to reducing the economic preponderance of the Republic in their economies. Their eventual success in achieving this objective inevitably induced other states, such as Prussia, Sweden, and Denmark, to follow suit. (de Vries and van der Woude, 1997: 341)

Thus, first England and then France sought to shut down Dutch shipping and fishing access to home markets, an effort enforced by new mercantilistic policies and a sequence of wars that continued from 1651 to 1720. After 1720,

a number of Baltic states also began emulating Anglo-French mercantilistic intervention policies. In the process, the Dutch lost control of markets around
the world in Asia, the Americas, the Mediterranean, the Baltic, and Atlantic
Europe. Israel (1989) dates the end of Dutch trade primacy to 1740 (a year
marked by the onset of another round of Anglo–French commercial rivalry and
warfare), but by this time the Dutch position had been deteriorating for nearly
a century.

Trade primacy, productive efficiency, and technological innovation all
interacted in the Dutch case. As Israel (1989) observes, Dutch skills in processing and manufacturing were due in part to technological innovation, but
they were also greatly facilitated by a Dutch monopoly on the trade of the raw
materials on which processing and manufacturing were dependent:

> Dutch superiority in dyeing, bleaching, grinding, and refining was hard
> to challenge when it was the Dutch who had the stockpiles of dyestuffs,
> chemicals, drugs and rare raw materials on which all these processes
> depended. Thus, there was a high degree of interdependency between
> the Dutch commerce in high value commodities and Dutch industry,
> each continually reinforcing the other. (410)

Throughout history, an uncommon degree of access to raw materials has provided states a definite advantage over competitors. History also indicates that
such edges tend to be finite in time. Either the access is lost through depletion or
other actors develop strategies to undermine that access and the cost advantages
enjoyed by a singular leader. The Dutch case was further handicapped by a small
domestic market, with industrialization dependent on foreign markets (Smit,
1974: 62). Once the trade was interrupted, industrialization shriveled in response to reduced demand. Investment began to look for greener pastures and
higher returns and found them, among other places, in the British economy.

Agrarian Development

Generally, the Netherlands' poor soil and high costs of growing food were offset
after 1500 by a combination of an expanding population, rising prices, and
growing urbanized demand. The availability of inexpensive Baltic grain imports,
which were originally designed to supplement local food shortages, encouraged
Dutch farmers to specialize, adopt fertilizer and crop rotation to improve productivity, and participate in internationalized commerce. These incentives
worked to expand agrarian output through about 1650. After that date (and
through about 1750), agricultural depression became widespread throughout

Europe and in the Netherlands thanks to war, falling urban demand, and crop failures.[17]

Nonetheless, it is estimated (de Vries and van de Woude, 1997: 232) that Dutch agricultural output increased by about 2.4 times between 1510 and 1650. Since total population doubled in the same time period, food supply appears to have outgrown population expansion. Since the supply of agrarian labor did not improve at the same rate, Dutch agriculture must have become more efficient. This efficiency paid off in helping Dutch agriculture become more commercialized, thereby contributing to the economic foundation on which the Dutch lead was based.

Urbanization

Urbanization was fairly high in the Netherlands at a very early point. De Vries and van der Woude (1997: 60–62) claim that nearly a third of the Dutch population (31 to 32 percent) resided in cities by 1525. Van Bavel and van Zanden (2004: 504) assert that these percentages grew from 15 percent in 1300 to 45 percent in 1500. De Vries and van der Woude reserve the 45 percent figure for 1675, after which the urbanization trend turned negative and remained so into the nineteenth century.[18] Whichever figures are correct, there is little question that the Netherlands was highly urbanized and most likely the most urbanized area of Europe in this early modern era.

Taylor, Hoyler, and Smith (2012), working with Jane Jacobs' (1969, 1984) premise that city networks are the key to dynamic economic growth because their interactions lead to specialization and divisions of labor that increase the economy's complexity and productivity, have looked for cities with explosive growth (defined as 1 percent per year or more in fifty-year intervals). A rule of thumb that the Taylor group has devised is that clusters of growth spurts (several cities expanding quickly at the same time) should serve as an approximation of economic dominance, bookended by periods of ascent and decline. Table 6.3 summarizes a pattern that fits this approach quite well. Amsterdam is the sole Dutch entry in the 1500–1550 column. Four different cities (Amsterdam, Haarlem, Leiden, and Rotterdam) are seen to have expanded quickly in the 1550–1650 period. It is during precisely this period that most observers accord the Netherlands the peak status of European economic and technological leader. Only one Dutch city—and hardly any place else in Europe—expanded in the 1650–1700 interval, a period of Dutch decline, according to most analysts. Population decline presumably responded to the deterioration of economic prosperity.

Table 6.3 **European Cities with Explosive Growth, 1500–1700**

1500–1550	*1550–1600*	*1600–1650*	*1650–1700*
Lisbon	London	**Amsterdam**	Seville
Seville	**Amsterdam**	**Leiden**	**Rotterdam**
Augsburg	**Haarlem**	**Rotterdam**	
Antwerp	**Leiden**	London	
Magdeburg	Bordeaux	Paris	
Amsterdam	Cuenca	Lyon	
Hamburg	Vicenza	Hamburg	
London	Milan	Marseilles	
Lecce	Torino		
Rouen	Paris		
Venice	Jerez		
Catania			

Source: Taylor, Hoyler, and Smith (2012: 25); Dutch cities in bold.

Transportation and Communications

The Netherlands was naturally endowed with a number of rivers that over the years were improved by short canals subject to local sovereignty and multiple tolls. Increasing emphasis on maritime ports led to harbor construction projects instead of the improvement of canal connectivity. It was not until 1631 that a concerted canal construction effort to enhance intercity connections got underway. The project ended in 1665. While it failed to prove very useful for freight traffic, it did manage to improve passenger and mail movement.

Technological Innovation

Davids (2008: 268) notes that Dutch technological leadership was not based on any breakthrough innovations that catapulted the Netherlands ahead of its neighbors. Instead, it resulted from continuous incremental gains in a number of sectors. Some of the gains have to be credited to increasing investment and specialization, and not just the adoption of new techniques.

One of the early focuses of innovation involved herring. The Little Ice Age made North Sea waters colder, triggering a migration of Scandinavian fish

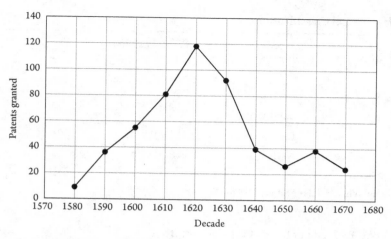

Figure 6.3 Dutch Patents. Source: Based on data reported in Davids (1993: 95).

south to English waters and closer to the Netherlands. Dutch factory ships, the "herring busses," emerged to catch the fish, remove their entrails, and salt them onboard. More durable, salted herring could then be kept longer at sea and moved through and into European markets as opposed to rushing fresh-caught fish with short shelf lives to coastal ports. In the latter part of the fifteenth and the early part of the sixteenth centuries, 200 to 250 such busses were in operation. By the end of the sixteenth century, the numbers had doubled to 400 to 450 and reached the 500 range by their mid-seventeenth-century peak (van Zanden, 1993: 8).[19] Extensive linkages to supporting industries on shore made these operations one of the principal sectors of Dutch industry. Figure 6.3 presumably captures the shape of Dutch technological innovation in general as a process that peaked sometime in the early seventeenth century.

Fuel Innovation and Power-Driven Machinery

Table 6.4 underscores the basic problem with Dutch peat: with less carbon content, its use was limited to heat conversion. It was superior to wood, especially in a largely deforested context, but it could not generate the type of heat associated with coal. Wrigley notes, "As a source of energy capital the Dutch peat deposits fell part way between the use of virgin timber stands on the one hand and the opening up of a major coalfield on the other in the size of the stock of energy available, and therefore the scale and duration of the boost to economic growth that they could sustain" (1988: 113). He goes on to explain that an unexploited forest could be utilized for making charcoal for a few decades

Table 6.4 **Coal Classifications**

Type	Percent Carbon
Peat	57
Lignite	70
Sub-bituminous	80
Bituminous	85
Anthracite	94

Source: Whitten and Brooks (1972: 87–88).

Table 6.5 **Estimate of Dutch Peat Consumption**

Period	Annual Peat Consumption (Ha)
1300–1550	30
1550–1600	140
1600–1750	200
1750–1860	125
1860–1950	135

Note: A ha, or hectare, is roughly equivalent to 2.5 acres.

before new timber would need to be found. A coalfield would also be exhausted eventually, but in the meantime it could generate a great deal of powerful energy for possibly several centuries. A large peat field could support economic expansion for at best a century or so, which would approximate well the Netherland's one-and-a-half-century lead.

Nonetheless, De Zeeuw (1978) portrays peat as the key to the Netherlands' technological lead in the seventeenth century. Peat is a fossil fuel that was once readily available and inexpensive to Dutch consumers. His estimates of peat consumption (table 6.5) suggest that at the least peat usage covaried with economic ascent and decline.

But Unger (1984) argues that De Zeeuw's calculations are biased in a number of ways and that they exaggerate the reliance on peat by a factor of five. Even so, peat was the principal source of energy for Dutch heating and industry in the Netherlands' golden age. Gradually, coal was added to the mix and eventually became the most important source in the eighteenth century. In the seventeenth century, though, peat provided at least three times the amount of energy supplied by coal. Therefore, it has to be credited with the lion's share of the Netherlands' lead in per capita energy consumption during this period.

The main caveats to this type of generalization involve wind. Dutch trade was heavily reliant on wind for its sailing vessels. Land industries also benefited from several thousand windmills used to drain water and saw wood. One calculation credits these windmills with generating the energy equivalent to that produced by fifty thousand horses.[20] All of this machinery was critical if the Dutch were to survive against the elements (pumping water), energize their far-flung trade network (filling sails), and support the construction of the manufactures that underwrote the trading (sawing wood). But did these elements add up to the first modern economy, as de Vries and van der Woude (1997) contend? To be fair, here is what those authors (693) say about the criteria of a modern economy:

> A "modern economy" need not be one with the outward attributes of a twentieth-century industrial economy; rather, it should incorporate the generic features that make those outward signs possible. Foremost among those features are:
>
> - markets, for both commodities and the factors of production (land, labor, and capital), that are reasonably free and pervasive;
> - agricultural productivity adequate to support a complex social and occupational structure that makes possible a far-reaching division of labor;
> - a state which in its policy making enforcement is attentive to property rights, to freedom of movement and contract, and at the same time is not indifferent to the material conditions of life of most inhabitants; and
> - a level of technology and organization *capable* of sustained development and of supporting a material culture of sufficient variety to sustain market-oriented consumer behavior.

De Vries and van der Woude go on to suggest that the United Provinces of the Netherlands satisfied the fourth criterion by the continuity of its sustained development and its leadership in creating the conditions for European economic modernity. Yet the claim to sustained development is dubious: when circumstances changed, trade-driven economic growth collapsed. Most importantly, it did not lead Europe into an industrial revolution. The Dutch accomplishments certainly stimulated the English/British (and the French) to catch up, but they did not encompass the steam engine–coal combination that was most critical to the creation of the modern industrial economy. The Dutch economy, for that matter, was slow to adopt steam engines once they emerged across the Channel. Sustained development had to await the next iteration.

For a period of time, roughly between 1550 and 1700, the Netherlands could certainly claim technological leadership in Europe. One could also say that Dutch economic achievements contributed disproportionately to the establishment of the conditions for European economic modernity. An abundance of peat was one of the underlying assets of this leadership. Peat, though, fell short in spurring industrialization because of its limited heat conversion potential. Its power, in conjunction with the harnessing of wind power, sufficed to assist the Dutch in moving the European technological frontier beyond what it had been in the sixteenth century. The threshold of economic modernity, assuming that truly sustained economic growth required a full energy transition and industrialization, was not crossed for another century.[21] As Wrigley puts it,

> Holland was perhaps more completely "modern" than England throughout the period from, say, 1550 to 1750. Specialization of economic function was far advanced at an early date in both industry and agriculture. Holland possessed a custom-made internal transport network superior to anything to be found in England. . . . She was the common carrier of Europe. Her cities were numerous and prosperous, and the percentage of the population living in towns was higher than in England and far higher than in most other countries. The bourgeoisie possessed great political influence. Capitalism was perhaps less impeded by legal and institutional handicaps than anywhere else. Real wages were the highest in Europe throughout the later sixteenth and seventeenth centuries, and for much of the eighteenth century also. And yet there was no early industrial revolution in Holland; indeed it was unusually late in making an appearance there.
>
> . . . The transition that produced the change in prospects was the move from an advanced organic to a mineral-based energy economy. . . . Above all, a source of energy was needed whose scale would make feasible a rise in output per worker which remained beyond reach as long as his own muscles and those of his domesticated animals were almost the sole means of lifting, pulling, moving, beating, stretching and pressing material objects; and as long as he was dependent upon organic raw material for all purposes, including that of raising heat. Such an energy source was not to be found within the confines of an organic economy (1988: 103–104).

In short, peat did not supply enough energy to do what needed to be done to make the transition from Wrigley's organic economy to a mineral-based one.

In some respects, the Netherlands in the seventeenth century resembled the success of Italian manufacturing in the late medieval and early Renaissance era. Building on its earlier commercial wealth, northern Italy expanded its manufacturing output, primarily in textiles, as well as its banking and shipping services. But this expansion was undercut by lower labor and commodity costs elsewhere in western Europe. As recounted by Cipolla (1952, 1974), Italian investment responded by moving away from manufacturing into agriculture. By the end of the seventeenth century, "Italy was a poor and predominantly agricultural country, importing manufactured goods and exporting mainly agricultural goods such as wine, oil, and raw silk" (1974: 9).

The Italian and Dutch cases thus underscore Goldstone's efflorescence argument. Temporary successes were conceivable given the right circumstances, but these early successes were not established on the type of foundations that could be sustained indefinitely. They were highly vulnerable to the disappearance of these facilitating circumstances as their operating environment changed. In both the Italian and the Dutch cases, being undercut by neighbors and rivals did not merely set back economic growth, but caused economic development to move in an entirely different and less industrial direction.

Business Organization

In the 1590s, Dutch merchants began breaking the Portuguese monopoly on spices by sending their own ships to the area in which the spices originated. In this effort they were too successful in the sense that they brought back enough spices to drive their price down. To reduce inter-Dutch competition in the Asian market (and to better control European prices for Asian commodities), the Dutch merchants involved in the Asian trade were brought together within one organization, the Vereenigde Oostindische Compagnie (VOC), in 1602.[22] This new organization was designed to be a hybrid commercial–state agency. It had the power to establish forts, maintain armies and navies, and negotiate treaties. Its primary purpose was to make money in trade, but it was also intended to fight and push out the Portuguese, Spanish, and English organizations already engaged in Asian trade.

In some respects, the VOC foreshadowed the later corporatization of commerce by charging its managerial group with pursuing VOC interests, in both the long and short run, as opposed to maximizing returns on an ad hoc partnership among traders engaged in a specific voyage to Asia and back (Steensgaard, 1982). But to the extent that modern corporations have their own foreign policies, the VOC usually worked closely with Dutch politicians

Table 6.6 **Presence and Absence of Key Economic Growth and Technological Centrality Factors — Seventeenth-Century Dutch Case**

Frontier Exploitation	Agriculture	Transportation/ Communication	Trade	Urbanization	Population Growth	Technological Innovation	Energy Transition	Power-Driven Machinery
Present	Present	Present	XPresent	Present	Present	Present	Partial	Present

as a vehicle for military and economic expansion outside Europe. Toward that end, the VOC established its headquarters in Batavia in the Spice Islands and set about constructing a trading network that stretched from the Persian Gulf to Japan (de Vries and van der Woude, 1997: 385–396). A second, less successful organization, the Verenigde West Indische Compagnie (WIC), was set up in 1621 to manage American commerce. However, establishing a monopoly in the more competitive Atlantic environment proved to be much more difficult and, ultimately, less successful.

Conclusions

Genoa and Venice made good use of their central positions and sea power to dominate the marketing of Asian goods and innovations in Europe. The Portuguese developed a way to circumvent the Venetian–Mamluk monopoly. In the process, the Mediterranean became less significant to Europe, replaced by the Atlantic Ocean as a gateway to the route around Africa and access to the resources of the New World.

The Netherlands fits into this narrative by its combination of Baltic and Atlantic activities to construct a European trade regime that greatly overshadowed the earlier transitional efforts. Buttressed by the development of agrarian and industrial technology and a heavy reliance on peat and wind as energy sources (summarized in table 6.6), the Netherlands became Europe's unquestioned technological leader in the latter sixteenth and seventeenth centuries.

The way in which these ingredients were combined seem to have been idiosyncratic to the Dutch case. Dutch frontier exploitation involved creating a land base by draining its water. Agricultural innovation was focused primarily on creating an export base, given the limitations of the available land, as opposed to expanding agrarian output to feed an expanding population. Trade is often important to leadership, but in the Dutch case, trade was crucial. Once neighboring states cut back on this trade, the economic platform of the Dutch state shrank rapidly. The base was too small to compensate for or adjust to the trade losses. Most critically, the energy transition was only partial. Based on wind and peat, clear advances were made in some power-driven machinery, as in the case of lumber sawing, and in the focus on technological innovation in industries that required heat for production purposes. Yet the heat and energy that were expanded remained constrained by the inherent limitations of the energy sources.

Britain copied the Netherlands' agrarian success, trumped its reliance on peat with coal, and went on to become the first modern industrialized economy. How all that came together is the focus of the next chapter.

Britain: The First Modern Industrial Economy

Combining Technology and Energy

The British Industrial Revolution is one of the most famous economic growth stories. Once a peripheral economy, Britain later became the center of the world economy, occupying a position of global technological centrality for an extended period of time. It was not always responsible for inventing new ways of doing things, but Britain did tend to disproportionately control the innovation—putting inventions into practice—of much new technology. Yet for all of this transformation's renown, the information on how Britain managed to climb to the top of the world economy's hierarchy is both highly uneven and much disputed. Scholars have been dissecting the British Industrial Revolution for a century and a half. At various points in time, something like a consensus on causation has seemed to emerge, only to be broken up by new revisionist research. Thus, scholars still do not agree on why Britain's Industrial Revolution occurred—any more than they do on why it happened in Britain first.[1]

As a consequence, we have far too much information and too many different arguments on the British case. So much has been written on the British case that it is hard to imagine saying something new. Here we employ a variant of the two-phase model that we used in chapters 4, 5, and 6. The only real difference is that in this chapter, the energy transition variable is fully activated. In the first phase of growth, population, frontier exploitation, trade, urbanization, agrarian development, and transportation/communications interact in such a way as to stimulate economic growth. These interactions can take place wholly within an agrarian setting and may suffice to allow a state to assume technological/economic leadership if the ingredients are sufficiently powerful in one country and less so in the economies of rivals. These are the agrarian efflorescences about which Goldstone's theory (outlined in chapter 3) speaks. Growth becomes more sustainable only when new types of energy sources are utilized and suitable technology that makes use of the new fuels is innovated. Even then, sustainability is finite because of the tendency for other economies eventually to eclipse their predecessors with larger markets, resource endowments, and technological proficiency.

Deconstructing the British Case

Wrigley (1988) argues that eighteenth-century Britain replicated the Netherlands' construction of the strongest "organic" economy possible, given the constraints of traditional economies.[2] The Netherlands and eighteenth-century Britain both combined population and agrarian growth, urbanization, international trade, and proto-industrial textile manufacturing to acquire the status of lead European economy. When the British moved into a mineral-based economy via their embrace of coal, they were able to move beyond the traditional constraints of organic economies. This second phase was truly revolutionary and produced the sustainability that had eluded the Dutch.

Basically, we agree with this argument—it sounds quite compatible with the model sketched in figure 7.1—although we would give more credit to the Netherlands for venturing somewhat beyond the constraints of the "organic" economy. In our view, it just did not go (and could not have gone) far enough with its peat and wind experimentation. We also underline the interaction between technology and energy as opposed to the shift in energy per se. As long

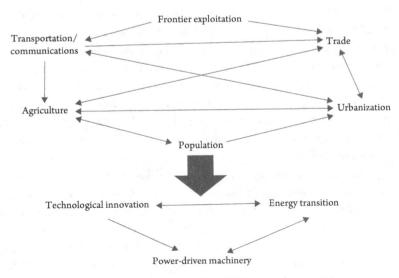

Figure 7.1 Factors Underlying Technological and Economic Leadership.

as coal's usage was restricted to heating homes, its revolutionary potential was constricted. When it was combined with steam and iron, the effects were quite transformative. Finally, we also link elements of Britain's organic phase to what transpired in its mineral-based phase. Trade and frontier exploitation, for instance, helped set up Britain's movement to the next phase, but they also continued to interact with other factors in the mineral phases as well.

Frontier Exploitation and International Trade

Britain's initial frontier lay in its preindustrial territorial possessions in North America. Before it became a colonial power, the state's economy had focused on providing wool for Dutch textiles, and its relative military standing in comparison to its European neighbors had been fairly weak. It was not a coincidence that England became a genuine island state only after being forced out of its extensive French territorial holdings in the fifteenth century. Even then it took a while for English decision-makers to adjust to England's new status as an island located not far from the European continent.[3] But one of the advantages of this insularity was that it encouraged the English to focus more attention on acquiring colonies in North America and the Caribbean, which together constituted England's first empire.

In the process, England became a significant sea power early on and enriched itself on slave-cultivated sugar and tobacco crops that were imported to the mother country and beyond. This foundation sufficed to underpin Britain's first "term" as global system leader. How one should evaluate these developments in terms of their contribution to Britain's ascent to technological preeminence in its second term as global system leader depends on the approach adopted. The now classical Wallersteinian world-system perspective (Wallerstein, 1974, 1980, 1989, 2011) is perhaps among the most extreme in arguing that the wealth of the British core was entirely due to exploitation of the periphery via unequal exchange—that is, without exploitation, there would have been no core wealth. The other extreme is to argue that the periphery really contributed little in terms of economic wealth to the core (O'Brien, 1982).

Assuming the truth actually lies in between these extreme positions leads to two other prominent interpretations, both of which emerged at about the same time. Chinese historian Pomeranz's view (2000) is the more prominent of the two, and the one that comes closest to the world-system extreme of the continuum. He asks why eighteenth-century Britain experienced an industrial revolution when eighteenth-century China did not, particularly given that the Lower Yangzi Delta in China at this time was fairly similar to Britain in many respects—deforestation, "proto-industrial" handicraft manufacturing, income per capita, and, most importantly, similar agrarian constraints that blocked further economic growth.

According to Pomeranz, Britain/Europe resolved its dilemma in part by making use of peripheral resources in the Caribbean and North America in a way that was not open to the Chinese.[4] In the New World, Old Worlders could exploit slavery (after decimating the indigenous populations with disease), obtain raw materials that were either not available at home or would have had to be developed anew at the expense of agrarian cultivation, and provide some export cushion while attracting proto-industrial, handicraft workers to Old World industrial factories. Colonies, then, in addition to coal, explain the divergence between East and West.

Pomeranz's thesis is attractive, but it works better for Britain than it does China. Basically, the argument can be read as saying that in the eighteenth century China was not doing what Britain was doing. For our purposes, it would be more plausible to suggest that in the eighteenth century Britain was doing some of the things China had done in the Sui–Tang–Song era. China was no longer following this track.

Inikori (2002) revives older emphases on the trade-driven economic growth of Britain to develop a strong empirical case for the expansion of textiles and iron, which he considers the two main conventional carriers of the Industrial Revolution, as being linked to trade demand in several direct and indirect ways. Innovations in iron and textile production took place in parts of Britain that were focused primarily on servicing trade to the West African–Caribbean–North American triangle (as opposed to domestic British demand for these products). Hence, the driver for innovations that allowed production expansion was the increasing centrality of the Atlantic economy to British concerns.

Table 7.1 brings this facet out by contrasting Britain's trade direction in the 1699–1701 period and the 1772–1774 period and showing that the American trade had diminished in proportional significance. Forty-two percent of Britain's exports came from America in the early 1770s, compared to 12 percent at the beginning of the eighteenth century. Furthermore, the cotton raw materials used in British textile production came from slave-based plantations in the American colonies, and British slavers, prior to the nineteenth century, were also prominent in delivering Africans to New World markets.[5] Thus, in Inikori's view, the British Industrial Revolution was driven ultimately by trade interests and based considerably on energy generated by slaves. Presumably, the Industrial Revolution would have been much less likely to have occurred in the absence of the need to respond to the expanding demands of the Atlantic-centered trade system.

Esteban (2004: 47) promotes the trade factor as the principal key to the rise of Britain to military and economic preeminence in the eighteenth century,

Table 7.1 **British Trade Directions as Reflected in Proportional Values (£1,000)**

	1699–1701				1772–1774			
	World	*Europe*	*East*	*Americas*	*World*	*Europe*	*East*	*Americas*
Exports	4,433	3,772	122	539	9,853	4,960	717	4,176
Imports	5,849	3,986	756	1,107	12,735	8,122	1,929	2,684
Re-exports	1,986	1,660	14	312	5,818	4,783	63	972
Imports								
Pepper			103				33	
Tea			8				848	
Sugar				630				2,360
Tobacco				249				518

Source: Based on Harley (2004: 177); Harley's data in turn are based on Davis (1954, 1962).

noting that by 1787, "British centres of power were well on their way to controlling the lion's share of non-European resources and markets. In 1716, their
claims to pre-eminence had already been considerable. Britain's trading system
encompassed some of the most promising areas of Asia and North America."
In the late seventeenth century, Britain had managed to hang on in India after
nearly being expelled by the Mughal Empire. Calico cloth, originally derived
from India, had by that time become an important trading commodity. In 1713,
Britain acquired exclusive access to Spanish America. And throughout the seventeenth and eighteenth centuries, the British North American and Caribbean
holdings were expanding their production of sugar and tobacco.[6] As the eighteenth century wore on, Britain's trading position only improved. American demand for British exports and re-exports also expanded. Britain's closest rival,
France, on the other hand, saw its own trading position decline with each subsequent loss in the wars that broke out during this period on the continent.

As in the case of Dutch trade dominance, Britain's trading preeminence is
mirrored by its disproportionate share of world maritime carrying capacity (see
table 7.2). As early as 1670, British shipping accounted for about 18 percent of
estimated world capacity. A century or so later, its share had improved to 25 percent. After the Napoleonic Wars, it controlled over 40 percent. That commanding
share declined over the first half of the nineteenth century but improved in the
second half thanks to the advent of steam-powered ships that proved to be faster
and more dependable than the traditional sailing ships.

Table 7.2 **British Maritime Carrying Capacity**

Year	Sailing Ships (#)	Steam-Powered Ships (#)	Carrying Capacity (# of ships)	World Capacity (#)	British Share
1470	n.a.	0	n.a.	320	n.a.
1570	51	0	51	730	6.9%
1670	260	0	260	1,450	17.9%
1780	1,000	0	1,000	3,950	25.3%
1820	2,436	3	2,448	5,880	41.6%
1850	3,397	168	4,069	14,600	27.9%
1900	2,096	7,208	30,928	96,100	32.2%
1913	843	11,273	45,935	171,000	26.9%

Source: Based on Maddison (2001: 95).

Transportation and Communications

The strongest claim for transportation as an essential ingredient of the British Industrial Revolution is advanced by Szostak (1991), who argues that Britain was the site of the first industrial revolution because it had the best internal transportation network in the world. Improved transport accomplished five things: (1) it widened the market, (2) it standardized product distribution, (3) it accelerated delivery speeds and made them more reliable, (4) it reduced the cost of obtaining raw materials, and (5) it enhanced technological innovation thanks to the first four operations. Mainly, though, these improvements seem to have increased the scale of production by cutting costs and expanding demand, all of which are certainly hallmarks of an industrial revolution.

Yet in arguing that the British road system was greatly improved in the first half of the eighteenth century, we wonder if the main advantages Britain enjoyed was that it was relatively small and it was encompassed by coasts with multiple rivers feeding into the coastal areas. Most of Britain was accessible by water of some sort (i.e., coastal shipping, rivers, canals).[7] These advantages do not mean that British industry could rely on Mother Nature for transportation services. They do suggest, however, that the task of developing ways of getting raw materials and finished products into circulation was less imposing in Britain than it was in most other places.[8]

The significance of transportation as a causal factor depends in part on whether one views the British Industrial Revolution as primarily a product of endogenous or exogenous demand. Szostak (1991), for instance, emphasizes domestic demand as the principal driver and focuses on roads. If external trade receives priority, one would focus more on British shipping, some portion of which was devoted to moving coal from one part of Britain to other parts. Either way, the transportation and communication networks can be said to have at least been facilitative of the political–economic changes of Britian in the eighteenth and nineteenth centuries.

Agrarian Development

There is a small subliterature on the "agricultural revolution" that supported the British Industrial Revolution, but it is characterized by rival arguments and weak data.[9] For instance, one argument is that enclosure practices led to larger farms, more farm output, and less farm labor.[10] These developments led to the expansion of cities and the economic growth associated with urbanization. Allen (2009), however, prefers a much different story in which expanding British trade led to the growth of London and proto-industrialization that in turn increased wage levels and seduced a number of farmers with small plots of land to move to cities. The ones that stayed behind (presumably those with both large and small acreages) were encouraged by the same high wages to improve their output.

If enclosures had all occurred at one time, it would be easier to assess their impact. But they did not. They occurred throughout much of the second millennium, although they may have increased in terms of the amount of land affected in the eighteenth century. By the second half of the nineteenth century, there was little left to enclose. Table 7.3 summarizes the most recent interpretation of British agricultural output. According to these data, output markedly expanded in the second half of the sixteenth century (probably too early for a linkage to enclosures, even though the Tudor era did witness this phenomenon), expanded slowly in the 1700s, and then expanded even more markedly in the nineteenth century.[11] One might wish to credit some of the eighteenth-century expansion to enclosure, yet it seems more likely that enclosure was simply one of several changes that facilitated it. It is not clear whether the amount of arable land dramatically changed during this period, which might be one anticipated outcome of turning pasturage into cultivation area, or whether it more gradually expanded (as shown in table 7.3).

Agricultural responses to the commercial incentives of an expanding and more affluent population would also seem to be a supportable argument for the causes of the so-called British agricultural revolution. English/British farmers did emulate Dutch agricultural techniques. Land was reclaimed. Arable land

Table 7.3 **Selected Agricultural Data Indexes**

Decades	Arable Area	Total Agricultural Output	% Increase
1500s	n.d.	77	
1550s	68	84	9.1
1600s	70	124	47.6
1650s	76	154	24.2
1700s	75	167	8.4
1750s	83	206	23.4
1800s	88	336	63.1
1850s	103	509	51.4
1860s	109	560	10.0

Source: Broadberry et al. (2015: 125–126). The first two columns are percentages of ouput in 1300.

was expanded by reducing fallowing. New crops, fertilizer, and better equipment (plows) were introduced, and some regional specialization took place. Enclosures creating larger farms could also easily be considered an innovation, as long as they do not claim too much of the credit.

Clearly, multiple arguments on what caused the agricultural revolution can find corroboration. For our purposes, whether there was something called an "agricultural revolution" or not does not really matter. British agricultural output expanded. The proportion of the workforce engaged in agriculture declined to about a third by 1800 (Overton, 1996). Therefore, agricultural production increased and became more efficient at a time when the population was expanding. This co-evolutionary movement certainly facilitated the changes occurring simultaneously in technology and industry. At the same time, it seems difficult to exaggerate agriculture's influence on the Industrial Revolution. The absence of expanded agricultural output would have restricted population growth if food had not been imported in greater amounts. This is exactly what happened later in the nineteenth century when population growth exceeded agricultural expansion. Earlier agricultural expansion at the very least made the Industrial Revolution less expensive and more feasible.

Population

One of the hallmarks of a prosperous and wealthy economy is population growth, albeit subject to postindustrial constraints. At the same time, considerable population growth in an agrarian context can become a Malthusian constraint in its own right. English growth was relatively modest until the second half of the eighteenth century and explosive after that (see figure 7.2).

Broadberry et al. note succinctly:

> Economic growth can be either extensive or intensive. Extensive growth arises where more output is produced in line with a growing population but living standards remain constant, while intensive growth arises where more output is produced by each person. In the former case, there is no economic development, as the economy simply reproduces on a larger scale; in the latter, living standards rise as the economy goes through a process of economic development (2015: 3).

Which case describes Britain? Broadberry et al. (2015) argue strongly for intensive growth prior to industrialization, counter to Malthusian expectations. In this view, the English population recovered slowly from the impact of the Black Death in the fourteenth century, due in part to recurring plagues. By the late

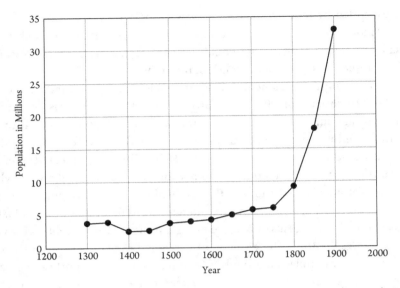

Figure 7.2 British Population Growth. Source: Based on McEvedy and Jones (1978: 43); data refer to England and Wales only.

fifteenth century, real wage rates had begun to decline in response to population growth, but the household response was to work more hours. In conjunction with other factors, ranging from literacy gains to expanded food supply, individual welfare levels, as measured by gross domestic product per capita, on average improved rather than deteriorated. Broadberry et al. remark: "In one of history's great ironies, the British economy finally broke free from Malthusian constraints half a century before Malthus's birth. By the time he published the first edition of his *Essay on the Principle of Population*, population growth was increasing fast but output was increasing faster" (2015: 275).

In addition to the overall expansion of the British population, we also need to call attention to a population shift. Probably more than a million people moved to North America and the Caribbean prior to the American Revolution.[12] Profitable commodities such as sugar and tobacco were sent back from these regions to the metropole. As the number of colonists expanded, their demand for British products also expanded. Both dimensions fed into the ascendancy of Britain in the eighteenth century and beyond.

Urbanization

Urbanization in England may have been strongly concentrated in London, but it still outpaced the rest of Europe in the critical eighteenth century. In 1700,

Table 7.4 **Urbanization in England and Europe (Population in Towns with 10,000+ Inhabitants)**

	1500	1600	1650	1700	1750	1800
England	3.2	6.1	10.8	13.4	17.5	24.0
Europe Minus England		8.1		9.2	9.4	9.5

Source: Based on Wrigley (2010: 59).

as table 7.4 shows, the English were well ahead of their European counterparts in city-dweller densities. By 1750, the rate of British urbanization was twice the rate found across the Channel. In 1800, it was 2.5 times the European rate. Urban density, in the Boserup (1965) tradition, is the key to technological innovation, because urban settings are so much more conducive than rural settings to both needing and encouraging change.

As in the case of the Netherlands, Taylor, Hoyler, and Smith's (2012) analysis of city growth spurts as an indicator of increasing complexity among a network of cities is summarized in table 7.5. If the existence of city networks is suggested by the existence of cities with growth at or exceeding 1 percent per year in fifty-year intervals, Britain had a longer run of economic dominance than the Netherlands. Between 1700 and 1750, five of the seven fastest-growing cities in the world were British; between 1750 and 1800, four of the six fastest-growing cities were British. Five British cities were among the fastest growing in the 1800–1850 period, with a sixth (London) falling below Taylor and colleagues' "top-twelve" cutoff point. Only one British city made the top twelve in the 1850–1900 interval, but another five British cities qualified for the "top forty."

There are several ways to interpret this distribution of city growth spurts. The Modelski–Thompson (1996) approach sees two periods of British leadership bracketed by periods of warfare in 1688–1713 and 1914–1945 and separated by the 1792–1815 combat of the French Revolution and Napoleonic Wars. Only the second of the two periods of leadership (post-1800 in table 7.5) fully involved the products of the Industrial Revolution, although the 1750–1800 interval also overlapped with the onset of this transformation. The first period was based more on colonial and maritime predominance. Still, it is the northern industrial cities of Birmingham, Manchester, and Glasgow that show up in the early columns of table 7.5, suggesting a long gestation period for industrialization. Another way of looking at table 7.5 is to see it as reinforcing Broadberry et al.'s (2015) argument that significant British economic growth preceded industrialization in the late eighteenth and early nineteenth centuries.

Table 7.5 **Cities with Explosive Growth, 1700–1900**

1700–1750	1750–1800	1800–1850	1850–1900
Liverpool	**Manchester**	New York	Chicago
Birmingham	**Liverpool**	Baltimore	Buenos Aires
Cadiz	**Glasgow**	Philadelphia	Leipzig
Cork	**Birmingham**	Boston	Pittsburgh
Manchester	Barcelona	**Liverpool**	New York
Glasgow	Moscow	**Manchester**	Berlin
Bristol		**Birmingham**	**Newcastle**
		Glasgow	Dresden
		Bombay	Boston
		Rio de Janeiro	Budapest
		Brussels	Hamburg
		Newcastle	Rio de Janeiro
		London (15)	**Birmingham** (15)
			Manchester (19)
			Glasgow (27)
			London (29)
			Liverpool (37)

Source: Taylor, Hoyler, and Smith (2012: 26). British cities in bold. Numbers in parentheses indicate cities that qualify (and the rank order of their qualification) only if the emphasis on the top 12 is relaxed to include cities below the top 12.

Technological Innovation, Fuel Transition, and Power-Driven Machinery

British patents are an imperfect index of technological innovation inasmuch as patents are sought to protect new technologies.[13] The "takeoff" in patent activity clearly occurred after 1760, as seen in figure 7.3. The number of patents issued in the 1770s was double the number granted in the 1760s. Likewise, the number issued in the 1780s was double that reported for the 1770s. To be sure, the full impact of some of the more successful patents probably was not registered until sometime in the next century. But clearly there was much more activity in the second half of the eighteenth century than in the first half.

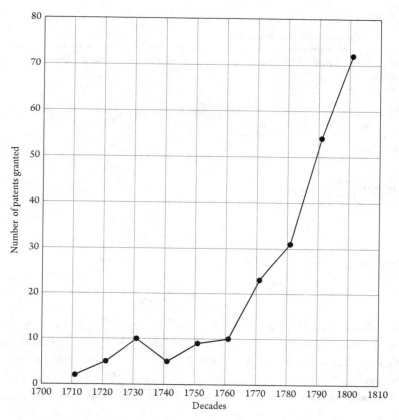

Figure 7.3 British Patents, 1702–1801. Source: Based on data from Rostow (1985: 132).

An alternative approach is to count the innovations that constituted the first Industrial Revolution. Dudley (2012) does this by listing 117 innovations of various magnitude, 23 of which are also major innovations identified by Mokyr (1990) and Lipsey, Carlaw, and Bekar (2005). As delineated in table 7.6, all of these innovations were not British in origin, but nearly two-thirds of them were. Arguably, the table implicitly makes a case for viewing the 1750–1849 "century" as the epicenter of this first industrial revolution.[14]

In studying industrial revolutions, there are two divergent choices. One can develop rather complex models with many variables (see, e.g., Szostak, 1991: 29), or one can reduce the transformative processes to a limited set of those factors that seem most crucial. While we have nothing against complex models and are in fact using a multifactor model to compare our four main cases, the complications of technological innovation we think are best treated reductively as long as a case can be made for simplification. In this respect, our preferred approach of pairing technological innovation with innovation in energy fuels is

Table 7.6 **Temporal and Geographical Distribution of British Industrial Revolution Innovations**

Total Inovations	France	Germany	Britain	Switzerland	United States	Denmark	Italy
1700–1749	2	1	10				
1750–1799	13	1	34	2	3		
1800–1849	9		32		8	1	1
Major Innovations							
1700–1749	1		3				
1750–1799	5		6		1		
1800–1849	1		5		1		

Source: Data from Dudley (2012: 61, 82–84, 110–112).

best realized in the block models put forward by Kander, Malanima, and Warde (2013). Four block models altogether are advanced: an iron–coal–steam block, which drove the first industrial revolution; an internal combustion engine–oil block and an electricity block, which together drove the second industrial revolution; and an information technology block, which is driving a third ongoing revolution. The iron–coal–steam block emerged first in Britain; the other three are largely U.S. developments and will be discussed in the next chapter.

The underlying thesis of this approach is that agrarian societies faced a ceiling on what could be accomplished by relying on photosynthesis and solar energy. To overcome the agrarian trap, they needed to develop a new source of energy with greater power potential than that what had prevailed for millennia (solar, wind, water, and human and animal muscle power). The new source of energy needed to be abundant, portable, and cheap. Coal was not a new source of energy, but technological innovation involving steam engines created a new technology–energy combination and transformed a bottleneck situation into one of economic growth possibilities. As Malanima notes:

> The agricultural energy basis of past civilizations was the main obstacle to their economic progress. Since the metabolism of their system depended on the availability of soil, which is limited, labor productivity declined as human beings grew in number and the ratio of population to natural resources and animals increased as a consequence. This resulted in decreasing energy for converters to translate into motion and work. Improvement in the division of labor, and the invention of

more effective implements, could stretch these limits, but not remove them, within the boundaries imposed by the dominant energy system. Only the passage to the new, modern system, starting in the nineteenth century, opened up new potentialities for growth to the agricultural civilizations. (2013: 80)

Coal and steam were two parts of a triangle that included iron (see figure 7.4). None of the three would have been sufficient to have a transformative effect. It was the interactions among the three that were the principal carriers of the British Industrial Revolution in the second half of the eighteenth century and the first half of the nineteenth century—hence the block designation. Steam engines were developed initially to remedy coal mining drainage problems at a time when coal was used primarily for home heating purposes. While the new engines were able to remove water from ever-deeper mines, they were notoriously inefficient and required considerable amounts of coal fuel. If coal had been scarce or expensive, the steam engines might have been abandoned as a clever idea that was less than cost-effective. Instead, it took about a century for steam engines to become sufficiently efficient and powerful to be employed in a variety of circumstances. In these respects, the interaction between coal and steam is clear. Steam was needed to obtain more coal; more coal was needed to make use of steam as its applications widened.

Although draining water from mines was one of the first practical applications of the steam engine, neither the engine itself nor the first steam engine was constructed to perform any specific practical task. This feature of steam engine development can be linked to the argument that one of the prerequisites for industrial revolution in Europe was the emergence of science and scientific inquiry in that region (see Mokyr, 2002, 2009; and Lipsey, Carlaw, and Bekar, 2005). Much of the tinkering that led to the improvement of the steam engine seems

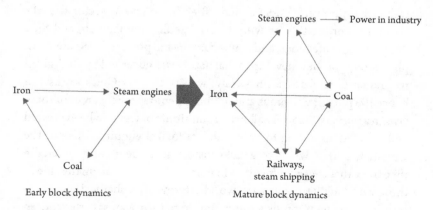

Figure 7.4 The Iron–Coal–Steam Block. Source: Based on Warde (2013: 174–175).

to have been done on the job as opposed to in a laboratory. However, it is worth noting that the steam engine's first appearance probably was dependent on scientific tinkering in Italy, the Netherlands, and Germany, which produced the prototype without identifying a specific purpose several years before it was put to work in the English mines. Persson (2010: 92) gives specific credit for this invention to work on atmospheric pressure, air weight, and vacuums done by Galileo Galilei (1564–1642), Evangelista Torricelli (1608–1697), Christiaan Huygens (1629–1695), and Otto von Guericke (1602–1686). However, Persson also argues that the steam engine was the exception that proves the rule that most of the early technological innovations of the Industrial Revolution were not based on new science. Since the first steam engine emerged only after the decline of the Netherlands, it may contribute a small piece of information to the puzzle of why the British were the first to industrialize, as well as why the Dutch missed out. The timing of the development of the understanding needed to make the first steam engine emerged at a time that favored the British and worked against the Dutch, who had already peaked by the mid-seventeenth century.

As we noted in chapter 6, Lipsey, Carlaw, and Bekar (2005) take this argument even further to argue that Britain was the ultimate beneficiary of multiple research programs in Europe that unfolded over several hundred years prior to the Industrial Revolution(s). This image flies in the face of the notion that Britain was merely lucky to possess vast coalfields. It was lucky, but the steam engine was not a fluke that emerged from nowhere. Rather, it emerged within a complicated context that was not evident elsewhere. As Lipsey, Carlaw, and Bekar note:

> The medieval period saw the development of a pluralistic society, which ultimately freed natural philosophers to pursue a uniquely powerful form of science that explained the world in terms of mechanical laws. In society, a division developed between lay and religious areas of jurisdiction. In government, many competing nation states arose, as well as many powerful independent cities. In the private sector, the self-governing corporation grew up to insulate first the Church, and then universities, professions, and crafts from the full power of the state. . . . In philosophy, the view developed that nature was governed by God-given natural laws. To discover these laws was to discover God's works and hence the pursuit was pious and not blasphemous. The search for these laws in a pluralistic society allowed a multitude of views to be expressed and debated according to strict rules of logical enquiry. This put the Christian church, which by a lucky historical accident had avoided the theocracy that caused difficulties in many other societies, on the side of those who sought to explain the world in terms of mechanical laws of nature. Then as the Catholic Church started to turn against early modern

science, the Reformation created a new branch of the Christian religion that welcomed it, at least in some Protestant areas—probably to some extent because welcoming it was anti-Catholic. (2005: 258–259)

In short, Britain's societal context, reflected in its government, science, and religion, facilitated the emergence of the ideas that would prove useful for the technological revolutions inherent in subsequent waves of industrialization. Lipsey, Carlaw, and Bekar's perspective on the "medieval period" may be a bit rosy-hued, but it is difficult to argue with the notion that northwestern Europe was the epitome of these supportive changes leading into the early modern era. We would repeat that Britain's timing was good as well, and better than that of the Netherlands in terms of the maturation of the scientific research programs that gave birth to the steam engine. That is not to suggest that the Dutch would have produced steam engines if their scientific research programs had been accelerated. They might have, but the British still had more incentive to spend a century improving the applications of the new machinery in their coal mines, which were absent from the Dutch scene. Relatedly, they also had more inexpensive coal than the Dutch. Advantages in timing, location, and motivation are hard to beat.

Coal and iron worked together via the intermediation of coke (or transformed coal) to create superior iron inexpensively and on a massive scale. Inexpensive and high-quality iron made better steam engines, which were improved in the 1770s from devices that could only run machinery in an up-and-down motion to devices that could rotate and drive wheels. This step in the evolution of the steam engine was necessary for the extension of its application into non-coal-mining industries as a source of machinery power. The diffusion of steam engines to transportation applications (railroads and steamships) made coal even cheaper and more readily available on an extended geographical scale while also increasing the demand for iron to construct locomotives, rails, and ships. Increasingly, bulk goods of all sorts could be transported over long distances more quickly and less expensively than before. As a consequence, the coal–steam–iron triangle in figure 7.4 evolved over the nineteenth century into a more complex block that included steam-driven transportation and other industrial applications. Coal-driven steam power ultimately trumped what wind, water, and animal power could accomplish.

The transition to coal and steam power is demonstrated to some extent by the estimates of changing dependence on different types of energy displayed in table 7.7. Dependence on human muscle power, estimated as 23 percent of all energy consumption in 1561–1570, dropped to less than 4 percent in 1850–1859. Animal muscle power became even less important, dropping from 32 percent in 1561–1570 to less than 3 percent in 1850–1859. Firewood and water

Table 7.7 **Annual Energy Consumption Per Head of Population (Megajoules)**

Decade	Human	Draft Animals	Firewood	Wind	Water	Coal	Total
1561–1570	4,373	6,210	6,324	59	162	2,039	19,167
1600–1609	4,161	4,647	4,729	85	152	3,153	16,925
1650–1659	4,521	4,802	3,849	153	156	6,772	20,253
1700–1709	4,789	5,744	3,939	238	173	14,719	29,602
1750–1759	4,519	5,113	3,429	427	198	21,403	35,089
1800–1809	4,233	3,471	1,877	1,282	111	41,373	52,347
1850–1859	3,564	2,633	118	1,280	89	88,779	96,462

Source: Based on Wrigley (2010: 94); the 1850–1859 figure for firewood actually refers to 1840–1849 because the data for firewood stopped in 1849 given the low level of consumption.

virtually disappeared as measurable contributors to total British energy consumption. The use of wind improved only slightly. Coal made the most dramatic gains, moving from 11 percent of all energy consumption in the mid-sixteenth century to 61 percent in the mid-eighteenth century and to 92 percent in the mid-nineteenth century. The meaning of these numbers are offset somewhat, however, by switching the emphasis to what these energy sources could accomplish in terms of power. Warde (2013: 183) notes that the power transition was more gradual than the energy consumed . In 1800, British steam engines could generate 30,000 horsepower, a figure that rose to 200,000 by 1840, 2 million by 1870, and 9 million by 1900.[15] Thus, the real transition probably occurred at some point between 1840 and 1870.

Was coal absolutely necessary to these changes? It is sometimes argued that other, more traditional, fuel sources might have been utilized with similar effects (see, e.g., Clark and Jacks, 2007). Other economies that did not have ready access to coal and some that did used firewood to run their steam engines. Might firewood have been substituted for coal in Britain's ascent to technological dominance? Table 7.8 suggests quite strongly that it could not have. Britain had already consumed much of its firewood in earlier centuries. It is conceivable that if Britain had regrown its forests and then denuded them for industrial and heating purposes, it might have been able to sustain its technological development partway through the nineteenth century—but only partway, because later in the century the sheer volume of the fuel demands, let alone the heat potential needed, was simply too great to be supported by firewood, even if it had been imported in great quantity.[16]

Table 7.8 **Coal Versus Firewood, Europe**

	Actual Energy		Counterfactual (No Coal)		
	% Firewood	% Coal	Firewood Equivalent (Million m³)	Land Area Required (Million km²)	% of Total Land Area
1850	58	42	388.4	1.29	58
1870	23	77	698.8	2.53	96
1900	5	95	1,492.9	5.28	201

Source: Warde (2013: 230).

Note: For this table, Europe = England and Wales, France, Spain, Sweden, the Netherlands, and Germany. Data on Italy and Portugal are added for 1870 and 1900.

We have noted Pomeranz's (2000) frustratingly simple "coal and colonies" argument in an earlier section dealing with frontier exploitation. The problem is that there are several ways to view the Pomeranz argument. For our purposes, it puts too much emphasis on coal and not enough on steam engines. By emphasizing the abundance of coal in England, the first Industrial Revolution comes across largely as a case of fortuitous geography—even though coal was also abundant elsewhere, particularly in China. Yet Pomeranz does recognize the significance of steam engines, as indicated by the following passage:

> The steam engine represented an even more important breakthrough than the slow and steady progress in tunneling for coal or learning how to keep its smoke from spoiling beer, glass, and iron. We have already seen that in this sense, Britain was fortunate to have the mining problem it did—a need to pump out water, rather than prevent explosions— since it led to engines with many other crucial applications. (2000: 67)

Pomeranz goes on to elaborate that the steam engine required a lengthy sequence of incremental improvements to make it reasonably effective, and that that too was a function of geography, since a European technological edge in instrumentation, not tools or machines, favored such modifications. But the fact is that this sequence led quite emphatically to a British technological edge in machines, and that is what we should be focusing on—not whether Europeans or the Chinese were generally better at making machines earlier. Moreover, the steam engine was indeed more important than coal per se, just as Pomeranz observes in the above passage. Perhaps if the Pomeranz argument were altered to "coal, steam engines, and colonies," the frustration with the salience of his interpretation would be much less. What differentiated China and Britain in the eighteenth century is that while both had plenty of coal, Britain developed steam engines and China did not. Why this occurred was a function not of race, culture, or inevitability, but of different technical problems occurring in different contexts leading to different resolutions. Pomeranz says precisely this, but his message remains framed in an argument couched to demonstrate that China and Europe or Britain were fairly similar in the eighteenth century, and that the probability of an industrial revolution taking place at either end of Eurasia therefore was pretty much the same. With the advantage of hindsight, though, we can say that this was not the case. An industrial breakthrough predicated on the interactions between fossil fuels and new technology (steam engines) could have happened in Song China but did not and was probably unlikely in eighteenth-century Qing China. It did happen (or start) in eighteenth-century Britain because conditions (mainly that people looking for a technical solution to mining problems found a newly invented device that might help) favoring such a breakthrough were more propitious in eighteenth-century Britain than they were at other times and places.[17]

Actually, we could argue that Tang and Song China did have colonies and coal. Their early manifestation of "colonies" was the Chinese south, into which northern population migrated and from which resources were extracted. The coalfields near Kaifeng were definitely exploited in the Northern Song era. Yet "colonies and coal" were not sufficient in the eleventh and twelfth centuries to transform the Chinese energy regime. What was missing was the steam engine, the technology part of the equation.

The steam engine breakthrough might also have happened in the seventeenth-century Netherlands, with its highly salient drainage issues, but did not. The close comparison between the seventeenth-century Dutch and the eighteenth-century British should suffice to put an end to claims about European superiority, however conceptualized, being important to the economics of ascent and decline. Europeans, and fairly successful ones at that, in the Dutch golden age had also failed to respond to problems in their working environment in a way that represented a permanent break from the agrarian trap. Many other Europeans, of course, failed even more overtly to make much progress along these lines until after some success was achieved in Britain. Of course, once the British Industrial Revolution was underway, different parts of Europe experienced differential success in catching up to the British breakthrough, depending in part on their access to abundant and inexpensive coal and their ability to apply steam engines to making machines run.

What then should we make of Allen's (2009) argument that Britain's Industrial Revolution was driven fundamentally by the combination of expensive labor and cheap energy? There is no question that Britain was a high-wage economy, not unlike the Netherlands. Costly labor should theoretically stimulate the search for labor-saving technology, and no doubt it does encourage the replacement of expensive people with machines or, at least, less expensive people. But high wages can also be symptomatic of an expanding, prospering economy. How much credit for innovation stimulation should we give to the expanding economy itself? The answer is not clear and would be difficult to test precisely. However, it also hinges on what one thinks is most important about the Industrial Revolution. Is it the change in energy source or the power-driven machinery? Both have considerable significance and are not easily separable, but if one points to the energy shift as the premiere facet of industrialization, high wages seem somewhat less central to the causal processes at work. The century-long interaction between coal and improvements to the steam engine was more about attaining efficient access to deep coal deposits and reducing the costs of supplying the demand for coal than it was about substituting machinery for coal miners. In this respect, high wages become something of a red herring in the prioritization of causal influences.[18]

A second problem with higher-wage explanations is that the higher wages found in northwestern Europe were initially a product of Black Death mortality rates (Pamuk, 2007), an effect that seems to have persisted through at least the fifteenth century. In the sixteenth century labor costs declined but did not return to pre–Black Death levels. Depending on which real wage series one examines, labor costs began increasing again at some point in the seventeenth century.[19] The hesitation to buy into the high wage–labor-saving incentive explanation only matters in this context because Allen (2009) argues that the high wages were due to the profits gleaned from American colonial markets. While this argument would provide a nice linkage between frontier exploitation and technological innovation, it remains unclear just how strong the connection really is.

The answer to the question of energy versus power-driven machinery is different if one gives the same weight to textiles as we have been giving to the coal–steam–iron triangle. There is no question that textile production benefited from industrialization. This fact is clearly underlined in table 7.9, which provides estimates for industrialization in three industries in Britain. Textile output doubled or nearly doubled several times, with growth occurring in this sector earlier than in iron and coal (compare the movement from the 1650s to the 1700s). For that matter, textile output consistently outpaced total industry output beginning in the 1500s. Through the eighteenth century, textile production was growing faster than iron and coal production. Yet early gains in textiles were also driven by water-powered machinery. Midway through the next century, when steam engines really took charge, iron and coal production outstripped textile production.

Moreover, imagine if British industrialization between 1750 and 1850 had been restricted to textile production. Would we be as equally in awe of the

Table 7.9 **Estimates of Industrial Growth, Britain (as percentages of 1700 output)**

Decades	Iron	Coal	Textiles	Total Industry
1500s	9	8	23	22
1550s	36	27	34	31
1600s	124	50	68	51
1650s	108	77	57	61
1700	100	100	100	100
1750s	153	154	170	132
1800s	678	456	398	271
1850s	7,154	2,366	2,124	1,163
1860s	10,329	3,254	2,246	1,480

Source: Broadberry et al. (2015: 138–139). The entries reflect percentages of 1700 output.

transformation wrought by changes in the British economy? Granted, the nature of the proposed counterfactual—restricting changes to textile production mechanization—is unrealistic. But the point is that there might very well not have been an industrial revolution if it depended solely on putting out more and cheaper cloth.[20] Yet this is the type of industry in which high wages would have been significant. Letting machines do what women with looms had once done much more slowly and in far less volume is the pluperfect example of the advantages of mechanization of an industry. In and of itself, though, textile mechanization probably would not have been as transformative if we could not have added the iron–steam–coal complex, especially if textile production was not allowed to make the transition to steam power.

Business Organization

As in the case of the Netherlands, the opportunity to engage in direct trade with the sources of spices led to a number of probes by English traders in the later sixteenth century. To regulate competition among English merchants and to better compete with merchants from other countries, a royal monopoly was granted to the British East Indies Company in 1600. This corporation foreshadowed the modern multinational corporation, although it operated more like a nation-state with its own armies, navies, bases, and, eventually, extensive territorial control in

Asia.[21] In this respect, the corporation clearly facilitated, as well as demonstrated, the rise of Britain as a trading power in the eighteenth century. When its mastery of India was jeopardized by the nineteenth-century Indian Mutiny, however, territorial control of India had to be taken over by the British state.

Otherwise, British firm structure remained primarily family-based. The increasing obsolescence of this traditional approach awaited the economic changes encountered in the late-nineteenth-century U.S. context. Some of these changes were associated with moving from coal to petroleum.

Conclusions

The British Industrial Revolution has received quite a bit of attention, with many good arguments and interpretations that have been advanced. From our perspective, Britain combined several factors (see table 7.10) to create a strong base for economic growth that might have remained Smithian in nature. It had an American/Caribbean frontier to exploit, a relatively small island base from which it was easy to move resources and commodities by sea, a commitment to maritime trade, and an innovative agrarian platform that could sustain population growth and urbanization. No doubt it also helped that Britain enjoyed some security from external invasion in the form of the English Channel when it counted most.[22]

What propelled Britain beyond the Smithian trajectory was the combination of ample, inexpensive coal and steam engines, which were initially needed to drain coal mines. After a century of steam engine development, itself predicated on European advances in the basic scientific principles underlying the engine's operation, steam engines could be put to other uses as the prime movers of the nineteenth century.

It is sometimes argued that if Britain had not brought together the necessary ingredients, some place else in Europe would have done so. Perhaps, but it is not that obvious that an alternative industrial revolution would have occurred quickly or even at all. In this respect, the contingent element is hard to deny. As has been noted earlier, Britain enjoyed a strong lead for much of the nineteenth century, in part because it proved difficult to replicate the Industrial Revolution in other parts of Europe immediately. This fact leads to the conclusion that "the British energy system in the early nineteenth century could not be immediately exported because only in Britain were the necessary economic, social and natural factors brought together which, elsewhere in Europe, were dispersed" (Debeir, Deleage, and Hemergy, 1991: 103). The first Industrial Revolution was certainly influenced by European developments, but it was not a pan-European phenomenon. It took place in Britain because

Table 7.10 Presence and Absence of Key Economic Growth and Technological Centrality Factors—British Case

Frontier Exploitation	Agriculture	Transportation/ Communication	Trade	Urbanization	Population Growth	Technological Innovation	Energy Transition	Power-Driven Machinery
Present	XPresent	Present	Present	Present	Present	Present	Present	Present

of the very distinctive package of facilitative factors that were brought together at the right time in a particular place. Britain may have been responsible for the first Industrial Revolution, but that event would not be the last one. At least two more have followed. Each of these more recent industrial revolutions have been associated with Britain's successor as the lead economy, the United States—the focus of the next chapter.

8

The United States: Emulating and Surpassing Britain

In contrast to the much-argued British case, the United States' economic growth story curiously has received far less attention—perhaps in part because there are fewer U.S. economic historians left to give it attention.[1] The last time there were multiple U.S. economic history texts in circulation—back in the 1970s— the stories they told were markedly similar, suggesting some amount of descriptive consensus. Given the relative paucity of U.S. economic historians these days, there is far less professional incentive to revise the prevailing paradigm. Instead, popular treatments of the U.S. ascendancy, often praising some dimension of exceptionalism and told largely through serial anecdotes, are now more common than serious academic debate based on theory and evidence.[2] The extraordinary wealth of the U.S. resource base and its rapid growth in the late nineteenth and early twentieth centuries have lent themselves quite readily to these exceptionalist beliefs and explanations.[3] Yet while U.S. economic growth has exceeded anything experienced before on the planet, that alone should not encourage us to think that its trajectory is unlike earlier cases of technological leadership.

Fortunately, there is a general interpretation that is quite compatible with the perspectives that we have employed in the previous cases. Wright (1990) and Nelson and Wright (1992) view U.S. economic growth as a two-stage process. In the first stage the United States acquired dominance in mass-production industries that were contingent on not only technological innovation but also an unusually rich resource endowment and an equally distinctive domestic market. While the large domestic market made increases in the scale of production possible, the nature of the United States' resource endowment ensured that raw materials remained inexpensive. The combination of innovation, cheap raw materials (including energy), and a very large domestic market pushed the United States into an economic leadership position by World War I. But the second stage of the process, the rise to world technological leadership

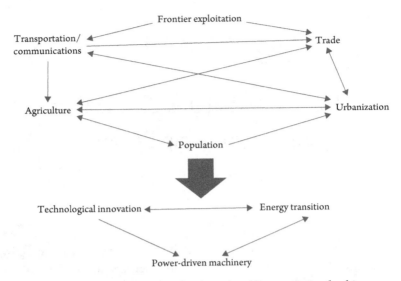

Figure 8.1 Factors Underlying U.S. Technological and Economic Leadership.

(see figure 8.1), did not begin until after World War II because it was based on science, and it took longer for the United States to acquire the lead in scientific research. In other words, the nature of technological innovation had by this time evolved more toward reliance on university and corporate laboratory experimentation and findings as opposed to the construction of more powerful and efficient power-driven machinery for manufacture and transportation purposes. Of course, at the outset, none of these factors were evident in the U.S. case. The nation's resource endowment, market size, and technology all had to be acquired and developed. David and Wright (1997) note that while the United States resource endowment always existed, it was not until the mid-nineteenth century that mineral exploration truly intensified. Thus, while the size and variety of the endowment may be seen as a matter of geophysical luck, it still had to be discovered and exploited by agents responding to increasing demand. By the latter decades of the nineteenth century, it was increasingly recognized that the United States led the world in mineral resource reserves.

Frontier Exploitation, Population Shifts, and Growth

The American frontier was huge once control over it was wrested from Britain, France, Spain, Mexico, Russia, and a large number of indigenous tribes. The original thirteen colonies occupied about 0.37 million square miles, but ultimately the United States grew to encompass 3.8 million square miles. Thus, one could say that the ultimate size of the frontier was some ten times the size of the original country. Most importantly for economic growth purposes, this frontier turned out to possess an impressive natural resource endowment. In 1783, when U.S. independence was recognized, no one was much interested in petroleum, coal, or tungsten. By the time people had become interested because of these resources' importance to industrial growth, the United States controlled a disproportionate share of them. Table 8.1 serves as a quick illustration of this endowment advantage, depicting the U.S. share of world production and its overall production rank. Immediately prior to World War I, the United States was the number one producer of many of the most significant natural resources needed for industrial production. It did not necessarily possess more of everything than anywhere else, but it was definitely in the best position to exploit its material foundation for industrial growth. These raw materials could have been obtained from other countries, but they would have cost more. The huge frontier thus bestowed a major cost advantage on U.S. industrial production as long as the country retained its natural resource lead. Not only were the resources relatively

Table 8.1   **U.S. Natural Resource Production, 1913**

Natural Resource	*% of World Production*	*Production Rank*
Natural Gas	95	1
Petroleum	65	1
Copper	56	1
Phosphate	43	1
Coal	39	1
Bauxite	38	2
Zinc	37	1
Iron Ore	36	1
Lead	34	1
Silver	30	1
Salt	20	1
Gold	20	2
Tungsten	17	1

Source: Based on Wright (1990: 661). France was ranked number one in bauxite production, and the Transvaal in gold production.

Table 8.2 **Natural Resource Production Shares over Time, Percent**

	U.S.			Other Industrial States			Developing States		
	1910	*1950*	*2006*	*1910*	*1950*	*2006*	*1910*	*1950*	*2006*
Bauxite	43.8	18.3	0.2	56.2	21.4	38.7	0.0	60.3	61.1
Copper	29.2	36.9	8.6	60.1	15.5	24.0	10.7	47.5	67.4
Gold	23.8	10.3	11.8	3.5	20.0	28.7	72.7	69.7	59.1
Iron	40.1	42.2	0.9	57.8	52.0	30.6	2.1	5.8	66.5
Lead	31.9	29.3	13.1	34.9	18.3	32.3	33.2	55.0	54.7
Phosphate	55.1	58.9	20.3	0.0	0.0	9.2	44.9	41.1	68.9
Silver	28.1	25.0	5.9	18.3	16.2	45.1	53.6	58.7	48.9
Tin	0.0	0.0	0.0	0.0	1.1	2.1	99.9	98.9	98.0
Zinc	0.0	30.4	1.9	80.9	35.2	8.2	19.2	34.4	54.2

Source: Based on Barbier (2011: 485, 567).

close at hand and not subject to supply interruptions, but U.S. producers could forgo oceanic freight charges and import duties.

Even though the frontier was considered settled by 1890, much of the U.S. resource endowment, with the exception of petroleum, remained relatively intact. However, as many more discoveries were made outside the United States, often by American geologists, access to resources became more commonplace elsewhere, as demonstrated in table 8.2. In the process, U.S. producers increasingly had to pay world prices for their raw materials and lost their initial resource cost edge, especially during and after the 1970s.

A second advantage of possessing a huge frontier was the ability to draw populations from abroad seeking affordable land. Over time, an initially small population about the size of that of the seventeenth-century Netherlands expanded to become one of the largest in the world, making the United States one of the few affluent states to possess an expanding population (see figure 8.2).

Closely linked to the population advantage was the ability to feed that expanding population through cultivation of a "western" region that continued to move west from, initially, the Ohio valley to the Pacific Ocean, as depicted roughly in table 8.3. Of course, this western movement had a strongly negative dimension as well. Morris (2012: 307) calls it an exercise in land spoliation. As farmland was used up quickly, farmers would simply move west to find new land to till until it was time to move on. Given this unsustainable approach, it was

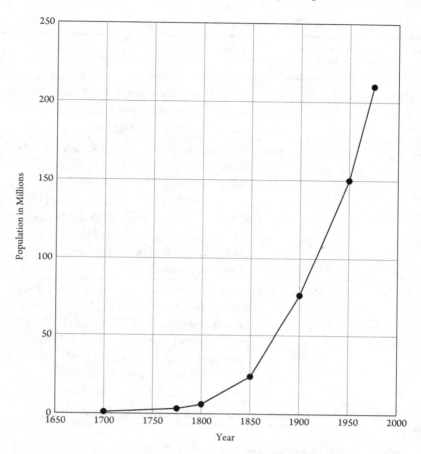

Figure 8.2 U.S. Population, 1700–1975. Source: Based on McEvedy and Jones (1978: 287).

fortunate for the U.S. economy, if not its ecology, that there was so much land to abuse.

A fourth advantage the United States enjoyed was that it was fairly easy to protect this frontier from external attack up to and even beyond the late 1940s thanks to the bracketing Atlantic and Pacific Oceans and relatively weak neighbors. Military protection costs, focused largely on naval coastal defense and the maintenance of scattered army forts throughout the west, were limited for most of the nineteenth century.

Meinig (1993: 255) sums up the American frontier in four characteristics: (1) it was a very large expanse of inexpensive and high-quality land, (2) it was essentially empty, (3) it was subject to very limited public control, and (4) it was well-connected by ever-improving transportation technology. As he concludes, "No other settlement frontier opened on the several continents during [the

Table 8.3 **U.S. Western Expansion**

Years	Population	States
1700–1775	1–3.25 million	Connecticut, Delaware, Georgia, Maryland, Massachusetts, New Hampshire, New Jersey, New York, North Carolina, Pennsylvania, Rhode Island, South Carolina, Virginia
1776–1850	3.25–23.5 million	Above plus Vermont (1791), Kentucky (1792), Tennessee (1796), Ohio (1803), Louisiana (1812), Indiana (1816), Mississippi (1817), Illinois (1818), Alabama (1819), Maine (1820), Missouri (1821), Arkansas (1836), Michigan (1837), Florida (1845), Texas (1845), Iowa (1846), Wisconsin (1848), California (1850), District of Columbia
1851–1950	23.5–150 million	Above plus Minnesota (1856), Oregon (1856), Kansas (1861), West Virginia (1863), Nevada (1864), Nebraska (1867), Colorado (1876), North Dakota (1889), South Dakota (1889), Montana (1889), Washington (1889), Idaho (1890), Wyoming (1890), Utah (1896), Oklahoma (1907), New Mexico (1912)
1951–1975	150–210 million	Above plus Alaska (1959), Hawaii (1959)

Source: Based on information in McEvedy and Jones (1978: 289–290).

nineteenth] century came close to offering so much to so many under such little restraint" (255).

Agrarian Development

The American colonies' early agrarian system was generally characterized by subsistence-level farming, especially in the northern colonies and along the western frontier. Farms were too far apart and inaccessible to expect much more prior to the development of networks of roads, canals, and, ultimately, railroads. The southern colonies had their share of subsistence farmers but also developed plantation crops of tobacco and cotton destined for British markets. After independence, the role of cotton expanded considerably thanks to the invention of the cotton gin, which reduced processing costs and increased British textile

Table 8.4 **The Agrarian Contribution**

Year	% of GDP	% of Labor Force	Output Value (US Dollars in 1840 Prices)	Increase
1800	60+	80	200 million	
1850	33–40	60	800 million–1 billion	4–500%
1897–1901	c. 22	40	6 billion	600%
1920	13–14	26	6.9 billion	15%

Source: Based on Vedder (1976: 227–228).

demand. Cotton subsequently became the predominant cash crop of the south and the principal U.S. export through at least the first half of the nineteenth century. Further regional specialization was enhanced by the northeast becoming the center for export shipping and manufacturing, initially through the construction of cotton textile mills based on British models.[4] The early west (which later became the Midwest) increasingly focused on supplying the northeast with food as transportation improvements made delivery conceivable and technological innovations made higher yields feasible. Among these innovations were improved plows (1840s and 1860s), mechanical reapers or harvesters pulled by horses (initially developed in the 1830s but expanding dramatically in the 1860s), and combines (1890s). The upshot of this mechanization was what had taken sixty-five to seventy hours per acre (sowing, cutting, and threshing) in the 1830s and 1840s had been reduced to about nine hours by the 1890s (Hacker, 1970: 105). The amount of wheat cultivated ballooned accordingly. Wheat and wheat flour exports increased from an annual average of 19 million bushels in 1852–1856 to 197 million bushels in 1897–1901 (Hacker, 1970: 228).[5]

In 120 years, the United States economy managed to move from a labor force in which 80 percent of workers were agricultural to one in which only 26 percent were (see table 8.4). Overall, the value of the nation's economic output in 1920 was thirty-five times its output in 1800, representing roughly twice the rate of expansion of the population over the same time period. So, the agrarian sector more than contributed its share to nineteenth-century economic growth by becoming more efficient and more productive. The expanding population could be fed even while the workforce shifted from an agricultural to a nonagricultural focus. This shift did not occur evenly throughout this period, however. Table 8.4 indicates that its growth slowed down considerably toward the end of the 120 years. But agriculture was also becoming less important as a share of gross domestic product with manufacturing taking over as the predominant sector.

Urbanization

Urbanization proceeded apace in the nineteenth century, as demonstrated in table 8.5. Between 1800 and 1840, the number of city dwellers increased more than fivefold. This number doubled again in each of the next two decades. By 1870, a fourth of the U.S. population was urbanized. City expansion interacted with agricultural and industrial expansion. The increased food supply fed the growing urban population, which in turn warehoused the food surplus and facilitated the concentration of urban labor for manufacturing and industrialization purposes. In sum, population density increased. As Gray and Peterson (1974: 156–157) observe, "In spite of vast additions to territory, the United States more than doubled its population per square mile from 4.5 in 1790 to 10.6 in 1860."

Table 8.6, which highlights the fastest-growing cities in the world as described in the last two chapters, emphasizes the early growth of the eastern coastal cities. Chicago and Pittsburgh, which were more industrial in focus, joined the list in the second half of the nineteenth century. The next half-century pulled in Los Angeles, Houston, Dallas, Detroit, Seattle, and Atlanta, giving the United States the distinction of possessing half of the twelve fastest-growing cities in the world. Approaching the end of the twentieth century, however, only the administrative capital city, Washington, D.C., made the list. The shape of this cycle over two hundred years, which overlaps with the British cycle, is well delineated by the number of quickly growing U.S. cities in each interval: four, five, six, and one.

Table 8.5 **U.S. Urban Population, 1800–1870 (Millions)**

Year	Number of Cities with population of 2500 or more	Urban Population	% of Total Population
1800	33	0.3	6.7
1840	131	1.8	10.7
1850	236	3.5	15.3
1860	392	6.2	19.8
1870	663	9.9	25.7

Source: Based on Hacker (1970: 103).

Table 8.6 **Top Twelve Fastest-Growing Cities, 1800–2005**

1800–1850	1850–1900	1900–1950	1970–2005
New York	**Chicago**	**Los Angeles**	Beijing
Baltimore	Buenos Aires	**Houston**	Shanghai
Philadelphia	Leipzig	**Dallas**	**Washington, D.C.**
Boston	**Pittsburgh**	Hong Kong	Osaka
Liverpool	**New York**	**Detroit**	Seoul
Manchester	Berlin	Sao Paulo	Singapore
Birmingham	Newcastle	Shanghai	Budapest
Glasgow	Dresden	Seoul	Madrid
Bombay	**Boston**	**Seattle**	Vienna
Rio de Janeiro	Budapest	Buenos Aires	Berlin
Brussels	Hamburg	**Atlanta**	Tokyo
Newcastle	Rio de Janeiro	Toronto	Hamburg

Note: In the 1850–1900 interval, Philadelphia and Baltimore were ranked twenty-second and twenty-fifth in the top thirty-nine cities; in the 1900–1950 interval, Washington, D.C., San Francisco, New York, Boston, and Philadelphia ranked fourteenth, sixteenth, twenty-fourth, thirty-second, and thirty-third in the top thirty-nine, respectively; in the 1970–2005 interval, Los Angeles, Miami, and Chicago were ranked fifteenth, twentieth, and twenty-eighth in the top thirty-five. U.S. cities appear in bold.

Source: Based on Taylor, Hoyler, and Smith (2012: 28).

Transportation and Communications

When the thirteen colonies gained independence in 1783, they were poorly connected with one another, and connections within each state were equally underdeveloped. Three phases characterized subsequent improvements in transportation. The first forty years after independence were devoted to improving roads in the vicinity of cities, often in the form of privately owned turnpikes, and making use of rivers for moving bulk cargo. After 1825, canal construction emerged as a way to supplement the nation's dependence on the natural course of rivers.[6] While not all of the canals that were built proved to be profitable, one estimate of their enhanced efficiency is the claim that horse-drawn canal barges couldcarry fifty times the loads associated with horse-drawn wagons (Menon 2011: 53). Rates for moving freight via canals were perhaps one-fifth the rates associated with road carriage. But canals could not easily be constructed everywhere, and they were subject to seasonal freezing. The use of steamboats on natural rivers proved the next phase in transportation infrastructure, but this innovation was considered complementary to the continuing expansion of canals.

Railroads supplanted canals in the 1850s as a transportation mode that could go practically anywhere faster and less expensively year-round (Marcus and Segal, 1999: 79). More specifically, Hacker (1970: 234) credits the railroads with providing the "greater stimulus to the manufacture of iron and steel and railroad equipment and the production of coal and timber . . . the opening up of the Plains country to wheat and cattle, the development of primary markets for agricultural goods, and a national market for the goods and services of the whole growing economy."[7]

At the beginning of the American Civil War, the United States had laid more than thirty thousand miles of rails focusing largely on the railroad network between the eastern and midwestern regions (Atack and Passell, 1994: 429). Although this network represented half of the world's total rails laid by that time, it would expand over the next four decades by a factor of more than six (432). By 1900, much of the U.S. rail network had already been established.

Transportation innovations thus contributed directly to the construction of a large domestic market that was critical to U.S. economic growth and leadership by literally and figuratively paving the way west while also linking urban centers and their hinterlands.[8] Railroads were thus a scale enabler for the entire nationalized American economy. As Goddard has observed:

> America's first big business, by opening up mass markets, made other large enterprises possible. A comparatively few people engaged in mechanized agriculture could raise the food to feed the city dwellers, who made the machines that mechanized agriculture. Moving goods quickly over large distances let small factories produce more, creating economies of scale, which made their rapid growth inevitable. (1994: 18)

The telegraph, which began to spread in the late 1840s, often paralleling railroad networks in placement and function, melded the transportation and communications sectors. Railroads used the telegraph to control their traffic. Information used by journalists, the military, and business decision-makers could also travel more quickly (Fite and Reese, 1965: 202–203).

Communications innovations contributed to U.S. economic growth in another, less recognized fashion (Marcus and Segal, 1999: 127–132). In seeking to construct something called "harmonic telegraphy," Alexander Graham Bell created the telephone, which initially competed with the telegraph and helped to make it an obsolete technology. The competition between the telegraph and the telephone was inadvertent, but radio was initially created to challenge the long-distance communication monopoly held by the telephone. This sequence illustrates the central substitution process driving technological change. Existing ways of doing things (or old innovations) can often be improved by new innovations.[9]

Technological Innovation, Fuel Transition, and Power-Driven Machinery

The three categories of technological innovation, fuel transition, and power-driven machinery are combined here because that configuration mirrors the way they actually interacted. Without the discovery of new fuel sources, the power-driven machinery that emerged would have been much less powerful. Without technological innovations, these new fuels would not have worked as well, if at all. Klein (2007: 83) captures this interaction well in the following passage:

> The creation and sources of new power laid the foundations for the new technologies that transformed transportation, communication, and production. It hastened the settling of the continent, multiplied the productivity of a people short on labor, and became the indispensable engine driving material progress. Between 1870 and 1920 American consumption of energy increased about 440 percent, and its sources changed dramatically. In 1870 wood accounted for about 73 percent of all energy used, with coal supplying nearly all the remainder. By 1920 wood provided less than 8 percent of energy used, coal soared to 73 percent, oil contributed 12 percent, and natural gas chipped in 4 percent. By the 1880s a growing proportion of energy went into producing a new source of power that became the most vital technology of the twentieth century: electricity.
>
> Without new sources of power, the industrial revolution would never have occurred. Without plentiful new sources of fuel, the power revolution would have stalled out.

As an index of increased power, we can look at the history of dramatic changes in energy consumed in the United States. According to the U.S. Energy Information Agency (2013), wood consumption never exceeded about 3 quadrillion British thermal units (Btu). The move to coal led to an early peak consumption around 1920 of 15 quadrillion Btu, or a fivefold increase. Subsequent coal usage in the early twenty-first century was approximately 23 quadrillion Btu. Natural gas consumption exceeded 25 quadrillion Btu more or less at the same time that petroleum consumption exceeded 40 quadrillion Btu. Thus, going back to about 1840, before the new fuels began to be introduced in quantity, U.S. energy consumption was something less than 3 quadrillion Btu. Adding coal, natural gas, and petroleum consumption just before the latest recession (2007–2008) would put U.S. energy consumption in the vicinity of 86 quadrillion Btu. Throwing in nuclear and other renewables would easily add another 10 quadrillion Btu. In about 160 years, then, U.S. energy consumption increased a considerable amount, breaking through the agrarian constraints in place prior to the American Civil War.

Without this shift to new energy sources, the industrialization that the United States experienced could not have occurred. There are several ways to demonstrate the truth of this generalization. At the beginning of the twentieth century, U.S. per capita consumption of wood as the primary energy source would have required 1 billion acres of forest—reserves that were no longer possible to sustain after 1630. In 1920, the 16.5 million animals used in the United States for economic service required the use of about one-fourth of all cultivated land as pasture. But at the same time, the U.S. economy produced 704 million horsepower in engines and motors. To achieve the same horsepower level with animals would have required far more pastureland to feed them than was conceivable. Alternatively, the U.S. economy would have needed fifteen acres of forest per capita to supply the wood necessary to generate the amount of heat needed in 1970. But by that time, only 2.7 acres per capita were available.[10]

Jones (2014: 73) puts this idea another way. In his view, the energy consumed to underwrite U.S. industrial development involved (1) heating homes and factories in increasingly dense cities, (2) making possible new patterns of movement of people and goods through the use of steamships and railroads, and (3) smelting iron in a fashion that was both quick and conducive to expansion. If the U.S. economy had been restricted to organic or noncarbon sources of energy, it might have been able to accomplish one of these three activities, but not all three.

Certainly, not all of this increased energy consumption reflects the power of new machinery used to produce commodities. Some of it reflects the comforts offered by innovations in air-conditioning and heating, for instance.[11] Yet even in these cases, power-driven machinery was used to produce the cooler and warmer air desired for greater comfort depending on the season. Moreover, as in the British case, some of the new fuels acted as substitutions for older energy sources. One might argue that many of the same results could have been achieved with older energy sources, such as wood and running water. Running water was important to U.S. textile mills, just as American railroads depended on firewood to a greater extent than their British counterparts. Yet running water and firewood were not always available or of sufficient power to do the work desired.[12] Licht (1995: 110) captures the indispensability of coal to American economic growth in the nineteenth century as follows:

The importance of coal in American industrialization cannot be over-stated. A more efficient fuel than wood, coal allowed for expanded use of steam engines in transportation and manufacture. Industrial plants were no longer bound to water sites, with steam engines and coal in this way promoting the geographical expansion of industry. Steam engines also permitted large-scale manufacturing, which in turn fostered cor-porate development. There is thus a direct connection between coal, mass industry, and the rise of the bureaucratic corporation. Coal could also be transformed into other products, and various derivatives of coal proved essential in industrial progress. For example, coke, a distillate of coal, was the required fuel in steelmaking. Burned coal produced methane gas which was employed in street lighting. Finally, anthracite coal, in particular, burned slowly and cleanly and had significant use in home heating.

This point is driven home in table 8.7, which uses data from Atack, Bateman, and Margo (2008) to show how coal-fueled steam replaced water in American manufacturing between 1850 and 1880. Their data show that small firms could get by with more traditional sources of energy, but larger firms led the shift to steam. Relying on water, however, was a major constraint in moving toward the ability to produce on a larger scale.[13]

By the end of the nineteenth century, U.S. coal consumption exceeded that of the economy that had initiated the shift to coal—Britain. Figure 8.3 places that transition point very near 1900. The U.S. economy went on to double the amount of coal Britain had consumed at its peak just prior to World War I.

But just as was the case in the first (British) Industrial Revolution, energy alone could not and did not carry the U.S. economy to new heights of produc-tivity. Technological innovation was essential. This transition is captured well

Table 8.7 **The Displacement of Water Power in American Manufacturing, average horsepower**

All Firms	*1850*	*1860*	*1870*	*1880*
Steam Only	6.8	14.6	20.1	20.5
Water Only	26.4	24.1	14.8	12.3
Larger Firms				
Steam Only	17.7	24.1	40.8	50.9
Water Only	26.6	25.9	17.1	4.7

Source: Based on Atack, Bateman, and Margo (2008: 189).

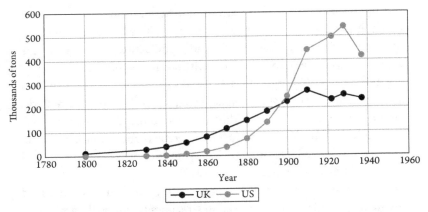

Figure 8.3 British and U.S. Coal Production, 1800–1937. Source: Based on data from Etemad and Luciani (1991: 6, 12).

in table 8.8, which lists the United States' leading industries between 1860 and 1920. In 1860, the top industries were various types of consumer goods appropriate for an agrarian economy, along with some machinery (ranked sixth). By 1880, machinery and iron/steel had become first and second on the list, with machinery production's value increasing by more than three times what it had been in 1860. By 1920, machinery's value-added had expanded to five times its 1880 value. In addition to machinery and iron/steel, shipbuilding, automobiles, general shop construction, and electrical machinery occupied six of the top ten industry categories in 1920.

Smil (2005) argues that the five decades prior to World War I constituted the most innovative period in human history, at least in terms of the concentrated number of innovations. Most of these innovations were American in application, if not invention. Table 8.9 lists some of the ones Smil views as among the most significant of this era. Not all of these innovations had their full impact in the nineteenth century, but they are representative of those that were crucial in assisting the United States to seize the leadership of world manufacturing in durable goods by the end of the nineteenth century.

Gordon (2015) makes a kindred argument. His thesis is that the economic changes wrought in the 1870–1970 period were truly revolutionary. Prior to 1870 and after 1970, innovations were or have been much less radical and broad in impact. The first Industrial Revolution, based on inventions formulated between 1770 and 1820 and primarily linked to the steam engine, predominated throughout most of the nineteenth century. Focusing primarily on electricity and the internal combustion engine—both initially developed in the late nineteenth century—these inventions had their maximum impact between 1920 and 1970, influencing "virtually the entire span of human wants and needs"

Table 8.8 **The Ten Leading Industries of the U.S. Economy**

Rank	1860	1880	1920
1	Cotton goods (58.8)	Machinery (111.0)	Machinery (575.6)
2	Lumber—sawed (54.0)	Iron and steel (105.3)	Iron and steel (492.8)
3	Boots and shoes (52.9)	Cotton goods (97.2)	Lumber—sawed (393.4)
4	Flour and meal (43.1)	Lumber—sawed (87.1)	Cotton goods (363.7)
5	Men's clothing (39.4)	Boots and shoes (82.0)	Shipbuilding (348.8)
6	Machinery (31.5)	Men's clothing (78.2)	Automobile (347.3)
7	Woolen goods (26.6)	Flour and grist milling (63.6)	General shop construction (327.7)
8	Leather (24.5)	Woolen goods (59.8)	Printing and publishing (267.7)
9	Cast iron (22.7)	Printing and publishing (58.3)	Electrical machinery (245.9)
10	Printing and publishing (19.6)	Malt liquor (44.2)	Men's clothing (239.2)

Source: Based on Atack and Passel (1994: 461, 467); numbers in parentheses represent value added in 1914 U.S. dollars, in millions.

(Gordon, 2015: 320).[14] In contrast, the third industrial revolution, predicated on information technology, has been in progress for some fifty-five years now. It has revolutionary characteristics, but its impact has been relatively narrow, focused more on entertainment, communications, and information. These ongoing changes are also handicapped by four "headwinds"—rising inequality, stagnating educational attainment, an increasing share of the population in retirement and a smaller share in the workforce, and expanding federal debt—that are conspiring to choke continued U.S. economic growth.

While Smil (2005) emphasizes technological change, Gordon (2015) is more concerned with technological change's impact on output and living standards. This difference of emphasis probably reflects the fact that Smil is trained as an engineer and Gordon is an economist. Smil does not assume that future technological change can never match what emerged between 1870 and 1914—only that it has not done so yet and, possibly, may not ever compare in its scope to the changes of the late nineteenth century. Gordon, in contrast, is more insistent that the changes wrought between 1870 and 1970 could only be done once, in

Table 8.9 **Key Inventions and Innovations, 1867–1914**

Years	Innovations
1867–1880s	First practical designs of dynamos and open-hearth steelmaking furnaces, definite formulation of the second law of thermodynamics, dynamite, telephones, sound recordings, lightbulbs, practical typewriters, chemical pulp, reinforced concrete
1880s	Reliable incandescent electric lights, electricity-generating plants, electric motors and trains, transformers, steam turbines, gramophone, popular photography, practical gasoline-fueled four-stroke internal combustion engines, motorcycles, cars, aluminum production, crude oil tankers, air-filled rubber tires, steel-skeleton skyscrapers, prestressed concrete
1890s	Diesel engines, x-rays, movies, liquefaction of air, wireless telegraph, discovery of radioactivity, synthesis of aspirin
1900–1914	Mass-produced cars, first airplanes, tractors, radio broadcasts, vacuum diodes and triodes, tungsten lightbulbs, neon lights, common use of halftones in printing, stainless steel, hydrogenation of fats, air-conditioning, Hammer-Bosch ammonia synthesis for fertilizer

Source: Based on Smil (2005: 22–25).

the sense that these shifts effected extremely fundamental lifestyle changes that ultimately affected all or almost all of the population in fairly quick order.[15] In his view, slower growth post-1970 was the inevitable outcome and is most unlikely to be accelerated by new technology that is applied relatively narrowly.

Both authors cannot be completely right in their interpretations, but their general point remains similar: the U.S. ascent was predicated on a unique concatenation of technological changes that was unlikely to be sustained and is unlikely to be duplicated in the future. Since these changes were destined to run their course, relative decline at some point was highly probable. From an international relations perspective, it is easy to appreciate the transformational power of the energy–technology package linked to the second Industrial Revolution. But the immediate question is: Could a future energy–technology revolution either vault a country into the lead economy position or restore the incumbent to the gigantic lead over others it once enjoyed?

In the abstract, the answers to both questions seem positive. It is conceivable that a new lead economy could emerge as it has in the past, and it is also at least imaginable that the United States could regain the type of lead it once possessed. The main reservations, however, are that (1) the type of energy–technology revolution that is most likely to occur (a combination of nonfossil fuels or much greener carbon-based energy and a less narrow application of information technology) has encountered considerable resistance within the incumbent lead economy, and (2) should such a transformation emerge, it will be difficult to monopolize for very long. The U.S. lead was long in duration because it took so long for other economies to catch up. The ones that have caught up— basically Organisation for Economic Co-operation and Development (OECD) countries—do not possess the resource base or ambition to make a bid for the lead economy status. The states with the ambition may or may not have an adequate resource base but still have some way to go to catch up, let alone seize the leadership role in driving radical economic transformation. But once the next radical economic transformation occurs, a number of other states should be able to copy it in less time than it took to catch up to the United States in the twentieth century. So, we might anticipate a wave of new energy–technology interactions that rivals the late-nineteenth and early-twentieth-century phenomenon, but without the same implications for altering the stratification of power in the international system.

Returning to the story underlying the emergence of the U.S. lead economy, figure 8.4 offers a plot of U.S. patent activity that underscores the hyperactivity of the second half of the long nineteenth century (through 1920) in American economic growth. It is difficult to distinguish among the decades from the 1860s to 1920 because the innovations kept appearing. Even so, steel production, the replacement for iron production; early electrification; and the initial stages of

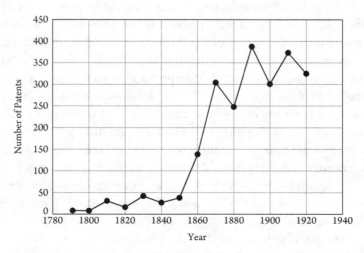

Figure 8.4 U.S. Patents Issued per Million Population. Source: Based on data from Vedder (1976: 280).

automobile production probably dominated this late-nineteenth- and early-twentieth-century cluster of technological change.[16] In this period, the United States established itself as the world's manufacturing leader "based on the high consumption of energy, high labor productivity, superior output, and an unprecedented collection of technological and organizational advances" (Smil, 2013: 44).

While steel and autos have tended to receive better press, Smil (2013) argues that the iconic analogue to the earlier steam engine was the electric motor, which offered a number of advantages over the now-refined steam engine. Klein (2007: 89–103) provides an excellent summary of the general advent of electricity applications that captures quite well one of the prime reasons energy transitions have led to sustained economic growth: the technology they lead to can usually be improved upon. Steam engines, for example, are characterized by a number of liabilities. They are complex in terms of their multiple parts and therefore not compact; they are noisy, dirty, and not portable; they cannot do some things directly; they are bad for assembly lines; and they are dangerous if they explode. Moreover, mechanization was benefited by the electric motor's ability to control the flow of oil precisely (Jones, 2014: 152). Oil lubricants could also be used to move power faster and with less friction. Petroleum-driven motors could be smaller than steam engines and utilized in more flexible circumstances. Alternative sources of power, as a consequence, were an attractive proposition. Both internal combustion engines and electricity emerged to replace the imperfect steam devices.

Experiments on ways to convert electricity into mechanical energy and vice versa were conducted in the 1820s and 1830s. Yet knowing how to produce electricity did not resolve the problem of producing enough electricity to accomplish a specific task.[17] Nor did it solve the problem of how to move the electricity once it was produced. Early applications in the form of the telegraph and telephone did not require much energy. Replacing gas lighting with electricity did. First, the electric bulb had to be created. Then power stations to distribute electricity to the bulb and other appliances had to be developed. Incandescent lightbulb inventor Thomas Edison insisted on committing to direct current (DC). Later it was proved that it made more sense to go with alternating current (AC), but that meant that the early commitment to DC had to be overcome. Another application involved replacing horse-drawn vehicles in cities with electric trolleys. Once lighting and trolleys were in place, more powerful generators and transmission systems had to be built to handle the increased demand. Further applications yielded turbo generators and electrochemical cells (batteries), and made factory assembly lines more feasible. Once better ways to assess usage and expand the usage load over the full twenty-four-hour cycle were discovered, it became possible to increase consumption at lower prices. This process led to the development of even larger generators and efforts to make the delivery process more efficient and transmittable over longer distances as greater proportions of the population and industry were brought within electric grids.

In 1899, only 4 percent of U.S. industry was powered by electric motors. By 1910, that figure had increased to 10 percent, jumping to 50 percent by 1918 and 75 percent by 1929. Jones (2014: 287) and Schur and Netschert (1960: 187) point out that it was World War I that stimulated the adoption of electric motors in American industry. At the outbreak of war in 1914, 39 percent of industrial machinery was driven by electricity. By 1919, that proportion had risen to 55 percent. With a bit of a lag, much the same thing happened in the residential sphere. Only 8 percent of American households had access to electricity by 1908, but by 1930 68 percent did (Smil, 2013: 51–52).

Automobile usage paralleled the electrification of the American economy, again subject to a lag. Table 8.10 compares automobile ownership in four states, the United Kingdom, France, Germany, and the United States. Most of the initial development of autos took place in the first three of these states, especially France and Germany, but the large size of the American market, in conjunction with Henry Ford's application of the assembly line process to automobile production in 1913, quickly swung leadership in this industry to the United States.[18] The timing of World War I, with its concomitant demand for trucks, hardly hurt the expansion of this new specialization either.

In this context, it should not be surprising that figure 8.5 includes both the internal combustion engine (ICE), the core innovation of the automobile industry, and electricity. These innovations proved to be the two most critical development blocks after the coal–iron–steam block that ushered in the Industrial

Table 8.10 **Automobile Ownership in Selected States (Millions)**

	United Kingdom	France	Germany	United States
1920	0.187	0.157	0.061	8.132
1930	1.056	1.109	0.489	23.035
1950	2.258	2.150	0.469	40.339
1960	5.526	5.546	4.788	61.682
1970	11.515	12.900	15.100	89.200
1980	14.772	19.130	25.870	121.600
1990	19.742	23.550	30.685	143.600
2000	25.067	28.060	42.840	213.000

Source: Based on Kander (2013: 297).

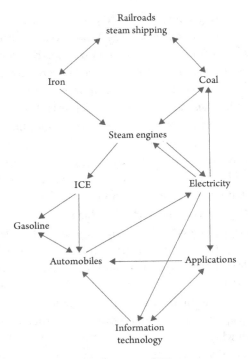

Figure 8.5 Coal, Steam, Iron, ICE, Electricity, and IT.

Revolution.[19] The United States adapted the first, British-based block and then forged ahead with the next two blocks of the late nineteenth and early twentieth centuries to supplant Britain as the world technological leader in the 1890s. As previously noted, the drawbacks associated with steam engines led to the development of the ICE and electric motors. Both of these prime movers generated a number of applications. The ICE led to the development of cars, trucks, and airplanes. Automobiles ultimately led to the supremacy of gasoline fuel, because early electrical vehicles could not operate reliably beyond relatively short distances (Black, 2012), although they may return to electricity as a source of energy in the twenty-first century if battery constraint and recharging infrastructure issues are resolved. The applications of electrification were diffused throughout industry and households. Initially electrification relied on coal to a great extent, but it has evolved more recently toward nuclear and natural gas as its fuel sources.

In any event, the United States was able to draw upon its resource abundance, large market, and innovations to maintain its production/technology lead through two world wars that were won to varying extents because the U.S. economy could supply one side with the fuel, weapons, and money needed to defeat its opponents.[20] Smil (2013) calls the 1865–1899 era the "creation" phase of American ascendance. The scope of this creation was very impressive, leading to industrial if not technological predominance by the turn of the century. As Atack and Passell note:

> In the late nineteenth century America was transformed from a predominantly rural-agrarian economy into an urban-industrial powerhouse.... Production became increasingly concentrated both industrially and geographically. By 1900 the United States was the dominant industrial power. American firms spanned the globe, and American technology and management techniques increasingly became the standard around the world. (1994: 489)

The subsequent years leading up to World War II represented a "consolidation" phase in Smil's (2013) interpretation.[21] A third phase, lasting from 1941 to 1973, is termed the "dominance" phase. From Smil's perspective, this last era was a unique period, because it combined elements that were unlikely to be duplicated. The United States came out of World War II in much better shape than the rest of the world, which had been badly damaged by intensive warfare.[22] In the immediate postwar era, the United States had no real economic competitors. It did have a strategic competitor, the Soviet Union, but it was able to develop a fairly stable relationship with this state. Best of all, the U.S. economy retained its resource abundance and access to cheap energy. As a consequence, it was well situated to lead the development of the information technology (IT) block, shown in figure 8.5, by developing transistors, microchips, and personal computers.[23]

Nebeker (2009: 474–475) suggests that the emergence of electrical engineering, electronics, and computing should be seen as stages (or phases) of electricity exploitation. Electrical technology emerged in the second half of the nineteenth century. The first half of the twentieth century saw electronics penetrate a number of industrial domains. In the second half of the twentieth century (and beyond), computers penetrated most technologies. In each phase, existing industries were transformed and new industries were created. Leadership in earlier phases up to a point facilitated leadership in the next phase.[24] These connections, in any event, help explain the arrow from electricity to information technology in figure 8.5.

Science is closely related to IT. While some of IT's breakthroughs have been achieved in garages, it is an area closely tied to university and corporate laboratories, as are its multiple and still unfolding applications in biotechnology and nanotechnology. In addition, it has a number of "backward" linkages to automobiles and electronics, which are being transformed by IT applications.[25] Yet as strong as the U.S. economy was in the early twentieth century, it could not claim world leadership in science at that time. One indicator of this lag is demonstrated in figure 8.6, which tracks the nationality of Nobel Prize winners in chemistry and physics.[26] Even acknowledging the inherent delay in the recognition accorded to Nobelist achievements, figure 8.6 suggests that Germany, the United Kingdom, and France had more outstanding scientists than the United States through almost all of the first half of the twentieth century. Only in the late 1960s did U.S. scientists begin to dominate the prizes. This scientific leadership was built on a number of decades of governmental support for universities, with special attention to boosting research in agriculture and engineering. But corporate laboratories had been developing since the late nineteenth century as well. World War II proved to be a turning point in the U.S. acquisition of a lead in research and development activities. Not only did the war effort stimulate science, which was seen as a vehicle for winning the war, but returning veterans were encouraged to acquire university degrees. It probably did not hurt that most of the nation's rivals in scientific competition were set back by the war, especially those states that lost.[27] As late as 1965, the U.S. economy had approximately 6.5 scientists and engineers per 1,000 involved in research and development, while the United Kingdom, Germany, France, and Japan all had ratios ranging between 2 and 2.5 per 1,000 population (Nelson and Wright, 1992: 1952). Add in the much larger U.S. population size, and it is clear that the U.S. scientific lead was in part attributable to having many more people engaged in science for several decades after the war.

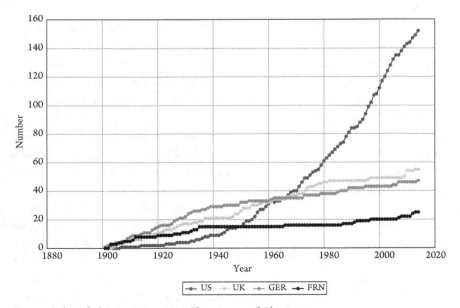

Figure 8.6 Nobel Prize Winners in Chemistry and Physics.

In more recent years, that particular gap has closed. While the U.S. ratio climbed to a high of 10 per 1,000 in 2003 and then began to decline, the European Union's ratio improved from 5 per 1,000 in 1995 to 7 per 1,000 in 2010. The Japanese ratio remained roughly constant at 10 per 1,000 in the 1990s and the first decade of the 2000s, while South Korea attained its peak of 12 per 1,000 in 2011 (U.S. National Science Board, 2014).[28] Only Russia has shown a persistent decline in research and development scientists over the past two decades. Otherwise, the data suggest that some parts of the world are catching up to the U.S. lead in numbers of scientific personnel. Figure 8.7 plots more recent numbers for a similar indicator tracked by the World Bank: workers in research and development (R&D) per million population. This R&D indicator is not restricted to scientists per se, since it also encompasses individuals who create or manage new knowledge products and therefore includes individuals with PhDs in a variety of fields. Clear convergence in researcher numbers between the United States and Europe (as demonstrated by a composite average of France, Germany, and the United Kingdom) is demonstrated after 2007.[29]

Similar figures have been found for spending on research and development. The U.S. share declined from 37 percent in 2001 to 30 percent in 2011. European spending on research and development remains about three-fourths of that of the U.S., while Chinese share improved from less than 6 percent of US

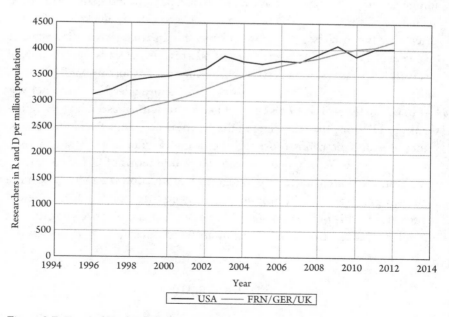

Figure 8.7 Research and Development Workers Per Million. Source: Data from the World Bank's World Development Indicators (WDI).

R&D expenditures in 1995 to about 49 percent in 2011. Convergence has yet to happen in this area, but the trend line is heading in that direction selectively.[30]

A partial explanation for these trends is put forward by Arora, Belenzon, and Pataccconi (2015), who find that U.S. corporate research and development has declined considerably in large U.S. firms since the 1990s.[31] Yet over the same period, an emphasis on corporate patents has increased. These tendencies appear to be related to Chinese import penetration. Large corporations have responded to heightened penetration with less innovation and more patent protection efforts, presumably to protect their profits and keep stockholders reasonably happy.

In the less scientifically oriented industrial fields, the United States has lost even more of its lead. This loss can be attributed in part to two environmental changes. After 1973, the United States lost its access to inexpensive energy after its own oilfield production peaked in the late 1960s. Increasing reliance on imported petroleum came at higher and higher prices, in terms of not just the petroleum itself, but all fuel prices. Those industries that were most dependent on the price of raw materials found themselves in jeopardy if they could not adapt by becoming more energy-efficient. The second change involved the appearance of multiple genuine economic competitors in Europe and Asia that were less reluctant to adapt to rising production costs. According to Smil (2013), it should not have been surprising that the first industrial leads lost were in steel and automobiles. Not only were these industries closely related, but they were among the most energy-intensive and least adaptive of industries. Moreover, the nature of the American market had encouraged U.S. automakers to develop a "technically retrogressive" culture of larger and heavier gas-guzzling vehicles that were not very reliable.[32] The losses of other industrial leads were reinforced by overly hasty moves to cut costs by offshoring and outsourcing. Smil labels the years after 1974 years of "retreat," as one manufacturing lead after another was lost to competitors. The 1990s seemed like a return to an ascending trajectory thanks to IT gains; the stumbling of the Japanese economy, the United States' principal economic competitor; and the death of its principal strategic rival, the Soviet Union. Yet nothing else had changed in terms of U.S. competitiveness. Even the United States' lead in high-tech production was reduced as more high-tech products have been imported than exported since 2002. Different approaches to this problem might yet be tried, but the prospects for turning around the "retreat" from manufacturing are not promising.

International Trade

In the first sixty or so years of the United States' existence, international trade became a significant component of its economic growth. War in Europe contributed to this expansion initially, since American firms could profit from neutral shipping—at least until both sides of the Napoleonic conflict developed animosity toward neutral ships. As long as sailing vessels remained the primary carriers of freight, U.S. shipping could focus heavily on moving cotton from southern fields to British textile mills. On this score, Gray and Peterson (1974: 161) contend that "the evidence suggests that trade was the key factor behind American development in most of the antebellum years. Prosperity based on trade generated the capital accumulation and changes in economic organization upon which later growth hinged." What they have in mind is the regional specialization that emerged as the south focused primarily on cotton and the northeast concentrated on commerce and shipping. Without the decades of cotton export experience accumulated and capital earned, the northeast might not have been as ready to support the emergence of manufacturing as it proved to be at the time of the American Civil War.

The advent of oceangoing steamships gave the freight-carrying edge to faster British shipping, which undercut the U.S. position as the primary mover of cotton across the Atlantic in the second half of the nineteenth century. The expansion of the U.S. economy, in any event, increasingly depended on the domestic market and internal transportation networks. Trade certainly continued, but it gradually became less significant to overall wealth accumulation in the second half of the nineteenth century and through much of the twentieth century as well.

Business Organization

Small, family-owned firms did not disappear as the U.S. economy transformed itself, but they were forced to compete with the very large firms focused largely on manufacturing high-volume products that emerged (see table 8.11).[33] Because these new firms needed considerable capital investment to underwrite the expansion of their production activities, they acquired corporate status partially in order to give investors limited liability for the firm's activities and allow for the coming and going of different investors. The size and complexity of these business activities encouraged the development of a hierarchy of administrators, with each level of administration specializing in managerial decision-making for different types and locations of activity. Profits and market control could be maximized, moreover, if each firm could complement its production with the acquisition of needed raw materials and the subsequent marketing of the finished products as well. This vertical integration of raw materials, production, and marketing could be further complemented by horizontal integration whenever

Table 8.11 **The Evolution of U.S. Business Firms**

1860	1900
Small	Large
Family owned and operated	Corporately owned and bureaucratically managed
Specialized	Multifunctional
Labor-intensive	Capital-intensive
Producers of small batches of goods sold locally or regionally	Marketers of mass-produced items sold nationally and internationally

Source: Based on Licht (1995: 133).

firms could get away with it. The fewer competitors for market share there were, the better the chance of truly controlling the marketplace.

Later, these large corporations became multinational. In this transition, headquarters, management, and profit repatriation tended to continue to be identified with the home country within which the corporation initially emerged; "multinational" only meant that corporate operations were more likely to be conducted in multiple states, as opposed to the home market. Large U.S. corporations, especially those that were vertically integrated, were natural vehicles for multinational activities. Reflecting the political–economic structure of the world economy, U.S. multinationals encountered little competition in the immediate aftermath of World War II. Rising competition and resistance to U.S. firms abroad has covaried with the slow relative decline of the United States as the leading technological power in the international system.

Conclusion

All of the key factors in economic growth and technological centrality can be seen to have been present in the U.S. case, as shown in table 8.12. The frontier exploitation involved in the U.S. case is impossible to ignore, given the scale of resources it has made available. The integrative impacts of canals, railroads, and highways, coupled with the innovations of the telegraph and telephone, equally stand out in the transportation and communications sectors. Agricultural innovation and expansion, as in the Chinese and British cases, easily sustained population and city growth, as well as providing important exports. While the Dutch and British invented new corporate forms for their overseas activities, the U.S. economy transformed the very nature of corporations in order to cope

Table 8.12 **Presence and Absence of Key Economic Growth and Technological Centrality Factors—U.S. Case**

Frontier Exploitation	Agriculture	Transportation/ Communications	Trade	Urbanization	Population Growth	Technological Innovation	Energy Transition	Power-Driven Machinery
Present	Present	Present	Only present early on	Present	Present	Present	Present	Present

with the increased scale and integration of business activity. Only trade was of minor significance in U.S.'s rise to leadership. Cotton exports contributed to economic growth in the first half of the nineteenth century, but afterwards internal economic growth stimulated by market expansion and increased production became the main driver.

U.S. economic growth emulated Britain's coal-centric trajectory and outdid it by the end of the nineteenth century. As electricity and petroleum began to be utilized in the latter years of the nineteenth century, they reshaped the nature of American industry, heating, and transportation, pushing the United States ahead of the rest of the world. Technological innovation and power-driven machinery increasingly provided the intermittent stimuli needed for the United States to fully embrace carbon-based energy sources that initially were relatively inexpensive. Centrality in technology innovation, science, and world economic growth followed.

Clearly, each of the four main cases are different. It would be easy to exaggerate just how different they are. But idiosyncracies aside, how does our analysis of the U.S. case and the other three predecessors inform our understanding of economic growth, technological leadership, and the role of energy in achieving systemic leadership is the focus of the next chapter. Their comparison reveals a straightforward answer: the key lies in the ways technology and energy interact.

9

Comparing the Four Main Cases

In chapters 5 through 8, we examined nine system leaders put forward by Modelski and Thompson (1996), although we focused primarily on four of the most prominent cases. No two system leaders were identical in their claims to being the most innovative states in their respective zones, eras, and periods of leadership. Nonetheless, three general categories emerge: maritime commercial leadership,[1] a pushing of agrarian boundaries, and sustained industrial and economic growth. Only two states fall in the third category, and their breakthroughs, of course, redefined the modern world, just as other leaders played contributory roles along the path to modernity.

But what are the implications of our analysis? How does it inform our understanding of economic growth, technological leadership, and the role of energy in these processes? First, we can acknowledge the many idiosyncrasies of each contender for leadership. Medieval China's story does not resemble what happened in fifteenth-century Portugal or the twentieth-century United States. At the same time, however, we have been able to impose a single framework on our analysis of the four major cases. This framework does not privilege one or two variables but incorporates a mix of interacting variables that appear to generate different levels and intensities of economic growth and technological leadership. Yet it is not a matter of choosing different variables to highlight in each case. In none of the cases do the variables work identically. China's commercial edge was a belated product of its technological lead, for instance, whereas in most of the other cases, the commercial leads came much earlier (except in the U.S. case, in which other factors were more significant). All of the system leaders capitalized on some source of energy other than the agricultural standard of solar power. Many relied only on wind to propel their sailing vessels. The Netherlands used peat much more than the others did. For a time, Britain used more coal than the rest of the world combined. And the U.S. cornered the market on petroleum.

We might continue listing the idiosyncratic factors that affected each case, but it would serve our analytical purposes better if we focused more specifically on the model factors (table 9.1). Frontiers were critically important in all four

Table 9.1 **Presence or Absence of Model Factors in the Four Main Cases**

Model Factors	China	Netherlands	Britain	United States
Frontier Exploitation	Present	Present	Present	Present
Transportation/Communication	Present	Present	Present	Present
Trade	Present	Present	Present	Partially present
Agriculture	Present	Present	Present	Present
Urbanization	Present	Present	Present	Present
Population	Present	Present	Present	Present
Technological Innovation	Present	Present	Present	Present
Energy Transition	Absent	Partially present	Present	Present
Power-Driven Machinery	Absent	Present	Present	Present

cases, but not in exactly the same way. In the Chinese and U.S. cases, the population moved toward and into the frontier in order to exploit its underutilized resources. One could say that this description applies to the Dutch case as well, although in the seventeenth-century Netherlands, the frontier and the state were nearly coterminous because the early settlers had to literally create the state from marshlands. In the British case, the frontier lay on the other side of the Atlantic and could be exploited from some distance as a set of American colonies.

Major improvements in transportation/communication facilitated economic growth in all four cases. How much effort was necessary to create these networks varied. Effort was greatest in the Chinese and U.S. cases and less in the Dutch and British cases. The Dutch had natural waterways within their state's boundaries. The British could rely on the seas surrounding their island, in addition to improved internal waterways and highways, to move goods and information. Transportation and communication developments (or "revolutions") made interactions over long and short distances more feasible and less expensive.

The importance of the trade factor varied considerably among the four cases. Trade was always important to the Dutch and the British. It became more important to the Chinese as their land trade alternatives were eliminated. In the U.S. case, trade was important at the outset but gradually diminished in overall significance. In contrast, agriculture was critical to all states across the board. Only in the Dutch case did this factor operate slightly differently, since the less than ideal soil of the Netherlands encouraged agricultural specialization as opposed to the more typical focus on growing food to feed an expanding population. Nonetheless, an expanding population was present in all four cases, even if the scale of increase varied from case to case. Population growth and shifts to cities forced agriculture to become more efficient and provided labor for nonagricultural pursuits. Similarly, urban demands stimulated or encouraged other processes such as regional specialization, technological innovation, and energy intensification.

Expanding populations and urbanization thus played important roles in expanding the size of domestic markets, which contributed in turn to scalar increases in production. Just how large the scalar increases were depended on the interactions among technological innovation, power-driven machinery, and energy transition. Even without an energy transition, the Song Chinese could still increase iron production considerably. With only a partial energy transition, the Dutch could increase the production of various commodities marketed to foreign consumers. It was the British and the Americans, thanks to their full energy transitions and their possession of technology to make use of those new and cheap energy sources, who experienced the most impressive production increases. Ultimately, the combination of technological innovation, energy shifts, and greatly expanded production led to corporate organizational change that, aside from the companies that operated in the East and West Indies, was absent in the first three cases.

Thus, while the four cases' histories exhibit various differences, their overall stories are not so different. Various places and their populations benefited from access to relatively underdeveloped reserves of one kind or another. Eventually, the stimulus of frontier exploitation wore off as the resources were either exhausted or their extraction was routinized. But until that happened, economic growth benefited from easy and inexpensive access to raw materials. Similarly, trade regimes strongly concentrated around the activities of one state proved highly vulnerable to changing environments and an increase in the number of strong competitors. The Netherlands is perhaps the best example of what can happen to a trading lead that develops while other possible rivals are distracted. In this case, when the rivals, which were larger in population and military capabilities, became less distracted, the trade regime built around the Netherlands eroded and eventually collapsed.

None of the changes detailed so far led automatically to technological leadership. Such leadership depended in part on the nature of the external competition. While lead status was never gained by default, it helped to have few rivals. As more serious rivals emerged, technological leaderships became harder to maintain. While factors such as frontier exploitation, trade success, urbanization, and so on did lead to Smithian economic growth, Schumpeterian growth depended in part on the kinds of bottlenecks societies faced and how local actors responded to them. China had many mouths to feed, and many of its innovations, not surprisingly, were oriented toward expanding the food supply. The Dutch were heavily invested in land reclamation, fishing, and trade. Many of their innovations consequently focused on moving water and shipbuilding technology. The British had a problem with water in coal mines that produced convenient and inexpensive energy to meet urban heating demands in a relatively deforested context. The solution for that problem eventually led to the development of steam engines, but this innovation required some foreknowledge of how pistons worked and another hundred years of experimentation to make it more suitable for other applications.

The Chinese had had similar mining problems but developed different solutions to them before the external threat environment altered their northern urban landscape (and affected its intensified demand for coal). The Dutch certainly had issues with excess water, but their solutions were developed prior to late-seventeenth-century experimentation with piston machinery and made use of the resources that were abundant in the Netherlands—wind and peat, not coal. Thus, there is something to be said for being in the right place at the right time, which is the quickest way to summarize why Britain was the first state to industrialize.

Two features of the four leadership ascendancy stories are most striking. One is that it was neither technological innovation nor energy sources alone that propelled these outstanding states upward in the hierarchy. Rather, such an ascent required an interaction between technological innovation and energy sources that allowed the state to break through the constraints of an agrarian economy. China and the Netherlands both had plenty of technological innovation and access to carbon fuels. But in neither case were carbon fuels and technological innovation brought together in a package that could alter the economy in a fundamental way. In Britain, the interaction between coal and the steam engine transformed the British economy. The same combination transformed the U.S. economy, which went on to harness petroleum to the automobile, electricity to a range of applications, and, eventually, electricity to information technology to produce multiple transformations. Electricity is not a carbon-based fuel, of course, but it is a secondary energy source that historically has been primarily generated by the utilization of carbon-based fuel. One major conclusion that can be drawn from this analysis is that while technological leadership could be gained in the past without marrying innovation to carbon-based fuels, the most successful cases did exactly that. Moreover, those lead states that did adopt carbon-based fuels dominated the world of the past two centuries in ways that earlier system leaders could not have imagined.

The second predominant feature of this analysis is that all four cases demonstrate in different ways that systemic leadership is increasingly predicated on access to abundant and relatively inexpensive carbon fuels. Nonetheless, this factor is not simply a matter of the costs and benefits associated with energy fuels. It is complicated by external interactions that have the potential to alter the lead economy's energy platform.

The loss of northern China to Jin invaders turned Song society in a different energy direction altogether because it deprived the state of ready access to the major coal deposits then being utilized. Consequently the Southern Song lost the demand stimulus generated by increasing urbanization in Kaifeng. China did not lose its technological lead or ability to innovate. Instead, the Southern Song became more oriented toward oceanic trade as it lost access to more traditional land routes. China, however, did probably lose its opportunity to break free of agrarian constraints once its intensifying dependence on coal for heating was undermined by intruders.

In the Netherlands, wind and peat were abundant and inexpensive. A number of industries requiring heat for production purposes could be supported. Coal was available elsewhere but was more expensive and only gradually replaced peat. Still, it does not appear that the Dutch decline was a result of wind and peat becoming less available or more expensive. Rather, the reliance on wind and peat set limits on how much power could be generated and thus what the Dutch economy could do. When the outside world intervened, it pulled the rug out from underneath a Dutch economy that was heavily dependent on external trade. The Netherlands' lead had developed in a context in which it could either defeat its competition (as in the struggle for Baltic trade with the Hanseatic League) or count on its potential competitors to be bogged down by internal warfare. Once France and England resolved their domestic problems, they turned on the Netherlands as the most obvious obstacle to their own ascendancies in the European and world economies. They set out to destroy the Netherlands' lead through protectionism and war. English and French elites admitted that they thought the Dutch had too much power and too much trade. They wanted bigger shares of both, and the most direct way of achieving those aims was to reduce the Dutch share. Ultimately, they succeeded.

The British seemed to do fine as long as coal and steam engines ruled. Yet Britain was also eclipsed, just as the Dutch had been by larger rivals, losing its technological lead to the Germans and Americans. The Germans represented one type of threat; the scale of the U.S. population and domestic marketplace was something else. While Britain's early commitment to petroleum for naval purposes indicated some recognition of what was coming, its reliance on petroleum never resembled its reliance on the inexpensive exploitation of large coal reserves at home. The United States, on the other hand, had relatively inexpensive access to ample reserves of coal and petroleum within its own borders. Similarly, Britain could make interesting automobiles that appealed to niche markets (something the Germans still do well), but the United States refined assembly line procedures to manufacture millions of standardized automobiles that could be sold around the world at fairly cheap prices. For some sixty to seventy years, the U.S. predominance in the car industry most closely linked to petroleum was uncontested. But this predominance was lost partially because U.S. automobiles did not respond very well in terms of size, style, or cost to increased petroleum prices. Product quality issues were also important. While the United States has yet to be eclipsed by a larger rival, its ability to manipulate the interaction between technological innovation and energy sources better than others has clearly diminished. How much of this problem is traceable to higher energy costs can be debated. Less debatable is that the problem became more evident only when energy costs escalated. Moreover, some industries went under or moved abroad in response to the loss of the United States' inexpensive energy/raw material platform.

Still, the inevitability of a lead state being eclipsed by a larger rival is not actually one of our findings. While the Netherlands was eclipsed by larger powers, China was eventually eclipsed as an East Asian technological leader by the smaller Japan within the eastern zone and by Britain outside that zone. And referring to Britain, Supple (1997: 15) observes that

> such a diminution of power could hardly have been avoided. A country with such a small proportion of the world's resources and population cannot indefinitely deal on equal terms with developed nations bigger by anything between 50 and 400 per cent. Indeed, Britain's transformation from imperial power to global innocuousness turned out to be a relatively and (surprisingly) sluggish process. And it is perhaps the slow pace, rather than the rapidity, of Britain's decline on the world scene that is the more interesting historical problem.

In some respects, much the same could be said about the Dutch. The verdict is still out on the fate of the United States. Two out of three does not quite constitute a pattern.

If we add Genoa, Venice, and Portugal to the mix, we can see that Venice did not eclipse Genoa in the fourteenth century but barely defeated it once it had been weakened. Portugal had a larger population than Venice in the fifteenth century but was not as wealthy. The Portuguese coup at Venice's expense was more of an end run than an eclipse. The Dutch had a larger population than Portugal, but by the time the Netherlands supplanted Portugal as the Western technological leader, Portugal was technically part of the even larger Spanish Empire. Then there is the problem of mixing technological leaders that specialized in naval or maritime activities and commerce with those technological leaders that also generated substantial industrial production. Suffice it to say that eclipses in terms of relative size have definitely occurred, but not in every case.

More interesting is the question raised by what Mokyr (1993) calls "Cardwell's law" and others (Swart, 1974: 47–48) have referenced in terms of Jan Romein's "law of interrupted progress." The more general Romein argument is that lead economies will eventually encounter barriers to further growth that will make it less probable that they will be responsible for the next breakthrough; instead, another economy with fewer obstacles will be more likely to spearhead such a breakthrough. Romein's law seems more fitting for our earlier cases. Northern Song China had relatively easy access to coal, but Southern Song China did not. The Dutch had easy and inexpensive access to peat and wind but not coal. Britain had good access to cheap coal but not petroleum. Britain might well have been eclipsed by the United States and Germany in a world where King Coal still prevailed, but its transition to petroleum was also hampered by adjustment and financial problems. Along these lines, we can ask: Is a United States with plenty of coal and natural gas and an unexpected increased supply of petroleum courtesy of fracking the most likely leader of a movement to eliminate dependence on fossil fuels? In this case, the Cardwell argument, which stipulates that groups that anticipate losses from a new innovation becoming successful will lobby political decision-makers to suppress or limit the innovation, seems to provide the better fit. Of course, one could say something similar about America's Chinese rival, given its own heavy dependence on coal and foreign oil, albeit for different reasons.[2]

Yet it is also clear that inexpensive and abundant energy was characteristic of the technological leaders that produced industrial goods. Therefore, it might be possible to restate the "law" to read that some economies are able to do well within one energy regime but can be seriously handicapped if or when the regime shifts. We might go even further and say that system leaders rise on a resource foundation that includes access to inexpensive energy. When that access is blocked, interfered with, or terminated, the system leader's continued functioning will be jeopardized, and it may or may not be able to make the transition to whatever comes next. But even if it does survive the transition, its capability foundation for systemic leadership may be seriously undermined in the process.

It is not so much that a given type of energy source is deterministic at any point in time. The energy sources upon which system leaders have relied often could have been replaced by something else up to a point. Steam engines, for instance, could have run on coal or wood. Automobiles could have run on steam, electricity, or petroleum. But the increased scale of production output associated with the Netherlands to some extent but especially Britain and the United States depended on these states' access to relatively cheap and plentiful energy. Without the ability to produce large quantities of the commodities on which their economies were based, their industrial preeminence would have been far less likely. The sheer power and reliability associated with fossil fuels have also been difficult to match. Britain did not have enough wood and would have been hard-pressed to acquire the wood equivalent of the coal it burned to produce its commodity mix in the nineteenth century. In the early twentieth century, automobiles and trucks simply operated better when they used petroleum than they did when they used alternative fuels. That may change, but airplanes still require petroleum in the form of jet fuel and may continue to do so long after automobiles have been converted to some other energy source. Similarly, various fuels can be used to generate electricity, but breaking free of coal or natural gas dependence has proven neither easy nor inexpensive. Renewables have certainly become less expensive, but not necessarily less expensive than fossil fuels. Nor have they yet become as reliable. Fossil fuels can work in the dark, unlike solar energy, and when the wind does not blow. It is also generally easier to store carbon energy than it is noncarbon energy.

These problems will probably be fixed in the future. The coal and steam engine combination was not very efficient at the outset either, and it took a century to make steam engines capable of being diffused beyond coal mines. Yet the point remains that there were very strong reasons to commit to fossil fuels once the Industrial Revolution was underway. It might have been possible to carry out some type of industrial revolution without relying on carbon fuels, but any such attempt would have encountered major constraints on heat transformation and production scale fairly quickly.

Only now is it apparent that there are strong reasons to move away from the consumption of these once-essential fossil fuels in great quantities. Initially, the impetus for this move was the probability of supply problems. The availability of carbon-based fuels is finite, which means that their relatively inexpensive nature depends to some extent on how much coal, petroleum, and natural gas can be readily and economically extracted in the future. While reserves have expanded with new discoveries, their size is unlikely to keep pace with fossil fuel consumption. At some point, petroleum extraction will have peaked, even if the peak keeps getting pushed further ahead in time.

It will take longer to run out of coal and natural gas.[3] But in the meantime supply questions have been pushed aside by alarm about the damage carbon-based fuels do to the environment and climate. The question is not so much whether we can find enough fossil fuels, but whether we can continue to use them without seriously damaging our ability to inhabit the planet. Nor is it really much of a question any more. What is not clear is how much future damage will be sustained by a continuing reliance on the fuels that made industrialization possible but have also contributed mightily to global warming.

A climate change crisis appears to be emerging. It requires some form of coordinated response, which does not usually emerge without leadership. We have sought to show that the economic and technological innovations of the past have led to the present climate change situation by breaking through the constraints of the agrarian economy. In other words, many of the same processes that have led to global warming were also closely linked to the emergence of states characterized by technological centrality and systemic leadership. It is now up to the systemic leadership to steer such a coordinated response in order to adapt to living on a planet undergoing environmental transition. We turn to this problem in the next four chapters.

PART III

THE FUTURE

10

Energy, Technology, and (Possibly) the Nature of the Next World Economy Upswing

Neither technological innovation nor long-term economic growth are continuous. Their development tends to be intermittent and highly concentrated in space and time. One state tends to dominate new innovations, which are diffused unevenly to other economies capable of absorbing new ways of doing things. Given this tendency for fluctuations in innovation and growth, it is only natural to ask what the next best thing might be. Assuming the historical pattern persists, what industries might be the center of a new round of radical innovations and in what industries are such innovations likely to emerge first?

The candidates for industries that will be the next major carriers of innovation are several and relatively well known, in part because they already exist. New innovations must first go through a start-up phase before being sufficiently developed to produce strong economic growth in a second, peak-growth phase. Candidates for growth-surge industries include information technology, biotechnology, nanotechnology, robotics, health, renewable energy, and environmental deterioration abatement. These fields overlap in various ways, and all of them could well contribute something significant to future major changes in the world economy. Indeed, if they all come into play more or less simultaneously, we can look forward to a massive upswing in economic growth.

We do not have an argument against any of these candidates other than noting that a transition to renewable energy seems a long way off—perhaps as long as the end of the current century, according to most forecasts. Instead, we simply make a case for another candidate with strong potential in the next few decades. Significant reductions in carbon emissions are needed to head off even greater escalation of global warming. One plausible interim strategy for achieving significant reductions involves a combination of increased fossil fuel efficiency, the use of decarbonized or green fuels to make electricity, and the electrification of transportation. The technology needed for these activities is not yet fully developed but appears to be emerging. Furthermore, the costs of such technology are quite high and will need to come down substantially to make these innovations fully feasible. But if these innovations can be applied on a great enough scale and soon enough, it just might be possible to limit the extent to which global warming makes the planet uninhabitable. Thus the incentives to adopt these innovations are high and possibly high enough to overcome the many types of resistance to their application. A revolution in making electricity and electrifying transportation conceivably could have a transformative effect on the world economy and its growth prospects.

In the last several upswings of the world economy, core innovations paired new engines with new fuels: steam engines with coal, internal combustion engines with petroleum, and numerous electricity-driven applications with fossil fuels. In each instance, the new fuels initially were inexpensive, abundant, and incredibly powerful but also damaging to the climate and environment. Now we need to develop engines that can run using decarbonized fuels to minimize CO_2 emissions.

We first review the evidence for global warming and its consequences. Next, we examine some of the possible policy responses to this issue. Finally, we relate macro-level fluctuations in world economic growth to policy responses focusing largely on electricity and transportation. Throughout, we emphasize the extent to which our observations are speculative. No one knows how bad global warming will become or when. Whether efforts to limit CO_2 emissions will suffice to limit the adverse consequences of global warming is also extremely difficult to say. It is equally unclear whether and when such attempts will become sufficiently serious to have a significant impact. Given the known unknowns, it may be simply wrong to contemplate an upswing in economic growth—but hope springs eternal.

Global Warming

The industrialization that allowed states to break through the constraints of the agrarian age has clearly come at a price. The increased power associated with the use of carbon fuels for numerous economic applications has increased the risk of human damage to the environment and possibly even human survival. Carbon dioxide emissions appear to be the major problem. As they accumulate in the atmosphere, they lead to changes in temperature, among other things. Figure 10.1 plots this relationship. The correlation between these variables is not perfect, but it is extremely close and difficult to overlook. Consequently, more carbon dioxide emissions mean warmer temperatures. Human activities are increasing the

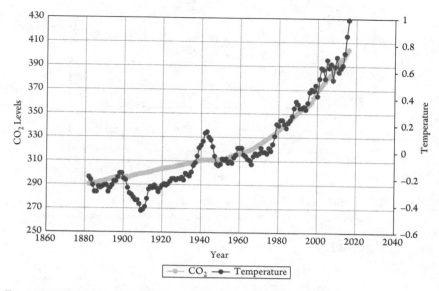

Figure 10.1 Global Temperature and CO_2 Levels, 1882–2016 Source: Etheridge et al. (2002).

millions of tons of carbon dioxide released into the atmosphere, about 80 percent of which is due to the use of fossil fuels. Therefore, we have already seen some temperature increase (less than one degree Celsius) and can anticipate more increases—perhaps in the range of two to six degrees C—depending in part on how much more carbon dioxide is emitted. The greater the future rise of carbon dioxide, the greater is the risk to the environment and the people who inhabit it.

Skeptics who claim that correlation does not demonstrate causation are correct methodologically, but it is important to note that in this case, the relationship between carbon dioxide emissions and temperature appears to be quite strong, expecially if viewed over a longer period. Figure 10.2 looks at the last millennium, precisely the period chapters 5 through 8 examine. The analysis of air bubbles in ice core samples indicates little rise in carbon dioxide prior to the second half of the eighteenth century, with an accelerating rise from the second half of the nineteenth century on. If we compare this development with the timing of the increase in carbon dioxide emissions displayed in figure 10.3, the close relationship seems all the more clear cut.

We can be also a bit more precise about the nature of the risk given the large number of quantitative forecasts that have been made. Such forecasts are hardly infallible: they can only say what might happen if we alter the values of known variables, and they cannot capture unknown variables, which include how people will respond to environmental problems.[1] Nonetheless, the risks of

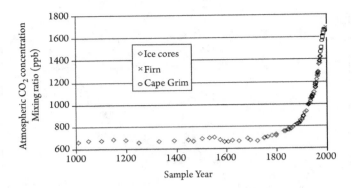

Figure 10.2 Carbon Dioxide Emissions Revealed in Air Bubbles, 1000–
2000. Note: Samples were drawn from ice cores and firn in Antarctica, with air samples from Cape
Grim, Australia.
Source: Etheridge et al. (2002).

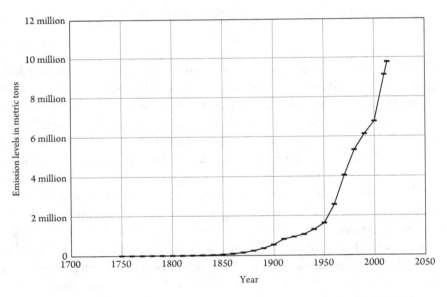

Figure 10.3 World CO_2 Emissions, 1750–2013. Source: Calculated using data from Boden,
Andres, and Marland (2016).

which we are already aware are manifold. Table 10.1 lists a number of them. The
first six entries are changes expected to vary linearly with the amount of temperature change. Increases in rain and storms along with decreases in ice, river
levels, and food crops will vary according to the extent of the global warming
experienced. Other problems are likely to be experienced above certain minimal

Table 10.1 **Global Warming Effects**

Estimates of Effects Per Degree Centigrade of Global Warming

5–10% change in precipitation

3–10% increase in heavy rainfall

1–4% increase in average intensity of tropical cyclones

5–10% change in streamflow of many river basins

5–15% yield reduction of a number of crops

c. 15% decrease in the extent of annually averaged Arctic and Antarctic sea ice

Estimates of More General Effects of Global Warming

Increases in the number of exceptionally warm summers (90% for about 3 degrees C)

200–400% increase in wildfire area burned

Increased coral bleaching and net erosion of coral reefs

0.5–1.0 meter sea level rise in 2100 (if 3–4 degree C increase), with associated increases in number of people at risk from coastal flooding and wetland and dryland losses

Decreased snowpack

Shrinking permafrost in Northern Hemisphere

Slowdown of Atlantic Ocean circulation, leading to less warmth in Northern Hemisphere

Increased ocean acidification

Increased number of maritime dead zones

Shifts in geographic range and frequency of agricultural growth, with associated increase in crop pests, weeds, and diseases leading to increased food prices (if warming above 2 degrees C and doubling if 5 degrees C) and increase in malnourishment

Increases in species shifts and die-offs

Increased demand for air-conditioning and decreased demand for heating

Increased risk of illness and death

Shifts in timing and geographical range of allergies and vector-borne diseases

Shifts and stress in forest processes

Source: Extracted from National Research Council (2011).

temperature increases. Warmer summers, more wildfires, more damage to the oceans, higher sea levels, less snow, and more species die-offs are some of the likely outcomes. So, too, are shifts in areas that can grow crops and significant increases in the costs of the food that will be grown. Both people and crops will be impacted by increased risk of various diseases and illnesses. All in all, the future does not look very attractive. It will be increasingly uncomfortable for some and deadly for many others.

It is too late to head off many of these effects. They are already occurring. Even if all carbon dioxide emissions were to cease immediately, it would still take decades, if not centuries, to deal with the greenhouse gases already in the atmosphere. The best that can be hoped for is that the severity of these effects can be constrained. The two degree Celsius increase that so many of the early proposals aimed at ameliorating seems pretty much guaranteed at this time. Now the question is: How much higher will the temperature rise—three degrees? Four degrees? Six degrees? Presumably, the answer will depend in part on how successful attempts are to curb emissions, the extent to which the emissions are curbed, and when that emission curbing begins.

Rojey (2009: 32), for example, argues that the increase might be limited to the two degree Celsius target if current CO_2 emissions are cut by 50 percent by 2050. If less developed countries (LDCs) are allowed to proceed with economic development involving relatively high CO_2 emissions, developed countries will have to cut their emissions to one-fourth of their current rate. Therein lie two of the major roadblocks to taking effective action. First, minor adjustments are not going to make much difference. Major adjustments are anathema to LDCs, as they tend to mean freezing their opportunities to develop economically. After all, these countries reason, the developed economies created the problem. Let them fix it at their own expense. However, the second roadblock is that developed countries are no more eager to sacrifice their economic growth prospects than anyone else.

The third major roadblock to doing something meaningful about global warming is that, ultimately, such solutions require states and their economies to effectively cut their reliance on carbon fuels. Carbon fuels—petroleum, natural gas, and coal—are not responsible for all CO_2 emissions, but they are their principal source. Making the transition away from carbon fuels will not be easy, nor will it occur anytime soon. One major reason is that the world has a high dependence on these fuels. Table 10.2 summarizes the world's and selected actors' energy mix. In 2015, carbon fuels generated about 86 percent of the world's energy. Developed countries tend to be a little less dependent on them (81.7 percent) than less developed countries (89.1 percent).

Not surprisingly, the two states that consumed the most energy in 2015, China and the United States, also produced the most CO_2 emissions.[2] As is shown in figure 10.4, which also contains data on the next two largest emitters

Table 10.2 **Energy Mix, World and Selected Actors, 2015 (million tons oil equivalent)**

	Oil	Coal	Gas	Carbon	Nuclear	Hydro-electric	Renewables	Total
World	4,331.3 (32.9%)	3,839.2 (29.2%)	3,135.2 (23.8%)	(85.9%)	583.1 (4.4%)	892.9 (6.8%)	364.9 (2.8%)	13,147.3
OECD	2,056.4 (37.4%)	979.2 (17.8%)	1,458.9 (26.5%)	(81.7%)	447.6 (8.1%)	314.6 (5.7%)	246.3 (4.5%)	5,503.1
Non-OECD	2,274.9 (29.8%)	2,860.7 (37.4%)	1,676.3 (21.9%)	(89.1%)	135.5 (1.7%)	578.3 (7.6%)	118.5 (1.6%)	7,644.2
United States	851.6 (37.3%)	396.3 (17.4%)	713.6 (23.6%)	(78.3%)	189.9 (8.3%)	57.4 (2.5%)	71.7 (3.1%)	2,280.6
China	559.7 (18.6%)	1920.4 (63.7%)	177.6 (5.9%)	(88.2%)	38.6 (1.3%)	254.9 (8.5%)	62.7 (2.1%)	3014.0
India	195.5 (27.9%)	407.2 (58.1%)	45.5 (6.5%)	(92.5%)	8.6 (1.2%)	28.1 (4.0%)	15.5 (2.2%)	700.5

Source: Based on data from British Petroleum (2016).

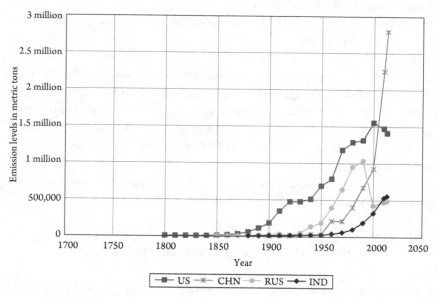

Figure 10.4 CO_2 Emissions of Selected Actors, 1750–2013. Source: Based on data from Boden, Andres, and Marland (2016).

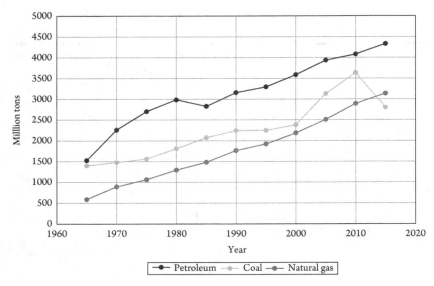

Figure 10.5 Carbon Fuel Consumption, 1965–2015. Source: Based on data from British Petroleum (2016).

(India and Russia), China surpassed the United States in emissions in 2011. In part, this was due to China's reliance on coal, the worse CO_2 offender of the three carbon-based fuels. Coal consumption comprised 66 percent of China's energy usage in 2014, compared to less than 20 percent of the United States' energy usage. It may also be that the U.S. emission rate has peaked while China's has not. (Nor, likely, has India's.)

Yet the problem cannot be reduced solely to China and the United States. The real problem is that petroleum and natural gas consumption are increasing, not decreasing, as shown in figure 10.5. Coal consumption had been increasing, but its trajectory, at least in the Northern Hemisphere, has been altered by natural gas substitution. Figures 10.6 and 10.7 do suggest that the carbon fuel increases are due to non-OECD consumption of petroleum and coal, led by China.[3] But not all developed countries, including the United States, are cutting back on their reliance on coal and petroleum all that quickly, even though Figure 10.8 shows that OECD natural gas consumption is increasing.

Possible Policy Responses and Implications

Obviously, the problem of carbon emissions has multiple facets. Developed countries are not cutting back on their carbon habits very rapidly. Less developed countries are increasing their carbon consumption in hopes of achieving

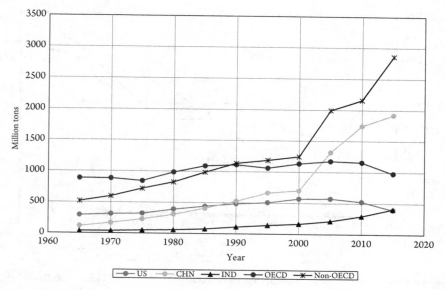

Figure 10.6 Coal Consumption by Selected Actors, 1965–2015. Source: Based on data from British Petroleum (2016).

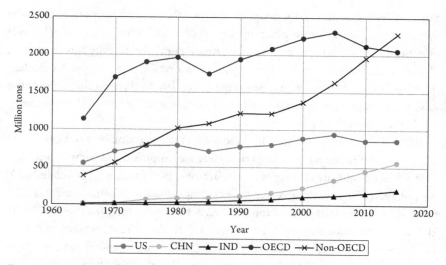

Figure 10.7 Petroleum Consumption by Selected Actors, 1965–2015. Source: Based on data from British Petroleum (2016).

developed status. Since there is no collective movement to cut reliance on carbon fuels, there is much less likelihood that CO_2 emissions will be reduced any time soon. Global warming effects will have to become more acute before any concerted action can be anticipated. The incentives for taking action certainly exist,

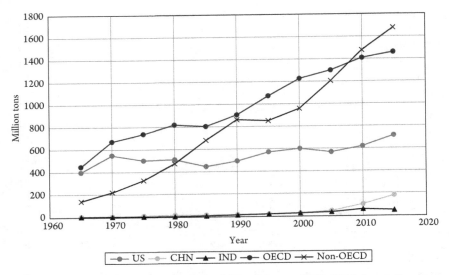

Figure 10.8 Natural Gas Consumption by Selected Actors, 1965–2015. Source: Based on data from British Petroleum (2016).

but they have not been fully grasped. The question is: Just how acute must the symptoms of global warming become before concrete action is taken? Whatever else they may have achieved, none of the multilateral, Kyoto-type agreements on climate change responses have managed to reduce CO_2 emissions. A corollary question is thus: Will such concrete steps be too late to stave off the worst of the possible temperature increases and their consequent impacts? Unfortunately, neither question can be answered at this point.

What we can do in the interim is to look at some numbers associated with International Energy Agency scenarios. Here we simplify these complex pictures as much as possible by looking at one indicator—how much energy-related CO_2 is expected to be emitted given certain assumptions about behavior. Table 10.3 provides 2013 emissions data for selected actors and compares them to 2020, 2025, and 2030 expectations depending on how radical the steps taken to reduce emissions are. The "INDC scenario" (INDC refers to "intended nationally de-termined contributions") is based on country pledges submitted in advance of the Paris COP21 meeting held in December 2015. The pledges are incomplete and, of course, are only promises to try to achieve certain mitigation goals (by, e.g., improving fuel efficiency, taxing the use of carbon-based fuels, or reducing the use of coal). The "450 scenario," in contrast, is predicated on what it might take to keep temperatures from exceeding two degrees C in the future.

Table 10.3 suggests that if current pledges to reduce carbon constitute all that states are willing to do, CO_2 emissions will rise slowly, but not exponentially, in

Table 10.3 **Energy-Related CO₂ Expectations in Two Scenarios (Gigatons)**

	INDC Scenario				450 Scenario		
	2013	2020	2025	2030	2020	2025	2030
World	32.2	33.9	34.3	34.8	32.4	29.6	25.6
U.S.	5.2	5.0	4.4	4.0	4.8	3.9	3.0
EU	3.4	3.0	2.8	2.4	2.9	2.4	2.0
Japan	1.2	1.0	0.9	0.9	0.9	0.8	0.6
China	8.7	9.6	9.9	10.1	9.1	8.0	6.4
India	1.9	2.3	2.6	3.0	2.2	2.3	2.3

Source: International Energy Agency (2015: 62). The INDC (intended nationally determined contributions) scenario is based on country pledges submitted in advance of the December 2015 Paris COP21 meeting. The 450 scenario is predicated on what it might take to keep temperatures from exceeding 2 degrees C in the future.

the next decade and a half. If the 450 scenario comes to pass, we will see a 20 percent decrease in world emissions by 2030. The point is that current policies, both those that have been put into action and those that have only been proposed, will be insufficient to head off increases of more than two degrees C. Leading emitters will either need to do more or face the prospects of a greatly warmer environment. The 2015 Paris Agreement is a step in the right direction, but only a step.[4]

A more aggressive scenario that also is more specific about what needs to be done is advanced in Williams et al. (2012). The Williams team was tasked with modeling a scenario that would lead to California meeting legislative targets for emissions reductions. Admittedly, California is only one of fifty U.S. states, but taken in isolation it is the world's fifth-largest economy and twelfth-largest CO₂ emitter, which puts it in the same league as Japan and the European Union.[5] More importantly, California has been in the vanguard of U.S. efforts to deal with carbon emissions and pollution, with Los Angeles being ground zero for the negative effects of automobile pollution. According to state law, California must cut its CO₂ emissions to 1990 levels by 2030 and ensure that its 2050 levels are no more than 80 percent of the 1990 levels. The scenario constructed by the Williams team would allow California to meet or exceed the 450 scenario mentioned in table 10.3.[6] Keep in mind that the entire planet needs to adhere to the 450 scenario to correspond to a 2 degree C increase but one must start somewhere.

Without going into every detail, the bulk of the plan focuses on energy efficiency, electricity decarbonization, and electrification of transportation and other sectors.[7] In brief, the scenario replaces the state's reliance on petroleum and natural gas with reliance on electricity generated by low-carbon fuels, as indicated in table 10.4. Most automobiles (75 percent) are switched to electrification. Most electricity (90 percent) is generated by decarbonized fuels. Renewables constitute somewhat less than a third of the fuel mix, partially based on the assumption that greater reliance on this type of energy is simply not technologically feasible for California by 2050.

If no mitigation takes place, the expectation is that CO_2 emissions associated with the use of energy fuels will increase by 69 percent by 2050. If the proposed mitigation does occur, energy fuel emissions could be reduced to about 16 percent of 2010 levels. In contrast, the 450 scenario envisages less reduction of carbon fuel usage and less emissions reduction in the same time period. Yet the

Table 10.4 **California's Primary Energy Consumption by Fuel Types in the Williams et al. (2012) Scenario for Cutting Greenhouse Emissions (exajoules)**

	2010	*Forecasted 2050 Without Mitigation*	*Forecasted 2050 with Mitigation*
Direct Fuel Use			
Natural Gas	2.73 (31%)	3.40 (25%)	0.38 (6%)
Gasoline	2.09 (24%)	4.36 (32%)	0.13 (2%)
Diesel	0.73 (8%)	1.23 (9%)	0.39 (6%)
Jet Fuel	0.04 (0%)	1.0 (0%)	0.04 (1%)
Biomethane and Biofuels	0.00 (0%)	1.0 (0%)	0.73 (11%)
Total Direct Fuel Use	5.59 (64%)	9.06 (67%)	1.67 (25%)
Electricity Generation			
Natural Gas (Non-CCS)	1.45 (17%)	2.90 (21%)	0.01 (0%)
Coal (Non-CCS)	0.49 (6%)	0.49 (4%)	0.00 (0%)
Fossil Fuel with CCS	0.00 (0%)	0.00 (0%)	2.18 (32%)
Nuclear	0.30 (3%)	0.26 (2%)	0.74 (11%)
Renewables and Hydroelectricity	0.71 (8%)	0.66 (5%)	2.04 (30%)
Other	0.16 (2%)	0.18 (1%)	0.16 (2%)
Total All Fuel Types	8.70 (100%)	13.56 (100%)	6.81 (100%)

Source: Williams et al. (2012: 56). CCS = carbon capture and storage.

California scenario is predicated on technology that, while already in existence, has not yet been commercialized. It does assume considerable gains in energy efficiency, but its main targets are easy to recognize and conceptualize—the decarbonization of transportation and electricity generation—if not easy to attain.[8]

Meanwhile, CO_2 levels continue to rise. Figure 10.9 plots U.S. governmental data on mean CO_2 levels for the recent past. In the past fifty years, CO_2 levels have risen more than 25 percent. Still this raises an unsettling point. If the current rate of increase continues, the CO_2 level will surpass 500 parts per million (ppm) by 2065. Of course, the rate of increase could also accelerate, given anticipated population increases and rising energy demands from developing countries. Furthermore, relatively weak efforts to reduce carbon emissions and isolated successes in states like Denmark and Germany may not end up having much impact on the rate of increase. If that is true, the goals of constraining the temperature increase to two degrees C and limiting the emissions level to 450 ppm may already be obsolete, meaning that our focus should instead be working on staving off even higher temperature and CO_2 increases.

An example of such a focus is suggested by a table constructed by Mark Lynas in 2008 and reproduced with slight modification in Table 10.5. The first two columns differentiate future temperature changes. Column three specifies what sort of policy changes are needed to hold the line at the temperature change indicated. Column four specifies the corresponding maximum CO_2 level. Table 10.5

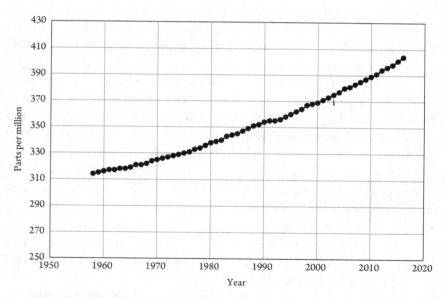

Figure 10.9 Atmospheric CO_2 Levels at Mauna Loa Observatory. Source: Data from CO_2Earth (2017).

Table 10.5 **The Lynas Estimated Schedule for Alternative Global Warming Futures**

Degree Change	Temperature Change	Action Needed	CO_2 Target
1	0.1–1.0 degrees C	Avoidance probably not possible	350 ppm (2008 level = 380 ppm)
2	1.1–2.0 degrees C	Peak global emissions by 2015	400 ppm
3	2.1–3.0 degrees C	Peak global emissions by 2030	450 ppm
4	3.1–4.0 degrees C	Peak global emissions by 2050	550 ppm
5	4.1–5.0 degrees C	Allow constantly rising emissions	650 ppm
6	5.1–6.0 degrees C	Allow very high emissions	800 ppm

Source: Based on Lynas (2008: 279).

is, of course, an estimate. It is not carved in stone that things will come to pass in exactly this way. However, in 2008, Lynas knew that we had passed the 350 ppm target, which meant that a one degree C change was unlikely to be avoided. Now we have passed the threshold associated with the second row (a two degree future change at 400 ppm), which implies that a two degree change is probably not avoidable. It is also clear that global emissions will not peak any time soon. Barring radical changes in energy consumption and policies, we appear to be on track to attain an emissions level of 450 ppm by 2040. Thus, the impacts of carbon-driven climate change will only be that much more severe in the future.

The possibility for more radical approaches is not entirely absent in the current period. Much will depend on what the two leading emitters agree to do. If the preferences of China and the United States cannot be harnessed to work in similar directions, fewer changes around the world can be expected. The European Union, which has led climate mitigation efforts in the past, cannot accomplish a great deal on its own, any more than California can. As table 10.3 shows, EU emissions amount to less than 11 percent of the world's total emissions. Adding the U.S., Chinese, and EU emission shares together, however, amounts to about 53 percent of the 2013 total—a very strong proportion of current CO_2 emissions.

The European Union has had some successes in decarbonizing, and it appears prepared to do more. The United States, once a leader on pollution and environmental degradation issues several decades ago, currently seems much less inclined to take a radical approach to climate problems, especially after the 2016 elections which placed climate change deniers in power. Today, multiple players in and out of government are working against strong responses to global warming. Global warming skeptics occupy key congressional posts, and the government maintains a heavy commitment to gas-powered automobiles and the oil industry in general. Furthermore, corporate lobbyists ensure that the interests of the wealthiest multinational corporations, of which a number are linked closely to the consumption of carbon fuels (e.g., petroleum and automobile producers, to say nothing of coal producers, which are active in a large number of U.S. states), are well represented in Washington. Barring spectacular technological breakthroughs, U.S. decision-makers appear to be anticipating a long and exceedingly slow transition to renewables.[9] China has also led opposition to mitigation efforts that spread the burden of reduced fossil fuel dependence throughout the whole world, arguing that since developed states brought about the problem, they should bear the main responsibility for fixing it. Its motto was develop now and worry about the environment later. Let OECD growth decline while less developed countries bring their economies into the modern, industrialized world.

Yet China's position may be shifting considerably. Extensive industrial pollution is believed to be killing more than a million Chinese people every year, and the state's last two five-year plans have featured significant efforts to reduce CO_2 emissions. Boyd (2012), based on a reading of government documents and the writings of Chinese energy scholars, argues that three things have changed. First, the first decade of the 2000s witnessed a strong increase in energy consumption but was also characterized by energy rationing, blackouts, and a greater recognition of the insecurity of energy supplies. Second, it became clear that there will be major costs for future economic growth in the long term if environmental degradation is ignored in the short term. Third, a stronger appreciation of the likelihood that renewable energy sources are the wave of the future, perhaps initiating a transition on the scale of the industrial and information revolutions, began to develop. If that is the case, why shouldn't China seize the leadership of this movement toward an energy transition?[10]

Boyd (2012: 12) contends that China's opportunity to assume energy transition leadership is widely accepted both among Chinese energy scholars and within the central government. If that consensus translates into Chinese policy, some willingness to accept greater restraints on future economic growth may be conceivable. China has become a leader in investing in renewables (see chapter 12). The logic that leading the way into the next energy regime is likely to be politically and economically advantageous is hardly alien to our own arguments. Perhaps the most beneficial outcome for the planet as a whole would be an intensive race between China and the United States to see which economy could become greener faster. Regardless of who actually won the race, the planet's environment would be a net beneficiary. Sadly, the evidence that a race of this sort will develop is lacking.

Development Surges

As we suggested earlier (chapter 2), technological innovation tends to cluster in time and space—and all the more so since Britain's industrial breakthrough. Table 10.6 tries to bring some of the more recent manifestations of these processes together in a relatively compressed fashion. We can argue about how far back in time these relationships have existed, but there is a fair amount of acceptance for the notion that technology, energy, and systemic leadership have become increasingly intertwined since the late eighteenth century.[11] Long-term economic growth has moved forward unevenly in clusters of radical change, followed by periods of more routine progress or worse (recession and depression).

Perez (2007) aptly calls the periods of radical change "development surges." Others refer to them as "Kondratieff" or "Schumpeterian cycles." But there are several problems with the "cycle" terminology. It instinctively raises the hackles of analysts trained to regard talk of cycles as dubious or requiring strict periodicity. Growth processes, at least as far as technological change goes, do not really operate in a binary fashion, rising and falling in exclusive sequence. Rather, earlier periods of fundamental change continue to influence subsequent periods, both because earlier innovations do not necessarily disappear and because the transformations wrought proceed so unevenly. The production of an innovation is pioneered in one place and then slowly diffused to other places, but not everywhere. At any given point in time, different parts of the world may be experiencing different development surges. Some parts of the world will be pioneering, while other parts will be gradually catching up with earlier innovations.[12] For that reason, the second column in table 10.6 makes no effort to provide precise dates. Instead, the crude dates that are supplied refer to periods of rapid growth in the more economically developed parts of the world.

Surges tend to be followed by more surges (or at least they have so far).[13] What differentiates them are the nature of the technologies that are introduced, their fuel requirements, and the increasing complexity of the world economy. Some

Table 10.6 **Development Surges, Technology, and Energy Changes**

Development Surge	Rough Timing	Technologies	Prime Movers	Primary Energy
1	Late 18th–early 19th centuries	Iron, textiles	Stationary steam engines	Coal, wind, water
2	Mid-19th century	Iron, mechanical equipment, steam engines, telegraph	Mobile steam engines	Coal
3	Late 19th–early 20th centuries	Steel, electricity, chemicals, telephone, radio	Steam turbines/ internal combustion engines	Coal, crude oil, electricity
4	Mid–late 20th century	Automobile, petrochemicals, television, jet airplanes, airlines	Gas turbines	Coal, crude oil, electricity, natural gas
5	Late 20th–early 21st centuries	Computers, telecommunications		Coal, crude oil, electricity, natural gas, nuclear, solar, wind
6?	?	?	?	?

Sources: Based on Smil (1994), Modelski and Thompson (1996), McNeill and McNeill (2003), and Perez (2007).

surges emphasize transportation innovations (moving people and commodities faster and in greater bulk), while others stress new ways to communicate.[14] The degree of revolution in how products are manufactured also varies over time. Changes in textile production were so radical that few other parts of the world could compete with the initial innovator (Britain). Similarly, the assembly line process ushered in by automobile production changed industrial production costs tremendously, and not just for automobiles.

Yet one of the primary reasons one surge follows another is that innovators have strong incentives to improve on the products of preceding surges. The marriage of coal and steam engines worked well, but hardly perfectly. Internal combustion engines and petroleum represented an improvement because they could generate more power more efficiently and their byproducts appeared to be less toxic to humans. That perception proved to be incorrect. The consumption of any or all carbon-based emissions, it turns out, is hazardous to human health, with large concentrations of CO_2 emissions producing major environmental effects.

Similarly, the automobile replaced the horse-drawn carriage, which had become a dirty and toxic transportation solution in its own right, inundating large cities with as much as a million tons of manure each year. As Kirsch (2000: 23) notes, new technological systems start out clean and become increasingly dirty as they expand in scale. Automobiles replaced one inefficient and smelly system that had grown too big, and it was not until a large number of automobiles were on the road that it became clear that gasoline-powered vehicles would also require replacement.

Thus a prime candidate for the next developmental surge involves substitutions for the coal- and petroleum-driven innovations of the past several surges. Presumably, this next cluster of technological innovation will revolve around reducing CO_2 emissions in a major way. Such reductions will most practically involve transforming coal, petroleum, and natural gas into greener energy sources, relying more on electricity and renewable sources of energy, and reducing considerably the reliance of transportation vehicles on carbon fuels.[15]

Suggesting that these particular technological innovations are logically next in line hardly guarantees that they will produce the next surge. However, they are currently already emerging. For instance, many new models of electric cars are coming on the market, making it possible to use less harmful carbon-based fuels and put more harmful ones aside. That does not mean that adoption of new models is extensive. It is not. Yet renewable sources of energy are becoming more commonplace as their costs decline. Improvements in electric cars, batteries, and electrical storage devices are in evidence.[16] If the next surge is waiting in the wings, we should be seeing a phase of experimentation and halting trials of the new technology before it moves center stage.

Electric vehicles provide one critical indicator. Although these vehicles technically have been around since the 1830s and once competed with ICE vehicles for adoption before losing the competition in the 1920s, they are now back, bidding once again to replace gasoline-based transportation. The problems of this innovation are clear cut.[17] Electric vehicles need to have a range similar to gasoline vehicles (about three hundred miles), be competitively priced, and have ready access to recharging stations. Currently, their range is at best around two hundred miles, but it is moving toward what gasoline vehicles can claim.[18] Battery prices, one of the principal expenses of electric vehicles, are falling. Development of the recharging infrastructure is lagging everywhere and has some way to go if we are to make a successful transition to electrification. However, electric vehicles have so far only constituted a very small proportion of vehicle production—less than 3 percent of U.S. production in the first decade and a half of the twenty-first century. If forecasts are correct, that situation is about to change.

Forecasts, especially those involving electric vehicles, need to be taken with the proverbial grain of salt. They tend to be produced by people who very much want their predictions to come true. Still, their claims are worth considering in part because they do not seem all that implausible. One forecast predicts that electric vehicles will account for 7 percent of world vehicle production by 2020.[19] Another predicts that the worldwide electric battery–electric vehicle value chain could be worth roughly 390 billion U.S. dollars by 2020.[20] A third suggests that ICE-driven vehicles will account for only 40 percent of world production by 2035.[21] The Chinese government anticipates that electric vehicle sales in China in 2020 will be six times higher than 2015 sales (PWC 2017: 5).[22]

Whether these numbers hold up remains to be seen. There has been substantial commitment to, and investment in, older technology that will not evaporate overnight. However, the new technology, as noted, still needs more work to make electric vehicles attractive to consumers. Lower gas prices in recent years are not helping either. Nonetheless, the sample of forecasts provides some hint of the possible revolutionary changes coming to a world vehicle fleet that, even long before China and India reach their peak fleet potential, currently numbers more than 1 billion units.

What is far less clear is who will dominate this surge, should it be realized in the next few decades.[23] The historical pattern has been that one economy predominates in bringing these surges to fruition. Objectively, China has the most incentive to develop ways to make coal less damaging to the climate and environment. Its dependence on coal is declining, but this fuel remains its principal energy source. Coal is also China's main CO_2 emitter (about 80 percent of emissions) and is estimated to be responsible for 50 to 60 percent of its pollution. Finally, China has been an early leader in making coal cleaner.[24]

In electrifying the transportation sector, the United States, largely thanks to California's strenuous regulatory efforts, has led the way in electric car development and claims the world's largest electrified fleet of vehicles. Yet the electrification process has become highly politicized in recent years, with Republicans attempting to block government intervention in the automobile industry and subsidization of electric car efforts. American auto producers and consumers remain wedded to the sport utility vehicle concept. Fracking has also reduced U.S. concerns about energy independence. Moreover, in a country in which long driving ranges are more conceivable than in most parts of the world, the electrical charging infrastructure lags considerably behind electric vehicle sales.

The second-largest electric vehicle producer, Japan, has embraced emissions reduction goals similar to those found in California but is burdened with a stagnant economy and is still feeling the impact of a set of recent natural disasters (a tsunami that wreaked havoc on its nuclear energy program and floods in Thailand that set back battery production). European efforts in this sphere are expanding quickly but so far encompass a much smaller number of drivers (and far less CO_2 emissions) than are found in the United States and Japan. That leaves China, which has openly professed a strategy of leapfrogging conventional auto production and seizing the lead in electric vehicle production. Yet, as discussed in Tillemann (2015), Chinese leapfrogging plans have not quite worked out as hoped. Chinese firms have not yet been able to overcome technological problems that have already been dealt with elsewhere, and Chinese consumers have been less eager to buy their products than had been anticipated.

None of this precludes one economy ultimately attaining a clear lead in electric vehicle production or clean coal generation. It just means that it is far too early to anoint leaders yet. Furthermore, the lack of an evident leader may also suggest that this particular potential surge may not be as centralized as past technological/energy surges have been. Tables 10.7, 10.8 and 10.9 depict the early leads commanded by Britain in coal (table 10.7) and the United States in petroleum (table 10.8) and electricity production (table 10.9). To be sure, production is not the same thing as consumption, but some states with large

Table 10.7 **Coal Production (Thousand Metric Tons), 1800–1937**

Year	United Kingdom	United States	France	Germany	Japan
1800	11,960	98	844	300	
1830	27,180	784	1,753	1,368	
1840	38,488	2,242	3,026	3,032	
1850	55,711	7,998	4,133	5,133	
1860	79,813	17,618	8,165	12,629	
1870	113,530	36,588	13,017	27,515	
1880	147,330	70,762	18,198	45,896	888
1890	184,246	138,386	24,982	70,432	2,729
1900	224,994	246,973	32,204	106,489	7,761
1910	270,979	441,128	37,757	152,814	16,121
1922	233,294	496,306	32,344	105,917	27,624
1928	252,850	539,101	52,312	155,867	33,383
1937	235,662	416,216	45,359	176,400	45,248

Source: Based on data from Etemad and Luciani (1991).

Table 10.8 **Petroleum Production (Thousand Metric Tons), 1860–1980**

Year	United States	Russia	Saudi Arabia	Iran	Venezuela
1860	116	4			
1870	652	25			
1880	3,282	608			
1890	6,012	3,812			
1900	8,448	10,308			
1910	27,252	9,257		15	
1922	80,501	4,600		3,049	397
1928	128,394	11,867		5,585	14,631
1937	161,859	28,700	26	9,673	26,250
1950	266,708	37,878	26,649	32,260	77,901
1960	347,975	147,859	64,524	53,491	149,358
1970	475,289	353,039	188,408	191,296	194,305
1980	424,196	603,207	495,898	72,667	114,788

Source: Based on data from Etemad and Luciani (1991).

Table 10.9 **Electricity Production (Million Kilowatt-Hours), 1890–1980**

	United States	France	Germany	United Kingdom	Japan
1890			40		
1900	5,969	325	1,150		
1910	24,752	1,033	5,400		616
1922	61,909	5,897	16,465	4,573	5,601
1928	108,736	14,038	27,889	10,461	13,631
1937	141,479	19,679	48,930	23,825	29,935
1950	388,674	33,025	44,466	66,385	46,266
1960	844,188	72,118	116,418	136,970	115,497
1970	1,639,771	140,564	242,750	249,016	359,538
1980	2,354,384	246,415	368,770	284,937	577,521

Source: Based on data from Etemad and Luciani (1991).

coal- and petroleum fields held energy advantages for many decades. Britain was not surpassed in coal production until the 1890s. U.S. petroleum production led until the 1970s. U.S. electricity production remains in a league of its own. Economic electrification in the twenty-first century cannot take the same shape. There are simply too many contenders around the world jostling to produce the electric car that emulates the Model T's success in an earlier era.[25]

The technological developments involved in decarbonizing electricity and transportation have hardly been autonomous national efforts, but they have been marked by unusually strong tendencies to avoid dependency on foreign firms. Yet even as the United States has discouraged Chinese participation in energy-intensive activies, the U.S./California process has been heavily reliant on Japanese innovation and batteries produced in Asia. The Chinese process has been reliant on technology developed elsewhere as well, despite attempts to keep foreign firms at bay in this particular sector. There is also a strong sense of U.S.–Chinese competition, given the size of their existing and potential fleets and carbon emissions, for the lead in electrification. But if one party actually wins the leadership, it is not clear that it will be in a position to export its technology to rivals and other lagging economies, as has been the approach in the past.

If so, a race between the two largest emitters could be useful in goading both economies (and political systems) into more strenuous efforts without necessarily generating a traditional global economic payoff. At the same time, without U.S. and Chinese success in drastically reducing carbon emissions, the goal of decarbonizing to head off the most serious environmental deterioration cannot succeed either. If significant reductions in CO_2 generation can only be achieved at the cost of a major shift in the way new technology enters the world economy, such an alteration, in the form of Schumpeter's intermittent disruptions and the Kondratieff wave, seems acceptable.[26] It could be that if decarbonization does not figure prominently in the next technological upswing, there will be no such upswing in the twenty-first century. Unfortunately, even that potential outcome has been insufficient to produce a high probability of decarbonization of electricity and electrification of transportation becoming the next technological surge. Despite the usual strong resistance from people and organizations committed to older technologies and the technological hurdles still to be overcome, the prospects seem quite promising.[27] What about fracking? Some would say that the United States already has a path to renewed economic vigor by ramping up oil and gas production to a level harking back to the 1950s. Is it possible for the United States to ride fossil fuels back to the top? We think not. Our rationale is developed in the next chapter.

11

Fracking, Warming,
and Systemic Leadership

The American oil boom wrought by fracking and the shale revolution has been sold as a major game changer in world politics.[1] If the United States is able to attain energy independence as a result of the shale oil and gas boom, it could reduce some of the tensions inherent in the scramble for scarce commodities. But will America's energy independence prolong its tenure as the predominant power in the international system? Should we expect the possession of more oil to help states maintain or regain systemic leadership?[2] Just as important, will ameliorating the dire nature of oil shortages discourage the U.S. search for energy alternatives? That is, will increased access to less expensive but older sources of energy decrease the incentives to develop alternative forms of energy and protract the petroleum age? The ongoing U.S. shale fracking boom thus has serious global implications for the peak oil argument, as well as the issues associated with a protracted petroleum era, U.S. movement away from petroleum dependence, and world sustainability.

These issues are hardly confined to the United States. They are global in impact because the increased power that has resulted from the use of fossil fuels in a host of technological and economic applications has led to a greenhouse gas problem that poses an acute threat to the planet's fundamental way of life. Is American fracking a positive or negative contribution to the ongoing struggle with decarbonization? Should we expect it to accelerate or retard the adoption of greener approaches? Most specifically, will fracking help or hinder vital U.S.– Chinese collaboration in efforts to reduce carbon dioxide and other emissions while these nations compete in developing pathways toward the construction of decarbonized lead economies?

As with many new interactions between technology and energy, observers of the hydraulic fracturing (fracking) phenomenon can be clustered into two camps—optimists and pessimists. The optimists claim that U.S. fracking and the resulting increases in oil and gas production will revive the U.S. economy, allow the nation to achieve energy independence, dispel fears of U.S. leadership decline, and contribute significantly to the reduction of carbon dioxide emissions and thereby help reduce the extent of global warming in future decades. While pessimists concede that U.S. fracking will lead to increased oil and gas production, they maintain that full U.S. energy independence is unlikely, fracking's contribution to U.S. economic growth will be modest, the tendency toward U.S. leadership decline will persist, and fracking per se (by increasing the natural gas supply) is unlikely to reduce global warming. On the contrary, it is likely to make it worse. Neither camp talks much about U.S.–Chinese energy collaboration. The optimist position implies that revived U.S. relative power will render cooperation less necessary. The pessimist position suggests that fracking could handicap cooperation. We find that the evidence in general provides more support for the pessimist position.

In examining the impact of U.S. fracking, there are three main questions to address. First, will fracking put the U.S. economy in a better position, and, if so, just how much of a better position? Second, will fracking contribute to the fight to keep global warming to ostensibly tolerable levels, or will it make the impending environmental crisis worse? Finally, given the answers to these two questions, will fracking reinforce, neutralize, or have no effect on U.S. systemic leadership? Our answer is that fracking will be advantageous in the short term but much less so when it comes to longer-term considerations such as global warming and systemic leadership. In subsequent sections, we tackle each of the three questions sequentially after first outlining the nature of the current boom.

The Fracking Boom

The latest twist in the energy acquisition story is the emergence of new reserves of oil and gas within U.S. territory thanks to extraction techniques involving the injection of water and other ingredients into the ground to fracture the rock encapsulating fossil fuels. While fracking techniques have been employed for some time, it is only fairly recently that they have begun to pay off. In the last decade, they have led to an unexpected supply of oil and gas in such significant amounts that U.S. oil and gas prices have declined. The new supply of natural gas is thought to be laying the groundwork for an economywide shift to this fuel source as an inexpensive and less CO_2-emitting alternative that could revitalize U.S. manufacturing and make the U.S. economy less vulnerable to oil supply disruptions.[3]

The recent American oil/gas boom has been sold by some as a way to turn back the clock to the preeminence enjoyed by the United States prior to the early 1970s. In this view, the United States will supplant Saudi Arabia and other major oil producers as the new leading oil producer and will no longer need to worry about peak oil turning points. Energy independence will be secured. Turmoil in the Middle East will cease to be of any concern to U.S. decision-makers and citizens, because the region will simply become irrelevant to American interests. Energy prices will plummet. Manufacturing will return home from the venues to which it had been outsourced. Thanks to all of these developments, constituting a mini industrial revolution via accelerated economic growth, the United States will return to its position at the top.

It sounds great in a way that is reminiscent of Ronald Reagan's "Morning in America" narrative, an earlier response to similar frustrations. Turning the clock back to before 1973 is something many U.S. citizens would welcome. However, the immediate question is, Are things really likely to work out this way? The answer, we think, is that some approximations of these developments may take place, but that ultimately the picture of the energy boom as a new industrial revolution and a herald of the United States' return to unquestioned geopolitical hegemony is probably mostly hype. Part of the problem is that the popular forecasts assume a short-term and fairly narrow perspective. For instance, lower energy costs in North America would mean much lower energy costs for U.S. producers only if North American oil and gas producers ignore the profits that might be made from selling their product abroad. Oil and gas produced in the United States could not legally be exported from 1975 to 2015 but political pressures to revise these prohibitions led to the change in policy. Alternatively, if lower energy costs mean factories using U.S. labor could once again be competitive in the world market, what these factories would produce becomes critically important. If they returned to the production of Detroit-made cars with long fins and terrible gas mileage or large sport utility vehicles, the outcome would not prove all that favorable to the United States. So, it is not simply a matter of revived factories, but, more importantly, whether the revived factories focus on sunrise or sunset industries. Finally, some analysts claim that if the United States had no need to import oil, it could abruptly abandon its involvement with foreign oil-producing areas as largely irrelevant to American national interests. But that contention seems to assume that (a) U.S. petroleum imports are heavily Middle Eastern in origin, and/or (b) U.S. foreign policy concerns related to the Middle East stem primarily from U.S. energy dependency on the Middle East. Neither is the case. The U.S. focus on the Middle East stems from systemic leadership perceptions of the responsibility to keep oil flowing into the world economy. Abandoning Middle East concerns would mean abandoning system leadership, not maintaining it.

The United States' position as system leader—a position that in turn is predicated on technological centrality in the world economy—is in serious doubt. Reviving its technological lead will take more than making petroleum more abundant or reviving old-school manufacturing. What effect should we expect greater quantities of less expensive oil in North America to have? Our answer is much less than the "Morning in America" hyperbole would suggest. That the oil/gas boom will have effects is not in doubt. But where those effects fit within larger-scale changes that are also underway is not clear. In particular, it is important to ask whether the boom is likely to detract from another dimension of leadership—showing the way to the development of a decarbonized economy before environmental stresses become overwhelming.

Fracking and Economic Growth

Not surprisingly, journalist treatments of the fracking boom and its implications tend to be limited in detail and structured argument. Some arguments with greater complexity, however, have appeared. Morris (2012) sees an energy bonanza as encouraging an ongoing process of "reshoring" in which American manufacturers return to U.S. production sites as Asian labor costs rise and U.S. production costs decline. In turn, this manufacturing resurgence would lead to improvement of the nation's economic infrastructure and help revitalize the healthcare industry. The central driver in this argument is expanded economic growth that leads to renewed public support for infrastructure and healthcare expenditures. This version of the economic renaissance is not dependent on cheap energy, although cheap energy certainly helps by encouraging reshoring and the reduction of costs in general. The expected outcome is a return to the type of U.S. industrial preeminence enjoyed in the 1950s and 1960s.

Kurtzman's (2014) argument on "unleashing the second American century" is similar but not identical. He contends that economic growth in the twenty-first century will be a function of four factors: (1) creativity/innovation leadership, (2) massive new energy reserves, (3) expanded access to capital for investment purposes, and (4) unrivaled manufacturing depth. Several economies can claim the presence of one or more of the four factors, but only the United States possesses strong links to all four. Moreover, its massive new energy reserves and ready capital pool will support manufacturing depth by encouraging the return of offshore manufacturing. Energy independence will allow the United States greater flexibility in defending the continued flow of Gulf petroleum and essentially underwriting undesirable regimes in Saudi Arabia, Nigeria, and Venezuela.

In this interpretation, the U.S. centrality and primacy of the first American century were undone by the nation's increased dependence on other states for energy and financial investment. Energy independence will be an important contributor to the reversal of this dependency and the restoration of U.S. centrality and primacy in a second century. But is it possible to return to a pre-1973 hierarchical structure? The answer to this question depends on how one interprets the fracking boom phenomenon.

Like Morris and Kurtzman, Morse et al. (2012) are quite bullish in their approach to the fracking boom. Their detailed argument is informed by an understanding of the economics of energy processes. But their perspective is also clearly more short-run (a decade) than is desirable for transitional purposes and, as it turns out, much less fracking- and petroleum-centric than one might imagine. Still, their argument incorporates many of the promises often associated with the fracking boom.

Their interpretation is that higher energy prices in the first decade of the twenty-first century led to an increased emphasis on exploration and innovation in order to increase the supply of oil and gas. Exploration and innovation in turn led to the United States becoming the fastest-growing producer of fossil fuel for at least the remainder of the century's second decade. With the expansion in the supply of petroleum, forecasts of production peaks were pushed back in time, and affordable energy-intensive production in the United States became possible. Looking forward, the Morse team predicts that a combination of expanded production, more use of natural gas as an energy source, and less consumption of energy in general will create new jobs, decrease petroleum imports and trade deficits, increase gross domestic product, and enhance the value of the dollar. The influence of the Organization of Petroleum Exporting Countries (OPEC) on oil supply and pricing, moreover, will be eclipsed by the new production centrality of the United States, Canada, and Mexico. It follows for them, therefore, that

> it is unclear what the political consequences of this might be in terms of American attitudes to continuing to play the various roles adopted since World War II—guarantor of supply lanes globally, protector of main producer countries in the Middle East and elsewhere. A US economy that is less vulnerable to oil disruptions, less dependent on oil imports and supportive of a stronger currency will inevitably play a central role globally. But with such a turnaround in its energy dependence, it is questionable how arduously the US government might want to play those traditional roles. (Morse et al., 2012: 84)

The Morse et al. interpretation broadens the phenomena linked to the fracking boom. In this view, a production boom is still central to but is not the singular driver of all the beneficial effects attributed to fracking. Fracking is seen as contributing to reduced costs and increased supply of both oil and natural gas. It is primarily the cost advantages of gas, not petroleum, that will lead to industrial revitalization and, when coupled with changing consumption habits, the equivalent of an industrial revolution. This interpretation assumes that gas, some of the

Table 11.1 **Fuel Production and Consumption, 2012, 2025, 2040**

	Crude Oil/Natural Gas Plant Liquids (quadrillion BTUs)			Dry Natural Gas and Supplements (tcf)		
Year	Production	Consumption	Deficit	Production	Consumption	Deficit
2012	17.08	35.87	−18.7	24.12	25.64	−1.51
2025	23.03	36.28	−13.25	31.93	28.35	3.58
2040	19.99	36.07	−16.08	37.61	31.63	5.98

Source: U.S. Department of Energy (2014: 17).

production of which will be shale-based, increasingly will be used to generate electricity, serve as a substitute for heating homes, and alter how transportation is fueled on both land and water. Changes in consumption habits hinge on a number of plausibly contingent factors, such as the development of more efficient vehicles, greater availability of vehicles that do not rely on petroleum for fuel, an aging population that drives less, and a decrease in suburban commuting as more people move to cities.

While some analysts believe these changes will be realized by 2020, U.S. Energy Information Administration (EIA) forecasts depict a longer process. Table 11.1 summarizes the EIA's production and consumption estimates for 2012, 2025, and 2040. According to these figures, the need to import crude oil will persist. The anticipated 2040 deficit is not much less than the shortfall in 2012. The difference is that domestic petroleum production is seen as continuing to expand through 2016–2020 before approximating a production high reached in 1970 and then slowly declining thereafter. These data show that the United States will have more natural gas than it needs by at least 2025. At the same time, petroleum consumption will remain roughly constant, while natural gas consumption will increase over time (56 percent between 2012 and 2040).

In terms of economic growth, the average annual growth of real gross domestic product (GDP) during this period (2012–2040) is projected to be 2.4 percent, which would be a marked improvement on the 2000–2012 period (1.75 percent) but less than that seen during the 1990–2012 period (2.5 percent).[4] After the initial decline, prices for oil and gas will increase.[5] Electricity prices will also reflect increases, but at a slower rate (for a now dated forecast see table 11.2). Future energy price advantages thus could occur, but not indefinitely. Figure 11.1 offers a good perspective on this phenomena by beginning the oil price series before 2000. Petroleum prices are expected to decline from a peak just before 2012 to a low that is still much higher than was experienced in the 1990s and then resume an upward trajectory from roughly 2020 on.

Table 11.2 **Expected Energy Pricing**

Prices	2012	Various	2040
Average annual Brent spot crude oil prices	$112/barrel	2017: $54 /barrel ($3.03/gal)	$141/barrel ($4.73/gal)
Henry Hub spot price gas	$4.80/million Btu	2020: $4.38/million Btu	$7.65/million Btu
Electricity	$.098/kwh	2030: $.104/kwh	$.111/kwh

Source: U.S. Department of Energy (2014: 18). Price forecasts represent a splitting of differences between low and high expectations.

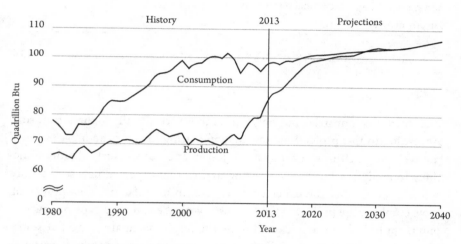

Figure 11.1 Total Energy Production Versus Consumption, 1990–2040. Source: U.S. Department of Energy (2015: 17).

Will all these changes in production, consumption, and pricing lead to U.S. energy independence? The answer, at least according to the U.S. Department of Energy's forecast, is almost. As shown in figure 11.1, fracking, in conjunction with other changes, is expected to cut the gap between consumption and production significantly. This gap, which had been growing over the last decade and a half, should abruptly narrow in the near future (2028) and eventually become one-fourth (3–4 percent) of what it was in 2012 (16 percent). Even so, U.S. reliance on the Middle East for energy fuel imports began diminishing well before 2012 and is expected to continue decreasing as the United States turns toward fuels that are American (North and South) in origin.

The anticipated job expansion associated with the increased supply of oil/gas is broken down in table 11.3. About two-thirds of forecast new jobs are

Table 11.3 **Hiring Forecast Linked to the Fracking Boom**

Employment Sectors	Millions of Jobs
Manufacturing: fabricated metals; transportation equipment; machinery; paper products; computers and electronics; chemicals; stone, clay, and glass; petroleum refineries; primary products; iron and steel mills and products; alumina and aluminum products	1.2
Industrial nonmanufacturing: about half in oil/gas extraction	1.1
Goods and services: health care/social assistance, professional and business services, retail trade, leisure and hospitality, financial activities, construction, wholesale trade, transportation and warehousing, educational services, information, federal government, agriculture	1.3

Source: Based on Morse et al. (2012: 87). Sectors are listed in order of size, with sectors expected to grow most listed first.

categorized as industrial, but only half of these are actually in manufacturing. According to this projection, new manufacturing jobs for the most part will not be in new cutting-edge industries. Job creation of any sort is hardly something to denigrate, but it is interesting to note that expected new service jobs actually outnumber the expected expansion in manufacturing employment. If we combine the projected GDP growth with the expected type of new employment linked to the fracking boom, the results seem attractive but somewhat less than revolutionary. Yet this evaluation may prove to be a matter of perspective. New employment increased in the United States through most of the twentieth century. Job gains in more recent years have been much harder to achieve. Three and a half million new jobs courtesy of the fracking boom would definitely be a positive development, even if it was still less than revolutionary.

In sum, the fracking boom is likely to be beneficial to the U.S. economy, at least in the short run, and barring major environmental disasters.[6] On average, it is expected to create more fuel, more jobs, more per capita income, smaller trade deficits, and lower energy prices in the second decade of the century.[7] These outcomes are not really predicated on the abundance of oil per se or on the United States supplanting Saudi Arabia as a leading oil producer. The expansion of the oil supply contributes something to the mix, but the effects are as much dependent on reducing petroleum consumption as they are on making more petroleum available. More importantly, they are also contingent on moving toward a natural gas–/electricity-centric economy.

However, Morse et al. (2012) offers one of the more optimistic scenarios, aimed at forecasting the maximum possible changes that could come about, as opposed to what might be more probable. Their forecasts are also restricted to a decade ahead—that is, the period most likely to be benefited by the fracking boom. All observers of the phenomenon see it as producing some type of short-term windfall. The question is, What is the longer-term effect?

A more comprehensive examination of the fracking effect has been put forward by Houser and Mohan (2014). In table 11.4, some of their forecasted effects based on empirical modeling are summarized in three contexts: pre-shale, a conservative scenario, and an optimistic scenario. All that is different in the two alternative futures is the supply of energy resources, something that depends in part on investment in extraction infrastructure.

In the near future (2020), they anticipate limited changes in gasoline and coal pricing. Natural gas pricing is likely to be attractive, with decreased electricity

Table 11.4 **Estimated Alternative Futures (2020) with Fracking**

	Pre-shale	Conservative		Optimistic	
	Value	*Value*	*% Difference*	*Value*	*% Difference*
Gasoline (2010 USD per Gallon)	3.62	3.56	−1.7	3.35	−7.5
Natural Gas (2010 USD per Million Btu)	5.47	4.31	−21.2	2.77	−49.3
Coal (2010 USD per Short Ton)	41.10	41.00	−0.4	41.30	0.4
Electricity (2010 Cents per KWh)	9.98	9.63	−3.5	9.04	−9.4
Energy Expenditures					
Economywide (Billion 2010 USD)	1,438	1,403	−2.4	1,322	−8.1
Household (Billion 2010 USD)	5,377	5,263	−2.1	4,987	−7.3
Real GDP (Billion 2005 Chained USD)	15,293	15,389	0.6	15,620	2.1
Nonfarm Employment (Millions)	141.3	142.1	0.5	143.8	1.8

Source: Based on Houser and Mohan (2014: 47, 53).

costs less easy to predict. Overall energy expenditures are likely to be reduced, but not necessarily all that much. GDP and employment improvements are discernible, but also not as impressive as has been predicted. More specifically, Houser and Mohan (2014) predict that the main employment beneficiaries in manufacturing will be industries linked to drilling. Their simulations suggest that 73 percent of manufacturing firms will see no more than a 1 percent increase in employment, and that the increase will be less than 5 percent for 94.3 percent of the manufacturing sector.[8] They conclude that any renaissance in U.S. manufacturing will not be due to expanded employment, but that increased competitiveness thanks to reduced energy costs remains a possibility, especially in the chemistry industry, which makes direct use of fossil fuels.

In summary, Houser and Mohan (2014: 50) view the shale boom effect as similar to the effect of the American Recovery and Reinvestment Act on the U.S. economy after the recent Great Recession.[9] Annual GDP growth is likely to be at best in the 2-3 percent range for the near future. Greater improvement in the U.S. economy would translate into a smaller stimulus effect for shale oil and gas.

A longer-term question is whether the shale boom is likely to lead to major shifts in the types of fuel consumed in the U.S. economy. Table 11.5 suggests some changes of fairly modest scale by 2035, including reduction of coal consumption (15–18.9 percent of total consumption with fracking vs. 21.8 percent in the absence of fracking) and expansion of natural gas usage (25.6–31.1 percent with fracking vs. 20.9 percent without fracking). Oil consumption is not seen as changing all that much. Nuclear power and renewables usage are expected to be slightly less than might have been the case in the absence of a shale boom. Even more importantly, though, this mixed set of changes is not expected to alter CO_2 emissions all that much between 2011 and 2035, although energy

Table 11.5 **Estimated Future Energy Consumption with Fracking, by Percent**

Energy	Pre-shale			Conservative		Optimistic	
	2011	2020	2035	2020	2035	2020	2035
Coal	20.2	21.1	21.8	18.9	19.8	14.7	15.0
Oil	36.3	34.9	31.7	34.9	31.9	35.2	32.2
Natural Gas	25.5	23.8	20.9	26.2	25.6	30.5	31.1
Nuclear	8.5	9.4	10.5	9.3	8.7	9.0	8.2
Renewables	9.4	10.5	14.8	10.3	13.9	10.3	13.4

Source: Based on Houser and Mohan (2014: 109).

use–related emissions in 2035 are forecasted as being higher than in 2012 but less than at the 2007 peak.[10]

The Houser and Mohan analysis thus anticipates a short-term stimulus and little long-term effect. Yet "little long-term effect" has several different connotations for our research questions. In terms of U.S. economic growth, the effect is likely to be something less than an industrial and manufacturing game changer. The contribution of fracking to the reduction of CO_2 emissions is expected to be negligible. If the shale boom is unlikely to transform the American economy or its emissions problem, the prospects of the U.S. systemic leadership position being maintained or reinvigorated are rather slight.

Thus the fracking "evidence," which is based entirely on pre-2015 forecasting, suggests that the increased supply of oil and gas could very well be beneficial to U.S. economic growth in the short run. Energy costs overall could be lower for a few years as a result of expected oil and gas price decreases in the immediate future. National account deficits should decline to the extent that energy imports decrease. Energy exports may increase as well. Some new employment can be anticipated in response to the need to develop infrastructure for the transition to a new energy source, whatever that may be. All of these outcomes would be much different from those seen in recent years.

While not denying the overt benefits of fracking, analyses of the boom that focus on improved economic growth usually ignore the differences between intensive and extensive economic growth. Extensive growth involves the expansion of the economy through more consumers, more economic activity, or reduced costs. Intensive economic growth involves radical changes to the very nature of economic production such that new technologies replace old and increasingly obsolete technologies. Sailing ships gave way to steamships, which gave way to petroleum-fueled ships, which in turn gave way, in some spheres, to nuclear-propelled ships. Each shift in propulsion created ships that could do things that were not possible earlier, including moving much faster and carrying more cargo at reduced cost. Shipping activities, as a consequence, expanded intensively and extensively. If more sailing ships had simply been constructed, growth would have been merely extensive.

Lower costs, the employment of more people, and fewer imports and more exports can generate extensive economic growth, but they do not themselves generate intensive economic growth or something approximating a new industrial revolution, even if they do encourage the return of some offshore factories.[11] The agents of the next bout of intensive growth will most likely be innovations in information technology, biotechnology, and nanotechnology, as well as combinations of the three. The direct advantages for these areas of having more local sources of petroleum are not obvious.

Some authors have argued that economic growth is gradually being decoupled from increased energy consumption. One of the reasons for this phenomenon is that new industries are much less closely tied to expansions in fossil fuel consumption than steam and internal combustion engines were. Building more railroads in the nineteenth century or more automobiles in the twentieth century, for instance, meant greater consumption of coal and oil to make them run. Vehicles in the twenty-first century at some point will be propelled by some other type of fuel—as will other types of new technology that will rely on electricity and batteries. The point is that extensive economic growth generated by the fracking boom in and of itself is unlikely to significantly impact the advent of the next economic transition. At best, it might allow lower production costs for some types of innovative production and more disposable income for consumers to purchase the latest IT gadgets.

The fracking boom does seem to have derailed talk of peak oil. That does not mean that the concept of peak oil has lost all utility. Rather, it means that the peak in North America and perhaps elsewhere has likely been pushed further down the road. Earlier discoveries and reestimations of reserves had already had this protracting effect prior to the fracking boom, producing an iteration of peaks in which each successive peak was a few years later than the earlier one. Given the lack of public information on the size of reserves, such reestimating and re-guesstimating are not surprising. While consumption had been increasing faster than new discoveries prior to the onset of the fracking boom, it is possible that more major discoveries will follow as a result of increased access to areas formerly buried in ice (the Arctic, Antarctica) and further innovations related to extracting oil located deeper underground and farther offshore.

Of course, one thing early forecasts missed was OPEC's decision to keep the oil supply high, thereby driving the price of oil even lower and making U.S. fracking less profitable and therefore less likely to persist (Cooke, 2015; McBride and Sergie, 2015; Tully, 2015; LeVine, 2016; Klare, 2016). The immediate effect of this implicit price war among oil producers has been to undercut fracking operations in the United States. Yet this effect too is likely to be short-term, depending on how long Middle Eastern oil producers can weather their own reduced revenues. In late 2016, OPEC oil ministers agreed to move toward reducing the supply of petroleum (El Gamal, Lawler, and Ghaddar, 2016), which immediately led to an increase in the price of oil. Just how this situation will play out remains to be seen, but it seems safe to presume that U.S. fracking efforts will continue and perhaps increase.

Fracking and Global Warming

There is a general consensus that global warming is a product of greenhouse gases released by industrialization's reliance on fossil fuels. This warming is manifested by a movement toward more variable and extreme climate characterized by increased pollution and heavily damaging storms. As it proceeds, some agricultural areas, including those among the most heavily populated regions of the planet, will become too warm for food production. At the same time areas hitherto too cold or frozen should become more amenable to producing food. Likewise, resources, including petroleum, in areas once covered by ice may become more exploitable. Ocean levels will rise as ice caps melt, threatening the existence of coastal populations. Some low-lying states could disappear altogether. Other densely populated areas will suffer from a lack of access to potable water. Some of the areas currently considered most attractive for fracking, an activity that depends heavily on water availability, (California, China) already face serious limitations on their water supply.

Just how far this environmental transition proceeds will depend on the increase in average temperatures. A three-degree increase will make for a more extreme and devastating transition than an increase of two degrees. To the extent that the increasing temperatures of the past century are due to industrialization, the scope of climate change will also hinge on whether the harmful effects of industrialization are modified, and to what degree. So far, there has not been a great deal of movement on this front, which would seem to guarantee that environmental deterioration, which is already underway, will occur more quickly and be more damaging than otherwise might have been the case. These warnings were highlighted in the 2014 report by the United Nations Intergovernmental Panel on Climate Change (IPCC), which found that major carbon-emitting countries are still spending large amounts of money subsidizing fossil fuels, thus slowing down the transition to renewable energy. Despite growing political willingness to tackle climate change and falling emissions levels in some of the wealthiest economies in recent years, most countries are still dragging their feet when it comes to reducing emissions. If countries continue with their current rates of emissions until 2030, the UN report suggests, the risks of climate change will be impossible to reverse with existing technologies (Intergovernmental Panel on Climate Change, 2014).

Increasing the supply of oil will likely have two effects on the movement away from fossil fuels. By making petroleum and gas more readily available, it will reduce incentives to find alternatives, other things being equal. Reduced incentives will prolong the gradual movement away from hydrocarbons. More oil will not stop the movement, but it could slow the pace of transition. The other effect is less direct. If petroleum and gas are made more available and less costly, it is likely that more of these carbon-intensive fuels will be consumed. If so, this indirect effect would also be expected to slow the pace of energy transition in the twenty-first century.

If more petroleum is consumed because it is more readily available and less expensive than it has been, however temporarily, it is reasonable to expect the boom to aggravate the environmental transition. Maugeri (2010) has described vicious boom-and-bust cycles in oil pricing that he thinks are a product of a number of interacting factors: limited spare capacity; perceptions of imminent decline in reserves; unreliable information about supply, demand, and inventories; overestimation of future demand; geopolitical tensions related to oil-producing states; and technical problems in refining petroleum. Whether his complicated mix of factors is right or wrong, his conclusion that low prices for petroleum tend to lead to paradoxical behavior seems well supported by historical evidence.[12]

> History has shown that low prices for petroleum or excessive uncertainty about future price movements are the worst enemies of research and development into alternative energy sources. Low prices for crude oil also foster unacceptable consumption habits and discourage energy efficiency. In brief, cheap oil tends to kill sustainable development. A less volatile and more predictable petroleum market would be a reasonable goal, but in practice, it is a chimera. (Maugeri, 2010: 31)

The increase in the oil supply thus is a "too little, too late" phenomenon in an era in which petroleum is losing economic centrality. At most, it could hasten environmental changes and slow the movement away from oil if it leads to more petroleum being consumed. Oil will not fuel the next wave of economic innovations, and therefore it cannot energize or reenergize the systemic leadership for very long. At the same time, an expanded supply of oil will divert the U.S. economy from its search for alternatives to fossil fuels. Arnsdorf (2014) notes that investment in renewables declined 5 percent in 2013 and may have discouraged the likelihood of Congress passing wind tax credits.[13] Support for renewables development could languish in the absence of an energy crisis situation. If the expanded oil supply discourages the U.S. search for renewables, the lead in developing these types of resources could well pass permanently to other economies.

Moving to gas would not stop the energy transition away from fossil fuels, but it could slow it down considerably. Natural gas is admittedly greener than oil or coal, but gas also emits carbon dioxide—about half as much as petroleum and roughly two-thirds that of coal. One finding (described in Davenport, 2014) suggests that while natural gas produces nearly a third less carbon dioxide than diesel, the drilling and production of gas gives rise to methane leaks, which are greatly more damaging than carbon dioxide emissions (Hayhoe et al., 2002; Burnham et al., 2012; Howarth, Ingraffea, and Engelder 2011; Howarth, Santoro, and Ingraffea, 2011; Hultman et al., 2011; Brandt et al., 2014; Newell and Raimi, 2014; Sovacool, 2014).[14] Wigley (2011) is more emphatic, stating simply that methane leakages will offset any gains made by switching from coal to natural gas—assuming that gas becomes a substitute for coal, as opposed to a complement.[15] This conclusion also assumes that the unused coal is not simply exported abroad, which would merely transfer the emissions problem from one state to another.

If the ultimate goal is to move toward a primarily clean fuel, gas can only be an interim vehicle—a so-called "bridge"—especially if its contribution to reducing carbon emissions is not all that great (Davis and Shearer, 2014).[16] On this point, McJeon et al. (2014) find that between 2010 and 2050, abundant natural gas will have a –2 to 11 percent impact on CO_2 emissions, depending on a set of alternative assumptions about how the gas is employed. Transportation too is a very important contributor to greenhouse gases, because it is so dependent on petroleum. A large-scale conversion of vehicles to run on natural gas seems unlikely. Models have tended to find little impact of expanded natural gas supply on either the transportation (McJeon et al., 2014) or the electricity (Spencer, Sartor, and Mathieu, 2014) sector.[17] For that matter, fracking is not without its own environmental costs in terms of water contamination and increasing the likelihood of earthquakes (Colborn et al., 2011; Deyette et al., 2015; Jackson et al., 2014; Mason, Muehlenbachs, and Olmstead, 2015; Small et al., 2014).[18]

Moreover, Hughes (2011) argues that gas wells are not very productive, and that a great deal of expensive investment will be required to maintain the large supply of gas promised by shale boom optimists. Frackers could well be overestimating what they can access at an affordable cost. The incentive to overestimate is certainly there if substantial investment is required. If the supply cannot be maintained, the natural gas price will increase. The price will also rise if substantial amounts are exported abroad.

Finally, there is also a reasonable possibility that China could eventually apply fracking techniques to resolve some of its own serious energy problems.[19] But such a development, if it ever happens, is decades away, given the technological and resource barriers that the Chinese must first overcome. For now, the United States possesses a definitive fracking lead. Whether the boom will prove to be long-term remains to be seen. So far, the modeling forecasts do not seem auspicious.

The U.S. Fracking Boom and Systemic Leadership

Cho's (2014) basic argument is that the British Industrial Revolution was not a matter of luck. The Little Ice Age ensured that England's climate was cold in the middle of the last millennium. By this time, wood had become scarce on the island. Coal was initially readily available for heating purposes but gradually became more difficult to extract as a result of flooding of mines deep in the ground. Steam engines solved this problem by pumping water out of the mines and turned out to have an added bonus in helping move the coal to the country's large cities by rail. England, which by now had become Britain, rode the transition to coal and its associated new technology to establish an empire on which the sun never set.

Cho's model is that environmental change leads to energy transitions, which lead to technological innovation, which leads to political and economic success. Thus he does not claim that cold weather led to the British Industrial Revolution. Rather, cold weather combined with fuel scarcity contributed to an energy transition, which set the stage for the Industrial Revolution and imperial success. We can quibble with the details of this story while still acknowledging the argument that important processes have been interdependent in the past. We think they are also likely to be interdependent in the future, and that it is not coincidental that four types of transitions (environmental, energy, technological, and political–economic) characterized the British rise. Since the contribution of fracking to ascent dynamics is something of a novel topic, we cannot rely too much on historical analogies. The question then is whether it is possible to speculate on its potential contribution while its effects are ongoing.

System leaders sit at the apex of success, producing on the world economy's technological frontier. Their economies become the world's lead economies as a result of a near-monopoly on radical technological innovation that is gradually and selectively diffused to the rest of the world economy. System leaders also specialize in long-distance military capabilities that allow them to better protect their far-flung activities throughout the world. Instead of expanding their armies, system leaders cultivate naval and aerospace capabilities to control the global commons, which they use for interregional transactions.

The British Empire did draw on its technical ability to industrialize warfare, developing steamboats that could penetrate river systems and machine guns that could annihilate large numbers of indigenous opponents. But otherwise, Britain's territorial empire was more often a reflection of its failure to maintain its focus on being the workshop of the world. German and U.S. challenges to that workshop position led ultimately to the transition from the *Pax Brittanica* to the *Pax Americana*. The United States ascended to system leadership on the basis of its technological leadership, as Britain had, but its rise was built on a resource/

energy foundation based initially on coal and later on petroleum, electrification, and an economy geared toward the assembly line production of automobiles (sometimes referred to as the second industrial revolution). Just as in the British case, heading a winning coalition in a global war was also part of the ascent package.[20]

Although there is a clear relationship between systemic leadership and political–economic success, this relationship has not always existed. It emerged most clearly in the fifteenth century with the ascendance of the Portuguese, but its roots can be traced back to China and the Song dynasty. There also appears to be a similar linkage between systemic leadership and energy transitions. This relationship emerged in the seventeenth century with the ascendance of the Netherlands. Their lead economy was fueled by a creative combination of peat and wind. Britain's rise was fueled by coal. The United States' rise was based in part on, sequentially, coal, petroleum, and electricity. Should we then add petroleum and gas fracking to this tale of modern lead economy succession? Might a second interval of U.S. leadership be fueled by the technological innovation of hydraulic fracturing?

We think that the fracking boom is an unlikely foundation for renewed systemic leadership, with claims to the contrary demonstrating a mistaken understanding of the foundations of past systemic leaderships. In the past three hundred years, lead economies have been fueled by new, relatively cheap energy sources. Natural gas may be relatively inexpensive for a while, but it is not a new source of energy. Rather, the current situation represents an increased supply of an old source of energy. A historically minded critic might quickly interject that much the same thing characterized the shift from coal to petroleum, with one fossil fuel replacing another. The difference, however, is global warming. Fossil fuels are no longer desirable given their extreme costs in terms of greenhouse gas emissions and their impact on temperatures. Fossil fuels will be with us for some time to come, but it is essential that we move away from them as quickly as possible. A temporary expedient such as natural gas seems an unlikely foundation for a systemic leadership that will have as one of its missions the modeling of the transition to a carbon-free economy.

A second reason that fracking is unlikely to prove a foundation for renewed system leadership is more pragmatic. The "game changer" assertion seems oversold. While fracking may have been transformative for North Dakota's economy (at least for the first few years of activity), it does not appear likely to transform the U.S. economy as a whole. The boom probably will be nice for consumers for a while before prices rise again. It may help stimulate an underemployed economy still recovering from an intense recession, and it should reduce the U.S. balance of payments deficit, as long as reduced fuel imports do not lead to a strengthened dollar and reduced exports. But overall, the fracking boom does not appear to have much in the way of long-term implications for the United States, with forecast modeling showing neither impressive gains in long-term economic growth nor much lessening of greenhouse gas emissions.

It is widely recognized that the future of U.S. systemic leadership is seriously threatened by the emerging Chinese challenge and a variety of problems characterizing contemporary U.S. economics and politics. The United States appears to be less predominant than it once was, even if the decline has been rather gradual. The slow decline in itself does not translate into the imminent loss of the United States' lead position, but technological leadership as well as leadership in the shift to nonfossil fuels do appear to be up for grabs. If some other state than the United States assumes and maintains these leads, it is quite possible that the mantle of system leader will move accordingly to it. [21]

When we try to explain why one state is predominant over all others in a given system, the tendency is to look for edges that the predominant state possesses. The United States does have an edge over the rest of the world in fracking development, as indicated by drilling activity, appropriate technology, and access to the necessary capital to finance these activities. However, the United States does not possess the world's largest recoverable shale gas reserves (U.S. Department of Energy, 2013). That distinction is held by China, which also possesses the third-largest shale oil reserve (after Russia and the United States). But Chinese fracking development is still in its infancy and is expected to encounter serious technological and water supply problems.

Still, the United States' decisive edge in fracking operations over its most evident challenger does not necessarily translate into the maintenance or reinvigoration of its systemic leadership role. Although the path to systemic leadership is often taken for granted, it rests on a combination of several attainments. First and foremost, the system leader must establish itself as the world's lead economy. This does not mean that it must have the largest economy. Second, if lead economy status is gained by cultivating a technological edge sustained by a near-monopoly on radical economic innovations, the leader must be the first to put new and major inventions into practice and then export them. Third, these innovations must revolutionize the entire lead economy and put it well ahead of competitors for a finite period before other economies begin to catch up via emulation and diffusion. Revolutionizing the next lead economy means decarbonization, the embrace of clean/green energy, and a focus on electricity applications in the areas of transportation and information technology. In hindsight, fracking will probably be seen as a diversionary tangent away from these objectives.

In contrast, an alternative story is that U.S. political power and affluence encountered substantial "headwinds" after the 1973 oil embargo. The difficulties of obtaining petroleum after the Yom Kippur War and later the overthrow of

Iran's shah in 1979 ushered in a period of rising and volatile oil prices, jihadi terrorism, and increased U.S. involvement in the Middle East that included two Gulf wars and a long war in Afghanistan. If we equate some forty years of Middle Eastern turmoil with the U.S. loss of power and influence, the logical solution appears to be to reduce substantially U.S. military involvement in the region, its dependency on Middle Eastern oil, and the uncertainties of fluctuating energy prices. For a number of observers, these are some of the direct payoffs associated with the fracking boom.

The problem with this interpretation is not that Middle Eastern turmoil and the relative decline of U.S. influence are unrelated. The problem is that it is not clear whether one led to the other and, if so, which one did the leading. From our perspective, Middle Eastern turmoil is more or as much a consequence of U.S. relative decline than it is a primary cause of that decline. The decision by Arab states involved in the Organization of Arab Petroleum Exporting Countries (OAPEC) to punish the West for its support of Israel in 1973 was part of a longer process of Arab oil producers wresting control of their own natural resources away from international oil companies. The 1973 Arab-Israeli war provided an opportunity for these countries to gain more national control over petroleum and definitely constituted a challenge to the Western international order dominated by major oil companies. But it also reflected the peaking of U.S. oil production, a consequence of the U.S. decision to abandon the gold standard in 1971, and the informal end of the Bretton Woods era. The subsequently depreciated dollar reduced oil payments (which were paid in dollars) and gave producers ample incentive to increase oil prices if given an opportunity. That the 1973 war was just such an opportunity is underlined by the quadrupling of oil prices that took place then.

The 1979 overthrow of the U.S.-backed shah in Iran constituted another challenge to U.S. systemic leadership, which led to another oil price shock and a long war between Iran and Iraq in which Iraq may have been encouraged to act as a U.S. surrogate. Iraqi losses in the 1980s war led to its occupation of Kuwait in the early 1990s, a move that was perceived as a direct challenge to the very functioning of the Western economy. The challenge was suppressed by a large coalition but largely paid for by U.S. allies. The First Gulf War begat the Second Gulf War, although this outcome was not inevitable. Ironically, the Second Gulf War may have been fought for the same reason as the First Gulf War—to ensure the continuing flow of Middle Eastern oil to Western consumers.[22] Yet increased war and threats of war in the Gulf area have to take some share of the responsibility for oil price volatility. Increased U.S. involvement in the Middle East and especially its support for conservative autocrats there also led to the United States becoming one of the main targets of jihadi terrorism.

The Gulf wars turned out to be highly asymmetrical affairs, with the militarily powerful United States rapidly defeating its Iraqi opponents. Yet the United States' need to rely on coercion to achieve its goals reflected its diminishing political influence in the area. Occupations of Iraq and Afghanistan that failed to accomplish much also did little to enhance U.S. prestige in the Middle East. In sum, some of the problems the United States has encountered in the Middle East after 1973 have been due to perceived U.S. vulnerabilities and relative weaknesses. Whether or not such perceptions are accurate, they represent challenges to a once-preponderant state rather than causes of decaying strength.

In the interim, the ultimate irony of increasing American energy security and independence is that despite the important role that breaking free of Middle Eastern problems has played in efforts to achieve these aims, such an outcome really does not alter the links between U.S. grand strategy and Middle Eastern turmoil (Bryce, 2008; Zubrin, 2009). The view that foreign policy concerns related to propping up Arab autocracies, resisting territorial expansion into Kuwaiti oilfields, and coping with the blowback from increased jihadi terrorism would all vanish if the United States could eliminate its need for Middle Eastern oil imports is much too narrow to withstand scrutiny. U.S. imports from the Middle East had already been reduced prior to the fracking boom without any perceived loss of official involvement in the region.[23]

Another irony is that the root cause of U.S. involvement in the Middle East is closely linked to systemic leadership processes. The United States intensely sought access to petroleum, officially and commercially, prior to World War II and entered that conflict controlling in one way or another 50 percent of the world's oil supply. In this competition for energy resources, its main commercial rival was Britain, the declining system leader. U.S. gains in the Middle East largely came at the expense of its closest political ally.

Access to oil was the initial driver of Middle Eastern involvement. Once the United States ascended to system leader status after World War II, the burden of policing sea-lanes that provided a conduit for world trade was added to its responsibilities. The Persian Gulf became more and more critical in that respect. Furthermore, European dependency on Middle Eastern oil became an increasing concern to the United States, especially as Western Europe's importance to the world economy was reestablished. In all these respects, the U.S. concern for regulating Middle Eastern turmoil is a legacy of the formative and peak power phases of its system leadership. The highly compressed observations of a Securing America's Energy Future (SAFE; 2013) document on Middle Eastern scenarios, developed by former high-ranking military and governmental officials, captures accurately the dual motivations at stake. On the one hand, petroleum remains important to transportation worldwide, and it is difficult to compartmentalize the havoc caused by fluctuating oil supply and prices. Even if one state

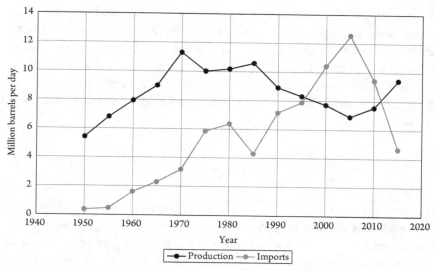

Figure 11.2 U.S. Petroleum Domestic Production and Net Imports, 1950–2015. Source: Based on data from U.S. Department of Energy (2016).

does not need to import oil (see figure 11.2), its economic activities will still be affected by the fluctuations. On the other hand, the United States has been not merely "one state," but the lead state. As the lead economy, its special concern for keeping the world economy afloat means that it must be prepared to project its power into the Middle East, regardless of its own energy concerns. Observers often recognize the first motivation without fully appreciating the second. As long as the United States seeks to act as system leader, it will be extremely difficult for it to disentangle itself from Middle Eastern problems. Consequently, SAFE (2013: 2) notes:

> Oil dependence has contributed to U.S. involvement in regions of the world that are often unstable and sometimes hostile to American interests. Domestic oil abundance will not end these involvements, largely due to the enduring importance of oil to the U.S. economy and transportation sector in particular. As such—and contrary to some predictions—instability in the Middle East will continue to pose economic risk for the United States, a fact that will influence national security policy. In fact, no matter how close the country comes to oil self-sufficiency, volatility in the global oil market will remain a serious concern.[24]

Where does a fracking boom fit into this system leader model based on technological innovation, the existence of a lead economy, global reach capabilities, and global war? The lead economy needs access to inexpensive energy to make its innovations function. A temporary increase in the supply of oil and gas may contribute to that economy's prosperity in lowering its basic operating costs. But oil is the energy of the last century's leadership infrastructure. Its central role has been slowly diminishing, even if it has yet to vanish and will still play some role for decades to come. Its lingering endgame should not be confused with a wave of the future.

Conclusion

The fracking boom is, or at least was, real and will lead to a mix of economic benefits and environmental liabilities for the United States and perhaps others. We think most of the economic benefits of this boom will be quite short-lived. They seem unlikely to generate or even contribute much to the next industrial revolution, since the next anticipated wave of new technology and produc- tion approaches will not depend on traditional fossil fuel energy sources. The boom, however, is likely to slow the energy transition away from petroleum, as the greater availability of oil and gas is unlikely to reinforce interest in sustaina- bility. Finally, we do not see how a fracking boom would either help maintain or revive systemic leadership. System leaders do need access to affordable energy, but they also need lead economies operating at the technological frontier. If the next set of pioneering industries are not propelled by petroleum or even nat- ural gas, it seems unlikely that hydrocarbon sources will provide the fuel needed for the next wave of radical change in economic production. Ready supplies of petroleum might even retard the development of some new industries—most particularly those related to transportation, one of the major sources of carbon dioxide emissions that lies at the heart of the movement toward environmental transition.

More important for system leadership is the development of a base for new sources of energy, not old. In the next chapter we turn to the question of who is ahead in the transition to renewable energy —China or the United States?

12

Racing to a Renewable Transition?

> The choice we face is not between saving our environment and saving
> our economy—it's a choice between prosperity and decline. The nation
> that leads the world in creating new energy sources will be the nation
> that leads the twenty-first-century global economy (Obama, 2009).

The above Obama citation accurately poses the central dilemma of the twenty-first century. Historical patterns of energy transitions over the past several hundred years suggest that systemic leadership transitions are tied to transitions in the primary source of energy—or so we argue. A relatively inexpensive energy source is critical to a state's development of technological and economic growth that outpaces, for a time, the rest of the world. The Dutch had peat, the British had coal, and the United States had coal, electricity, and petroleum. As the world transitions away from coal and petroleum in response to dwindling supplies and their harmful side effects, what might be the next big source of energy that will power the world economy and its lead economy (or economies)? The question is particularly compelling if we are in the early days of a political–economic transition in which China is set to surpass the United States at some point in this century. Which of the two lead economies, which today are also the world's biggest carbon emitters, are leading the world in replacing fossil fuels with alternative energy sources? And is the pace of their transition to the next energy regime fast enough to adequately address the fundamental threat of climate change?

In this chapter, we briefly scan the evidence for the linkage of energy transitions and technological leadership, as well as for the erosion of the incumbent regime. Turning to the question of systemic leadership transition, we examine the relative positioning of the United States and China in terms of renewables development. While it is clear that China is in the lead at present, we consider whether a competition between the two states over a small proportion of the total energy inventory would matter all that much. This question leads us to consider various forecasts for the relative consumption of different types of energy. If the technological leadership–energy transition argument and the forecasts are correct, there is little reason to anticipate a systemic leadership transition of any strength in this century. If the forecasts are wrong and overestimate the amount of fossil fuels remaining to be extracted, we are likely to be confronted with major energy problems by roughly midcentury. Either way, we may experience major energy problems alongside even more major environmental problems in about the same time frame.

Who's on First Base?

As the world depletes its supply of fossil fuels, what might be the next big source of energy that will power the world economy? More importantly, is the world's declining lead economy (the United States) or its aspiring heir apparent (China), which today are also the world's biggest carbon emitters, leading the race to replace fossil fuels with renewable alternatives? And is their pace fast enough to reverse or reduce the risks of climate change? China's prospects of succeeding the United States as the world's next leading global power would be greatly enhanced if it assumed the leadership of developing a new energy regime. To what extent has China embraced that role, given its current energy needs? This question is particularly compelling if we are in the early days of a political–economic transition in which China is set to surpass the United States at some point in this century. Similarly, if the United States wishes to maintain and renew its lead, it will need to assume the leadership of the development of a new energy regime. To what extent is the United States moving in this direction, given its own current energy and economic revitalization needs?

However, there are other possibilities. Some observers think that natural gas will lay the energy foundation for the next phase of advanced economic development. Increasing supplies of gas are already negatively impacting investment in renewables. The value of increased usage of natural gas is partly environmental—as gas is substituted for coal, the negative consequences of fossil fuel use for climate change are less than they might otherwise have been. If gas proves a halfway point in a transition toward genuinely greener energy sources, the next system leader will profit from ready access to it. In this sense, the shale gas boom, as discussed in chapter 11, could contribute to the United States at least holding on to its lead status somewhat longer than it would have otherwise. Furthermore, if increased natural gas supplies become instrumental in pioneering the next phase of industrial revolution, they could also lead to the United States succeeding itself as system leader, much as Britain did in the nineteenth century. Whether this is a strong possibility, though, is debatable.[1] If the gas wells are not all that efficient, high maintenance costs will be inescapable.

If the supply cannot be maintained, prices will increase. The price of natural gas will also rise if substantial amounts are exported abroad. Moreover, moving to natural gas will not resolve the global warming problem. While overall CO_2 emissions might be reduced by such a transition, no one has advanced an argument that such reductions would be sufficient to avoid warming greater than two degrees C. Natural gas usage also is accompanied by increased methane emissions, which are considered even more damaging than CO_2 emissions. If global warming persists or becomes even worse, what might the implications be for the world's lead economy in a global setting overwhelmed by environmental deterioration issues?

An expanded supply of natural gas, moreover, could divert the U.S. economy (or any other economy, including China's) from its search for alternatives to fossil fuels.[2] If more gas is consumed in the coming decades because it is more readily available and less expensive, support for renewables development could languish, especially in the absence of an acute energy crisis. If this diversion discourages the United States' search for alternatives, any lead in developing sunrise energy resources could well be assumed by another country. Consequently, we should not be surprised by increasing consumption of natural gas in the immediate future, but such a shift does not appear to be a long-term winning strategy, particularly for aspiring system leaders.

Another possibility for an energy transition is nuclear power. While some observers think it is unlikely that decarbonization will be achieved without substantial help from nuclear reactors, nuclear power suffers from huge construction costs and poor public relations (Anderson, 2015; Levitan, 2016; McGlynn, 2016; Pomper, 2016). New technology could make reactors less expensive and safer, but its development is currently largely limited to the drawing board and will not be implemented in the near future. In the absence of a major turnaround in the nuclear energy arena, the probable future of nuclear power over the next few decades is bimodal. Older, more affluent states will be reluctant to do much with nuclear reactors while emerging powers seem to be embracing nuclear reactors with considerable enthusiasm. The United States has more reactors than other states, but its plants are aging and may not be replaced. Other major economies, such as France, Japan, the United Kingdom, and Germany, are either abandoning nuclear projects altogether or contemplating doing so. In contrast, Russia, China, and India have big hopes for nuclear energy. Whether all of the reactors that these countries have planned actually come to fruition remains to be seen, of course, but the pattern unfolding is one of less nuclear development in the global North and the possibility of stronger nuclear development in the larger states of the global South. Very different bets on this situation are being made, and it is difficult to see how it will play out, barring major innovation. As a consequence, there is not much we can do with it at the moment. Suffice it to say that most energy forecasts do not predict much expansion of nuclear power in the twenty-first century.

The next most overt candidate for energy ascendancy is renewables, which usually primarily comprise hydropower and wind and solar technology. Dams, wind turbines, and solar panels can be constructed widely, generate energy that is free of CO_2 emissions, and can replace coal and gas in the generation of electricity. The technologies, of course, are not without major problems. Only so many new dams are likely to be built, especially in an era of water scarcity. Wind and sun energy are intermittent and need to be stored and transmitted to consumers, raising questions about their ultimate power potential. Yet renewables enthusiasts are convinced that this path is the best way to free the planet of its dependency on fossil fuels. Various plans have been developed that suggest that it would be feasible to shift completely to renewables by 2050 to 2070. Unfortunately, technical feasibility is not the major obstacle to be overcome. The cultivation and adoption of renewables will require considerable investment and governmental subsidization, particularly during the transitional phase. Considerable resistance to new energy sources must also be overcome. But these constraints tend to apply to all new energy sources, which are usually more expensive initially than conventional supplies and rarely receive endorsement as the next best thing.

Who Is Winning the Renewable Energy Race?

Given the expense and resistance associated with new energy sources, governments need to be more than mildly facilitative in encouraging their adoption. Political commitment and strong endorsement are necessary. The natural questions, then, are: Which governments are inclined to support renewables development, and (2) Which economies possess greater renewables capabilities? Not surprisingly, small, affluent states located in western Europe have tended to lead in this race. But these states are not contenders for systemic leadership. Confining the question to the most obvious candidates leads us to ask: Is China or the United States in the lead?

For most energy analysts, the answer to this question is clear. Relative to their economies, China is investing twice as much in renewable energy as the United States, and its support is rapidly expanding (see table 12.1). But China has not always been in the lead. In fact, the United States under the Carter administration was among the first to set a target for renewable energy usage. At a 1979 press conference, President Carter promised the American people that by the turn of the 21st century the United States would obtain one-fifth of its energy

Table 12.1 **US-China Investment in Clean Energy, 2012-15 (in US$ billions)**

Rank	Country	2012	2013	2014	2015
1	China	54.2	57.9	89.5	110.5
2	USA	36.7	40.3	51.8	56.0

Source: Bloomberg New Energy Finance

from solar power. The ideas that the world needed to transition to renewable energy and that the United States needed to lead that transition were largely a response to the oil crises of the 1970s, which revealed the advanced industrial economies' dangerous overreliance on Middle Eastern oil. The desire to avoid the disastrous consequences of another cutoff of supply paved the way for the current boom in renewable energy. However, Carter's promise was not realized. What followed his pledge instead were decades of stagnation. The extremely low oil prices of the 1980s and 1990s, combined with the ongoing shale revolution of the early 2000s, discouraged U.S. efforts to develop renewable energy. Consequently, even as late as 2015, renewables accounted for only about 9 percent of the U.S. energy supply—not much different from their share in 1980. If we discount hydropower (which has been in constant use for many years) and biomass, renewables in 2015 constituted less than 3 percent of the total U.S. energy supply (U.S. EIA, 2016).

While the U.S. solar industry became what the *Economist* described as "a commercial graveyard for ecologically minded dreamers," leadership in renewable energy was being established elsewhere in the world, first by Japan, then by Germany. With strong government support, both economies were motivated to revive the renewables industry for different reasons. Japan's economic growth in the 1960s and 1970s had been largely fueled by Middle Eastern oil, making it extremely vulnerable to any disruptions in the oil supply. Motivated by the need to reduce its dependence on Middle Eastern oil, the country launched a national initiative in the 1970s to develop solar energy. Japan's solar market took off, explains Yergin (2011: 536), thanks to large government subsidies "that helped consumers purchase solar panels, along with the most expensive domestic electricity rates in the world, plummeting costs, efficiencies of scale, and increased competition." Two decades later, leadership in renewables passed to another economy halfway around the world. In an effort to integrate East Germany's power system into West Germany's electric utilities grid after the fall of the Berlin Wall, Germany became a global leader in renewable energy in the 1990s. Despite the oversupply of oil that flooded the world market in the mid-1980s, forcing prices to plummet from a high of $34 per barrel to $10 per barrel in 1986, Germany was more concerned with the devastating consequences of another event that took place the same year—the nuclear power plant accident at Chernobyl. This disaster served as a mobilizing force for Germans who did not want to depend on nuclear energy, which up until then had been touted as the energy source of the future. By the early 1990s, wind turbines were proliferating across Germany. By the turn of the century, the government had "adopted a program to phase out all nuclear power, [which at the time was] providing over a quarter of Germany's total electricity", providing a further impetus for the development of renewables (Yergin, 2011: 539). In 2009, renewables' share of Germany's electricity consumption reached 14 percent, exceeding the country's 2010 goal. By 2012, Germany's solar photovoltaics (PVs) capacity accounted for nearly one-third (32 percent) of the global total. By contrast, the U.S. and China's share were very similar, at around 7 percent each (REN21, 2013: 40–41). However, two years later, Germany's early commanding lead had slipped to about 21 percent, while China's share had improved to almost 16 percent, and the U.S. share had increased more moderately, to a little over 10 percent of global capacity (REN21, 2016: 58–60).

China entered the renewables race in a significant way relatively late in the game. Even though it had laws in place that called for solar and wind energy as early as 1973, renewables were largely considered "antipoverty measures for the benefit of the rural poor" (Yergin, 2011: 543–544). But by the turn of the century, renewables had become a global business, and China wanted to play a major role in shaping it. By the mid-2000s, rapid economic growth had led to equally rapid growth in energy consumption, forcing China to import energy in order to respond to increasing electricity demand at home. The decisive change came with the Renewable Energy Law of 2005, followed by the Medium- and Long-Term Development Plan for Renewable Energy of 2007, which not only jump-started renewables in China but also set a specific target of renewables constituting 15 percent of the country's total energy by 2020. As a result of massive government stimulus spending during the 2008 global financial crisis, China's renewable energy industry "moved into high gear" (Yergin, 2011: 544). Within a decade, Chinese companies became the dominant manufacturers of solar panels, and China was second only to Germany in terms of cumulative installed solar PV capacity (see table 12.2).

To put things in perspective, in 1980, 85 percent of all solar modules were being produced in the United States. By 2005, the U.S. share had shrunk to less than 10 percent, with Japan, China, and Germany replacing the United States as the leaders in photovoltaics (Quaschning 2010: 113). China has also made significant inroads into the wind turbine industry, surpassing the United States and Germany as the global leader in cumulative installed wind power capacity in 2010 and maintaining its lead ever since (see table 12.3). Concerned with

Table 12.2 **Cumulative Installed Solar PV Capacity in Top Five Countries, 2000–2015 (Megawatts)**

Year	China	United States	Germany	Spain	India
1980	n.a.	8	0	0	0
1981	n.a.	18	0	0	0
1982	n.a.	84	0	0	0
1983	n.a.	254	0	0	0
1984	n.a.	653	0	0	0
1985	n.a.	945	0	0	0
1986	n.a.	1,265	0	0	0
1987	n.a.	1,333	5	0	0
1988	n.a.	1,231	15	0	0
1989	n.a.	1,332	27	0	0
1990	n.a.	1,484	62	0	0
1991	n.a.	1,709	112	5	39
1992	n.a.	1,680	180	50	39
1993	n.a.	1,635	335	60	79
1994	n.a.	1,663	643	70	185
1995	38	1,612	1,130	140	576
1996	79	1,614	1,548	230	820
1997	170	1,611	2,080	512	940
1998	224	1,837	2,875	834	1,015
1999	268	2,472	4,442	1,812	1,077
2000	346	2,539	6,113	2,235	1,220
2001	404	4,275	8,754	3,337	1,456
2002	470	4,685	11,994	4,825	1,702
2003	568	6,372	14,609	6,203	2,125
2004	765	6,725	16,629	8,263	3,000
2005	1,272	9,149	18,415	10,027	4,430
2006	2,599	11,575	20,578	11,623	6,270
2007	5,910	16,824	22,194	15,145	7,845
2008	12,020	25,076	23,826	16,689	9,655
2009	25,805	35,086	25,673	19,160	10,926

(*continued*)

Table 12.2 **Continued**

Year	China	United States	Germany	Spain	India
2010	44,733	40,298	27,097	20,623	13,065
2011	62,364	46,929	29,071	21,674	16,084
2012	75,324	60,007	31,270	22,784	18,421
2013	91,412	61,091	34,250	22,959	20,150
2014	114,609	65,879	39,165	22,987	22,465
2015	145,362	74,471	44,947	23,025	25,088

Source: British Petroleum (2014, 2015, 2016), modified from Roney (2014).

energy security and obsessed with controlling all aspects of energy production, China put in place policies requiring that as much as 70 percent of the parts for domestic wind installations had to be Chinese-made. Although the requirement was short-lived, such policies "gave Chinese wind-turbine suppliers time to expand the scale and sophistication of their operations and building on China's comparative advantage in manufacturing costs, to be more competitive with foreign companies and abroad" (Yergin 2011: 545).

In 2010, China also became the global leader in annual investment in renewable energy, taking that title from Germany, which had held it for several years (REN21, 2013: 47). Many scenarios anticipate that China will maintain its leadership in the coming decades. In 2014, China accounted for 45 percent of global new installed wind power capacity, compared to the United States, which accounted for less than 10 percent. In the same year, China accounted for about 31 percent of global cumulative installed wind power capacity, followed by the United States at about 18 percent (see table 12.3).

If we look across the board at the different types of renewable energy, China led at the beginning of 2016 in five of seven categories and placed in the top five in all but geothermal energy (see table 12.4). If one were handicapping a race, the odds of China leading the pack would be quite good. Still, the United States was ranked first or second in five categories and placed in the top five in all seven categories. The race's outcome, therefore, is not entirely a foregone conclusion.

Despite China's lead in the renewables race, the country's push to boost these energy sources faces serious challenges. For instance, in the view of one energy analyst, from 2000 to 2010, the increase in Chinese energy demand (just in terms of growth) was equivalent to double Latin America's entire energy consumption. In other words, in the span of a decade, the Chinese have created two continents' worth of energy demand, and they are expected to create another

Table 12.3 **Cumulative Installed Wind Power Capacity in Top Five Countries, 1980–2014 (Megawatts)**

Year	China	United States	Germany	Spain	India
1980		8			
1981		18			
1982		84			
1983		254			
1984		653			
1985		945			
1986		1,265			
1987		1,333	5		
1988		1,231	15		
1989		1,332	27		
1990		1,484	62		
1991		1,709	112	5	39
1992		1,680	180	50	39
1993		1,635	335	60	79
1994		1,663	643	70	185
1995	38	1,612	1,130	140	576
1996	79	1,614	1,548	230	820
1997	170	1,611	2,080	512	940
1998	224	1,837	2,875	834	1,015
1999	268	2,472	4,442	1,812	1,077
2000	346	2,539	6,113	2,235	1,220
2001	404	4,275	8,754	3,337	1,456
2002	470	4,685	11,994	4,825	1,702
2003	568	6,372	14,609	6,203	2,125
2004	765	6,725	16,629	8,263	3,000
2005	1,272	9,149	18,415	10,027	4,430
2006	2,599	11,575	20,578	11,623	6,270
2007	5,910	16,824	22,184	15,145	7,845

(*continued*)

Table 12.3 **Continued**

Year	China	United States	Germany	Spain	India
2008	12,020	25,076	23,826	16,689	9,655
2009	25,805	35,086	25,673	19,160	10,926
2010	44,133	40,298	27,097	20,623	13,065
2011	62,364	46,929	29,071	21,674	16,084
2012	75,324	60,007	31,270	22,184	18,421
2013	91,412	61,091	34,250	22,959	20,150
2014	114,609	65,879	39,165	22,987	22,465
2015	145,362	74,471	44,947	23,025	29,088

Source: Global Wind Energy Council (2015). Missing values modified from Roney (2014).

Table 12.4 **Total Installed Renewable Capacity by Source in Top Five Countries, 2015**

Rank	Renewable Power (w/Hydro)	Renewable Power (No Hydro)	Biopower	Geothermal Power	Solar PV Power	Wind Power	Hydropower
1	China	China	United States	United States	China	China	China
2	United States	United States	China	Philippines	Germany	United States	Brazil
3	Brazil	Germany	Germany	Indonesia	Japan	Germany	United States
4	Germany	Japan	Brazil	Mexico	United States	India	Canada
5	Canada	India	Japan	New Zealand	Italy	Spain	Russia

Source: Based on REN21 (2016).

continent's worth of demand every five to six years (Herberg 2013). This pace of growth is detrimental to the global climate, particularly since up to two-thirds of the Chinese energy supply comes from coal. The biggest challenge for China is thus to acquire enough energy to feed the juggernaut that its economy has become since the late 1990s.

Even as China's wind and solar power generation capacities rapidly expand, they may together account for just 5 percent of China's total electricity generation in 2020. Although China is moving fast on renewables, it has been burning 10 percent more coal each year just to keep up with the annual growth in energy demand. Air pollution from burning coal, however, has encouraged some retreat from this energy source. Yet renewables cannot become China's primary source of energy any time in the near future, because China's economy will continue to demand more energy than renewables can supply. Nuclear power and natural gas, both seen as cleaner alternatives to coal and oil, will inevitably be used, but so will petroleum and coal. As one observer notes:

> Whether China can become a true energy innovator will determine the country's economic future. If it is successful, it will ease the country's rise to great-power status and aid the global fight on climate change. If it is not, the Chinese dream might see an unpleasant awakening, as China throws off the shackles of poverty only to see them replaced by the shackles of energy imports that have long plagued Western foreign policy. (Huenteler 2014)

Of course, China is hardly alone in being far from developing a reliance on renewables. The United States has been plagued by major policy disagreements about how best to stimulate economic growth. New U.S. leads in petroleum and natural gas production thanks to the introduction of shale extraction techniques, as discussed in chapter 11, are rather difficult to ignore in this context, even if the gains are unlikely to be long-term in nature. Most of the world is in a similar position. With the exception of a very few small countries, most states have much further to go than they have come in making the transition to a full commitment to renewables. Table 12.5 singles out only four states (Norway, Paraguay, Iceland, and Tajikistan) that have been deemed close to halfway in making this transition. Much of the rest of the world is far behind although recent information (REN21 2017) suggests some states are making better-than-expected headway. Still, the two potential leaders, the United States and China, are both judged to be less than 5 percent along the way toward a full transition to an economy based on renewables.

These trends are more than sobering and suggest that the renewables age (despite current investments and installed capacities) may well not emerge before the twenty-second century. China and the United States may be leading the race, but they are leading it at a snail's pace, which may not be good enough, given the impending climate crisis. So while we have been asking, Who is ahead in the renewables race—the United States or China? the more important question is: Are they leading fast enough? In 2013, renewables accounted for 10.1 percent of global energy consumption, whereas fossil fuels covered around 78.3 percent

Table 12.5 **Percent Attainment of Commitment to Renewables, 2014**

% Attained	States
50+%	Norway, Paraguay
40–49%	Iceland, Tajikistan
30–39%	—
20–29%	Portugal, Sweden
10–19%	Costa Rica, Switzerland, New Zealand, Montenegro, Georgia, Spain, Kyrgyzstan, Albania, Uruguay, Canada, Denmark, Greece, Bosnia and Herzegovina
5–9%	Armenia, Turkey, Ireland, Austria, Romania, El Salvador, Colombia, Slovenia, Brazil, Sri Lanka, Italy, Venezuela, Germany, Zambia, France, Latvia, Mozambique, Panama, United Kingdom, Bulgaria, Cambodia, Kosovo, Nicaragua, Peru, Chile
1–4.9%	Croatia, Australia, Argentina, Vietnam, Japan, Sudan, Ecuador, Myanmar, Slovak Republic, Macedonia, North Korea, United States, Honduras, Congo, Guatemala, Philippines, Serbia, Syria, Ghana, Finland, China, Namibia, Russian Federation, Dominican Republic, Kenya, Azerbaijan, Estonia, Iraq, Morocco, Czech Republic, Mexico, Cyprus, Belgium, Cameroon, Poland, India, Bolivia, Congo Dem. Rep., Zimbabwe, Ethiopia, Angola, Netherlands, Pakistan, Cote d'Ivoire, Ukraine, Nepal, Malaysia, Iran, Lithuania, Gabon, Lebanon, Luxembourg, Israel
0–0.9%	All others

Source: Based on rank orders reported in Jacobson et al. (2015: 14).

of the world's primary energy needs (REN21, 2016: 27). It is not enough to lead the renewables race if the lead economies are not making systemic changes along the way. More importantly, if neither the United States nor China is transitioning from fossil fuels to renewable energy–based economies fast enough, then new systemic leadership, which we argue is based on a complex of new technology and new fuel, is less likely to happen in the next half-century or so.

To help answer these questions, we have to know what the current map of U.S. and Chinese renewable energy consumption patterns looks like and what it might look like by 2050. In the face of the climate crisis, the idea of an inexhaustible and environmentally friendly energy source is deeply appealing. Yet currently both lead economies heavily rely on fossil fuels to power their economies. Since the 1990s, China's consumption of coal, most of which is produced domestically, has grown rapidly, providing more than two-thirds of its total energy and four-fifths of its electricity. This rate of growth is unsustainable—something that even Chinese decision-makers now acknowledge. Data from the World Energy Council show that, based on figures for 2011, China's proven coal reserves will last thirty-four years given its annual production rates. As Huenteler (2014) has noted, "That is down from about 100 years just a decade ago and means China will have exhausted its reserves by 2049, if it keeps going at the current rate."[3] But the longer-term scarcity problem is overshadowed by the nearer-term costs in environmental and human welfare within China. The severity of Chinese public health problems that are due to its dependence on coal have given central decision-makers strong incentives for rethinking their approach.

The fear of an unwavering commitment to coal (at least through 2030) on China's part may not reflect what is sometimes called the "new normal" growth model (Green and Stern, 2015). An intensive effort to rapidly reverse China's lack of economic development has been successful in some respects, but it also has led to the previously noted environmental and public health problems. Less emphasis on quantitative growth and more emphasis on qualitative growth—that is, the new normal—may lead to a more rapid abandonment of coal than has been planned in the past. Such a move would address the environmental degradation problem at the same time that it prepares the Chinese economy for a switch to more high-tech economic production.[4] Time will tell how this new normal model plays out.

What we do know at this juncture is that the demand for fossil fuels remains fairly high. Our collective appetite for energy is so great that most of the known fossil fuel deposits could be used up during the twenty-first century. For decades, peak oil pessimists have been warning about the imminent end of fossil energy reserves. Yet this end never quite seems to be in sight, and most people take no heed of the warnings as long as gas prices remain relatively low. This tendency has been exacerbated because in the past, technological advances in the exploitation of oil and natural gas have consistently resulted in revisions of the forecasts for how long reserves will last. The large coal reserves still available worldwide could enable us to use fossil energy sources for decades. But the number of new finds, especially of oil, has declined substantially in recent years, and new supplies cannot be exploited fast enough to meet rising demand. For instance, in 2016, global oil consumption grew by 1.6 million barrels per day, while global oil production grew by only 0.4 million barrels per day (British Petroleum 2017). In that same year, the United States consumed 19,531 thousand barrels per day (20.3 percent of world total) while China consumed 11,986 thousand barrels per day (12.8 percent of world total). Yet China has maintained the lead in the rate of growth in consumption through at least 2016 by increasing its 2014-2016 consumption by 687,000 barrels per day compared to the U.S. increase of 425,000 barrels. Table 12.6 shows that global consumption of petroleum, coal,

Table 12.6 **US-China Fossil Fuel Consumption, 2010–2016**

Petroleum (thousand barrels per day)

	2010	2011	2012	2013	2014	2015	2016
United States	19,180	18,882	18,490	18,961	19,106	19,531	19,631
China	9,436	9,796	10,230	10,734	11,209	11,986	12,381
World	88,722	89,729	90,675	91,114	92,025	95,003	96,558

Coal (million tons of oil equivalent)

	2010	2011	2012	2013	2014	2015	2016
United States	525	495.4	437.9	454.6	453.5	391.8	358.4
China	1,748.9	1,903.9	1,927.8	1,969.1	1,954.5	1,913.6	1,887.6
World	3,635.6	3,807.2	3,817.3	3,887	3,889.4	3,784.7	3,732

Natural Gas (billion cubic meters)

	2010	2011	2012	2013	2014	2015	2016
United States	682.1	693.1	723.2	740.6	753	773.2	778.6
China	111.2	137.1	150.9	171.9	188.4	194.8	210.3
World	3,187.6	3,245.9	3,323.1	3,383.8	3,400.8	3,480.1	3,542.9

Source: British Petroleum (2017); petroleum is measured in thousand barrels daily, the coal metric in million tons of oil equivalent, and natural gas in billion cubic meters.

and natural gas are all still on the rise. China's coal consumption may actually have peaked, but its demand for natural gas continues to grow. The decline in U.S. coal consumption is offset by the country's increased use of natural gas.

Oil remains the world's leading fuel, still accounting for about a third of global energy consumption in 2016 (British Petroleum, 2017). As long as fossil fuels remain attractively priced thanks to ample supply and enjoy subsidies larger than those granted to renewables, they are likely to continue to dominate the global energy mix. Non-hydro renewables now account for less than 3 percent of global total energy consumption.

We may well be in the early days of an energy transition, but it seems likely to be slow and protracted. This makes it difficult to imagine that renewable energies will become the primary source of energy in the next half-century. The production and use of renewable fuels has grown more quickly in recent years as a result of higher prices for oil and natural gas and a number of government incentives for renewable energy development. The use of renewable fuels is expected to continue to grow over the next thirty years, although most forecasts project that during this period we will still rely on nonrenewable fuels to meet most of our energy needs.

Table 12.7 supports this generalization. Forecasts are based on scenarios, and some forecasters like to develop conservative and liberal sets of assumptions (hence the range of outcomes separated by a slash in table 12.7). Yet none of these forecasts can envision more than a third of the world's energy being supplied by renewable sources as late as 2060. Thus the renewables age is unlikely to emerge before the advent of the twenty-second century.

Nonetheless, even the "liberal" entries in table 12.7 are generally conservative. Oil companies, industry groups, and government agencies all tend toward conservative estimates, usually restricting their renewables proportion to about 20 percent of the total supply. Estimates that boost the renewables proportion to as much as 40 percent tend to focus on climate mitigation concerns. Anything higher is reserved for renewables advocates who claim that renewables could become the main source of energy as early as 2050 if governments and populations are prepared to make the shift.[5]

We remain unconvinced that the conservative estimations will prove good guides to the future of fossil fuel consumption. For one thing, the predictions for lingering petroleum reliance are contingent on dubious Middle Eastern claims about reserves and the expectation of continuing oil discoveries. New oil discoveries may in fact have peaked in 1965, according to Hughes (2012), and so far, the potential for Arctic oil exploitation seems limited. Even so, there are very good reasons to expect that any transition to renewables will entail an extraordinary level of investment and the overcoming of significant political resistance. However, if the supply of carbon-based fuels can somehow be prolonged

Table 12.7 **Forecasted World Proportions of Renewables in Future Energy Mixes**

	2020	2025	2030	2035	2040	2050	2060	2100
U.S. EIA (2013)					12% (U.S.)			
International Energy Agency				12–23%				
British Petroleum (2014)				7%				
British Petroleum (2015)				17% (U.S.)				
British Petroleum (2016)				10% (China)				
Exxon Mobil (2014)		15%			15%			
Shell Global (2008)			11.5%		16.3%	22.8%		
Shell Global (2013)	9.5/9.6%		9.8/11.5%		12.2/18.2%	16.7/18.2%	19.6/32.7%	
World Economic Council (2013)						20–30%		
Bloomberg New Energy Finance (2013)			16–22%					
Matias and Devezas (2007)								100%
Li (2014)								100%
Hartley et al. (2014)								100

into the future, conservative estimates may prove reasonably accurate. If so, a new source of energy would seem unlikely to become fully available during the next half-century, and perhaps not until the twenty-second century.

At the same time, current plans for responses to global warming threats that hinge on an accelerated decarbonization by 2050 (as exemplified by Guerin, Mas, and Waisman, 2014; and Jacobson et al., 2015) do not call for a full movement to renewables. These plans call for a mix of fuel sources that would vary from state to state depending in part on development level, differential access to various energy sources, and a focus on electrification of building heating/air-conditioning and transportation. For instance, the U.S. energy mix (Williams et al., 2014) might be composed of 39 percent renewables (including hydro-power), 30 percent nuclear power, and 30 percent gas and coal that have been treated for carbon capture and storage. The Deep Decarbonization Project's Chinese plan (Teng et al., 2015) is less specific about energy combinations but appears to propose a China in 2050 that resembles an OECD country in 2010, with much less emphasis on coal that has not been treated for carbon capture and storage. These 2050 plans are scenarios that allow for variable combinations of energy sources.[6] We suspect that this more flexible approach is more likely to reflect 2050 conditions than is a scenario linked to a continued petroleum or new renewables age. Yet some form of intensive decarbonization by 2050 presumes a widespread and serious response to global warming and climate change, and that, we recognize, remains an iffy assumption.

If we are right about the historical pattern of new and inexpensive energy providing a base for systemic leadership, the future's economic context does not appear to be favorable to the rise of a new systemic leadership, whether a renewed version led by the United States or a new version championed by China. Barring some type of unpredictable game changer, China may grow relatively richer than it has been and the U.S. lead may continue to diminish slowly without any radical or fundamental shift in relative power distribution. This outcome will be unfortunate if new systemic leadership is crucial to a serious and widespread response to climate change problems. At best, one might hope for U.S–Chinese cooperation on this issue—a relationship that may be emerging but will always be vulnerable to the vicissitudes of their ongoing rivalry and the twists of domestic politics.

Thus, the immediate future could very well be more of what we are currently experiencing: increasing verbal acknowledgement of a serious problem at least in some quarters and maybe movement toward dealing with the issue in some meaningful way(s). The 2015 Paris climate summit was more positive than earlier meetings in Copenhagen or Kyoto, yet it still was unable to spur concrete action, partly because of U.S inability to obtain legislative ratification for concrete measures. This secondary problem reflects less a lack of systemic leadership than it does political polarization within the United States which ultimately led to the United States disavowing the Paris goals.[7] Still, the two processes are not unrelated and, more generally, do reflect current weaknesses in the evolution of systemic leadership—hence our expectation of more of the same (or worse) in the immediate future. One difference, however, is that the future is likely to be characterized by approaching exhaustion of the world's hitherto relatively inexpensive fossil fuels and continued and perhaps escalating problems with greenhouse gas emissions. More renewable energy will become available for sure. What remains unclear is how much is needed and by when, how long the transition away from fossil fuels will take, and whether systemic leadership—old or new—will be able to cobble together an effective response to global warming.

Conclusion

> The great energy transition from fossil fuels to renewable sources of energy is under way. As fossil fuel prices rise, as oil insecurity deepens, and as concerns about pollution and climate instability cast a shadow over the future of coal, a new world energy economy is emerging. The old energy economy, fueled by oil, coal, and natural gas, is being replaced with an economy powered by wind, solar, and geothermal energy. The Earth's renewable energy resources are vast and available to be tapped through visionary initiatives. Our civilization needs to embrace renewable energy on a scale and at a pace we've never seen before. (Brown, 2012: 3)

Most everyone concerned with the health of the environment would agree with Brown's assertion that the time to transition from fossil fuels to renewable energy is past due. However, despite Brown's optimism, a new world economy sustained by renewables is hardly emerging quickly. Given the current rate at which the global energy transition is proceeding, it may be the dawn of the twenty-second century before renewable alternatives constitute the primary source of global energy.

Over the past several hundred years, systemic leadership transitions (from the Dutch to the British to the Americans) have been tied to transitions in primary energy sources (from peat to coal to petroleum, respectively). That is because historically, lead states have had a commanding lead in energy and its associated infrastructure. System leaders need cheap energy to fuel their economic leads. The technology that they pioneer tends to rely on new sources of energy that are critical to operating at the production frontier. Thus, energy transitions have profound and long-lasting implications for economic growth, which itself exerts considerable influence on the international system's power hierarchy.

In the past, systemic leadership in the West emerged first in Europe and then in the United States at least partially because these countries adopted fossil fuels after China and the Netherlands failed to fully do so. To go beyond agrarian constraints, lead economies needed additional sources of energy. While wind and peat were important parts of the rise to systemic leadership, it took coal for the British and petroleum for the Americans to become predominant powers in the international system. Systemic leadership transitions ultimately hinged on the development of a combination of technological leadership and access to relatively inexpensive energy that fit the radical new technology. Assuming that the radical new technology of the mid- to late twenty-first century will be IT-based, that energy will at least be whatever is useful for generating electricity. Yet petroleum, if not coal, presumably will be much scarcer by 2050 and therefore more expensive. Of course, the major new wrinkle in this energy transition story is that the use of carbon-based fuels has caused major environmental problems, which will only become more severe as more such fuels are used. Hence, renewables are the cleanest source of energy for both the environment and system leadership. In this chapter we have argued that as the world's relatively inexpensive fossil fuel reserves approach exhaustion, the ascendance of new systemic leadership will hinge on a transition to non–fossil fuel energy sources. Thus, who is ahead in the renewables race matters. But if there is only a small gap between competitors, a low probability of a politico–economic transition occurring in the twenty-first century seems more likely. The absence of new or reinvigorated systemic leadership in turn bodes poorly for the formulation of a global response to global warming. Not only do system leaders need to negotiate a global consensus to make changes in this area, but they must also lead in radically transforming their own economies. So far, it has proven easier to accomplish the former than the latter. Yet maintaining the consensus has also proven to be quite difficult.

13

Denouement: World Politics, Systemic Leadership, and Climate Change

We began this undertaking with three goals. First, we wanted to improve our understanding of the patterns underlying the evolution of world politics over the past one thousand years. How did we get to where we are now? Where and when did the "modern" world begin? How did we shift from a primarily agrarian economy to a primarily industrial one? How did these changes shape world politics? A second goal was to examine more closely the factors that led to the most serious attempts by states to break free of agrarian constraints—medieval China, the seventeenth-century Netherlands, nineteenth-century Britain, and the twentieth-century United States. Toward this end, we developed an interactive model of the factors that we thought were most likely to be significant— with not all factors necessarily being equally significant in each case. Finally, a third goal involved examining the linkages between the systemic leadership that emerged from these historical processes and the global warming crisis of the twenty-first century. How was systemic leadership linked to bringing about the crisis in the first place? What is the likely systemic leadership role in responding to the crisis? We have sought to address all three goals. Now it is time to recapitulate what we have found.

The first goal aimed to enhance the Modelski–Thompson (1996) interpretation of the evolution of global politics over the past millennium. The hallmark of this approach is its focus on the intermittent ascendance of lead economies that corner the market on economic innovation for a period of time. During this ascendancy, they become technological centers and global system leaders that command global reach capabilities until they are eclipsed by new lead economies. This view stresses the distinctions between actors that are more concerned with traditional territorial expansion in their home regions and global actors that specialize in long-distance maritime commerce and high-tech industrial production and by and large attempt to stay clear of regional power plays. Lead economies are the most technologically advanced of the global actors. World politics is thus characterized by differential levels of power concentration at the global and regional levels. Occasionally, global and regional activities have become linked when attempts to take over the European region have threatened lead economies and other global actors. From 1494 to 1945, these threats to system leadership were resolved in global wars that became increasingly lethal.

A major amendment to this framework revolves around distinctions among the various lead economies that have risen to power over the past one thousand years. The main distinction drawn here was between those actors in the West that focused on maritime commerce and naval technology and those that introduced transitions to new energy regimes. China, Genoa, Venice, and Portugal did not usher in new energy regimes. The Netherlands, using peat and wind, almost did but ultimately failed to do so, while Britain and the United States successfully inaugurated transitions to carbon fuels. As a consequence, the power of their economies—and their system leads—was much greater than those of their predecessors.

The second goal of this examination was to demonstrate the degree to which inexpensive energy has been a major component of a state's rise to systemic leadership. Toward this end, we examined case studies of the emergence of lead economies in China, the Netherlands, Britain, and the United States within a framework designed to highlight the contributions of those factors considered most salient to a particular economy's rise. This work does not represent the first time that these four states have been compared in terms of economic development, but it may well be the first time that they have been treated as four roughly successive lead economies within a single model emphasizing their ascendance to technological centrality.

Chapters 5 through 9 ended up accomplishing a variety of tasks. First, a rather large number of arguments about economic growth, the rise of the West conundrum, and global inequality had to be reviewed. As much evidence as was available and pertinent also had to be evaluated. Ultimately, the comparison of the four cases was facilitated by the imposition of a standard model that essentially demarcates a two-phase development of Smithian factors coupled with a cluster of Schumpeterian energy considerations. This model posits that, à la Goldstone's efflorescence theory, outstanding economic growth can be achieved up to a point and for only a finite period within the agrarian regime. Ultimately, these gains cannot be sustained unless a second phase involving an interaction between new technology and new energy sources takes place. Once that occurs, a state can achieve a breakthrough from the agrarian regime to the industrial regime. Economic growth can then be more or less sustained, if for no other reason than because there are strong incentives to improve the imperfect technology in use and make the use of energy more efficient.

The energy sources used by lead economies have not been as substitutable as economists like to think. Britain could not have carried out the Industrial Revolution relying solely on wood. The amount of wood that would have been needed to fuel what Britain accomplished in terms of industrial production was impossible to obtain. This wood was not available locally, could not have been imported in sufficient quantities, and could not have generated sufficient heat to make iron, textiles, and railroads. Much the same can be said about the U.S. growth trajectory. It could never have accomplished what it ended up producing with traditional sources of energy. Unlike Britain, the United States had plenty of wood, but this energy source would not have been sufficient to allow the United States to surpass British achievements. For that, it needed electricity and petroleum.

Moreover, these energy sources had to be relatively inexpensive to allow lead economies to reach the production scales that were so critical to industrial leadership. Scalar changes in production levels could not be attained with costly energy sources. When energy became considerably more expensive or could no longer be obtained locally without expensive importation, the ability of the lead economy to maintain its production edge suffered. Some other economy (or the same firms with transplanted production sites) could make the same products more cheaply elsewhere and did. This observation is not meant to sound like a single-variable explanation of rise and fall. Energy does not explain everything, but it does appear to be more crucial than is often recognized. Easily accessible, inexpensive energy was important to the ascents of the Dutch, the British, and the Americans between the seventeenth and twentieth centuries. In the absence of some revolutionary game changer, we should expect this factor to still remain significant in the twenty-first century.

The third goal of this work was to address the relationship between system leadership and climate change. Climate change means that traditional energy platforms for system leadership—coal, petroleum, and natural gas—have become counterproductive. While they are still capable of generating power, they also produce greenhouse gases that make climate change more likely. The ultimate irony is that we thought that the harnessing of carbon fuels made us invulnerable to climate fluctuations, when the exact opposite turns out to be true. The more carbon fuels are consumed, the greater is the damage done to the atmosphere.

Decarbonization, preferably within the next few decades, if we hope to avoid doing even greater damage to the planet, seems desirable. To date, the best plans involve an intensified program of electrification, especially in terms of transportation, and decarbonization of the fuels used to generate electricity. Renewables will be part of that program, but it will be a very long time before renewables replace other energy sources entirely—if they ever do. In the interim, the decarbonization of coal and natural gas will probably be critical. The problem is that this approach has not been much attempted, and the technology required is costly. Ideally, further technological research and innovation will improve this approach, just as improvements in wind turbines and solar panels have decreased the cost of renewables. More research and innovation are also needed in the renewables sector to improve our abilities to store and distribute energy derived from wind and the sun.

In contrast, U.S. shale discoveries appear attractive in the short term but much less desirable in the long term. Extending access to fossil fuels reduces immediate energy costs, but if it discourages efforts to move away from fossil fuels, the money saved will prove to have been deceptive. Mitigation of the climate changes that are anticipated will be quite costly as well. Attempts to weigh short-term benefits and long-term costs are difficult, since we can only guess about the future. But given that the future will probably be much warmer (probably by more than two degrees C) than the present, it is hard to see how cheaper gasoline today is worth the likely environmental problems down the road.

In any event, and returning more explicitly to the issue of systemic leadership, it is more than fortuitous that both the incumbent system leader, the United States, and its possible heir, China, are seeking radically altered economies at the same time. The U.S. economy is bogged down by twilight industries that once made the United States great but now are less than competitive in global markets. It needs to expand into new industries if it wishes to maintain its economic foundation for system leadership. The Chinese economy has made rapid strides toward economic development by providing the world with inexpensive labor for consumer manufacturing. Now, however, it needs to move beyond routine manufacturing into high-tech economic innovation if it wishes to construct a platform for system leadership in the future. Should one or both of these states lead the way to the next technological wave and/or energy regime, we will be better off. And the sooner that pathway is found, the more global welfare will improve. Whoever pulls off this feat will provide a model for the rest of the world to emulate. Leading the way to new ways of doing things is one variant of systemic leadership.

At the same time, China and the United States are the G2 of carbon emissions, the two greatest consumers and emitters of energy, together generating about 45 percent of global CO_2 emissions. Further Chinese economic growth threatens to make the problem even worse, while further increases in Chinese carbon pollution threaten to make China even less livable. So, China and the United States are major and indispensable parts of the climate change problem. Without their strong participation in responding to this problem, no climate change solution or collective response will be meaningful at the global level. With almost two hundred states in the world, all with different interests and different problems, political coordination is essential. Historically, system leaders, based on their technological centrality and global reach, have been the principal sources of international political coordination at the global level. They are still needed for global governance in the twenty-first century.

But the United States is no longer operating at full strength, and China is nowhere near full strength. There is some risk that we could find ourselves in the same structural context that bedeviled the twentieth-century interwar years (1919–1939), when systemic leadership was scarce and coordination difficult. At that time, Britain had lost much of its leadership foundation, and the United States was still assembling its platform. World economic depression and a second world war were the outcome. Fortunately, the comparison is not exact. The United States has been in relative decline in recent years, but its position is nowhere near as low as Britain's after World War I. It was also fairly clear after World War I that the United States was likely to succeed Britain at some point. China's prospects are less clear-cut. It may become the next global leader down the road, but it is also possible to conceive scenarios in which China's global succession does not occur.[1] It is even possible that no single system leader will emerge in the future, given the difficulties states face in getting ahead of the rest of the pack technologically and maintaining a lead for any length of time. Perhaps we have moved beyond the ability of one state to monopolize its lead for several generations.

Regardless of whether the comparison with the twentieth-century interwar period is appropriate, there is an opportunity for U.S.–Chinese collaboration on decarbonization. Such cooperation would require both states to be eager to engage in decarbonization and to accept the idea that the failure to eliminate fossil fuel use in coming decades will prove too costly. Decision-makers in both states seemed close to such a position in the months leading up to the 2015 Paris climate summit on reducing greenhouse gas emissions. But neither state is currently in a perfect position to collaborate. China still needs and wants more economic growth that cannot be achieved as quickly as desired if it cuts back on its energy consumption right away. The United States has political leadership that is at best intermittently committed to decarbonization, depending on which party holds the executive position, and is generally paralyzed when it comes to taking nonexecutive action. The party in power at the time of this writing is very much opposed to decarbonization efforts and publicly derides climate change problems as a hoax. Both the United States and China, of course, are also engaged in an increasingly globalized strategic rivalry. With both of the key actors handicapped and characterized by multiple tradeoff options, it will be interesting to see what they are able to accomplish, if anything, in coming decades.[2]

The traditional Chinese curse—may you live in interesting times—unfortunately comes immediately to mind.

Victor (2013) contends that it makes little sense to try to obtain agreement among 193 states on a response to climate change. Any transition to a new energy regime will be long and slow, lasting as much as seventy years. In his view, it would make more sense to focus first on achieving a consensus among a small club of the most enthusiastic proponents of decarbonization. This consensus should be aimed less at goals involving heading off a defined amount of warming and more on concrete measures for transitioning away from carbon fuels. Once this aim is accomplished, this group can work on winning over reluctant states while focusing on improving climate change technology and preparing for the inevitable problems associated with global warming beyond the magical two-degree C threshold.

We share Victor's (2013) pessimism about the prospects of a 193-member UN committee succeeding. We also think that the two degree ceiling on future warming is not realistic because not enough has been done to curb CO_2 emissions. We also have no argument with the prediction that any energy transition will be long and slow. Moreover, the club focus is appealing. As Victor (2013: 10) points out, a dozen states (if we count the European Union as one) account for more than three-fourths of the world's carbon emissions. Why not focus first on the principal emitters? But here we disagree. In many respects, the enthusiast approach has already been tried and achieved some success in parts of the European Union. The problem is that even if the European Union succeeded in making the transition to a decarbonized energy regime tomorrow, this move would not address the carbon emissions problem all that much, because the EU states are not the main emitters—China and the United States are. Without their participation (and probably India's as well) and leadership in working toward a new energy regime, it is unlikely that much progress will be feasible. Therefore, we suggest that it makes more sense to focus any club approach on the United States, China, and major enthusiasts.[3] If the United States and China could be counted among the enthusiasts, so much the better. But both states are likely to be, at best, reluctant enthusiasts, given domestic opposition to energy changes. After the November 2016 electoral surprise, the United States, of course, can no longer be placed even in the reluctant enthusiast category. How much damage the advent of President Donald Trump will do to the world response to global warming remains to be seen.[4]

At the same time, we strongly endorse the idea that more resources need to be devoted to improving climate change–related technology. Batteries for electricity storage and automobiles and carbon capture techniques for treating coal and gas should be given the highest priority. These aims are a matter not just of coming up with better gadgets to cope with climate problems, but of restructuring economies around a different approach to utilizing energy. Such restructuring cannot proceed very far without new and improved technology. As demonstrated in chapters 5 and 6 especially, energy transition and technological innovation must proceed hand in hand.

What might happen to world politics if cooperation and technological/energy changes are not forthcoming? Inadvertently, a possible answer is found in eight scenarios (listed in table 13.1) developed by Hillebrand and Closson (2015). We say "inadvertent" because Hillebrand and Closson's interests are different from those of this book. Their scenarios are structured around different combinations of three variables: the price of energy, the rate of economic growth, and geopolitical harmony/disharmony. They develop eight possible stories for what might happen between 2010 and 2050 within the constraints of the three variable mixes. In addition, they also calculate different empirical outcomes

Table 13.1 **Hillebrand and Closson's 2050 Scenarios**

No.	Name	Economic Growth	Conflict	Fossil Fuel Share	CO_2 Increase	World Temperature (C)
1	Catching Up to America	Strong	Low	81.3%	34.6%	16.0
2	Global Backtracking	Weak	High	84.6%	27.4%	15.8
3	Peaceful Power Transition	Strong	Low	69.3%	27.4%	15.8
4	Regional Mercantilism	Weak	High	67.1%	21.5%	15.6
5	A New Bipolarity	Strong	High	57.4%	29.0%	15.8
6	Eco World	Weak	Low	57.7%	19.7%	15.5
7	Ambition Fuels Rivalry	Strong	High	75.4%	28.7%	15.8
8	Natural Disasters Promote Unity	Weak	Low	79.7%	28.2%	15.8

Source: Based on Hillebrand and Closson (2015: 22, 131) and author calculations. Fossil fuel share is calculated by dividing the share of fossil fuels by the total of fossil fuels and renewables. CO_2 increase is based on the CO_2 parts per million increase over 2010. The 2010 world temperature was 14.7.

using variable forecasts based on the International Futures (IFs) model developed by Barry Hughes at the University of Denver.

Hillebrand and Closson demonstrate a strong interest in the U.S.–China transition, but within a fairly status quo energy regime. Renewables increase in every scenario (the 2010 fossil fuel share is 87.7 percent), but in four (numbers 1, 2, 7, and 8), the change is not very great. At best, the overall energy regime moves toward a roughly equal split between fossil and nonfossil fuels without actually getting there by 2050. As a consequence, CO_2 emissions and world temperature increase, even in the most environmentally optimistic scenario (number 6). Since the temperature increase is only about one degree C regardless of the scenario, the IFs model calculation may be conservative or optimistic. While we do not know exactly what might happen if CO_2 emissions continue to climb, there is some potential for even greater increases in temperature beyond the roughly one-degree increase that has occurred since the late nineteenth century.

Still, the point is that a large range of outcomes could occur. Conflict between the United States and China could escalate.[5] Economic growth could improve or continue to sputter. Natural disasters could also escalate. Systemic leadership, something that is virtually missing in all eight scenarios, could vanish. Given that the world economy in 2050 is likely to be built around technology and energy usage not all that dissimilar to what we observe today, we have to assume that that the planet will be worse off, conflict will be greater, and economic growth will continue to be slow. Those assumptions point to scenarios 2 (global backtracking) and 4 (regional mercantilism) as the most likely. In the global backtracking scenario, all of the lead economies go into a downward spiral. In the regional mercantilism scenario, most states turn inward, cooperation becomes scarce, and coal is used less in the global North but is simply exported to the global South.

Needless to say, scenarios 2 and 4 are among the least desirable outcomes in the array presented in table 13.1. They are futures that we should work to evade, just as we should seek to avoid increased consumption of fossil fuels, increased CO_2 emissions, and higher temperatures. Whether all of any of these undesirable futures will or can be prevented will hinge to some extent on systemic leadership. Either lead economies will serve as decarbonized models for emulation, or they will not. Either lead economies will facilitate coordinated responses to global warming, or they will not. Our argument is simply that the most undesired futures are more likely to be avoided if systemic leadership of some sort is evident. Systemic leadership is not a panacea for all the ills of the world, but it is a necessary ingredient for coping with those ills. Hopefully, we have made that inconvenient truth more evident.

NOTES

Chapter 1

1. The basic problem with forecasting, as Paltsev (2016) observes, is that predictions rely too much on the past. However, it remains to be seen how soon renewable sources can supply sufficient energy to rival coal, petroleum, natural gas, and nuclear energy (Moriarity and Hannery, 2012).

2. Part of the disagreement is due to the reluctance to disentangle global and regional systems. Global systems (over which system leaders preside) involve transregional transactions and activities—essentially, the global political economy. But not all great powers are capable of maneuvering in multiple regions, and thus one needs to differentiate between regional and global power structures. Analysts often mix global elites with regional elites. From the late eighteenth to the early twentieth century, for instance, Britain, Russia, and France were both global and regional elites, while Austria-Hungary was exclusively a regional elite power, and Germany and Italy were primarily European regional elite powers that sought to participate in the global system. Italy stayed close to home in North Africa, while Germany's non-European forays became more ambitious toward the end of the nineteenth century. Japan and the United States initially were elite powers in other, non-European regions. Thus, one analytical choice that is often made without a great deal of explicit consideration is between a single international system with one set of elites and an international system with multiple regions in which elites have various standings. In the latter conceptualization, the main distinction is between elite powers that show up in multiple regions as opposed to those that are significant in only one.

3. Peat could be said to be an inferior form of coal (or compressed vegetation).

4. In particular, and as noted earlier, one of the likely missing ingredients is a twenty-first-century energy transition.

5. The National Science Knowledge and Technologically Intensive (KTI) industries data are only released every two years, which means that 2016 data will not be available until 2018, and 2018 information won't be available until 2020.

6. The relative decline data in figure 1.1 would be much more apparent if the frame of reference also encompassed the second half of the twentieth century.

7. From a conflict perspective, both characteristics are beneficial for world peace.

8. Another possibility is nuclear power, but its history of accidents and the tremendous scope of construction sites for new reactors have worked against its widespread development. At best, nuclear power is likely to be avoided in the Northern Hemisphere and sought in the Southern Hemisphere. As a consequence, economic forecasts rarely pay much attention to its potential and tend to predict that its future prominence will be no greater than its current status. Even if new technology that permits safer-functioning reactors could overcome the reluctance in some parts of the world to expand this energy source, the current extraction of uranium from

mines is insufficient to fuel existing nuclear reactors. In the period between 1995 and 2005, the gap between supply of and demand for uranium was almost 50 percent. While some of the gap is currently being filled by the recovery of uranium from military stocks and old nuclear warheads, these stocks are a finite resource and cannot be seen as a definitive solution to the problem of insufficient supply. For a more detailed discussion of the uranium supply–demand gap, see Bardi (2014).

Chapter 2

1. Readers will not find a succinct expression of hegemonic stability in Gilpin (1975), but it is there nonetheless. One has to reconstruct it from shards of argument found in different parts of the text. In his later work, a different variation appears in Gilpin (1980), but the original reemerges, still somewhat ambiguously, in Gilpin (1987). Gilpin and Gilpin (2001) has a brief defense of hegemonic stability theory (HST) in response to various criticisms published in the 1980s and 1990s. Lake (1993), of course, wrote a celebrated epitaph for HST, but it was probably premature. Cohen (2008: 67–79) offers an interesting history of the HST argument. Much of the relevant literature of the 1980s and 1990s was focused on how to organize the world economy in the aftermath of hegemony, but these interpretations assumed that "hegemony" disappeared in the 1970s. It is probably more accurate to say that it declined significantly after this decade but also lingered well past its "due date." Hegemony is a variable that is difficult to operationalize as either present or absent, and thus dealing with the H part of the HST has been problematic. A second problem is that much of the criticism of the theory is pretty much beside the point. That is, a number of early critics (e.g., Snidal, 1985) argued that public goods were not dependent on a single leader but could be generated by multiple actors acting collectively. But as Gilpin and Gilpin (2001) notes, that is probably true in the abstract but hardly invalidates a world economy that tends to be shaped by one leader at a time. Thus, the HST argument has experienced a checkered history that has revolved around what might best be interpreted as errors of analysis in the sense that the main criticisms proffered to date should not really matter to an assessment of the theory's utility. The real question is how far one can go with an exceedingly simple univariate theory. Because it is simple and univariate, we should anticipate limits on its explanatory value. Yet it is not yet clear that we know enough to write off the theory as lacking in utility.

2. Leadership long cycle theory is not a derivation of hegemonic stability theory, yet as far as theories go, they are close cousins. They both emerged at about the same time, in response to the post-1973 disorder in the world economy, just as international political economy as a recognizable subfield and other approaches such as world systems analysis also all emerged at this time for similar reasons.

3. See, for instance, Modelski (1987), Modelski and Modelski (1988), Modelski and Thompson (1988), Thompson (1988), and Rasler and Thompson (1992).

4. Admittedly, some post-1815 analysts incline toward the end of the Napoleonic Wars rather than the British Industrial Revolution as the demarcation event.

5. Some of the overlap is due to the sheer prominence of the actors, with this prominence perhaps becoming less "sheer" as one moves back in time. But Modelski and Thompson (1996) read Gilpin and Wallerstein. Kindleberger was familiar with Gilpin and the pre-1996 version of the leadership long cycle theory. Maddison (2001) did not reveal what he had read to create his list of lead states.

6. External shocks such as war and discoveries can accelerate the cycle, depending on the response to the developments.

7. The Venetian Arsenal was essentially an early factory for turning out warships rapidly. The Dutch fluyt was a flat-bottomed ship that could transfer bulk goods from the Baltic to the Atlantic inexpensively with a small crew.

8. A naïve version of public goods would have the leader supplying them because the system needs them to function. A more realistic (or cynical) version would suggest that goods are supplied to keep functional a system that primarily benefits the supplier of the public goods.

9. S-shaped emergence means that the growth of new activities and industries starts off slowly, accelerates, and then levels off before declining. The waves of growth are thus really sequences of S-shaped activity.

10. Global wars did not take place prior to 1494 and may have ended in 1945. Phenomena that emerge need not persist. Whether global wars truly ended in 1945, however, remains to be seen.

11. Note that "global system" is not a synonym for the whole world. Global politics are about regulating and preserving interregional transactions that stem in large part from long-distance trade and commerce. Protecting and cultivating the world economy is the prime directive of those states that have the most to gain from a stable economic environment. In contrast, a respectable proportion of international relations is entirely intraregional and often oriented toward territorial control. In international relations analysis we have tended to fuse these two different universes to our analytical disadvantage. To be fair, however, the activities of decision-makers intermittently conflate these spheres as well. For example, periodic attempts to establish European regional hegemony have been seen as indirect threats to the functioning of the world economy. If the aspiring European regional hegemons had been successful, they would have created a foundation for a direct assault on the world economy that might have been difficult to resist.

12. The relative positions of the succeeding lead economies are based on measuring their production in the leading economic sectors of their respective eras, ranging from Asian spices to computers, as specified by the indicators listed in table 2.3.

13. To make an implicit point explicit, the phases were designated well in advance of developing the hypothesis that each lead economy experiences two growth spurts. It was not a matter of fitting the phases to the hypothesis to confirm it. At the same time, the initial phase identification was certainly a subjective undertaking, except for periods of global warfare.

14. The global reach indicators examined in figure 2.2 are restricted to naval capabilities. The U.S. portion of this figure shows less relative decline than what is portrayed in figure 2.1 because the earlier figure focuses instead on a combination of naval and nonnaval capabilities.

Chapter 3

1. Smil (2010a: vii) defines an "energy transition" as a change in the composition of the primary energy supply. It has been possible to have a lead without ushering in an energy transition, but the most impactful leads have entailed full transitions to new energy regimes.

2. A trifecta wager requires the bettor to pick the first three finishers in a race, usually involving horses or greyhounds.

3. According to Arrighi (2007: 49), Adam Smith constructed his understanding of economic development around the concept of "filling up" national containers. If the spatial container that constitutes a state is underdeveloped in terms of people and capital, the state's economy has considerable growth potential. If the national spatial container is already filled with people and capital, its growth potential is limited. Growth dynamics will become stationary and, in Elvin's (1973) sense, create a high equilibrium trap. In our context, underexploited frontiers resemble Smith's partially filled spatial containers. At some point, though, all frontiers will be fully exploited and will have little more to offer in terms of greatly stimulating economic growth. Other emphases on frontier exploitation may be found in Webb (1964), Meinig (1986), Turner (1986), di Tella (1982), David and Wright (1997), Wright and Czelusta (2004), and Barbier (2011).

4. The role of state intervention became more critical to attempts to catch up with lead economies at least as early as seventeenth-century France. It is also true that government intervention in the technological innovation process has become increasingly important in the nineteenth to twenty-first centuries. See, for example, Weiss (2014) and Mazzucato (2015). If we were focusing exclusively on twenty-first century cases, the role of state intervention would be very hard to ignore, but this examination does not have such an exclusive focus.

5. We freely admit to simplifying the political–economic evolution of the past millennium.

6. This outcome did not occur in China despite that economy's decreasing access to firewood, increasing emphasis on coal for heating purposes, and the problem of too much water in coal

mines. In Britain, steam pumps were developed to cope with the water problem. In China, the water problem seems to have encouraged miners to move to other, drier sites. We do not reduce the alternative trajectories these economies followed to simply this factor, but it seems to loom large in accounting for different reactions to a similar problem.

7. See, for instance, the arguments in Chase-Dunn et al. (2011), Grinin and Korotoayev (2014), and Thompson (2015).

8. A number of analysts, for instance, have the impression that the pace of technological development has accelerated in recent years.

9. For more discussion of this topic, see chapters 8 to 11.

10. Perhaps if Charlemagne's kingdom had persisted, the outcome of the Roman and Qin–Han empires would have been somewhat more similar, but it did not. Even so, Charlemagne's Holy Roman Empire was still something less than a restoration of the older Roman Empire.

11. It could have worked out differently. Alexander the Great might somehow have kept his Macedonian juggernaut moving into and beyond India, however unlikely that might have been. If the Romans had developed a way to beat the Parthians, the Chinese and Roman armies might have clashed somewhere along the Silk Roads. After the Mongols withdrew from central Europe to deal with succession politics, they might have attacked again in the north instead of focusing on the Middle East and elsewhere. The Ming Chinese fleets of Zeng He might have continued down the East African coast and entered the Atlantic and ultimately the Mediterranean. However, none of these things took place. Short of military conquest by Eastern or Western navies and armies, the two zones could evolve somewhat separately. Once one zone subordinated the other, separate development became most unlikely. Wilkinson (1987, 1991, 1993), Chase-Dunn and Hall (1997), and Morris (2010), for example, all agree that Western and Eastern systems did not become integrated prior to the nineteenth-century penetration of China.

Chapter 4

1. The truth of this statement depends on whether one interprets the Islamic expansion in the sixth and seventh centuries CE as a Western or a non-Western phenomenon. Since the West began in Mesopotamia in southwest Asia, it is difficult to write it off as somehow non-Western, even though that might be instinctual for many twenty-first-century observers.

2. Erdkamp (2015: 20) argues that the argument between the Finley camp of primitivists, who emphasized traditional inertia, and the modernist camp, who argued that economic growth and innovation were possible in the ancient world, was resolved in favor of the modernists. But, as Grantham (2015: 56–60) notes, even though this argument may be closed, there is still a great deal of uncertainty about how ancient economies actually worked.

3. Since so little is known about Roman population dynamics, we simply omit these variables, although they obviously played a role in both the ascent and the decline of Rome.

4. Ferrill (1991: 23) makes an interesting argument that few others mention, attributing the rising standard of living linked to the Pax Romana to Augustus's decision to fix his standing army at twenty-eight legions in 30–28 BCE. A very large number of military personnel had been mobilized for the civil wars of the latter part of the first century BCE. Many of these personnel needed to be demobilized to reduce military costs. The decision to operate with twenty-eight legions meant that Augustus was fixing the army's size at the number of legions he had been using for Italian operations, despite the empire having been expanded to include Egypt and regions to the east. By saving on potential military costs, there would be less drain on the economy. Yet it is rather hard to calculate how much legions foregone contributed to economic growth. Since the empire was no longer expanding much (see table 4.1), fewer troops should have been needed. However, Wilson (2013: 264) attributes the idea of a post–civil war peace dividend combined with the unification of the Mediterranean to Walter Scheidel. Clearly, this type of effect would amount to a fairly short-term stimulus, as opposed to a persistent contribution to economic growth.

5. Hopkins (1978: 7) estimated that as many as half of the peasant families in Roman Italy (some 1.5 million people) were forced to move from their land in the first century BCE, while some 2 million peasants in non-Roman areas were forced to move to Italy as slaves.

6. Kron (2012) contends that the best practices of Roman agrarian production were comparable to the best practices of northwest European agricultural production in the mid-nineteenth century. Presumably, this claim overlooks nineteenth-century farm machinery that was just beginning to be industrialized (although perhaps more in North American than in northern Europe). The Romans had some farm machinery, but with the debated exception of water mills, the degree of technological innovation appears not to have been great. The problem with water mills, based on either Greek or Egyptian models, which began appearing in greater numbers after the second century CE, is that we do not know how much difference they made (Wikander, 2008: 142). They may also have been limited to villas and, if so, were largely abandoned as the villa system broke down (Marzano, 2015). Interestingly, though, Wilson (2008: 362) thinks water-powered machines may have diffused from the Mediterranean to China before the first such Chinese innovation was adopted in the Mediterranean in 597 CE.

7. Poulter (2002) gives primary credit to the barbarian invasions for disrupting rural agriculture. Wilson (2013) nominates disease in the second century as the main exogenous shock halting economic growth. See also Saller (2002) and Koepke and Baten (2005) on this issue. Giardina (2007) adds less land under cultivation, population decline, increased taxes, and expanded welfare demands to the list of overlapping problems in the transition to "late antiquity." McCormick (2001) argues that labor shortages, along with malnutrition, malaria, leprosy, and a decline in life expectancy, led to substantial amounts of farmland not being worked in the fourth through sixth centuries. Then again, Potter (2009: 332) rather pessimistically suggests: "Just as there can be no single date for the 'end of the Roman Empire,' so too there is no simple or easy explanation for the progressive decline. Indeed more than 200 reasons ranging from superstition, celibacy, imperial absolutism, two-front war, excessive taxation, and the consumption of water passed through lead pipes have, at one time or another, been proposed to explain this."

8. Hopkins (1978: 8) said much the same thing when he argued that military conquest served the same function as technological innovation in the Roman era, but his emphasis was more on the disruptive nature of the activity than on novel ways of making products.

9. Hopkins (1980) was the first to promote this thesis.

10. There have been a variety of efforts to calculate ancient Roman gross domestic products and real wages, none of which contradict the notion of a one-time spurt of economic gains. See, e.g., Hopkins (1980), Goldsmith (1984), Mokyr (1990), Saller (2005), Temin (2006), Maddison (2007), Bang (2008), Allen (2009), Scheidel and Friesen (2009), Lo Cascio and Malanima (2009a, 2009b), Scheidel (2008), and Malanima (2011a). Bang (2002: 14) also notes that any estimate of the size of the Roman economy must be predicated on the size of its population, which peaked in the middle of the second century CE.

11. Grant (1996: 42) states that the army was twice as expensive by the end of the fourth century CE because of increases due to feeding horses.

12. Aberth (2011: 77) argues that the Antonine Plague (beginning around 165 CE) killed about 10 percent of the Roman population, but that it came at a time when external threats on two different fronts demanded increased military manpower. Thus the move to recruit barbarians for the army was stimulated by the onset of smallpox.

13. Adams (2012) suggests that scholars have tended to underestimate the amount of connectivity that was facilitated by road building. In point of fact, we lack data on much of what happened inside the Roman Empire, including the movement of people and goods.

14. Bes (2008) relates how Roman specialists have rebelled against the older idea (à la Finley) that no technology characterized traditional economies relying on slaves, but there are few "smoking gun" examples of new technology in Rome that had radical impacts on production or transportation. Wikander (2008) makes the strongest case for the exception to this generalization in his examination of the adoption of water mills later in the imperial era. But we do not know how much difference they actually made in terms of output.

15. The Romans worked with iron as well, but, unlike the Chinese, their furnaces did not become larger. Instead, Romans tended to build a larger number of small furnaces to produce their iron (Grantham, 2015: 80–82).

16. Roman engineering was very strong for its time. Presumably, this strength reflected military needs, and the army did not need technological innovation until Rome was too far gone to

defend itself or to generate innovations. Since the army was the central focus of so much of the activity of the Roman Empire, the high value given to engineering over technological innovation makes some sense and presumably was a factor in this difference between east and west Eurasia.

17. Morley (2007: 567) notes that Roman mining drilled as far as 200 meters below water tables, a feat that requires some extraction technology in addition to inexpensive labor. Schneider (2007) indicates that the deep-mining technology was borrowed from irrigation techniques for moving and lifting water.

18. Malanima (2011b: 8) suggests that probably only a few ancient Romans were familiar with earlier experimentation with processes related to steam engine principles.

Chapter 5

1. Adshead (2004) has a useful critique of Frank (1998). While we do not share all of his criticisms, we believe he is right to balk at Frank's arguments that (a) China has always been the strongest state in the world except for the past 150 years or so, and (b) bullion flows (especially silver in the era from 1400 to 1800) determine centrality in a singular world system. Adshead argues instead that China only ascended to technological preeminence in the era from 500 to 1000 CE, a view we share. Somewhat like Frank but not like Adshead, we are impressed by long-distance commerce but part company with both by placing technological preeminence and energy development at the center of our structural explanation of stratification in world politics. While we are also sympathetic to Frank's long-time interest in "systemness," we will argue later that it makes sense to treat Eurasia as being divided into two partially autonomous zones (East and West). Thus, we can acknowledge Chinese technological superiority in the pre–Industrial Revolution era without adopting a totally Sinocentric interpretation of the development of the world economy over the past thousand years.

2. Pomeranz (2000) acknowledges this; Frank (1998) does not.

3. These statements are not meant to imply that external invasion alone led to the demise of the Song dynasty. A number of different factors, including climate problems (see Brooke, 2014: 369–370), were involved.

4. For China, the demonstration came in the form of the First Opium War, when British iron-hulled, steam-powered gunboats penetrated up the Grand Canal (Headrick, 2009: 108–109). Japan was forcefully opened up to Western penetration after the arrival of the American "Black Ships" in 1854.

5. Exactly how far south southern China extended also broadened during this era.

6. Barbier (2011: 169–174) sees three Chinese frontiers: the northwest steppe, the western deserts, and the southeast—all of which offered potentials for trade and exploitation. The combination of southeastern internal resources and foreign trade based in southeastern ports made this frontier the most profitable one in the period from 1000 to 1500.

7. Curiously, though, Millward (1996) argues that the Qing expansion to the west should be viewed as a process similar to Russian and American frontier expansion. If so, it did not have the payoff realized in the American experience, or probably even the Russian experience.

8. It also has much utility for non-Chinese dynamics in the premodern era—and perhaps some use in the modern era as well. In the Chinese context, there is some irony in the fact that this interpretation stems from arguments made by Japanese scholars early in the twentieth century (sometimes referred to as the Naito hypothesis) in part to reinforce claims that Japan had eclipsed China after Chinese stagnation as a result of the cessation of inner Asian penetration. See, e.g., the discussions in Miyakawa (1955), Brook (1999), and von Glahn (2003). Chinese scholars conventionally have preferred to extoll the virtues of the Tang dynasty.

9. The Skinnerian reference is to Skinner (1977). The exact boundaries of Hartwell's macro-regions could vary over time, but he identified seven, each of which possessed a set of cores and peripheries: North China, Lower Yangtze, Northwest China, Upper Yangtze, Middle Yangtze, Lingnan, and Southeast China.

10. Kelly (1997) notes that most observers reflexively credit abrupt economic takeoffs to innovation, but that it is theoretically conceivable that specialization within an increasingly complex market can accomplish the same effect.

11. China not only escaped plague but also experienced only a limited threat from western nomadic "barbarians" in this era from 450 to 750. In contrast, Europe was overrun by tribes from Scandinavia and Central Asia.
12. On this point, see McNeill (1998: 33–34) and Barbier (2011: 270–271).
13. One of the consequences of ruralization was a decline in literacy during the Qing dynasty era (Adshead, 2000: 259).
14. Britain could be said to have been invaded successfully in 1066 by the Normans and in 1688 by the Dutch in support of William's claim to the English throne. Other attempts had been made from time to time but were consistently unsuccessful. As a consequence, Britain rarely had a strong land-based system of defense against invasion.
15. Lo (2012: 339) estimates that it took about three hundred years for China to become dominant in the seas adjacent to it and the eastern Indian Ocean.
16. They also employed former Song ships and crews.
17. The Greek fire was probably a Byzantine import, but cannons began to appear on naval decks in the East before they did in the West.
18. Temple (1986: 64–65) suggests the sixth century for smelting and the fourteenth century for the furnace bellows.
19. This assessment assumes that the British Industrial Revolution was carried by textile innovations. We will argue against this interpretation in chapter 6.
20. Bozhong (2003: 137) observes that every conceivable Malthusian check on population growth (military conquest, civil war, famine, epidemics, natural disasters, and climate cooling) took place during the Song to Ming transition.
21. However, Wong (1997: 17–22) sees several indicators of Smithian economic dynamics at work between the sixteenth and nineteenth centuries.
22. One possible avenue worth exploring is the interaction between regime type and threat environment. Jones (2002: 15) writes about something he calls "emergency marketization." He argues that Song (presumably Southern Song) rulers recognized that they needed to encourage market expansion in the face of increased threat from steppe invaders. Autocratic rulers, especially in preindustrial times, were inclined to extract as much as they possibly could from the economy, but heightened external threat can override predatory inclinations. This explanation appears to work for the Southern Song, but it is less clear whether it works for the Tang dynasty. Wong (1997: 54–55), in contrast, argues that Mokyr is simply wrong to emphasize government support or suppression of technological change as a major explanation because governments did not much care about technology and lacked the capability to monitor scientific inquiry very closely. Ultimately, though, Wong's position seems to be that since bursts of technological creativity are so rare in the first place, their disappearance should be expected and not puzzled over.
23. They rely strongly on Qian (1985) for parts of their argument.
24. Debeir, Deleage, and Hemery (1991: 55) suggest coal was used to smelt bronze in Eastern Zhou times some half a millennium or more earlier.
25. Hartwell describes Kaifeng functioning much like London did: as a catalyst for growth in both size and economic demands. What was needed was a concentration of sustained demand for large quantities of industrial products. He estimates that the value of trade going through Kaifeng at the end of the eleventh century was worth 150 percent of the trade going through London in 1711 (1967b: 144). This type of interpretation credits the scale of demand to the tendency toward increased technological innovation.
26. McNeill (1982: 32–33) attributes the lack of a reinvigorated iron production in the Yuan era to natural disasters that destroyed the canal system in northern China, which thereafter went unrepaired as a result of the Mongol defeat of the Southern Song, thereby localizing northern iron production.
27. Yet Debeir, Deleage, and Hemery (1991: 56) indicate that Peking was dependent on coal for heating in the Ming dynasty era. If so, this only really demonstrates that heating demands are not sufficient to bring about fuel transitions.
28. Feuerwerker (1995) actually refers to the three in which he is most interested (2-4 in table 4.5) but it seems clear from his discussion that number 2 was preceded by an earlier one and he does note the one that followed the fourth one in table 4.5 in China.

29. Feuerwerker (1995) might also have added climate changes associated with the periods of destabilization but did not.
30. Europeans moved to the New World and elsewhere, while Chinese moved to the south and east.
31. See, e.g., Lieberman's (2003, 2009) comparisons of Southeast Asian and European developments.
32. It is curious that Feuerwerker's (1995) interpretation is not better known in the debates about East–West technology transitions.

Chapter 6

1. Much of this section relies heavily on the arguments advanced in Modelski and Thompson (1996: chs. 6 and 10), since the Genoese, Venetian, and Portuguese cases are affected by the revision of these scholars' framework but are not major foci for the energy issue.
2. McNeill (1974) and Abu-Lughod (1989) note that trade along the central land route only expanded in the second half of the thirteenth century.
3. Other Italian city-states profited during this time period (Lane, 1973; Lopez, 1987; Verseth, 1990), but presumably not to the same extent as Genoa.
4. Not coincidentally, Champagne's aristocrats were also instrumental in organizing the Crusades of the latter twelfth century (Norwich, 1982).
5. Various authors put the decline of the Champagne Fairs between 1283 and 1300 (see Bernard, 1976; Abu-Lughod, 1989; Van der Wee, 1990).
6. Ashtor (1983) considers the fifteenth century's second quarter to have been the peak of Venetian growth in Levantine markets. Lane (1973) nominates 1430 as the peak of Venetian maritime expansion.
7. The rise of Timur (the Lame) in the latter decades of the fourteenth century and the later Ottoman movement on Constantinople, along with the eventual isolationism of the Ming dynasty, meant that the overland route remained less utilized in the fifteenth century.
8. Earlier galley lines had been focused on Romania and Cyprus.
9. Such a network constituted the transplantation of the Venetian model to the Indian Ocean.
10. Venetians assisted Mamluk and Ottoman efforts in this regard, although the Ottoman Empire absorbed Mamluk Egypt in 1516.
11. The spice profits started coming in just as West African gains were diminishing (Godinho, 1963–1965; Scammell, 1989). From 1591 to 1630, "many shipwrecks, poor returns to Lisbon, recurrent fiscal losses, and military defeats undermined confidence and discouraged further efforts" (Duncan, 1986: 18). Consequently, Portuguese attention shifted increasingly to Brazil.
12. This approach was abandoned in the 1540s, but by that time the Portuguese were less in control of Asian commodity flows to Europe.
13. In the process, as Braudel (1972: 480–481) says, Antwerp became the "true capital of the Atlantic."
14. This characteristic is an old emphasis in the relevant literature. For contemporary interpretations, see, e.g., Jones (1981) and Acemoglu, Johnson, and Robinson (2005).
15. It also connects readily to part of Feuerwerker's (1995) interpretation featured in the preceding chapter.
16. While the reclaimed areas were characterized by a high-wage economy and thus theoretically should have given rise to technological innovation to save labor costs, the re-application of most of the polder mills used to keep the land relatively dry to agricultural usages had to await higher grain prices to make the effort worthwhile (van Bavel and van Zanden, 2004: 513, 522). In other words, high wages did not suffice to incentivize the technological fix.
17. Ironically, the Netherlands was a net importer of food in the sixteenth century but a net exporter in the nineteenth century, reversing the more typical pattern of technological powers.
18. De Vries and van der Woude (1997) also note that the northern Netherlands' early high rate of urbanization resembled Venice's situation, but the Dutch accomplishment preceded the development of numerous trade connections. Later in their review of Dutch demographics, the same authors (80) observe that the rapid economic growth of the Netherlands would

have been inexplicable in the absence of the high urbanization rate that preceded the Dutch Revolt.

19. Davids (2008: 89) claims that there were nearly 800 such busses in operation in the early seventeenth century.

20. The Netherlands could support that many horses, but it could not meet the demand for horses in industry and warfare simultaneously (De Zeeuw, 1978; Davids, 2008: 370).

21. Prak (2005: 110) has a different take on this question of Dutch economic modernity. After listing all of the Netherland's attributes that were modern (urbanization, a large nonagrarian workforce, a high level of economic productivity, the division of labor, a high standard of living, and governments that favored property rights and economic development), Prak notes that the Netherlands was surrounded by traditional economies that tended to stifle economic growth in the Netherlands and elsewhere.

22. The English East Indies Company was established first, in 1600.

Chapter 7

1. For a period of time, econometric analysis even challenged whether Britain had experienced an industrial revolution. There does appear to have been a lag in productivity gains from the initial onset of shifts in textile and iron output.

2. Ormrod (2003) objects to purely national studies of economic development in favor of regional foci. The linkages between the Netherlands and Britain are quite close in many respects.

3. As Maddison (2001: 89) wryly put it, "From the eleventh to the mid-fifteenth century, British national identity was ambiguous. The monarchy and ruling elite were Anglo-French warlords whose property rights and income derived initially from territorial conquests in England and France. . . . The acquisition of land and loot in France was pursued by war and matrimony. British possessions were biggest in the second half of the twelfth century. . . . At that time, half of France was British . . . and at the end of the Hundred Years War in 1453, all that was left was Calais, which the French [recovered] in 1558.

4. In his argument Pomeranz shifts back and forth between developments in Europe generally and in Britain specifically (see on this point the useful review in Vries, 2001). The irony is that this reflex to compare Europe and China—which admittedly is an intermittent one in Pomeranz (2000)—seems to hark back to more traditional, Eurocentric approaches to the causes of the British Industrial Revolution that also generalized about Europe. To be sure, some of the changes ongoing in Britain at this time were also taking place on the European continent, but the question remains whether, in the absence of a Britain, some European state might have experienced the same economic transformation that took place there. If the answer is no or not likely, comparisons between Europe and China need to exercise considerable caution.

5. Dutch and Portuguese slavers had been prominent in their respective centuries as well.

6. The Dutch unintentionally facilitated some of these gains. In the early seventeenth century they had driven out their English competitors from the Spice Islands and had not been too concerned about their movement into Indian markets, which then seemed less appealing. Dutch sugar growers also introduced sugar into English colonies. The Dutch were later forced to surrender Manhattan and parts of New York to the English. The initial defeat of the perceived French threat (emanating from Louis XIV) in the combat of 1688–1713 involved a Dutch–English alliance in which the Dutch essentially installed William of Orange on the English throne to ensure English participation in continental warfare, only to end up as the junior partner in the subsequent war effort.

7. British canals, we should note, were constructed primarily to deliver coal, according to MacLeod (2004: 118).

8. Debeir, Deleage, and Hemery (1991: 99) stress that France was slow to adopt coal largely because of the high costs of transporting it. In the nineteenth century, prior to the development of a railroad network that could reduce fuel costs, French ports could obtain coal from Britain less expensively than from domestic sources.

9. See Overton (2002) for an overview and critical discussion.

10. Enclosures involved the fencing of what had been common pasturage land, thereby leading to the creation of larger farms.
11. Allen (1999) argues for a sixteenth-century expansion of agricultural output.
12. Four times as many people moved there after 1820.
13. The protection motivation encourages looking at patent rates. But the overall rate does not differentiate among the variable radicalness of new technology or its relative successful impact on economic growth, which may also be delayed.
14. At the same time, Dudley (2012) makes a good case for examining the gradual improvements made to steam engines beginning at the end of the seventeenth century as the run-up to the eventual revolutionary changes in steam power.
15. One steam horsepower is equivalent to the amount of work that can be accomplished by twenty-one men.
16. Sieferle (2001: 104) argues that wood substitutes for coal consumption after 1810 had already exceeded the total land area of England and Wales, and that British coal consumption in 1913 exceeded the land hypothetically available for wood by a factor greater than nineteen. He (107–109) estimates the amount of Baltic firewood that might have been imported at about 100 million cubic meters, which translates into enough wood to substitute for British coal consumption in 1820. But even if all British maritime tonnage of that time had been dedicated to hauling wood imports, only one-fifth of the state's 1790 coal consumption could have been replaced. Much larger ships like today's supertankers for moving petroleum were possible in theory but unlikely to have been feasible in the wooden ship era, because ship sizes were limited by the height of trees used for single pieces in their construction. Moreover, the price of wood would have had to rise to give importers sufficient incentive to move away from other higher-priced imports.
17. It is certainly conceivable that it took several hundred years of acquaintance with piston principles, which were first discovered in China, to arrive at the first steam engine, just as it took five hundred years to develop infantry guns, also begun in China, into effective weapons.
18. Keep in mind, of course, that Allen does not argue that it is only high wages that drive technological innovation or that they drove the British Industrial Revolution. High wages would certainly have helped diffuse the new technology throughout the economy.
19. See Broadberry et al. (2015: 251, 254) for the depiction of several long wage series from England/Britain.
20. Sieferle (2001: 134) concurs with this point when he describes textiles as more of an outgrowth of the agrarian system than a pioneer of the new industrial era. What he means is that most of the material and energy involved in textile production did not need coal, iron, or steam. The machinery used in production was not made of iron. The power used was mainly hydraulic. The raw materials needed were wool and cotton. Ultimately, a steam engine–less textile industry would have hit a production ceiling. Significant gains in textile production were also found in the economies of postmedieval Venice and the golden age Netherlands without leading to modern industrialization. Put another way, it was possible to engage in moderate forms of industrialization without experiencing radical industrial revolutions.
21. See, among others, Steensgaard (1975), Furber (1976), Chaudhuri (1978), Andrews (1985), and Robins (2006).
22. The British Isles had been invaded many times (by Romans, Saxons, Danes, and Normans) in earlier eras. The one "invasion" that it did experience in later times—the Dutch in 1688—proved beneficial to the ascendance and technological centrality of the British over the Netherlands.

Chapter 8

1. Americans also tend to take their phenomenal economic success for granted. Hence, they see less need to explain it.
2. Lind (2012) is a major exception among the contemporary economic histories aimed at popular consumption, because his work is guided by an unusual appreciation for the temporal clustering of new technology and its repercussions.

3. Johnson (2014: 12) argues, for instance, that since the U.S. economy rarely, if ever, experienced anything resembling Malthusian constraints, the population was inoculated against believing in the idea of ecological limitations operating in North America.

4. Meyer (2003) argues that the genesis of American manufacturing was largely endogenous to the northeastern region and did not rely on inputs from other regions or any division of labor.

5. Other farm products became increasingly available for export as well: during the same time frame, corn and corn meal increased from 7 to 192.5 million bushels, beef products from 25 to 357.9 million pounds, and pork products from 103.9 to 1.5 billion pounds. All of these increases contributed to the United States' post-1870s switch from a country that imported more than it exported to the converse situation (Hacker, 1970: 228).

6. Freese (2003: 88–89, 119–120) suggests that the primary purpose of the earliest canals was moving coal to large cities. Much the same thing had occurred in Britain earlier.

7. Hacker (1970: 239) later notes that using steel to build railroad rails and locomotives "increased the carrying capacity of trains (from 200 tons in 1865 to 2500 tons in 1900) and their speed (from 25 miles an hour in the earlier years to 65 in the later). In contrast, British trains were heavier and carried much less cargo. American railroad costs, as a consequence, were 50 percent lower than in Britain."

8. There is a famous (or infamous) debate among economic historians about the precise value of the railroad in American economic development, a dispute that sometimes employs rather dubious assumptions. See Jenks (1944), Fogel (1964), Fishlow (1965), McClelland (1968), Rostow (1971), and Williamson (1975).

9. Buck (2015) notes that the wagons used to support the early-nineteenth-century canals were converted in the middle of the century to transport settlers across the U.S. Plains. Demand was sufficiently high to encourage the production of standardized wood and iron parts and the construction of wagon factories, of which at least one (Studebaker) was later converted to build automobiles in a similar way.

10. See Johnson (1914: 20, 24) for these calculations and the comment that total U.S. energy consumption in 1920 could be compared to having the energy of 3 billion slaves at one's disposal.

11. This comment is not meant to suggest that air-conditioning and heating are exclusively optional, luxury items, but only that U.S. consumption of them probably exceeds what is absolutely necessary for getting by.

12. Similarly, it is difficult to imagine canals being constructed from the Mississippi River to the Pacific Ocean as a counterfactual to the significance of railroads to nineteenth-century growth.

13. Coal had to first become sufficiently inexpensive for it to be widely adopted. Otherwise, waterpower was more attractive from a cost perspective. Canals became the initial conduit for lowering the price of coal in the northeastern U.S. (Nye, 1998: 76).

14. Gordon (2015: 320) singles out as wants and needs "food, clothing, housing, transportation, entertainment, communication, information, health, medicine, and working conditions."

15. Nonetheless, it remains unclear why comparably fundamental and rapid changes in individual lifestyles are so unlikely in the future—even if they are not introduced in the United States. Many, if not all, of the categories that Gordon reviews have potential for further transformation.

16. Steel rails for railroads lasted considerably longer than iron rails. The first steel boom was focused on this rail substitution process.

17. Podobnik (2006: 59) suggests that the advent of electrification was delayed because coal and petroleum garnered the lion's share of available investment money for much of the nineteenth century.

18. Informed observers (Hounshell, 1984; Podobnik, 2006) like to point out that the employment of assembly line techniques in the United States dates back to 1790 and the manufacture of weapons. At the time, this approach to mass production was referred to as the "American system of manufacturing." But it is also true that the assembly line developed by Henry Ford required electrification: "Subdivision of labor, interchangeable parts, single-function machines, sequential ordering of machines, and the moving belt defines the assembly line [and] factory

electrification was necessary before [each of] these elements could be improved individually and then brought together in a new form of production" (Nye, 1998: 143).

19. The development block conceptualizations are found in Kander (2013).

20. As noted in chapter 2, this propensity to subsidize and supply allies is important to systemic leadership and was not a novelty introduced in the twentieth century.

21. Adams (1996: 206–211) emphasizes that the U.S. turn toward a greater emphasis on science was a process that was accelerated by the abrupt need to mobilize support for the U.S. entry into World War I in 1917. World War II later proved "the most significant watershed of changing direction for U.S. science and technology" (216). Once again, the stimulus was the need to gear up for a world war.

22. From our perspective, this development was not unique to the United States in 1945. Lead economies tend to profit more from global wars than other states do.

23. See, e.g., Cortado (2004: 7–9) for a quick overview of the evolution of "digital" technology.

24. However, see Chandler, Hikino, and von Nordenflycht's (2001) autopsy of the death of the consumer electronics and computer industries and the loss of U.S. leadership.

25. Electricity had backward linkages to steam engines via turbo generators.

26. Nationality in this figure is awarded to the country in which the Nobelist's home institution was located. Needless to say, Nobelists and potential Nobelists are attractive targets for academic acquisition. Their home institutions are therefore not always good predictors of individual nationality. However, we are more interested in where the Nobelists choose to work than in where they might have been born. Our hunch is that Nobelists are more likely to move after their award than before, and to the extent that this is true, it will not bias the picture sketched by figure 8.6.

27. One can see the French and German award trajectories become flatter after World War II in figure 8.6.

28. Chinese figures from U.S. National Science Board (2014) are difficult to interpret because of the state's different standards for who should be counted.

29. According to more recent World Bank data for 2005–2015, the European trio had an average ratio of 4,278 researchers per million population compared to the U.S. ratio of 4,019 researchers per million, approximately what is shown for 2012.

30. This paragraph represents an update of an argument first made by Nelson and Wright in 1992.

31. Their main indicator is scientific publication, which, of course, is only a proxy and is subject to some interpretation. But their argument certainly seems plausible.

32. Smil (2013) also gives credit/blame to other factors, such as high labor costs and government support, especially in terms of the automobile industry.

33. See also Chandler (1962, 1977, 1990) and Atack (1985) on factors responsible for the emergence of the new kinds of corporations. Of particular interest to our current examination is Podobnik's (2007: 80–81) argument that nineteenth-century coal companies faced fewer organizational challenges than twentieth-century oil companies. Oil company needs involving refineries, the marketing of multiple products, and constant exploration encouraged the development of vertically integrated multinationals, while coal companies tended to exploit mines by digging deeper shafts in the same places to yield one primary product.

Chapter 9

1. Most of these commercial leaderships were restricted not just in time, but in space. Genuinely global leaderships in trade only emerged in the nineteenth century when East and West lost their separate identities.

2. The Chinese case might reflect both versions of the "law" in question.

3. Coal will be available for much longer than it can be used without considerable decarbonization transformation (roughly a century and a half). Natural gas reserves have actually expanded slightly faster than natural gas consumption (reserves expanded by a factor of 2.59 from 1980 to 2013, while consumption increased by a factor of 2.33).

Chapter 10

1. Primarily for that reason, some analysts (see, e.g., Smil 2003) suggest that such forecasts have always been wrong and that we should forgo them altogether. While it is true that models do not usually include such potentially game-changing events as the rise of fundamentalist Islam after the 1970s, the emergence of fracking technology, or some as-yet unknown way of building smaller automobile batteries, it seems difficult to refrain from using the data that we currently possess to estimate what might happen in the future, *ceteris paribus*. Of course, we must keep in mind that such estimates are only based on "what ifs" and currently known model parameters. Estimations may well exaggerate the extent of future problems by not taking into consideration various factors that are difficult to foresee. They may also downplay future problems by not taking interactions and nonlinear relationships among the variables fully into consideration.

2. CO_2 emissions related to carbon-based fuels are highly concentrated. In 2012, China, the United States, and India were responsible for nearly half of world CO_2 emissions from fossil fuel use. Ten states account for about two-thirds of the world total. The other seven include Russia, Japan, Germany, South Korea, Canada, Iran,and Saudi Arabia (International Energy Agency, 2015: 27).

3. China's economy is not a major consumer of natural gas as yet.

4. See, as well, the data and discussion in Peters et al. (2017), Green (2017), and Sanderson and Knutti (2017).

5. The California scenario also assumes that the state will experience a hefty 49 percent increase in population between 2010 and 2050. This figure probably exceeds world population gains, which are more likely to be in the range of 33 percent. Yet most of the world's population gains will take place in less developed countries, while the California scenario is very much geared toward developed economies.

6. The 450 scenario, developed by the International Energy Agency and the Intergovernmental Panel on Climate Change, is designed to reach 450 ppm in the atmosphere, thereby keeping the global temperature increase to two degrees C.

7. Roughly two-thirds of the targeted reduction in CO_2 emissions is achieved by changes in the three identified areas.

8. Improved energy-efficiency measures account for about 29 percent of the projected 2050 CO_2 emissions reductions. The decarbonization of electricity generation is linked to 27 percent of the reductions, while the electrification of transportation contributes another 16 percent. Keep in mind that plans are one thing, but executing them is often something else. In early 2017, California's decision-makers are struggling to meet their decarbonization goals and may well prove less than successful.

9. Of course, just how long and slow this transition is depends on what governments are willing to do in order to hasten the ultimate outcome.

10. Boyd (2012) singles out Hu Angang as a leader of this argument for China capturing the lead in the movement toward renewables. Hu argues that, historically, a few states were able to improve their positions within the international system considerably by making use of new energy technologies before others caught on. China, moreover, was increasingly marginalized by failing to exploit the new energy technologies. Now it is in a position not only to exploit the new technologies but also to lead the rest of the world in phasing out carbon-based fuels in the transition to renewable sources of energy. See also Chen Dezhao (2011) for similar sentiments.

11. All of these processes can be found taking place and interacting in fourth- to third-millennium BCE Mesopotamia. Modelski and Thompson (1996), however, contend that the linkage between technological change and systemic leadership started to become continuous after Song China in the tenth and eleventh centuries CE, as discussed in Thompson and Zakhirova (2013). Even so, no one would argue that the temporal concentration of technological innovation was equally evident throughout the second millennium CE. It does become more pronounced after the Industrial Revolution.

12. This unevenness in particular characterizes the use of energy. While some parts of the world are beginning to make the transition away from petroleum dependence, other parts are still reliant on wood and coal.
13. It is conceivable that these surges of technological clustering have ended, but there does not appear to be any salient theoretical reason to assume that they will not or cannot continue into the future.
14. As a consequence, we should not assume that the impact of each surge is identical. Some are fundamentally transformative, while others are less radical. Consider, for example, the differences between assembly line production and changes in social media technology. The impacts of the former presumably have been much greater than the impacts of the latter, even though both have involved major changes.
15. For instance, there are a number of ways to reduce coal's harmful effects, including removing its mineral content, capturing and storing CO_2 underground, and transforming coal into gas. See BBC News (2005).
16. There does not seem to be any reason to assume that the type of batteries with which we are most familiar today will be prevalent a decade or two down the road. See, e.g., Schlesinger (2010: ch. 13).
17. For elaboration, see Lee and Lovelette (2011); and Dijk, Orsato, and Kemp (2013).
18. In the fall of 2015, Porsche Voelk claimed that its new electric concept car, called Mission E, had a three-hundred-plus-mile range. Supposedly, it is five years away from production.
19. See Marcacci (2013) and International Energy Association (2013).
20. This forecast is summarized at www.energycentral.com/endse/electricvehicles/news/vpr/ 8256/PRTM-Analysis-Shows-Worldwide-Electric-Vehicle-Value-Chain-to-Reach-300b-by-2020-Creating-More-than-1-Million-Jobs. Billmaier (2010: 91) suggests that "cleantech" in general will produce 20 million jobs worldwide over the next two decades and be worth 6 trillion US dollars but provides little in the way of details. Nonetheless, the overall point is that an electrification surge could be quite large in impact.
21. See Green Car Congress (2015), although this forecast actually minimizes the role of electric vehicles in favor of hydrogen fuel cells. Even so, as much as 71 percent of the existing vehicle fleet (as opposed to sales) in 2035 would still be ICE vehicles.
22. See www.prweb.com/releases/2013/prweb0560078.htm. It is worth noting that Chinese plans in 2011 called for 1 million vehicles to be sold in 2015 and 10 million in 2020. By 2012, the plans had been scaled down to 0.5 million and 5 million, respectively.
23. This surge, should it come, also seems likely to involve heavy investment in robotics for production purposes and automobile-linked information technology.
24. See Bradsher (2009), Fallows (2010), Shobart (2014), and Zhidong (2014).
25. A less centralized technological innovation pattern could make for greater increased prosperity earlier in the development process than has been seen in the past. It might also help reduce CO_2 emissions more quickly.
26. The shift may also be unavoidable if radical technological innovation in general is less highly concentrated in one economy than it has been in past surges. In such a case, there may still be obvious technological leaders, but there will likely also be a number of "follower" economies far more ready to adopt pioneering technologies than has previously been the case.
27. The increasing number of electric models coming online is one indicator that the automobile industry may be moving away from its reluctance to abandon gasoline-powered vehicles.

Chapter 11

1. See, e.g., Ignatius (2012); Cockerham (2013); Drezner (2013); Knowles (2013); Kurtzman (2014); McSwain (2013); Mills (2013); Morris (2013); Spenser (2013); Blackwill and Sullivan (2014); Jones, Steven, and O'Brien (2014); Naim (2014); and Nicks (2014). Sernovitz (2016) refers to fracking as the equivalent of the "internet of oil." While all of the claims that have been made are not identical, they all suggest that an energy revolution should end talk of U.S. decline.
2. Mills (2013) wins the enthusiasm prize by comparing the 21st century United States to the United States surpassing the British economy in the 19th century and its navy in the 20th century.

3. Hausman and Kellogg (2015: 6) report a 25 percent increase in natural gas supply between 2007 and 2013, accompanied by a 47 percent decrease in natural gas prices. Some uncertainty exists at the time of this writing (2015) as to whether the currently ample supply of low-cost oil and gas will lead to less shale drilling—and therefore a smaller supply of shale oil and gas.

4. The historical GDP growth rates are based on estimates found in Williamson (2011). Note that Houser and Mohan's (2014) simulations of U.S. economic growth suggest that the energy boom will have a gross national product–boosting effect similar to that of the American Recovery and Reinvestment Act (ARRA), which was enacted to respond to the 2008 Great Recession. Its timing is expected to be quite good, because the effects of the ARRA stimulus will be fading away as the energy boom picks up strength in the 2013–2020 era. But Houser and Mohan also emphasize that the energy boom effect will be a one-time shock and therefore will have only a limited impact in the long term.

5. The International Energy Agency predicts that the supply increase in petroleum due to North American fracking will "run out of steam in the 2020s." See International Energy Agency (2014: 13).

6. Fracking contaminates the water supply and may be responsible for increased risks of earthquakes. Industry spokesmen claim that these problems can be managed. Critics say the opposite. Whatever the case, a major catastrophe on the order of a nuclear reactor meltdown could easily lead to a ban on fracking activities. Some protest movements have already been successful in limiting or excluding fracking activity in some American states.

7. Houser and Mohan (2014) predict that as energy imports decrease, dollar appreciation could be expected to reduce nonenergy exports, possibly offsetting improvements to the trade balance.

8. Mathilde, Spencer, and Sartor's (2014) modeling concurs in finding that the gas-intensive sectors that would benefit most from low gas prices comprise only about 1.2 percent of U.S. GDP, with the long-term impact of the shale boom over the 2012–2040 period being 0.575 percent on average. Huntington's (2013) estimate is slighltly lower (0.46 percent), but more or less of the same magnitude. Such figures are nothing to ignore, but they fall short of an industrial renaissance. Celasun et al. (2014) forecast a meager 1.5 percent increase in U.S. manufacturing as a consequence of the new oil and gas discoveries.

9. Spencer, Sartor, and Mathieu (2014) find something quite similar. They estimate the short-term 2007–2012 stimulus value to have been 0.88 percent of GDP and the long-term shale boom impact to be 0.84 percent of GDP.

10. This prediction is roughly the same whether the conservative or optimistic scenario is employed. Spencer, Sartor, and Mathieu (2014) find much the same stagnation in emission levels prevailing through 2040 in their model.

11. Houser and Mohan (2014) more simply point out that greater consumption of the same energy, even if at a lower price, is less than transformative in effect.

12. See Securing America's Future Energy (2012: 25) for a similar argument about spare capacity and oil prices.

13. The Ivanpah solar project that came on line in the western United States in 2014 may be an indicator of attitudes toward renewables. Questions remain about whether there are better ways to generate solar power than relying on several square miles of mirrors to generate steam turbines in order to make electricity, but even if the project proves successful, the waning federal support and vanishing tax credits may make any replication unlikely (see Cardwell and Wald, 2014).

14. United Nations Environment Programme (2012: 4) suggests that methane's harmful effects as an emission are seventy-two times greater than those of CO_2 within a twenty-year gestation period. Over a longer period of time, its effect reduces to only twenty-five times the damage done by CO_2.

15. There is at least one problem in estimating the effect of methane leakage from gas infrastructure: leakage varies considerably across different producers (Brandt et al., 2014; Moore et al., 2014).

16. Should the United States allow its natural gas to be exported, Hausman and Kellogg (2015) argue that producers will gain at consumers' expense, and, more importantly, its U.S. price would rise, thereby reducing the U.S. price advantage.

17. Houser and Mohan (2014), however, do find some gains in transportation and electricity applications.
18. There is some possibility that fracking techniques will move away from their reliance on water injection, which could reduce some of their harmful byproducts.
19. Chinese oil and gas reserves that might be accessed through fracking are believed to be greater than those that exist in the United States (U.S. Department of Energy, 2013). However, the combined reserves that exist in Mexico, the United States, and Canada are thought to exceed those that might be tapped in China.
20. British political–economic leadership was manifested in the French Revolution and the Napoleonic Wars, while U.S. coalition leadership was most evident in World War II.
21. Another possibility (Grinin and Korotayev, 2014) is that the world system will outgrow the tendency to maintain a lead economy. If new waves of technological innovation were no longer concentrated in one place and occurred roughly simultaneously in multiple locations, a systemic leadership transition would still occur, but it would be toward a new regime with no singular leader—something that has not been experienced for several hundred years. Our reflexive approach to transition questions is that past patterns will persist into the future, but there is no reason to assume that that will be the case if it is not the only possibility.
22. The motivations for the Second Gulf War will continue to be disputed for some time to come, in part because there are a number of plausible interpretations of the multiple factors involved. However, on the issue of maintaining the flow of oil (as opposed to the more conspiratorial idea that the war was fought to expand corporate interests), compare Muttitt (2012) with the more conventional approach taken in Yergin (2012: ch. 7).
23. The shift in the U.S. stance on Iran is often attributed to the greater abundance of North American oil, but one might have thought that a relaxation of the need for imports would have led to greater rigidity on sanctions, not less.
24. See also Yetiv (2015: ch. 5).

Chapter 12

1. Helm (2012: 199–216) recommends a quick but temporary transition to natural gas in order to replace coal, but he also realizes that this strategy can only work for a limited time. Smil (2015) anticipates that natural gas will become more important in coming decades but balks at claims that natural gas will enjoy a golden age in the mid-twenty-first century.
2. Smil (2015: 141) summarizes the consensus on Chinese shale prospects as hampered by a lack of technical experience, scattered and deep formations with many faults, poor mapping, competition over scarce water supplies, and bureaucratic resistance. None of these factors preclude Chinese shale exploitation, but they make it more likely that such exploitation will develop slowly and be less productive than sometimes forecasted.
3. Chinese energy statistics have been revised in recent years to reflect even greater consumption rates than were reported earlier.
4. Chinese decision-makers appear to be aware that many high-growth LDCs have stalled mid-point in their development trajectories by failing to move from low-tech to high-tech innovation and production.
5. See, e.g., Williams et al. (2014); Williams, Haley, and Jones (2015); Jacobson et al. (2015); Teng et al. (2015); Ackerman, Comings, and Fields (2016); and Labor Network for Sustainability (2016).
6. As a consequence, 2050 decarbonization plans are often accompanied by multiple scenarios that reflect variable mixes of energy inputs but arrive at the same end.
7. The problem is complicated. For a cursory treatment of the serial fluctuations in U.S. and Chinese positions on climate change measures at meetings prior to Paris, see Darwall (2013).

Chapter 13

1. For a discussion of the reasons that might get in the way of China becoming the world's system leader, see Griffiths and Luciani (2011), Beardson (2013), Fenby (2014), and Hung (2015).

2. The traditional Chinese curse "May you live in interesting times" seems particularly apt in considering the likelihood that the future will be cursed by interesting times for climate change and climate change responses.

3. It would be wise to also include some of the next generation of problem emitters, such as India, lest any approach worked out in one decade need to be revised completely another decade or two down the road. Reading between the lines in newspaper accounts of the 2015 Paris negotiations, one gets the impression that something like this strategy is already in play but still has some way to go.

4. Some observers contend that state plans (mainly in California and New York) and investment decisions already in play will keep the U.S. economy moving away from fossil fuel dependence. But as Sanderson and Knutti (2017) argue, U.S. governmental delays in participating in the 2015 Paris Accords could be fatal to the agreement attaining its goals in time to head off greater warming.

5. One of the interesting variations on this theme is the question of whether a new Cold War might encourage the two main protagonists to accelerate their efforts to transform their economies in order to beat their rival. Or is technological/energy transformation more likely if the two states cooperate in their competition to transform their economies? Somehow, the latter approach seems more promising, particularly in light of what transpired in the last Cold War.

REFERENCES

Aberth, J. 2011. *Plagues in World History*. Lanham, MD: Rowman and Littlefield.

Abu-Lughod, J. L. 1989. *Before European Hegemony: The World System, A.D. 1250–1350*. New York: Oxford University Press.

Accenture. 2014. "The Electric Vehicle Challenge: Electric Vehicle Growth in an Evolving Market Dependent on Seven Success Factors." https://www.accenture.com/us-en/~/media/Accenture/Conversion-Assets/DotCom/Documents/Global/PDF/Industries-15/Accenture-Electrics.

Acemoglu, D., Johnson, S., and Robinson, J. A. 2005. "Institutions as a Fundamental Cause of Long Run Growth." In *Handbook of Economic Growth*, ed. P. Aghion and S. N. Durlauf. Amsterdam: Elsevier.

Ackerman, F., Cumings, T., and Fields, S. 2016. "The Clean Energy Future Appendix." Cambridge, MA: Synapse Energy Economics. http://synapse-energy.com/sites/default/files/Clean-Energy-Future-Appendix-15-054.pdf.

Adams, C. 2012. "Transportation." In *The Cambridge Companion to the Roman Economy*, ed. Walter Scheidel. Cambridge: Cambridge University Press.

Adams, R. M. 1996. *Paths of Fire: An Anthropologist's Inquiry into Western Technology*. Princeton, NJ: Princeton University Press.

Adshead, S. A. M. 2000. *China in World History*, 3rd ed. New York: St. Martin's Press.

Adshead, S. A. M. 2004. *T'ang China: The Rise of the East in World History*. New York: Palgrave.

Allen, R. C. 1999. "Tracking the Agricultural Revolution in England." *Economic History Review* 52: 209–235.

Allen, R. C. 2009. "How Prosperous Were the Romans? Evidence from Diocletian's Price Edict (AD 301)." In *Quantifying the Roman Economy*, ed. Alan Bowman and Andrew Wilson. Oxford: Oxford University Press.

Anderson, R. 2015. "Nuclear Power: Energy for the Future or Relic of the Past?" *BBC News*, February 27. http://www.bbc.com/news/business-30919045.

Andrews, K. R. 1985. *Trade, Plunder and Settlement: Maritime Enterprise and the Genesis of the British Empire, 1480–1630*. Cambridge: Cambridge University Press.

Arnsdorf, I. 2014. "Fracking Sucks Money from Wind While China Eclipses U.S." *Bloomberg News*, May 29. https://www.bloomberg.com/news/articles/2014-05-29//fracking-sucks-money-from-wind-while-China-eclipses-u-s-.

Arora, A., Belenzon, S., and Patacconi, A. 2015. "Killing the Golden Goose? The Decline of Science in Corporate R & D." NBER Working Paper Series 20902. Cambridge, MA: National Bureau of Economic Research.

Arrighi, G. 2007. *Adam Smith in Beijing: Lineages of the Twenty-First Century*. London: Verso.

Ashtor, E. 1983. *Levant Trade in the Later Middle Ages*. Princeton, NJ: Princeton University Press.

Atack, J. 1985. "Industrial Structure and the Emergence of the Modern Industrial Corporation." *Explorations in Economic History* 22 (1): 29–52.

Atack, J., Bateman, F., and Margo, R. A. 2008. "Steam Power, Establishment Size, and Labor Productivity Growth in Nineteenth Century American Manufacturing." *Explorations in Economic History* 45: 185–197.

Atack, J., and Passell, P. 1994. *A New Economic History of American History*, 2nd ed. New York: W. W. Norton.

Bang, P. F. 2002. "Romans and Mughals: Economic Integration in a Tributary Empire." In *The Transformation of Economic Life Under the Roman Empire*, ed. Lukas De Blois and John Rich. Amsterdam: J. C. Gieben.

Bang, P. F. 2008. *The Roman Bazaar: A Comparative Study of Trade and Markets in a Tributary Empire.* Cambridge: Cambridge University Press.

Bang, P. F. 2009. "Commanding and Consuming the World: Empire, Tribute, and Trade in Roman and Chinese History." In *Rome and China: Comparative Perspectives on Ancient World Empires*, ed. Walter Scheidel. Oxford: Oxford University Press.

Bang, P. F. 2012. "Predation." In *The Cambridge Companion to the Roman Economy*, ed. Walter Scheidel. Cambridge: Cambridge University Press.

Barbier, E. B. 2011. *Scarcity and Frontiers: How Economies Have Developed Through Natural Resource Exploitation.* Cambridge: Cambridge University Press.

Bardi, U. 2014. *Extracted: How the Quest for Mineral Wealth Is Plundering the Planet.* White River Junction, VT: Chelsea Green Publishing.

BBC News. 2005. "Clean Coal Technology: How It Works." November 28. http://news.bbc. co.uk/2/hi/science/nature/4468076.stm.

Beardson, T. 2013. *Stumbling Giant: The Threats to China's Future.* New Haven, CT: Yale University Press.

Bernard, J. 1976. "Trade and Finance in the Middle Ages, 900–1500." In *The Fontana Economic History of Europe: The Middle Ages*, ed. Carlo M. Cipolla. New York: Barnes and Noble.

Bes, P. 2008. "Technology in Late Antiquity: A Bibliographic Essay." In *Technology in Transition*, ed. Luke Lavan, Enrico Zanini, and Alexander Sarantis. Leiden: Brill.

Billmaier, J. 2010. *Jolt! The Impending Dominance of the Electric Car and Why America Must Take Charge.* Charleston, SC: Advantage Media Group.

Black, B. C. 2012. *Crude Reality: Petroleum in World History.* Lanham, MD.: Rowman and Littlefield.

Blackwill, R. D., and Sullivan, M. L. 2014. "America's Energy Edge: The Geopolitical Consequences of the Shale Revolution." *Foreign Affairs* 93 (2): 102–114.

Bloomberg New Energy Finance. 2013. "Global Renewable Energy Market Outlook 2013." http://about.bnef.com/presentations/global-renewable-energy-market-outlook-2013-fact-pack/.

Boden, T., Andres, B., and Marland, G. 2016. "Global, Regional, and National Fossil-Fuel CO_2 Emissions." Oak Ridge, TN: Carbon Dioxide Information Analysis Center, Oak Ridge National Laboratory. http://cta.ornl.gov/data/chapter1.shtml.

Boserup, E. 1965. *The Conditions of Agricultural Growth: The Economics of Agrarian Change Under Population Pressure.* London: Allen & Unwin.

Boyd, O. T. 2012. "China's Energy Reform and Climate Policy: The Ideas Motivating Change." CCEP Working Paper 1205. Melbourne: Crawford School of Public Policy, Australian National University.

Bozhong, L. 2003. "Was There a 'Fourteenth-Century Turning Point'? Population, Land, Technology, and Farm Management." In *The Song-Yuan-Ming Transition in Chinese History*, ed. Paul J. Smith and Richard von Glahn. Cambridge, MA: Harvard University Press.

Bradsher, K. 2009. "China Outpaces U.S. in Cleaner Coal-Fired Plants." *New York Times*, May 10. http://www.nytimes.com/2009/05/11/world/asia/11coal.html.

Brandt, A. R., Heath, G. A., Kort, E. A., O'Sullivan, F., Petron, G., Jordaan, S. M., Tans, P., Wilcox, J., and Gopstein, A. M. et al. 2014. "Methane Leaks from North American Natural Gas Systems." *Science* 343 (14): 733–735.

Braudel, F. 1972. *The Mediterranean and the Mediterranean World in the Age of Philip II*, vol. 1. New York: Harper and Collins.

Bray, F. 1984. "Agriculture." In *Science and Civilization in China*, vol. 6, part 2, ed. Joseph Needham. Cambridge: Cambridge University Press.

Bray, F. 1986. *The Rice Economies*. Oxford: Blackwell.

Bresson, A. 2006. "La Machine d'Heron et Le Cout de L'energie dans Le Monde Antique." In *Innovazione Technica e Progresso Economico nel Mondo Romano*, ed. E. Lo Cascio. Bari: Ledipuglin.

British Petroleum. 2014. *BP Statistical Review of World Energy 2014*. http://www.bp.com/content/dam/bp/pdf/Energy-economics/statistical-review-2014/BP-statistical-review-of-world-energy-2014-full-report.pdf.

British Petroleum. 2015. *Statistical Review of World Energy 2015*. www.bp.com/en/global/corporate/about-bp/energy-economics/statistical-review -of-world-energy.html.

British Petroleum. 2016. *Statistical Review of World Energy 2016 Workbook*. http://www.bp.com/statisticalreview.

British Petroleum. 2017. *Statistical Review of World Energy 2016 Workbook*. https://www.bp.com/content/dam/bp/en/corporate/pdf/energy-economics/statistical-review-2017/bp-statistical-review-of-world-energy-2017-full-report.pdf.

Broadberry, S., Campbell, B. M. S., Klein, K., Overton, M., and van Leeuwen, B. 2015. *British Economic Growth, 1270–1870*. Cambridge: Cambridge University Press.

Brook, T. 1999. "Capitalism and the Writings of Modern History in China." In *China and Historical Capitalism: Genealogies of Sinological Knowledge*, ed. Timothy Brook and Gregory Blue. Cambridge: Cambridge University Press.

Brooke, J. L. 2014. *Climate Change and the Course of Global History: A Rough Journey*. Cambridge: Cambridge University Press.

Brown, L. 2012. "The Great Transition: Part I: From Fossil Fuels to Renewable Energy." Earth Policy Institute. http://www.earth-policy.org/plan_b_updates/2012/update107.

Brown, P. 1971. *The World of Late Antiquity, AD 150–750*. New York: W. W. Norton.

Bryce, R. 2008. *Gusher of Lies: The Dangerous Delusions of "Energy Interdependence."* New York: Public Affairs.

Buck, R. 2015. *The Oregon Trail: A New American Journey*. New York: Simon and Schuster.

Burnham, A., Han, J., Clark, C. E., Wang, M., Dunn, J. B., and Palou-Rivera, I. 2012. "Life-Cycle Greenhouse Gas Emissions of Shale Gas, Natural Gas, Coal and Petroleum." *Environmental Science and Technology* 46 (2): 619–627.

Cardwell, D., and Wald, M. L. 2014. "A Huge Solar Plant Opens, Facing Doubts About Its Future." *New York Times*, February 14. www.nytimes.com/2014/02/14/business/energy-environment/a-big-solar-plant-opens-facing-doubts-about-its-future.html?r=0.

Celasun, O., Bella, G. D., Mahedy, T., and Papageorgiou, C. 2014. "The U.S. Manufacturing Recovery: Uptick or Renaissance?" IMF Working Paper 14/28. International Monetary Fund

Chandler, A. D. 1962. *Strategy and Structure: Chapters in the History of the American Industrial Enterprise*. Cambridge, MA: MIT Press.

Chandler, A. D. 1977. *The Visible Hand: The Managerial Revolution in American Business*. Cambridge, MA: Harvard University Press.

Chandler, A. D. 1990. *Scale and Scope*. Cambridge, MA: Harvard University Press.

Chao, K. 1977. *The Development of Cotton Textile Production in China*. Cambridge, MA: Harvard University Press.

Chase-Dunn, C., and Hall, T. D. 1997. *Rise and Demise: Comparing World-Systems*. Boulder, CO: Westview Press.

Chase-Dunn, C., Kwon, R., Lawrence, K., and Inoue, H. 2011. "Last of the Hegemons: U.S. Decline and Global Governance." *International Review of Modern Sociology* 37 (1): 1–29.

Chaudhuri, K. N. 1978. *The Trading World of Asia and the English East India Co., 1660–1760*. Cambridge: Cambridge University Press.

Cho, J. 2014. "The Little Ice Age and the Coming of the Anthropocene." *Asian Review of World Histories* 2 (1): 1–16.

Christian, D. 2011. *Maps of Time: An Introduction to Big History*, 2nd ed. Berkeley: University of California Press.

Cipolla, C. M. 1952. "The Economic Decline of Italy." *Economic History Review* 5 (2): 178–187.

Cipolla, C. M. 1974. "The Italian 'Failure.'" In *Failed Transitions to Modern Industrial Society: Renaissance Italy and Seventeenth Century Holland*, ed. Frederick Krantz and Paul M. Hohenburg. Montreal: Interuniversity Centre for European Studies.

Clark, G., and Jacks, D. 2007. "Coal and the Industrial Revolution 1700–1869." *European Review of Economic History* 11 (1): 39–72.

CO2Earth. 2017. "NOAA Monthly CO_2 Data." https://www.co2.earth/monthly-co2.

Cockerham, S. 2013. "Fracking-led Energy Boom Is Turning US into 'Saudi America.'" *Miami Herald Nation*, December 3, www.miamiherald.com/2013/11/28/3765669/fracking-led-energy-boom-is-turning.html.

Cohen, B. J. 2008. *International Political Economy: An Intellectual History*. Princeton, NJ: Princeton University Press.

Colborn, T., Kwiatowski, C., Schultz, K., and Bachran, M. 2011. "Natural Gas Operations from a Public Health Perspective." *Human and Ecological Risk Assessment* 17 (5): 1039–1056.

Cooke, K. 2015. "Plummeting Oil Price Casts Shadow Over Fracking's Future." *Guardian*, January 6. https://www.theguardian.com/environment/2015/jan/06/oil-price-casts-shadow-over-frackings-future.

Cornell, T. J. 2003. "Warfare and Urbanization in Roman Italy." In *Urban Society in Roman Italy*, ed. T. J. Cornell and Kathryn Lomas. London: Routledge.

Cortado, J. W. 2004. *The Digital Hand: How Computers Changed the Work of American Manufacturing, Transportation, and Retail Industries*. Oxford: Oxford University Press.

Darwall, R. 2013. *The Age of Global Warming: A History*. London: Quarter Books.

Davenport, C. 2014. "Study Finds Methane Leaks Negate Benefits of Natural Gas as a Fuel for Vehicles." *New York Times*, February 14.

David, A. P., and Wright, G. 1997. "Increasing Returns and the Genesis of American Resource Abundance." *Industrial and Corporate Change* 6: 203–245.

Davids, K. 1993. "Technological Change and the Economic Expansion of the Dutch Republic, 1580–1650." In *The Dutch Economy in the Golden Age: Nine Studies*, ed. Karel Davids and Leo Noordegraaf. Amsterdam: Het Nerderlandsch Economisch-Historisch Archief.

Davids, K. 2008. *The Rise and Decline of Dutch Technological Leadership*, 2 vols. Leiden: Brill.

Davis, R. 1954. "English Foreign Trade, 1660–1700." *Economic History Review*, 2nd ser., 7 (2): 150–166.

Davis, R. 1962. "English Foreign Trade, 1700–1774." *Economic History Review*, 2nd ser., 15 (2): 285–303.

Davis, S. J., and C. Shearer. 2014. "Climate Change: A Crack in the Natural-Gas Bridge." *Nature* 514 (7523): 436–437.

Debeir, M. J. C., Deleage, J. P., and Hemery, D. 1991. *In the Servitude of Power: Energy and Civilization Through the Ages*. Trans. John Barman. London: Zed Books.

Devezas, M. T. C., and Modelski, G. 2008. "The Portuguese as System-Builders: Technological Innovation in Early Globalization." In *Globalization as Evolutionary Process: Modeling Global Change*, ed. George Modelski, Tessaleno C. Devezas, and William R. Thompson. London: Routledge.

De Vries, J., and van der Woude, A. 1997. *The First Modern Economy: Success, Failure and Persistence of the Dutch Economy, 1500–1815*. Cambridge: Cambridge University Press.

Deyette, J., Clemmer, S., Cleetus, R., Sattler, S., Bailee, A., and Rising, M. 2015. "The Natural Gas Gamble: A Risky Bet on American's Clean Energy Future." Union of Concerned Scientists. http://www.ucusa.org/sites/default/files/attach/2015/03-natural-gas-gamble-full report. pdf.

De Zeeuw, J. W. 1978. "Peat and the Dutch Golden Age: The Historical Meaning of Energy-Attainability." *AAG Bijadragen* 21: 3–31.

Dezhao, C. 2011. "China's Position and Policy on Climate Change." In *Chinese Climate Policy—Institutions and Intent*, ed. William C. Ramsay and Jacques Lesourne. Paris: Institut Francaises Relations Internationales.

Dijk, M., Orsato, R. J., and Kemp, R. 2013. "The Emergence of an Electric Mobility Trajectory." *Energy Policy* 52: 135–145.

di Tella, G. 1982. "The Economics of the Frontier." In *Economics in the Long View*, ed. Charles P. Kindleberger and Guido di Tella. London: Macmillan.

Dreyer, E. L. 2007. *Zeng He: China and the Oceans in the Early Ming, 1405–1433*. New York: Longman.

Drezner, D. W. 2013. "While Britain Stagnates, America is Roaring Back." *Spectator* June 29.

Dudley, L. 2012. *Mothers of Innovation: How Expanding Social Networks Gave Birth to the Industrial Revolution*. Newcastle, UK: Cambridge Scholars.

Duncan, T. B. 1986. "Navigation Between Portugal and Asia in the Sixteenth and Seventeenth Centuries." In *Asia and the West: Encounters and Exchanges from the Age of Exploorations*, ed. Cyriac K. Pullapilly and Edwin J. VanKley. Notre Dame, IN: Cross Cultural Publications.

El Gamal, R., Lawler, A., and Ghaddar, A. 2016. "OPEC in First Joint Oil Cut with Russia Since 2001, Saudis Take 'Big Hit.'" Reuters, 1 December.

Elvin, M. 1973. *The Pattern of the Chinese Past*. Stanford, CA: Stanford University Press.

Erdkamp, P. 2015. "Structural Determinants of Economic Performance in the Roman World and Early Modern Europe: A Comparative Approach." In *Structure and Performance in the Roman Economy: Models, Methods, and Case Studies*, ed. Paul Erdkamp and Koenraad Verbouen. Brussels: Editions Latomus.

Esteban, J. C. 2004. "Comparative Patterns of Colonial Trade: Britain and Its Rivals." In *Exceptionalism and Industrialisation: Britain and Its European Rivals, 1688–1815*, ed. Leandro Prados de la Escosura. Cambridge: Cambridge University Press.

Etemad, B., and Luciani, J. 1991. *World Energy Production, 1800–1985*. Geneva: Librarie Droz.

Etheridge, D. M., Steele, L. P., Francey, R. J., and Langenfelds, R. L. 2002. "Historical CH_4 Records Since About 1000 A.D. from Ice Core Data. In Trends: A Compendium of Data on Global Change." Oak Ridge, TN: Carbon Dioxide Information Analysis Center, Oak Ridge National Laboratory, Department of Energy.

ExxonMobil. 2014. "The Outlook for Energy: A View to 2040." http://corporate. exxonmobil. com/en/energy/energy-outlook.

Fallows, J. 2010. "Dirty Coal, Clean Future." *Atlantic* (December). http://www.theatlatnic.com/magazin/archive/2010/12/dirty-coal-clean-future/308307.

Fenby, J. 2014. *Will China Dominate the 21st Century?* Cambridge, UK: Polity.

Ferrill, A. 1991. *Roman Imperial Grand Strategy*. Lanham, MD: University Press of America.

Feuerwerker, A. 1995. *Studies in the Economic History of Late Imperial China: Handicraft, Modern Industry, and the State*. Ann Arbor: Center for Chinese Studies, University of Michigan.

Finley, M. I. 1973. *The Ancient Economy*. Berkeley: University of California Press.

Fishlow, A. 1965. *American Railroads and the Transformation of the Antebellum Economy*. Cambridge, MA: Harvard University Press.

Fite, G. C., and Reese, J. E. 1965. *An Economic History of the United States*, 2nd ed. Boston: Houghton Mifflin.

Fogel, R. W. 1964. *Railroads and American Economic Growth*. Baltimore: Johns Hopkins University Press.

Frank, A. G. 1998. *ReOrient*. Berkeley: University of California Press.

Freese, B. 2003. *Coal: A Human History*. New York: Penguin.

Furber, H. 1976. *Rival Empires of Trade in the Orient, 1600–1800*. Minneapolis: University of Minnesota Press.

Gernet, J. 1982. *A History of Chinese Civilization*. Trans. J. R. Foster. Cambridge: Cambridge University Press.

Giardina, A. 2007. "The Transition to Late Antiquity." In *The Cambridge Economic History of the Greco-Roman World*, ed. Walter Schiedel, Ian Morris, and Richard Saller. Cambridge: Cambridge University Press.

Gilles, B. 1978. *Histoires des Techniques: Technique et Civilisations, Technique et Sciences*. Paris: Editions Gallimard.

Gilpin, R. 1975. *U.S. Power and the Multinational Corporation*. New York: Basic Books.

Gilpin, R. 1980. *War and Change in World Politics*. Cambridge: Cambridge University Press.

Gilpin, R. 1987. *The Political Economy of International Relations*. Princeton, NJ: Princeton University Press.

Gilpin, R. with Gilpin, J. M. 2001. *Global Political Economy: Understanding the International Economic Order*. Princeton, NJ: Princeton University Press.

Gizewski, C. 1994. "Romisch und alter Chinesische Geshichte im Vengleich I zur Moglichkeit eines gemeinsamen Altertums- begriffs." *Klio* 76: 271–302.

Global Wind Energy Council. 2015. *Global Wind Report 2015*. http://www.gwec.net/publications/global-wind-report-2/.

Goddard, S. B. 1994. *Getting There: The Epic Struggle Between Road and Rail in the American Century*. Chicago: University of Chicago Press.

Godinho, V. M. 1963–1965. *Os Discobrimentos e a Economica Mundial*. Lisbon: Editorial Presencas.

Golas, P. J. 1999. *Joseph Needham's Science and Civilization in China*, vol. 5, *Chemistry and Chemical Technology, Part XIII: Mining*. Cambridge: Cambridge University Press.

Goldsmith, R. W. 1984. "An Estimate of the Size and Structure of the National Product of the Early Roman Empire." *Review of Income and Wealth* 30: 263–288.

Goldstone, J. A. 2002. "Efflorescences and Economic Growth in World History: Rethinking the 'Rise of the West' and the Industrial Revolution." *Journal of World History* 13 (2): 323–389.

Gordon, R. J. 2015. *The Rise and Fall of American Growth: The U.S. Standard of Living Since the Civil War*. Princeton, NJ: Princeton University Press.

Grant, M. 1996. *The Climax of Rome*. London: Weidenfeld and Nicolson.

Grantham, G. 2015. "A Search-Equilibrium Approach to the Roman Economy." In *Structure and Performance in the Roman Economy: Models, Methods, and Case Studies*, ed. Paul Erdkamp and Koenraad Verbouen. Brussels: Editions Latomus.

Gray, R., and Peterson, J. M. 1974. *Economic Development of the United States*. Homewood, IL: Richard D. Irwin.

Green, C. 2017. "Half Full or Nearly Empty?" *Nature Climate Change*, February 7: 98–99.

Green, F., and Stern, N. 2015. *China's 'New Normal': Structural Change, Better Growth, and Peak Emissions*. London: Grantham Research Institute on Climate Change and the Environment and Centre for Climate Change Economics and Policy.

Green Car Congress. 2015. "Navigant Forecasts Global Annual Sales of LDVs of 122.6M by 2035, Up 38% from 2015." http://www.greencarcongress.com/2015/07/20150706-navigant.html.

Greene, K. 1986. *The Archaeology of the Roman Economy*. Berkeley: University of California Press.

Griffiths, R., and Luciani, P., eds. 2011. *Does the 21st Century Belong to China: Kissinger and Zakaria vs. Ferguson and Li*. Toronto: Anansi.

Grinin, L., and Korotoayev, A. V. 2014. "Globalization Shuffles Cards of the World Pack: In Which Direction Is the Global Economic-Political Balance Shifting?" *World Futures* 70 (8): 515–545.

Guerin, E., Mas, C. and Waisman, H. 2014. *Pathways to Deep Decarbonization*. New York: Sustainable Development Solutions Network and Institute for Sustainable Development and International Relations. http://unsdsn.org/wp-content/uploads/2014/09/DDPP_Digit.pdf

Hacker, L. M. 1970. *The Course of American Economic Growth and Development*. New York: John Wiley.

Haley, K. H. D. 1974. "Holland: Commentary." In *Failed Transitions to Modern Industrial Society: Renaissance Italy and Seventeenth Century Holland*, ed. Frederick Krantz and Paul M. Hohenberg. Montreal: Interuniversity Centre for European Studies.

Harley, C. K. 2004. "Trade: Discovery, Mercantilism and Technology." In *The Cambridge Economic History of Modern Britain*, vol. 1: *Industrialisation, 1700–1860*, ed. Roderick Floud and Paul Johnson. Cambridge: Cambridge University Press.

Hartley, P., Medlock, K. B., III, Temzelides, T., and Zhang, X. 2014. "Energy Sector Innovation and Growth." RISE Working Paper 14-009. Houston, TX: Rice Initiative for the Study of Economics.

Hartwell, R. M. 1962. "A Revolution in the Chinese Iron and Coal Industries During the Northern Sung, 960–1126 AD." *Journal of Asian Studies* 21 (2): 153–162.

Hartwell, R. M. 1966. "Markets, Technology, and the Structure of Enterprise in the Development of the Eleventh-Century Chinese Iron and Steel Industry." *Journal of Economic History* 26 (1): 29–58.

Hartwell, R. M. 1967a. *The Causes of the Industrial Revolution in England*. London: Methuen.

Hartwell, R. M. 1967b. "A Cycle of Economic Change in Imperial China: Coal and Iron in Northeast China, 750–1350." *Journal of the Economic and Social History of the Orient* 10 (1): 102–159.

Hartwell, R. M. 1971. *The Industrial Revolution and Economic Growth*. London: Methuen.

Hartwell, R. M. 1982. "Demographic, Political and Social Transformations of China, 750–1550." *Harvard Journal of Asian Studies* 42 (2): 365–442.

Hausman, C., and Kellog, R. 2015. "Welfare and Distributional Implications of Shale Gas." Brookings Papers on Economic Activity (March). Washington, D.C.: Brookings Institution.

Hayhoe, K., Keshgi, H. S., Jain, A. K., and Woebbles, D. 2002. "Substitution of Natural Gas for Coal: Climatic Effects of Utility Sector Emissions." Climate Change 54 (1–2): 107–139.

Headrick, D. R. 2009. Technology: A World History. Oxford: Oxford University Press.

Helm, D. 2012. The Carbon Crunch, rev. ed. New Haven, CT: Yale University Press.

Herberg, M. 2013. "China's Energy Future." USC US-China Institute video, 14:50. June 19. https://www.youtube.com /watch?v=NtMW_aa-r1I.

Hillebrand, E., and Closson, S. 2015. Energy, Economic Growth, and Geopolitical Futures: Eight Long-Range Scenarios. Cambridge, MA: MIT Press.

Hobson, J. M. 2004. The Eastern Origins of Western Civilization. Cambridge: Cambridge University Press.

Hodges, H. 1970/1996. Technology in the Ancient World. London: Michael O'Mara Books.

Hopkins, K. 1978. Conquerors and Slaves. Cambridge: Cambridge University Press.

Hopkins, K. 1980. "Taxes and Trade in the Roman Empire, 200 BC–AD 400." Journal of Roman Studies 70: 101–125.

Hopkins, K. 1995/1996) "Rome, Taxes, Rents, and Trade." Kodai 6/7: 41–75.

Hounshell, D. A. 1984. From the American System to Mass Production, 1800–1932: The Development of Manufacturing Technology in the United States. Baltimore: Johns Hopkins University Press.

Houser, T., and Mohan, S. 2014. Fueling Up: The Economic Implications of America's Oil and Gas Boom. Washington, D.C.: Peterson Institute for International Economics.

Howarth, R. W., Ingraffea, A., and Engelder, T. 2011. "Should Fracking Stop? Yes." Nature 477: 271–274.

Howarth, R. W., Santoro, R., and Ingraffea, A. 2011. "Methane and the Greenhouse-Gas Footprint of Natural Gas from Shale Formations." Climate Change 106: 679–690.

Huang, R. 1990. China: A Macro History. Armonk, NY: M. E. Sharpe.

Hucker, C. O. 1975. China's Imperial Past. Stanford, CA: Stanford University Press.

Huenteler, J. 2014. "China's Coal Addiction a Threat to Its Energy Security." South China Morning Post, May 14.

Hughes, J. D. 2011. "Will Natural Gas Fuel America in the 21st Century?" Post Carbon Institute. http://www.postcarbon.org/report/PCI-report-nat-gas-future.pdf.

Hughes, J. D. 2012. "The Energy Sustainability Dilemma: Powering the Future in a Finite World." http://www.eeb.cornell.edu/howarth/HUGHES%20Cornell%Ithaca% 20May%202%20 2012.pdf.

Hultman, N., Rebois, D., Scholten, M., and Ramig, C. 2011. "The Greenhouse Impact of Unconventional Gas for Electricity Generation." Environmental Research Letters 6 (4): 1–9.

Hung, H. 2015. The China Boom: Why China Will Not Rule the World. New York: Columbia University Press.

Huntington, H. 2013. "Changing the Game? Emissions and Market Implications of New National Gas Supplies." Energy Modeling Forum Report 26. Palo Alto, CA: Stanford University.

Ignatius, D. 2012. "An Economic Boom Ahead?" Washington Post, May 4.

Inikori, J. E. 2002. Africans and Industrial Revolution in England: A Study in International Trade and Economic Development. Cambridge: Cambridge University Press.

Intergovernmental Panel on Climate Change. 2014. "Climage Change 2014: Synthesis Report." https://www.ipcc.ch/report/ar5/syr/.

International Energy Agency. 2013. Global EV Outlook: Understanding the Electric Vehicle Landscape to 2020. https://www.iea.org/publications/freepublications/publication/GlobalEVOutlook_2013.pdf.

International Energy Agency. 2014. "World Energy Investment Outlook." https://www.iea.org/publications/freepublications/publication/WEIO2014.pdf.

International Energy Agency. 2015. World Energy Outlook 2015: Special Report on Energy and Climate Change. Paris: IEA.

Israel, J. I. 1989. Dutch Primacy in World Trade, 1585–1740. Oxford: Oxford University Press.

Jackson, R. B., Vengosh, A., Carey, J. W., Davies, R. J., Darrah, T. H., O'Sullivan, F., and Petron, G. (2014). "The Environmental Costs and Benefits of Fracking." Annual Review of Environment and Resources 39 (October): 327–362.

Jacobs, J. 1969. *The Economy of Cities.* New York: Random House.

Jacobs, J. 1984. *Cities and the Wealth of Nations: Principles of Economic Life.* New York: Random House.

Jacobson, M. Z., Delucchi, M. A., Bazouin, G., Bauer, Z. A. F., Heavey, C. C., Fisher, E., Morris, S. B., Piekutowski, D. J. Y., Venal, T. A., and Yeskou, T. W.. 2015. "100% Clean and Renewable Wind, Water, and Sunlight (WWS) All-Sector Energy Roadmaps for 139 Countries of the World." Stanford, CA: Department of Civil and Environmental Engineering, Stanford University.

Jenks, L. 1944. "Railroads as an Economic Force in American Development." *Journal of Economic History* 4 (1): 1–20.

Johnson, B. 2014. *Carbon Nation: Fossil Fuels in the Making of American Culture.* Lawrence: University Press of Kansas.

Johnson, S. A. J. 2017. *Why Did Ancient Civilizations Fail?* London: Routledge.

Jones, C. F. 2014. *Routes of Power: Energy and Modern America.* Cambridge, MA: Harvard University Press.

Jones, E. L. 1981. *The European Miracle.* Cambridge: Cambridge University Press.

Jones, E. L. 2002. *The Record of Global Economic Development.* Cheltenham, UK: Edward Elgar.

Jones, B., Steven, D., and O'Brien, E. 2014. "Fueling a New Order? The New Geopolitical and Security Consequences of Energy." Washington, D.C.: Brookings Institution.

Jongman, W. M. 2002. "The Roman Economy: From Cities to Empire." In *The Transformation of Economic Life Under the Roman Empire,* ed. Lukas De Blois and John Rich. Amsterdam: J.C. Geben.

Jongman, W. M. 2007. "Gibbon Was Right: The Decline and Fall of the Roman Empire." In *Crises and the Roman Empire: Proceedings of the Seventh Workshop of the International Network Impact of Empire,* ed. Olivier Hekster, Gerda de Kleijn, and Danielle Sloojus. Leiden: Brill.

Kander, A. 2013. "The Second and Third Industrial Revolutions." In *Power to the People: Energy in Europe over the Past Five Centuries,* ed. Astrid Kander, Paola Malanima, and Paul Warde. Princeton, NJ: Princeton University Press.

Kander, A., Malanima, P., and Warde, P., eds. 2013 . *Power to the People: Energy in Europe over the Past Five Centuries.* Princeton, NJ: Princeton University Press.

Kedar, B. Z. 1976. *Merchants in Crisis: Genoese and Venetian Men of Affairs and the Fourteenth Century Depression.* New Haven, CT: Yale University Press.

Kehoe, D. P. 2007. "The Early Roman Empire: From Cities to Empire." In *The Transformation of Economic Life Under the Roman Empire,* ed. Lukas De Blois and John Rich. Amsterdam: J. C. Geben.

Kelly, M. 1997. "The Dynamics of Smithian Growth." *Quarterly Journal of Economics* 112 (3): 939–964.

Kindleberger, C. P. 1996. *World Economic Primacy, 1500–1990.* Oxford: Oxford University Press.

Kirsch, D. A. 2000. *The Electric Vehicle and the Burden of History.* New Brunswick, NJ: Rutgers University Press.

Klare, M. T. 2016. "The Future of Oil Is Here—and It Doesn't Look Pretty." *Nation,* March 8. https//www.thenation.com/article/the-future-of-oil-is-here-and-it-doesn't-look-pretty/.

Klein, M. 2007. *The Genesis of Industrial America, 1870–1920.* Cambridge: Cambridge University Press.

Knowles, N. 2013. "Fracking Is Propping Up the US Economy." *NewStatesman* October 7.

Koepke, N., and Baten, J. 2005. "The Biological Standard of Living in Europe During the Last Two Millennia." *European Review of Economic History* 9: 61–95.

Kron, G. 2012. "Food Production." In *The Cambridge Companion to the Roman Economy,* ed. Walter Scheidel. Cambridge: Cambridge University Press.

Kurtzman, J. 2014. *Unleashing the Second American Century: Four Forces for Economic Dominance.* New York: Public Affairs.

Labor Network for Sustainability. 2016. "The Clean Energy Future." www.labor4sustainability. org/wp-content/uploads/2015/10/cleanenergy_10212015_main.pdf.

Lake, D. A. 1993. "Leadership, Hegemony, and the International Economy." *International Studies Quarterly* 37: 459–489.

Lane, F. C. 1973. *Venice: The Maritime Republic.* Baltimore: Johns Hopkins University Press.

Lane, F. C. 1987. "Technology and Productivity in Seaborne Transportation." In *Studies in Venetian Social and Economic History*, ed. B. G. Kohl and K. C. Mueller. London: Variorum Reprints.

Lee, H., and Lovelette, G. 2011. "Will Electric Cars Transform the U.S. Vehicle Market? An Analysis of the Key Determinants." Cambridge, MA: Belfer Center for Science and International Affairs, Harvard Kennedy School.

Levathes, L. 1996. *When China Ruled the Seas: The Treasure Fleet of the Dragon Throne, 1405–1433.* Oxford: Oxford University Press.

LeVine, S. 2016. "The US Bet Big on American Oil and Now the Whole Global Economy Is Paying the Price." *Quartz*, February 1. https://qz.com/604756/the-us-bet-big-on-american-oil-and-now-the-whole-global-economy-is-paying-the-price/.

Levitan, D. 2016. "Is Nuclear Power Our Energy Future, or in a Death Spiral? *Climate Control*, March 6. http://www.climatecontrol.org/new/nuclear-power-energy-future-or-dinosaur-death-squad-20103.

Lewis, A. R. 1988. *Nomads and Crusaders, A.D. 1000–1368.* Bloomington: Indiana University Press.

Li, M. 2014. *Peak Oil, Climate Change, and the Limits to China's Economic Growth.* London: Routledge.

Licht, W. 1995. *Industrializing America: The Nineteenth Century.* Baltimore: Johns Hopkins University Press.

Lieberman, V. B. 2003. *Strange Parallels: Southeast Asia in Global Context, c. 800–1830,* vol. 1: *Integration on the Mainland.* Cambridge: Cambridge University Press.

Lieberman, V. B. 2009. *Strange Parallels: Southeast Asia in Global Context, c. 800–1830,* vol. 2: *Mainland Mirrors: Europe, Japan, China, South Asia, and the Islands.* Cambridge: Cambridge University Press.

Liebeschuetz, W. 2002. "Unsustainable Development: The Origin of Ruined Landscapes in the Roman Empire." In *The Transformation of Economic Life Under the Roman Empire*, ed. Lukas De Blois and John Rich. Amsterdam: J. C. Gieben.

Lind, M. 2012. *Land of Promise: An Economic History of the United States.* New York: Harper.

Lipsey, R. G., Carlaw, K. I., and Bekar, C. T. 2005. *Economic Transformations: General Purpose Technologies and Long Term Economic Growth.* Oxford: Oxford University Press.

Lo Cascio, E., and Malanima, P. 2009a. "GDP in Pre-Modern Economics (1–1820 AD)." *Revista di Storia Economica* 25 (3): 391–419.

Lo Cascio, E., and Malanima, P. 2009b. "Ancient and Pre-Modern Economies: GDP in the Roman Empire and Early Modern Europe." www.paolomalima.it/default_file/Articles/RomanGDP.pdf.

Lo, J. P. 2012. *China as a Sea Power, 1127–1368.* Ed. Bruce A. Elleman. Singapore: National University of Singapore Press.

Lopez, R. 1987. "The Trade of Medieval Europe: The South." In *The Cambridge Economic History of Europe: Trade and Industry in the Middle Ages*, 2nd ed., ed. M. M. Postan and E. Miller. Cambridge: Cambridge University Press.

Lopez, R., and Miskimin, H. A. 1962. "The Economic Depression of the Renaissance." *Economic History Review*, 2nd ser., 14: 408–426.

Luzzato, G. 1961. *An Economic History of Italy.* Trans. P. Jones. London: Routledge and Kegan Paul.

Lynas, M. 2008. *Six Degrees: Our Future on a Hotter Planet.* Washington D.C.: National Geographic Society.

MacLeod, C. 2004. "The European Origins of British Technological Predominance." In *Exceptionalism and Industrialisation: Britain and Its European Rivals, 1688–1815*, ed. Leandro Prados de la Escosura. Cambridge: Cambridge University Press.

MacMullen, R. 1988. *Corruption and the Decline of Rome.* New Haven, CT: Yale University Press.

Maddison, A. 2001. *The World Economy: A Millennial Perspective.* Paris: Organisation for Economic Co-operation and Development.

Maddison, A. 2007. *Contours of the World Economy, 1–2030 AD.* Oxford: Oxford University Press.

Malanima, P. 2002. *L'Economie Italiana, Dalla Crescita Medievale alla Crescita Contemporanea.* Bologna: Il Mulino.

Malanima, P. 2011a. "The Long Decline of a Leading Economy: GDP in Central and Northern Italy, 1300–1913." *European Review of Economic History* 15: 169–219.

Malanima, P. 2011b. "Energy Consumption and Energy Crisis in the Roman World." Paper presented at the American Academy Environmental History Conference, Rome, June 15–16. http://www.paolomalanima.it/default_file/Papers/ENERGY-ENVIRONMENT.pdf.

Malanima, P. 2013. "Pre-Industrial Economies." In *Power to the People: Energy in Europe over the Past Five Centuries*, ed. Astrid Kander, Paola Malanima, and Paul Warde. Princeton, NJ: Princeton University Press.

Mann, M. 1986. *The Sources of Social Power*, vol. 1: *A History of Power from the Beginning to AD 1760*. Cambridge: Cambridge University Press.

Marcacci, Silvio. 2013. "Electric Vehicles Speeding Toward 7% of All Global Sales by 2020." *Clean Technica*, September 30. https://cleantechnica.com/2013/09/30/electric-vehicles-speeding-toward-7-global-sales-2020/.

Marcus, A. I., and Segal, H. P. 1999. *Technology in America: A Brief History*, 2nd ed. Fort Worth, TX: Harcourt Brace.

Marzano, A. 2015. "Villas as Instigators and Indicators of Economic Growth." In *Structure and Performance in the Roman Economy: Models, Methods, and Case Studies*, ed. Paul Erdkamp and Koenraad Verbouen. Brussels: Editions Latomus.

Mason, C. F., Muehlenbachs, L., and Olmstead, S. M. 2015. "The Economics of Shale Gas Development." *Annual Review of Resource Economics* 7 (1): 269–289.

Matias, J. C., and Devezas, T. C. 2007. "Consumption Dynamics of Primary-Energy Sources: The Century of Alternative Energies." *Applied Energy* 84 (7–8): 763–770.

Mathieu, M., Spencer, T., and Sartor, O. 2014. "Economic Analysis of the U.S. Unconventional Oil and Gas Revolution." *Vox*, Centre for Economic Policy Research. http://voxeu.org/article/limited-economic-impact-us-shale-gas-boom.

Maugeri, L. 2010. *Beyond the Age of Oil: The Myths, Realties, and Future of Fossil Fuels and Their Alternatives*. Trans. J. T. Hine, Jr. Santa Barbara, CA: Praeger.

Mazzucato, M. 2015. *The Entrepreneurial State: Debunking Public vs. Private Sector Myths*. New York: Public Affairs.

McBride, J., and Sergie, M. A. 2015. "Hydraulic Fracturing (Fracking)." Council on Foreign Relations (June 10). www.cfr.org/energy-and-environment/hydraulic-fracturing/p31559.

McClelland, P. 1968. "Railroads, American Growth, and the New Economic History: A Critique." *Journal of Economic History* 28 (1): 102–123.

McCormick, M. 2001. *Origins of the European Economy: Communities and Commerce, AD 300–900*. Cambridge: Cambridge University Press.

McEvedy, C., and Jones, R. 1978. *Atlas of World Population History*. New York: Facts on File.

McGlynn, D. 2016. "The Future of Nuclear Energy." *Phys.org*, November 28. https://phys.org/news/2016-11-future-nuclear-energy.html.

McJeon, H., Edmonds, J., Bauer, N., Clarke, L. Fisher, B., Flannery, B.P., Hilaire, J., Krey, V., Marangoni, G., Mi, R., Riahi, K., Rogner, H., and Tavoni, M. 2014. "Limited Impact on Decade-scale Climate Change from Increased Use of Natural Gas." *Nature* 514 (7523): 482–485.

McLaughlin, R. 2014. *The Roman Empire and the Indian Ocean: The Ancient World Economy and the Kingdoms of Africa, Arabia and India*. Barsley, UK: Pen & Sword Military

McNeill, J. 1998. "Chinese Environmental History in World Perspective." In *Sediments of Time: Environment and Society in Chinese History*, ed. Mark Elvin and Liu Ts'ui-jung. Cambridge: Cambridge University Press.

McNeill, W. H. 1974. *Venice: The Hinge of Europe, 1081–1797*. Chicago: University of Chicago Press.

McNeill, W. H. 1982. *The Pursuit of Power: Technology, Armed Force, and Society Since A.D. 1000*. Chicago: University of Chicago Press.

McSwain, D. 2013. "Fracking Energy Revolution Begins to Rock the World." *San Diego Union-Tribune*, May 25. www.utsandiego.com/news/2013/May/25/fracking-energy-revolution-rocks-world/.

Meinig, D. W. 1986. *The Shaping of America: A Geographical Perspective on 500 Years of History*, vol. 1: *Atlantic America, 1492–1800*. New Haven, CT: Yale University Press.

Meinig, D. W. 1993. *The Shaping of America: A Geographical Perspective on 500 Years of History*, vol. 2: *Continental American, 1800–1867*. New Haven, CT: Yale University Press.

Menon, R. V. G. 2011. *Technology and Society*. Delhi: Longman.

Meyer, D. R. 2003. *The Roots of American Industrialization*. Baltimore: Johns Hopkins University Press.

Mills, R. M. 2013. "Who's Winning the Great Energy Rat Race?" *Foreign Policy*, March 8. http://www.foreignpolicy.com/articles/2013/03/08/whos_winning_the_great_energy_rat_race_china_oil_importer.

Millward, J. A. 1996. "New Perspectives on the Qing Frontier." In *Remapping China*, ed. Gail Hershatter, Emily Honig, Jonathan N. Lipman, and Randall Stross. Stanford, CA: Stanford University Press.

Mitchell, B. R. 1980. *European Historical Statistics, 1750–1975*, 2nd rev. ed. New York: Facts on File.

Miyakawa, H. 1955. "An Outline of the Naito Hypothesis and Its Effects on Japanese Studies of China." *Far Eastern Quarterly* 14 (4): 533–552.

Modelski, G. 1987. *Long Cycles in World Politics*. London: Macmillan.

Modelski, G. 2003. *World Cities: –3000 to 2000*. Washington, D.C.: Faros 2000.

Modelski, G., and Modelski, S., eds. 1988. *Documenting Global Leadership*. London: Macmillan.

Modelski, G., and Thompson, W. R. 1988. *Sea Power in Global Politics, 1494–1993*. London: Macmillan.

Modelski, G., and Thompson, W. R. 1996. *Leading Sectors and World Powers: The Coevolution of Global Politics and Economics*. Columbia: University of South Carolina Press.

Mokyr, J. 1990. *The Lever of Riches: Technological Creativity and Economic Progress*. Oxford: Oxford University Press.

Mokyr, J., ed. 1993. *The British Industrial Revolution: An Economic Perspective*. Boulder, CO: Westview Press.

Mokyr, J. 2002. *The Gifts of Athena: Historical Origins of the Knowledge Economy*. Princeton, NJ: Princeton University Press.

Mokyr, J. 2009. *The Enlightened Economy*. New Haven, CT: Yale University Press.

Moore, C. W., Zielinska, B., Petron, G., and Jackson, R. B. 2014. "Air Impacts of Increased Natural Gas Acquisition, Processing and Use: A Critical Review." *Environmental Science and Technology* 48 (15): 8349–8359.

Moriarity, P., and Hannery, D. 2012. "What's the Global Potential for Renewable Energy?" *Renewable and Sustainable Energy Reviews* 16: 244–252.

Morley, N. 2007. "The Early Roman Empire: Distribution." In *The Cambridge Economic History of the Greco-Roman World*, ed. W. Scheidel, I. Morris, and R. Saller. Cambridge: Cambridge University Press.

Morris, C. R. 2012. *The Dawn of Innovation: The First American Industrial Revolution*. New York: Public Affairs.

Morris, C. R. 2013. *Comeback: America's New Economic Boom*. New York: Public Affairs.

Morris, I. 2010. *Why the West Rules—for Now*. New York: Farrar, Straus and Giroux.

Morse, E. L., Lee, E. G., Ahn, D. P., Doshi, A., Kleinman, S. M., and Yuen, A. 2012. *Energy 2020: North America, the New Middle East*. New York: Citi GPS: Global Perspectives and Solutions.

Muttit, G. 2012. *Fuel on the Fire: Oil and Politics in Occupied Iraq*. New York: New Press.

Naim, M. 2014. "America's Coming Manufacturing Revolution." *Atlantic*, April 21. https://www.theatlantic.com/business/archive/2014/04/americas-coming-manufacturing-revolution/360931/.

National Research Council. 2011. *Climate Stabilization Targets: Emissions, Concentrations and Impacts over Decades to Millennia*. Washington D.C.: National Academies Press.

Nebeker, F. 2009. *Dawn of the Electronic Age: Electrical Technologies in the Shaping of the Modern World, 1914–1945*. Hoboken, NJ: John Wiley.

Needham, J. 1959. "Mathematics and the Sciences of Heaven." In *Science and Civilisation in China*, vol. 3, ed. Joseph Needham. Cambridge: Cambridge University Press.

Needham, J. 1969. *The Grand Titration*. Toronto: University of Toronto Press.

Negri, T. O. 1974. *Storia di Genoa*. Milan: Aldo Martello.

Nelson, R. R., and Wright, G. 1992. "The Rise and Fall of American Technological Leadership: The Postwar Era in Historical Perspective." *Journal of Economic Literature* 30 (4): 1931–1964.

Newell, R. G., and Raimi, D. 2014. "Implications of Shale Gas Development for Climate Change." *Environmental Science and Technology* 48 (15): 8360–8368.

Nicks, D. 2014. "How the US Energy Boom Is Changing America's Place in the World." *Time*, February 7. http://www.nation.time.com/2014/02/07/fracking-energy-boom-natural-gas-geopolitics-iran/.

Norwich, J. J. 1982. *A History of Venice*. New York: Penguin.

Nye, D. E. 1998. *Consuming Power: A Social History of American Energies*. Cambridge, MA: MIT Press.

Obama, B. 2009. "Clean Energy Economy Fact Sheet." Obama White House Archives. https://obamawhitehouse.archives.gov/the-press-office/clean-energy-economy-fact-sheet.

O'Brien, P. K. 1982. "European Economic Development: The Contribution of the Periphery." *Economic History Review* 35 (1): 1–18.

Ormrod, D. 2003. *The Rise of Commercial Empires: England and the Netherlands in the Age of Mercantilism, 1650–1770*. Cambridge: Cambridge University Press.

Overton, M. 1996. "Re-establishing the English Agricultural Revolution." *Agricultural History Review* 44 (1): 1–20.

Overton, M. 2002. *Agricultural Revolution in England, 1500–1850*. Cambridge: Cambridge University Press.

Paltsev, S. 2016. "Energy Scenarios: The Value and Limits of Scenario Analysis." Cambridge, Ma.: MIT Center for Energy and Environmental Policy Research.

Pamuk, S. 2007. "The Black Death and the Origins of the 'Great Divergence' Across Europe, 1300–1600." *European Review of Economic History* 11 (3): 289–317.

Perez, C. 2007. "Great Surges of Development and Alternative Forms of Globalization." In *Long Duration and Conjuncture in Contemporary Capitalism*, ed. Theotorio Dos Santos and Carlos Eduardo Martins. Florianopolis, Brazil: Universidad Federal de Santa Catarina (English version at www.carlotaperez.org/papers/GreatSurges_ and_ Globalization. pdf).

Perroux, F. 1979. "An Outline of a Theory of the Dominant Economy." In *Transnational Corporations and World Order: Readings in International Political Economy*, ed. George Modelski. San Francisco, CA: W. H. Freeman.

Persson, K. G. 2010. *An Economic History of Europe: Knowledge, Institutions and Growth, 600 to the Present*. Cambridge: Cambridge University Press.

Peters, G. P., Andrew, R. M., Canadell, J. G., Fuss, S., Jackson, R. B., Korsbakken, J. I., Le Querc, C., and Nakicenovic, N. 2017. "Key Indicators to Track Current Progress and Future Ambition of the Paris Agreement." *Nature Climate Change* (February 7: 118–122).

Podobnik, B. 2007. *Global Energy Shifts: Fostering Sustainability in a Turbulent Age*. Philadelphia: Temple University Press.

Pomeranz, K. 2000. *The Great Divergence*. Princeton, NJ: Princeton University Press.

Pomper, M. A. 2016. "What Future Does Nuclear Power Have in an Era of Cheap Energy?" *World Politics Review* (December 5).

Poulter, A. G. 2002. "Economic Collapse in the Countryside and the Consequent Transformation of City into Fortresses in Late Antiquity." In *The Transformation of Economic Life Under the Roman Empire*, ed. Lukas De Blois and John Rich. Amsterdam: J. C. Gieben.

Potter, D.S. 2009. *Rome in the Ancient World: From Romulus to Justinian*. London: Thames & Hudson.

Prak, M. 2005. *The Dutch Republic in the Seventeenth Century: The Golden Age*. Trans. Diane Webb. Cambridge: Cambridge University Press.

Price, J. L. 1998. *The Dutch Republic in the Seventeenth Century*. New York: St. Martin's Press.

PWC. 2017. "PwC Automotive Industry Bluebook (2017 edition) China Automotive Market: Witnessing the Transformation." https://www.pwccn.com/cn/automotive/pwc-auto-industry-bluebook.pdf.

Qian, W. 1985. *The Great Inertia: Scientific Stagnation in Traditional China*. Beckenham, UK: Croom Helm.

Quaschning, V. 2010. *Renewable Energy and Climate Change*. West Sussex, UK: John Wiley & Sons.

Rasler, K., and Thompson, W. R. 1992. "Politico-Economic Tradeoffs and British Relative Decline." In *Defense, Welfare and Growth: Perspectives and Evidence*, ed. Alex Mintz and Steve Chan. London: Routledge.

REN21. 2013. *Renewables 2013: Global Status Report*. Paris: Institute for Sustainable Energy Policies. http://www.ren21.net/Portals/0/documents/Resources/GSR/2013/GSR2013_lowres.pdf.

REN21. 2016. *Renewables 2016 Global Status Report*. Paris: Institute for Sustainable Energy Policies. www.ren21.net/wp-content/uploads/2016/10/REN21_GSR2016.FullReport.en.11.pdf.

REN21. 2017. *Renewables 2017 Global Status Report*. Paris: Institute for Sustainable Energy Policies. http://www.ren21.net/gsr-2017/.

Reuveny, R., and Thompson, W. R. 2004. *Growth, Trade and Systemic Leadership*. Ann Arbor: University of Michigan Press.

Robins, N. 2006. *The Corporation That Changed the World: How the East India Company Shaped the Modern Multinational*. London: Pluto Press.

Rojey, A. 2009. *Energy and Climate: How to Achieve a Successful Economic Transition*. Columbus, OH: Wiley.

Romein, J. 1939. "Dialektik des Fortschrifts," In *Zweimonatsschrift fur freie deutsche Kultur*, ed. Thomas Mann and Konrad Falke, Vol. 2. Zurich: Oprecht.

Roney, J. M. 2014. "China Leads World to Solar Power Record in 2013." Earth Policy Institute. http://www.earth-policy.org/indicators/C47/solar_power_2014.

Rosenthal, J. L., and Wong, R. B. 2011. *Before and Beyond Divergence: The Politics of Economic Change in China and Europe*. Cambridge, MA: Harvard University Press.

Rostow, W. W. 1971. *The Stages of Economic Growth*, 2nd ed. Cambridge: Cambridge University Press.

Rostow, W. W. 1985. "No Random Walk: A Comment on 'Why Was England First.'" In *The Economics of the Industrial Revolution*, ed. Joel Mokyr. Totowa, NJ: Rowman and Allenheld.

Sallares, R. 2002. *Malaria and Rome: A History of Malaria in Ancient Italy*. New York: Oxford University Press.

Saller, R. 2005. "Framing the Debate over Growth in the Ancient Economy." In *The Ancient Economy: Evidence and Models*, ed. Joseph Manning and Ian Morris. Stanford, CA: Stanford University Press.

Sanderson, B. M., and Knutti, R. 2017. "Delays in US Mitigation Could Rule Out Paris Targets." *Nature Climate Change* (February 7: 92–94.

Scammell, G. V. 1981. *The World Encompassed: The First European Maritime Empires, ca. 800–1650*. Berkeley: University of California Press.

Scammell, G. V. 1989. *The First Imperial Age: European Overseas Expansion, circa 1400–1715*. London: Unwin Hyman.

Scaruffi, P. "A Time-line of the Roman Empire." http://www.scaruffi.com/politics/romans.html.

Scheidel, W. 2008. "Real Wages in Early Economics: Evidence for Living Standards from 2000 BCE to 1300 CE." Princeton/Stanford Working Papers in Classics, no. 110801.

Scheidel, W. 2009. "From the 'Great Convergence' to the 'First Great Divergence': Roman and Qin-Han State Formation and Its Aftermath." In *Rome and China: Comparative Perspectives on Ancient World Empires*, ed. Walter Scheidel. Oxford: Oxford University Press.

Scheidel, W. 2012. "Approaching the Roman Economy." In *The Cambridge Companion to the Roman Economy*, ed. Walter Scheidel. Cambridge: Cambridge University Press.

Scheidel, W., and Friesen, S. J. 2009. "The Size of the Economy and the Distribution of Income in the Roman Empire." *Journal of Roman Studies* 99: 61–91.

Schlesinger, H. 2010. *The Battery: How Portable Power Sparked a Technological Revolution*. New York: Harper Collins.

Schneider, H. 2007. "Technology." In *The Cambridge Economic History of the Greco-Roman World*, ed. Walter Scheidel, Ian Morris, and Richard Saller. Cambridge: Cambridge University Press.

Schurr, S. H., and Netschert, B. C. 1960. *Energy in the American Economy, 1850–1975*. Baltimore: Johns Hopkins University Press.

Securing America's Future Energy. 2012. *The New American Oil Boom: Implications for Energy Security*. Washington, D.C.: P.X. Kelly Center for Energy Security at SAFE.

Securing America's Future Energy. 2013. *Oil Security 2025: U.S. National Security Policy in an Era of Domestic Oil Abundance.* Washington, D.C.: P.X. Kelly Center for Energy Security at SAFE.

Sernovitz, G. 2016. *The Green and the Black: The Complete Story of the Shale Revolution, the Fight over Fracking, and the Future of Energy.* New York: St. Martin's Press.

Shell Global. 2008. "Shell Energy Scenarios to 2050." http://s00.static-shell.com/content/dam/shell/static/future-energy/downloads/shell-scenarios/shell-energy-scenarios2050.pdf.

Shell Global. 2013. "New Lens Scenarios: A Shift in Perspective for a World in Transition." http://s01.static-shell.com/content/dam/shell-new/local/corporate   /Scenarios/Downloads/Scenarios_newdoc.pdf.

Shobart, B. A. 2014. "The Key Drivers of China's Environmental Policies." In *China's Energy CrossRoads: Forging a New Energy and Environmental Balance,* ed. Clara Gillespie and Meredith Miller. Seattle: National Bureau of Asian Research.

Sieferle, R. P. 2001. *The Subterranean Forest: Energy Systems and the Industrial Revolution.* Cambridge, UK: White Horse Press.

Skinner, G. W. 1977. "Introduction: Urban Development in Imperial China." In *The City in Late Imperial China,* ed. G. William Skinner. Stanford, CA: Stanford University Press.

Slicher van Bath, B. H. 1982. "The Economic Situation During the 17th Century." In *Dutch Capitalism and World Capitalism,* ed. Maurica Aymard. Cambridge: Cambridge University Press.

Small, M. J., Stern, P. C., Bomberg, E., Christopherson, S. M., Goldstein, B. D., Israel, A. L., Jackson, R. B., Krupnick, Mauter, M. S., Nash, J., North, D. W., Olmstead, S. M., Prakash, A., Rabe, B., Richardson, Tierney, S. Webler, T., Wong-Parodi, G., and B. Zielinska . 2014. "Risks and Risk Governance in Unconventional Shale Gas." *Environmental Science and Technology* 48 (15): 8289–8297.

Smil, V. 2003. *Energy at the Crossroads: Global Perspectives and Uncertainties.* Cambridge, MA: MIT Press.

Smil, V. 2005. *Creating the Twentieth Century: Technical Innovations of 1867–1914 and Their Lasting Impact.* Oxford: Oxford University Press.

Smil, V. 2010. *Why America Is Not a New Rome.* Cambridge, MA: MIT Press.

Smil, V. 2010a. *Energy Transitions: History, Requirements, Prospects.* Santa Barbara: ABC-CLIO.

Smil, V. 2013. *Made in the USA: The Rise and Retreat of American Manufacturing.* Cambridge, MA: MIT Press.

Smil, V. 2015. *Natural Gas: Fuel for the 21st Century.* Chichester, UK: Wiley.

Smit, J. W. 1974. "Holland: Commentary." In *Failed Transitions to Modern Industrial Society: Renaissance Italy and Seventeenth Century Holland,* ed. Frederick Krantz and Paul M. Hohenberg. Montreal: Interuniversity Centre for European Studies.

Smith, P. J. 2004. "Eurasian Transformations of the Tenth to Thirteenth Centuries: The View from Song China." *Medieval Encounters* 10, 1-3: 279-308.

Snidal, D. 1985. "The Limits of Hegemonic Stability Theory." *International Organization* 39 (4): 579–614.

Sovacool, B. K. 2014. "Cornucopia or Curse? Reviewing the Costs and Benefits of Shale Gas Hydraulic Fracturing (Fracking)." *Renewable and Sustainable Energy Reviews* 37: 249–264.

Spencer, T., Sartor, O., and Mathieu, M. 2014. "Unconventional Wisdon: An Economic Analysis of U.S. Shale Gas and Implications for the EU." Institut du Developpement Durable et Des Relations Internationales, Sciences-Po (Paris), no. 2/14 (February). http://www.iddri.org/Publications/Collections/Analyses/Study0214_TSS%20al%20al._shale%20gaqs.pdf.

Spenser, R. 2013. "The US Fracking Boom Is Changing Geopolitics and Rearranging Global Alliances." *Daily Telegraph,* December 13. http://www.businessinsider.com/the-us-fracking-boom-is-changing-geopolitics-2013-12.

Steensgaard, N. 1975. *The Asian Trade Revolution of the Seventeenth Century: The East India Companies and the Decline of the Caravan Trade.* Chicago: University of Chicago Press.

Steensgaard, N. 1982. "The Dutch East India Company as an Institutional Innovation." In *Dutch Capitalism and World Capitalism,* ed. Maurice Aymard. Cambridge: Cambridge University Press.

Supple, B. 1997. "Fear of Failing: Economic History and the Decline of Britain." In *Understanding Decline: Perceptions and Realities of British Economic Performance*, ed. Peter Clarke and Clive Trebilcock. Cambridge: Cambridge University Press.

Swart, K. W. 1974. "Holland's Bourgeoisie and the Retarded Industrialization of the Netherlands." In *Failed Transitions to Modern Industrial Society: Renaissance Italy and Seventeenth Century Holland*, ed. Frederick Krantz and Paul M. Hohenberg. Montreal: Interuniversity Centre for European Studies.

Szostak, R. 1991. *The Role of Transportation in the Industrial Revolution: A Comparison of England and France*. Montreal: McGill-Queen's University Press.

Tang, A. M. 1979. "China's Agricultural Legacy." *Economic Development and Cultural Change* 28 (1): 1–22.

Taylor, P. J., Hoyler, M., and Smith, D. 2012. "Cities in the Making of World Hegemonies." In *International Handbook of Globalization and World Cities*, ed. Ben Derudder, Michael Hoyler, Peter J. Taylor, and Frank Witlox. Cheltenham, UK: Edward Elgar.

Temin, P. 2006. "Estimating GDP in the Early Roman Empire." in *Innovazione Tecnica e Progresso Economico nel mondo romano*, ed. E. Lo Cascio. Bari: Edipuglia.

Temple, R. 1986. *The Genius of China: 3,000 Years of Science, Discovery and Invention*. New York: Simon and Schuster.

Teng, F., Liu, Q., Chen, Y., Tian, C., Zheng, X., Gu, A., Yang, X., and Wang, X. 2015. *Pathways to Deep Decarbonization in China*. Sustainable Development Solutions Network and Institute for Sustainable Development and International Relations. http://deepdecarbonization.org/wp-content/uploads/2015/09/DDPP_CHN.pdf.

Thompson, W. R. 1988. *On Global War: Historical-Structural Approaches to World Politics*. Columbia: University of South Carolina Press.

Thompson, W. R. 2015. "Inching Toward the Primus Inter Pares Model and the End of Systemic Leadership As We Have Come to Know It?" Paper presented at the annual meeting of the International Studies Association, New Orleans, LA, February.

Thompson, W. R., and Reuveny, R. 2010. *Limits to Globalization and North-South Divergence*. London: Routledge.

Thompson, W. R., and Zakhirova, L. 2013. "Global Energy Transitions and the Future of Systemic Leadership." Paper presented at the annual meeting of the American Political Science Association, Chicago, August.

Tillemann, L. 2015. *The Great Race: The Global Quest for the Car of the Future*. New York: Simon and Schuster.

Tully, S. 2015. "The Shale Oil Revolution Is in Danger." *Fortune*, January 9. http://fortune.com/2015/01/09/oil-prices-shale-fracking/.

Turner, F. J. 1986. "The Significance of the Frontier in American History." In *The Frontier in American History*, ed. Frederick J. Turner. Tucson: University of Arizona Press.

United Nations Environment Programme. 2012. "Gas Fracking: Can We Safely Squeeze the Rocks?" Geneva: UNEP Global Environment Alert Service. http://www.unrep.org/pdf/UNEP-GEAS_NOV_2012.pdf.

Unger, R. W. 1984. "Energy Sources for the Dutch Golden Age: Peat, Wind, and Coal." *Research in Economic History* 9: 221–253.

U.S. Department of Energy. 2013. *Technically Recoverable Shale Oil and Shale Gas Reserves: An Assessment of 137 Shale Formations in 41 Countries Outside the United States*. Washington, D.C.: U.S. Department of Energy.

U.S. Department of Energy. 2014. *Annual Energy Outlook 2014 Early Release*. Washington, D.C.: U.S. Department of Energy.

U.S. Department of Energy. 2015. *Annual Energy Outlook 2015 Early Release*. Washington, D.C.: U.S. Department of Energy.

U.S. Energy Information Agency. 2013. "International Energy Outlook 2013." http://www.eia.gov/forecasts/reo/world.cfm.

U.S. Energy Information Agency. 2016. "US Production Crude Oil." www.eia.gov/dnav/pet/pet crd.crpden ede.mbbl.m.htm.

U.S. National Science Board. 2014. *Science and Engineering Indicators 2014*. Washington, D.C.: National Science Foundation. http://www.nsf.gov/statistics/seind14/.

U.S. National Science Board. 2016. "Science and Engineering Indicators 2016." https://www.nsf.gov/statistics/2016/nsb20161/#/.

Van Bavel, B. J. P., and Van Zanden, J. L. 2004. "The Jump-start of the Holland Economy During the Late-Medieval Crisis, c. 1350–1500." *Economic History Review* 3: 503–532.

Van der Wee, H. 1990. "Structural Changes in European Long-Distance Trade and Particularly in the Re-export Trade from South to North, 1350–1750." In *The Rise of Merchant Empires: Long Distance Trade in the Early Modern World, 1350–1750*, ed. J. D. Tracy. Cambridge: Cambridge University Press.

Van Zanden, J. L. 1993. "Economic Growth in the Golden Age: The Development of the Economy of Holland, 1500–1650." In *The Dutch Economy in the Golden Age: Nine Studies*, ed. Karel Davids and Leo Noordegraaf. Amsterdam: Het Nerderlandsch Economisch-Historisch Archief.

Vedder, R. K. 1976. *The American Economy in Historical Perspective*. Belmont, CA: Wasdsworth.

Verseth, M. 1990. *Mountains of Debt: Crisis and Change in Renaissance Florence, Victorian Britain and Post-War America*. New York: Oxford University Press.

Victor, D. G. 2013. *Global Warming Gridlock: Creating More Effective Strategies for Protecting the Planet*. Cambridge: Cambridge University Press.

Von Glahn, R. 2003. "Imagining Pre-modern China." In *The Song-Yuan-Ming Transition in Chinese History*, ed. Paul J. Smith and Richard von Glahn. Cambridge, MA: Harvard University Press.

Vries, P. H. H. 2001. "Are Coal and Colonies Really Crucial? Kenneth Pomeranz and the Great Divergence." *Journal of World History* 12 (2): 407–446.

Wagner, D. B. 2008. *Joseph Needham's Science and Civilization in China*, vol. 5: *Chemistry and Chemical Technology, Part XI: Ferrous Metallurgy*. Cambridge: Cambridge University Press.

Wallerstein, I. 1974. *The Modern World-System I: Capitalist Agriculture and the Origins of the European World-Economy in the Sixteenth Century*. New York: Academic Press.

Wallerstein, I. 1980. *The Modern World-System II: Mercantilism and the Consolidation of the European World-Economy, 1600–1730*. New York: Academic Press.

Wallerstein, I. 1982. "Dutch Hegemony in the Seventeenth Century World-Economy." In *Dutch Capitalism and World Capitalism*, ed. Maurice Aymard. Cambridge: Cambridge University Press.

Wallerstein, I. 1989. *The Modern World-System III: The Second Era of Great Expansion of the Capitalist World-Economy, 1730s–1840s*. San Diego, CA: Academic Press.

Wallerstein, I. 2011. *The Modern World-System IV: Centrist Liberalism Triumphant, 1789–1914*. Berkeley: University of California Press.

Warde, P. 2013. "The First Industrial Revolution." In *Power to the People: Energy in Europe over the Past Five Centuries*, ed. Astrid Kander, Paola Malanima, and Paul Warde. Princeton, NJ: Princeton University Press.

Webb, W. P. 1964. *The Great Frontier*. Lincoln: University of Nebraska Press.

Weber, M. 1930. *The Protestant Ethic and the Spirit of Capitalism*. Trans. Talcott Parsons. London: Allen and Unwin.

Weiss, L. 2014. *America Inc.? Innovation and National Enterprise in the National Security States*. Ithaca, NY: Cornell University Press.

Whitten, D. G. A., and Brooks, J. R. V. 1972. *The Penguin Dictionary of Geology*. London: Penguin.

Wigley, T. M. L. 2011. "Coal to Gas: The Influence of Methane Leakage." *Climate Change* 108 (3): 601–608.

Wikander, O. 2008. "Sources of Energy and Exploitation of Power." In *The Oxford Handbook of Engineering and Technology in the Classical World*, ed. John Peter Oleson. Oxford: Oxford University Press.

Wilkinson, D. O. 1987. "Central Civilization." *Comparative Civilizations Review* 17: 31–59.

Wilkinson, D. O. 1991. "Cities, Civilizations and Oikumens I." *Comparative Civilizations Review* 27: 51–87.

Wilkinson, D. O. 1993. "Cities, Civilizations and Oikumenes II." *Comparative Civilizations Review* 28: 41–72.

Williams, J. H., DeBenedictis, A., Ghanadan, R., Mahone, A., Moore, J., Morrow III, W. R., Price, S., and Torn, M. S . 2012. "The Technology Path to Deep Greenhouse Gas Emissions Cuts by 2050: The Pivotal Role of Electricity." *Science* 335 (January 6): 53–59.

Williams, J. H., Haley, B., and Jones, R. 2015. *Policy Implications of Deep Decarbonization in the United States*, vol. 2. Deep Decarbonization Pathways Project of the Sustainable Development Solutions Network and the Institute for Sustainable Development and International Relations.

Williams, J. H., Haley, B., Kahrl, F., Moore, J., Jones, A. D., Torn, M. S., McJeon, H., et al. 2014. *Pathways to Deep Decarbonization in the United States*. Deep Decarbonization Pathways Project of the Sustainable Development Solutions Network and the Institute for Sustainable Development and International Relations. http://unsdsn.org/wp-content/uploads/2014/09/US-Deep-Decarbonization-Report.pdf.

Williamson, J. 1975. "The Railroads and Midwestern Development, 1870–1890: A General Equilibrium History." In *Essays in Nineteenth Century Economic History*, ed. David C. Klingaman and Richard K. Vedder. Athens: Ohio University Press.

Williamson, S. H. 2011. "Annualized Growth Rate and Graphs of Various Historical Economic Series." *MeasuringWorth*. http://www.measuringworth.com/growth.

Wilson, A. I. 2008. "Machines in Greek and Roman Technology." In *The Oxford Handbook of Engineering and Technology in the Classical World*, ed. John Peter Oleson. Oxford: Oxford University Press.

Wilson, A. I. 2012. "Raw Materials and Energy." In *The Cambridge Companion to the Roman Economy*, ed. Walter Scheidel. Cambridge: Cambridge University Press.

Wilson, A. I. 2013. "The Mediterranean Environment in Ancient History: Perspectives and Prospects." In *The Ancient Mediterranean Environment Between Science and History*, ed. W. V. Harris. Leiden: Brill.

Wilson, A. R. 2009. "The Maritime Transformation of Ming China." In *China Goes To Sea: Maritime Transformation in Comparative Historical Perspective*, eds. A. S. Erickson, L. J. Goldstein, and C. Lord. Annapolis, Md.: Naval Institute Press.

Wong, R. B. 1997. *China Transformed: Historical Change and the Limits of European Experience*. Ithaca, NY: Cornell University Press.

World Economic Council. 2013. "World Energy Scenarios: Comparing Energy Futures to 2050." http://www.worldenergy.org/wp-content/uploads/2013/09/World-Energy-Scenarios_Composing-energy-futures-to-2050_Full-report.pdf.

Wright, G. 1990. "The Origins of American Industrial Success, 1879–1940." *American Economic Review* 80: 651–668.

Wright, G., and Czelusta, J. 2004. "Why Economies Slow: The Myth of the Resource Curse." *Challenge* 47 (2): 6–38.

Wrigley, E. A. 1988. *Continuity, Chance and Change: The Character of the Industrial Revolution in England*. Cambridge: Cambridge University Press.

Wrigley, E. A. 2010. *Energy and the English Industrial Revolution*. Cambridge: Cambridge University Press.

Yergin, D. 2011. *The Quest: Energy, Security, and the Remaking of the Modern World*. New York: Penguin Group.

Yetiv, S. A. 2015. *Myths of the Oil Boom: American National Security in a Global Energy Market*. Oxford: Oxford University Press.

Zakhirova, L., and Thompson, W. R. 2015. "The United States-China Race to Renewable Energy: Who Is Winning and Does It Matter?" Paper presented at the 11th International Conference on Environmental, Cultural, Economic, and Social Sustainability, Copenhagen, Denmark, January.

Zhidong, L. 2014. "Peak Coal in China: Rethinking the Unimaginable." In *China's Energy Crossroads: Forging a New Energy and Environmental Balance*, ed. Clara Gillespie and Meredith Miller. NBR Special Report #47. Seattle: National Bureau of Asian Research.

Zubrin, R. 2009. *Energy Victory: Winning the War on Terror by Breaking Free of Oil*. Amherst, NY: Prometheus Books.

INDEX